Visionary Strategic Leadership

Sustaining Success through Strategic Direction, Corporate Management, and High-Level Programs

Visionary Strategic Leadership

Sustaining Success through Strategic Direction, Corporate Management, and High-Level Programs

David L. Rainey
Rensselaer Polytechnic Institute

INFORMATION AGE PUBLISHING, INC.
Charlotte, NC • www.infoagepub.com

Library of Congress Cataloging-in-Publication Data

Rainey, David L., 1946-
 Visionary strategic leadership : sustaining success through strategic direction, corporate management, and high-level programs / David L. Rainey, Rensselaer Polytechnic Institute.
    pages cm
  ISBN 978-1-62396-313-2 (pbk.) – ISBN 978-1-62396-314-9 (hardcover) – ISBN 978-1-62396-315-6 (ebook) 1. Strategic planning. 2. Leadership. I. Title.
  HD30.28.R3454 2013
  658.4'092–dc23
                                                                2013012233

Copyright © 2013 Information Age Publishing Inc.

All rights reserved. No part of this publication may be reproduced, stored in a retrieval system, or transmitted, in any form or by any means, electronic, mechanical, photocopying, microfilming, recording or otherwise, without written permission from the publisher.

Printed in the United States of America

Contents

    List of Figures ix
    List of Tables xi
    List of Boxes xiii
    List of Abbreviations xv
    Introduction xix

1 Visionary Strategic Leadership 1
    Introduction 1
    Concepts of Visionary Strategic Leadership 2
        The Underlying Elements of Visionary Strategic Leadership 2
        Global Perspectives on VSL Pertaining to the Business Enterprise 8
        Principles, Values, Beliefs, and Ethical Standards 11
    The Critical Roles and Responsibilities of Corporate Leaders 14
    Reflections 21
    Notes 22
    References 22

2 Corporate Leadership and Management 23
    Introduction 23
    The Integrated VSL and CSM Framework 25
    The Main Elements of VSL and CSM 29
        Strategic Perspectives and Management Systems 29
        The Embedded Corporate Management System 31
        Creating a Logical Organizational Structure 34
        Underpinnings of Corporate Governance 35
    Overarching Management Constructs 38
        Select Management Constructs 38
        The Crucial Role of Sustainable Business Development 39

> *Philosophical Aspects of Corporate Social Responsibility* 42
> *Shifting Mindsets Pertaining to SBD and CSR* 44
>
> Reflections 50
> Notes 51
> References 52

3 Vision, Strategies, and Goals 53
> Introduction 53
> Corporate Vision 56
> The Overarching Strategic Perspective 60
> > *Linking the Overarching Strategic Perspective with the Corporate Vision* 60
> > *The Importance of an Overarching Strategic Perspective* 62
> > *The Fundamental Aspects of the Overarching Strategic Perspective* 63
>
> Corporate Strategies and Goals 67
> > *The Notion of Grand Corporate Strategy* 67
> > *Overarching Corporate Goals* 69
>
> Evaluating Corporate Performance and Communicating Outcomes 80
> Reflections 87
> Notes 88
> References 88

4 Corporate Plans, Actions, and Relationships 89
> Introduction 89
> Scenario Planning 91
> > *Definition and Purpose* 91
> > *Brief Historical Background Pertaining to Scenario Planning* ...93
> > *Strategic Implications of Scenarios* 95
> > *Scenario Planning Process* 97
> > *Gap Analysis Between Scenarios and Strategic Options* 105
>
> High-Level Corporate Plans and Actions 107
> > *Corporate Strategic Plans* 107
> > *Corporate Mergers and Acquisitions* 109
> > *Strategic Alliances and Joint Ventures* 113
> > *Strategic Innovations* 114
>
> Building Relationships with Partners, Customers, and Employees ...118
> > *The Theoretical Underpinnings for Building Corporate Relationships* 118
> > *Building High-Level Mutually Beneficial External Relationships* 120
> > *Reinforcing Internal Relationships* 123
>
> Reflections 128
> Notes 129
> References 129

5 High-Level Strategic Programs: Management and Implementation 131
Introduction 131
Program Management 134
    General Perspectives on Program Management 134
    Project Management Versus Program Management 137
    The Linkages Between Strategy Formulation and Program Management 143
Program Implementation 145
    Framework for Selecting, Defining, and Designing High-Level Strategic Programs .. 145
    Screening and Selecting the Most Attractive Candidates 147
    Defining the Architecture of the Selected Programs 151
    Designing the Program Elements and the Specifications 158
Reflections 174
Notes 175
References 176

6 High-Level Strategic Programs: Execution and Evaluation 177
Introduction 177
Program Execution 180
    Framework for Executing High-Level Strategic Programs 180
    Developing the Program and the First Actions of Program Execution 181
    Demonstrating the Solutions and Outcomes of the Program 189
    Deploying the Solutions and Outcomes of the Program 196
Program Evaluation 200
    Evaluating High-Level Strategic Programs 200
    Evaluating External Outcomes and Success 201
    Evaluating Internal Outcomes and Success 204
Reflections 213
Notes 214
References 215

7 Enterprise-Wide Risk Management 217
Introduction 217
The Concepts of Risk and the ERM Framework 220
    Fundamentals of Risks 220
    Basic Types of Risks 222
    Enterprise-Wide Risk Management Framework 225
Main Elements of ERM 227
    Risk Management System 227
    Risk Assessment 237
    Risk Strategies and Action Plans 248
Reflections 257
Notes 258
References 258

8 Reflections and Concluding Comments 259
Introduction 259
Being a Visionary Strategic Leader 261
Reflections on Visionary Strategic Leadership 265
Philosophical Perspectives 265
Rhetoric and Reality 266
Linkages between VSL and Sustainable Success 269
Concluding Comments 271
Note 275
Reference 275

List of Figures

Figure 1.1	The continuum of VSL and CSM: imagination, insights, and innovations	3
Figure 1.2	Global perspectives of visionary strategic leadership	10
Figure 1.3	Essential roles and responsibilities of visionary corporate leaders	16
Figure 2.1	The integrated VSL and CSM framework	26
Figure 2A.1	Canon's stakeholder model	49
Figure 2A.2	Canon's corporate governance structure (June 1, 2006)	50
Figure 3.1	The vision construct for company and enterprise transformations	59
Figure 3.2	The connections between the vision, the strategic direction, and the OSP	62
Figure 3.3	Corporate goals: categories and connections	71
Figure 4.1	van der Heijden's model pertaining to predictability and uncertainty	96
Figure 4.2	Schwartz's scenario planning process	99
Figure 4.3	Scenarios pertaining to economic growth/environmental concerns	102
Figure 4.4	Matrix form for depicting scenarios	104
Figure 4.5	The front-end of the radical innovation framework	117
Figure 5.1	U.S. space program outline	133
Figure 5.2	Linkages between strategy formulation and program management	144
Figure 5.3	Key elements and sub-elements of program implementation	147
Figure 5.4	Program screening process	150
Figure 5.5	A relative sense of project management versus program management	154
Figure 5.6	Selected examples of sequential forms	158
Figure 5.7	Example of a program with mostly concurrent sub-programs	159

Figure 5.8	Example of a hybrid form tailored to large corporations with business units	160
Figure 5.9	Example of a hybrid form tailored to small corporations	161
Figure 6.1	Key elements and sub-elements of program execution	181
Figure 6.2	Relative scope of actions during program implementation and execution	197
Figure 6.3	Essential aspects for managing high-level strategic programs	213
Figure 7.1	Main elements of the ERM framework	227
Figure 7.2	Simplified perspectives associated with risk-analysis methods	242
Figure 7.3	Relative level of risk-to-reward matrix	245

List of Tables

Table 2.1	Selected Perspectives Involving Paradigm Shifts in Management Thinking	47
Table 3.1	Selected Grand Strategic Goals and Their Advantages and Disadvantages	74
Table 4.1	Theoretical Relationships Between Scenarios and Strategic Options	106
Table 5.1	Examples of Types of High-Level Strategic Programs	136
Table 5.2	PMI's Elements and Sub-Elements of Project Management	139
Table 5.3	Comparison Between Project Management and Program Management	142
Table 5.4	Selected Criteria for Screening Candidates	149
Table 5.5	Important Considerations Pertaining to the Operating System(s)	167
Table 7.1	Examples of Some of the More Important Risk Categories (Areas)	231
Table 7.2	Preliminary Steps in System Design	233
Table 7.3	The Risk Identification Process	238

List of Boxes

Box 1	Strategic Leadership at General Electric	19
Box 2	Canon's Corporate Leadership, Governance and its "*kyosei*" Philosophy	48
Box 3	Sam Walton's Market and Financial Successes	82
Box 4	Ken Iverson and the Transformation of Nucor Steel through Corporate Actions	125
Box 5	Electric Boat and the USS VIRGINIA-Class Environmental Compliance Program: Pioneering the Way toward Sustainable Development	166
Box 6	George David's High-Level Strategic Programs at United Technologies Corporation	206

List of Abbreviations

10X	Factor of ten times
ACE	Achieving Competitive Excellence
AOL	America Online
B&N	Barnes & Noble
B/C	Benefit to cost
BHAG	Big Hairy Audacious Goals
BOP	Bottom of the [economic] pyramid
BMW	Bavarian Motor Works
BP	BP plc (Formerly British Petroleum)
BPR	Business process reengineering
BSR	Business for Social Responsibility
CAD/CAM	Computer aided design/computer aided manufacturing
CEO	Chief executive officer
C-level	Corporate level
CPM	critical path method
CRO	Chief risk officer
CSM	Corporate strategic management
CSR	Corporate social responsibility
DFES	Design for EHS
DfSS	Design for Six Sigma
DJSI	Dow Jones Sustainability Index
DoD	Department of Defense
EB	Electric Boat
EBM	Enterprise-wide [strategic] business model
ECT	Environmental compliance team
EEB	Energy Efficiency in Buildings

EHS	Environment, health, and safety
EMT	Environmental management team
EO	Executive order
ERM	Enterprise-wide risk management
EU	European Union
FMEA	Failure mode and effects analysis
GE	General Electric
GM	General Motors
HBS	Harvard Business School
HRA	Hazard risk assessments
HSP	High-level strategic programs
ICT	Information and communications technologies
IBM	International Business Machines
IPD	Integrated product development
IRM	Integrated risk management
ISO	International Organization for Standards
IT	Information technology
J&J	Johnson & Johnson
JV	Joint venture
KRA	Key results areas
LCA	Life cycle assessment
LCD	Liquid crystal displays
LED	Light emitting diode
LTA	Long-term agreement
M&A	Mergers and acquisitions
MIT	Massachusetts Institute of Technology
NASA	National Aeronautics and Space Administration
NGO	Non-governmental organization
OSP	Overarching strategic perspective
PERT	Project evaluation review technique
PC	Personal computer
P&W	Pratt & Whitney [aircraft engines]
PMI	Project Management Institute
RCA	Radio Corporation of America
R&D	Research & development
ROA	Return on assets
ROE	Return on equity
ROI	Return on investment
RPN	Risk priority number

SBU	Strategic business unit
SBD	Sustainable business development
SD	Sustainable development
SMART	Specific, measurable, achievable, realistic, and time-based
SME	Small- and medium-sized enterprise
SOA	Sarbanes-Oxley Act of 2002
TQM	Total quality management
UN	United Nations
US	United States of America
UTC	United Technologies Corporation
UTRC	United Technologies Research Center
VSL	Visionary strategic leadership
WBCSD	World Business Council for Sustainable Development
WBS	Work breakdown structure
WWII	World War II

Introduction

Overview

Visionary strategic leadership (VSL) is the highest level of strategic leadership of global corporations and small- and medium-size enterprises (SMEs) that involves inspiring people, leading change, and sustaining success. It includes establishing the vision, ensuring proper governance, crafting strategies, inventing new solutions, and building solid and enduring relationships. It also includes creating management systems and structures, executing high-level strategic programs, integrating the whole organization with the real world and future generations, and providing oversight. It is principally about having well-established principles, compelling aspirations, audacious goals, and moving the organization toward more fruitful strategic positions for a more sustainable future. It involves using imagination to address what ought to be done instead of what is being done, obtaining insights from the market spaces and the business environment, being innovative in developing new solutions, and integrating the whole business enterprise.

VSL necessitates that corporate leaders have a broad array of exceptional personal values, positive attitudes, outstanding qualities, and multifaceted capabilities. Moreover, they must be excellent learners and teachers. Such leaders have to be competent, confident, and courageous in leading and managing their organizations. They must be broad-minded and selfless and practice self-discipline. The desired attributes must include respecting people, upholding the highest ethical standards, and being the architect of the future. VSL involves having a high-level position, being responsible for the strategic leadership and management of a company or a strategic business unit (SBU), inspiring and leading the organization, and sustaining success. VSL also involves providing the guiding energy and wisdom for creating the strategies, solutions, systems, structures, technologies, products, and processes and for transforming them into successful outcomes. In the turbulent, dynamic and global business world of today, corporate leaders have to have the daring and willingness to lead in uncharted waters and go beyond the conventional management approaches. They have to understand the past, know the present, and create their future successes.

Fundamentally, VSL involves people and making them successful. It is underpinned by the concepts and constructs of corporate strategic management (CSM), which involves the theories, methods, and practices for managing corporations, subsidiaries, SMEs and joint ventures, and for achieving desired outcomes and excellent performance. CSM involves the high-level leadership and holistic management of the entire company and its business enterprises with all of the contributors and recipients. CSM is based on an embedded management system that involves the duties, obligations, roles, and responsibilities of corporate officers, the strategic leaders of the business units, and the functional leaders of the operating systems. CSM includes creating value for the company and whole business enterprise, protecting the well-being of people, protecting the natural environment, and sustaining success.

VSL and CSM are parallel constructs. While there may be different perspectives about what they exactly involve, it is often difficult to precisely separate what is strategic leadership and what is corporate management, especially at the corporate level. However, in a fundamental way, leadership is about people, and management is about things—assets, resources, goods, etc.

Corporate leaders are the executives, company officers, and other high-level strategic leaders who lead the organization; establish the vision and aspirations based on their insights, imagination, and innovativeness; provide the means and mechanisms for value creation; manage high-level corporate programs; and mitigate risks. They have to envision what customers and stakeholders demand and expect and then create value and beneficial outcomes that such people desire and enjoy. Value creation implies determining and fulfilling the underlying social, economic, ethical, technological, and environmental needs and wants. It involves realizing the desires and expectations through proactive strategies, strategic innovations, and decisive actions. Corporate leaders have to have incredible foresight and commitment in leading change and creating new solutions that resolve difficulties and challenges; taking advantage of the organization's capabilities, knowledge and learning; and producing positive outcomes across the market spaces and the business environment.

Corporate leaders have to be personally engaged in high-level strategic thinking like determining the strategic direction; in critical roles and responsibilities like assuring proper corporate governance; and in the company's systems, structures, and performance like walking, talking, and connecting with people at the core levels of the organization. Corporate leaders focus on the big picture, but they also pay attention to the grass roots operations and the realities of the global economy. They give due consideration to all of the essential requirements. Their roles and responsibilities span from the top to bottom, from the present to the future, from the origins of the supply networks to all of the customers, stakeholders, and shareholders, and from strategic innovations to the management of the end-of-life residuals and unintended side effects. Corporate leaders are the visionary strategic leaders who create and sustain success.

Visionary Strategy Leadership and Corporate Strategy Management

VSL and CSM are about high-level leadership, strategic direction, and corporate strategy. Corporate strategy involves determining what has to be done and how to achieve success. Corporate strategy is well understood by most corporate executives, strategic leaders, strategists, practitioners, and business scholars. It evolved from the theoretical and practical methodologies involving business policies and long-range planning developed at Harvard Business School (HBS) and Massachusetts Institute of Technology (MIT) during the 1950s and 1960s. HBS's Kenneth Andrews (1916–2005) and MIT's H. Igor Ansoff (1918–2002) were two of the pioneers of corporate strategy. Andrews defined it thusly:[1]

> Corporate strategy is the pattern of decisions in a company that determines and reveals its objectives, purposes, or goals, produces the principal policies and plans for achieving those goals, and defines the range of businesses the company is to pursue, the kind of economic and human organization it is or intends to be, and the nature of the economic and non-economic contribution it intends to make to its shareholders, employees, customers, and communities. In an organization of any size or diversity, 'corporate strategy' usually applies to the whole enterprise while 'business strategy', less comprehensively defines the choices of product or service and market of individual businesses within the firm. Business strategy, that is, is the determination of how a company will compete in a given business and position itself among its competitors. Corporate strategy defines the businesses in which a company will compete preferably in a way that focuses resources to convert distinctive competence into competitive advantages.

Per Andrews' concepts, corporate strategy includes upstream strategic planning, analysis of the conditions and trends in the business environment and the related opportunities, challenges, threats, and risks, and the selections of the vision for the future, the long-term objectives, and a grand strategy. Andrews clearly differentiated CSM from business unit strategic management. The former involves the whole company and its enterprises. The latter involves the individual SBUs within the company. For small companies and many SMEs as well, there may be little or no distinction between CSM and SBU strategic management. In particular, small companies usually have only one business unit, thus corporate leaders perform all strategic roles and responsibilities. However, visionary strategic leaders go beyond setting strategic direction because that is often the easy part. They make the vision real in the hearts and minds of the key contributors and recipients. They provide the means and mechanisms for realizing the vision and intended outcomes. Moreover, they develop the next generation of strategic leaders within the organization and across the enterprise; leaders who have the competencies, capabilities, mindset and willingness to lead change and to be at the forefront of transforming the company into a more sophisticated business enterprise.

Visionary strategic leaders are theoretical strategists and pragmatists who are open minded and multifaceted; ones who engage the whole not just the parts, embrace people not just things, and have global perspectives; ones who include broad-based social, economic, ethical, technological and environmental concerns, issues, and challenges.

They realize that the overarching objective of the company is sustainable success, not just satisfying customers and shareholders and making money. They are never willing to risk future successes to maximize short-term results, nor do they fail to obtain good performance in the short term to achieve success in the long term. They know that their personal success is predicated on the success of their customers, stakeholders, supply networks, partners, peers, superiors, employees, key contributors across the enterprise, and shareholders. They are aggressive in their quest for success, yet they are respectful of other people and recognize and reward them accordingly. Moreover, visionary strategic leaders take global perspectives.

Global perspectives are based on an expanded framework of a business enterprise that includes the corporation with all of its internal SBUs and their value chains, with all of the global entities of the supply networks, related industries, and partners, and all of the relationships with customers, stakeholders, and other constituents in the value networks. Global perspectives are holistic and involve examining the whole business enterprise when making decisions about objectives and strategies, developing plans and actions, building relationships, designing and developing high-level programs, selecting processes, and engaging in strategic implementation and execution. They involve ensuring that the best choices are made and that risks, problems, and negative impacts are mitigated, if not eliminated, to the fullest extent possible. Global corporations and most SMEs now more than ever before depend on external connections and relationships to create, produce, and deliver value and sustain success. Moreover, they are driven by global forces that impact decision making and outcomes. In simple terms, global perspectives include all of the entities and participants, i.e., the contributors and recipients within and outside the company. The external entities are referred to as the "extended enterprise." The term "extended enterprise" is an accurate reflection of what a business enterprise of today really is. The added descriptor is unnecessary since a business enterprise involves all of the direct and indirect participants.

The Purpose and Framework of the Book

The purpose of *Visionary Strategic Leadership: Sustaining Success through Strategic Direction, Corporate Management, and High-level Programs* is to provide insights and suggestions for corporate leaders of today and to offer guidance and direction for the young strategic leaders of tomorrow. While the book covers the main topics of VSL and CSM, it is not possible to include all of the salient elements of such complex subjects. The main perspectives focus on the strategic leadership, principles, strategies, innovations, actions, and management constructs of high-level (corporate) strategic leaders. Corporate strategic leaders, especially the chief executive officer and chief operating officer, are often referred to as C-level leaders. They are responsible for everyone and everything. They are referred to as corporate leaders hereinafter.

VSL and CSM are about the aspirations and dreams for the future, the possibilities for the present and future generations, and the pathways and management constructs for achieving sustainable success. Astute corporate leaders expand their strategic thinking and global perspectives rather than constricting them. They eliminate barriers and constraints and open the doors to more opportunities and possibilities. They explore the unexplored; they resolve the unresolved; and, they do the undoable. They are never satisfied with good results because good is simply not good enough. Visionary strategic leaders link all of the contributors and recipients into a fully integrated business enterprise that is interconnected, interrelated, and proactive. They ensure that solutions are designed, produced, and delivered on the basis of the intended recipients.

VSL and CSM are about creating a better world with enduring outcomes that are closer to the ideal. While the ideal is always a distant dream, corporate leaders do everything possible to get closer to it. Great corporate leaders are optimistic, yet they are realistic and action-oriented. They seek excellence in everything they do. Moreover, they realize that what may be impossible today may become possibilities tomorrow. For instance, a telephone with video transmission was believed to be impossible thirty years ago, but now such technologies are commonplace. Visionary strategic leaders use strategic innovations to translate aspirations into substance and their vision for the future into richer realities. Visionary strategic leaders lead from the front and are not afraid to be on the cutting edge. They build consensus within the organization and across the enterprise and ensure that everyone understands what has to be done and how to do it. They do not rely on the conventional or mainstream thinking to reinforce their decisions. Great visionary strategic leaders realize that they are pioneers and architects who create the pathways to success. It is the quest for excellence that differentiates great strategic leaders from rest of the pack.

The framework of the book flows from defining and articulating the concepts of VSL, CSM, corporate vision, and fundamental values and discussing high-level (grand) strategies, objectives, and actions to developing and managing high-level strategic programs and mitigating risks.

Chapters 1 and 2 lay the foundation and provide the broad perspectives pertaining to VSL and CSM. They discern the differences between leadership and management and discuss the key elements of each, including the governance of the company and organization. Corporate governance is critical for achieving and sustaining ongoing success. It has two main components: prescribed and derived. The prescriptive requirements include the directions from the board of directors; the rules and requirements that corporate officers have to follow according to the by-laws of the corporation, and the laws pertaining to corporations; and the laws and regulations of the political economies in which they operate. The derived components are generally self-determined and/or deduced from the demands and wishes of the shareholders; the policies and directives of the executive leadership team; the values and beliefs of the company; the broader views of the employees; and the social, economic, and environmental expectations of the market spaces and the business environment. In both cases, the key elements are not exactly one or the other; there is overlap. While corporate governance involves the fiduciary responsibilities of strategic leaders, the focus herein is on philosophies, principles, values, beliefs, and ethics. In terms of strategic leadership, the main discussions concentrate on the choices that visionary strategic leaders have discretion over rather than on the obligations that they have. They include the frameworks, systems, and structures. They also include the management constructs used to lead and manage.

Chapters 3 and 4 involve setting strategic direction and formulating and implementing strategies and action plans. Determining vision and formulating the corporate strategies and goals based on leading change as discussed herein involves VSL rather than traditional strategic management because it embraces what could be or should be rather than what is. It takes visionary strategic leaders to determine how the company creates its future and sustains success.

The focus is on understanding the driving forces of change, determining the opportunities for achieving success, and taking actions through insights and imagination. Insights are gleaned from external context and are used to create competitive advantages and sustainable success. They involve taking broad perspectives of the external context, not simply examining the markets and near-term opportunities. Insights are derived from an analytical understanding of reality that focuses on discovering the true nature of situations and events. Two of the most intriguing stories about insights involve former visionary strategic leaders at IBM. Thomas Watson Sr. realized the enormous opportunity that resulted from the establishment of the Social Security Administration in 1936. He created tabulating machines and protocols for processing the enormous amount of information and data. In the next generation, Thomas Watson Jr., the son, saw the huge potential of mainframe computers that could replace the tabulating machines that his father's strategies and innovations created. Insights and imagination are often realized when visionary strategic leaders have global perspectives that drill deep into the business environment, the social world, and the natural environment to uncover the underpinnings of reality and the true opportunities for change.

Chapters 5 and 6 discuss the development, execution and management of high-level strategic programs. They are the essential means and mechanisms for affecting change and realizing the corporate objectives and desired outcomes. Such programs are managed and controlled by strategic leaders and implemented by senior program managers who have multifaceted experiences and knowledge and have the capabilities to engage in transitions and transformations. A high-level strategic program is one that is intended to transition or transform the company or some significant strategic position(s) within it to realize the strategic direction and/or to develop high-level/cutting-edge organizational capabilities and constructs that provide competitive advantages. Such programs result in higher levels of sophistication allowing the corporation to outperform its peers and competitors across the business environment or with respect to critical strategic positions.

Chapter 7 covers risk management and risk mitigation. It involves making sure that the negative aspects of the business world are duly considered and managed to the extent possible. True visionary strategic leaders know that without managing and mitigating risks, it is difficult to achieve and sustain success; therefore, they create sophisticated ways to integrate the whole enterprise and to manage all aspects within the company and the enterprise and to eliminates one's risks and vulnerabilities.

Chapter 8 provides reflections on VSL and CSM and concluding comments. Ultimately, VSL and CSM are predicated on the social, ethical, economic, technological, and environmental dimensions. Corporations are social institutions run by people for people. Success is achieved when people are put at the forefront and making money is achieved as a result of good leadership, proactive strategies, great innovations, positive actions, extraordinary outcomes, and solid relationships. Great corporate leaders know that building relationships within the organizations and across the enterprise is one of the best ways to achieve sustainable success. It may be easy to copy products, but it is significantly harder to duplicate unique solutions and solid relationships.

Note

1. Kenneth R. Andrews, *The Concept of Corporate Strategy, Revised Edition* (New York, NY: Irwin, 1980, pp. 18–19). Andrews was a leading strategic management scholar. He pioneered the development of business strategy at Harvard Business School.

Reference

Andrews, Kenneth R. (1980) *The Concept of Corporate Strategy, Revised Edition.* New York, NY: Irwin.

1

Visionary Strategic Leadership

Introduction

Corporate leadership involves the whole company, all of the people, their activities, and their achievements. Corporate leaders/executives engage people from all directions, like the points of the compass, and ensure that everyone is contributing to sustainable success and providing the best solutions and outcomes possible. Creating, developing, tracking, measuring, monitoring opportunities and challenges, achieving positive outcomes, and ensuring success are among the most critical roles and responsibilities of corporate leadership. The desired outcomes are not just dictated by executives and obtained through strategies, actions, programs, operations, products, and processes. They are determined and realized through a broad array of contributions and actions by the whole organization and the extended enterprise(s).

Astute corporate leaders are not arrogant, dictatorial, or think that they know everything and can make every decision on their own. Great strategic leaders realize that other people have much to contribute. They recognize that the wisdom, innovativeness, and commitment of the entire business enterprise are generally greater than that of the small number of high-level leaders. Successful corporate leaders make others successful through respect, recognition, and rewards. They subordinate their professional and financial rewards to the broader success of the organization and enterprise.

Visionary strategic leadership (VSL) in a corporate setting involves comprehending where the driving forces of change in the business environment are going, not just what they are; understanding what the future effects, impacts, and related implications are, not just the present conditions and trends; being innovative and leading, not just responding and following external mandates and requirements; and having the qualities and capabilities to lead people and change and to achieve the desirable outcomes. VSL also involves the fiduciary responsibilities of strategic leaders to protect the assets, intellectual capital, the well-being of the company and its relationships with contributors and recipients, and to sustain success.

Determining the competencies, achievements, and successes of corporate leaders is difficult to measure and the metrics are imprecise, at least in the short term. Some of the most important metrics include the rates of organizational improvements and learning, the increases in intellectual capital and knowledge, and the capabilities of the organization and extended enterprise(s) to succeed in the long term. For instance, the rate of leadership development provides the means for businesses to grow and prosper in the long term. On the other hand, annual corporate profitability gives a good indication about the current financial outcomes, but does not provide a sense of the sustainable success of the company and its ongoing financial performance. Some corporate leaders maximize short-term profits by suboptimizing the future or by turning certain costs and expenses into liabilities through accounting loopholes or failures to deal with long-term challenges to resolve existing problems. True success is multifaceted and enduring.

The chapter includes the following main topics:

- Exploring the concepts of VSL
- Articulating the roles and responsibilities of visionary corporate leaders

Concepts of Visionary Strategic Leadership

The Underlying Elements of Visionary Strategic Leadership

VSL requires thinking beyond the norm and creating new ways of leading and managing. It necessitates being on the cutting edge of change using sophisticated leadership and management constructs. While there are many theories, methods, and practices associated with strategic leadership, most such constructs really pertain to strategic management, i.e., managing. While strategic leadership and corporate strategic management (CSM) become intertwined at the corporate level, VSL involves leading people and organizations from the front (not the top), engaging in global perspectives, and creating innovative pathways to the future. Figure 1.1 depicts the main elements of VSL and CSM in basic terms.

VSL and CSM are not opposites, but are really two related constructs that need to be integrated into effective mechanisms for leading and managing. They are critical for success and depend upon intellectual capital, intuition, integrity, and inspiration. Astute strategic leaders lead and manage concurrently. They are the intellectual capital; their capabilities and attitudes are critical factors for achieving success. They also use intuition, integrity, and inspiration. Intuition is important in determining what is appropriate and necessary. Integrity is a reflection of principles, values, and culture of the people and the company and their regard for honesty and proper behaviors.

Figure 1.1 The continuum of VSL and CSM: imagination, insights, and innovations.

Inspiration by leaders provides contributors with the desires to do what is best and to be the best.

Visionary strategic leaders inspire people to achieve exceptional outcomes. The essence of VSL is to envision, inspire, and achieve positive actions and outcomes and to facilitate the pathways to extraordinary performance rather than using dictatorial methods of command and control. It is easier to lead than to push or pull. It is better to focus on creating and providing great solutions in the first place than it is dealing with the negative effects and impacts afterwards through problem solving techniques. VSL is about being proactive and avoiding problems by creating solutions that have many positives and few negatives. While problem solving is a widely used management construct, it intuitively makes sense to avoid problems in the first place. Problem solving is a relatively poor management construct because it usually involves efforts to mitigate and eliminate the difficulties and their consequences after bad things have happened.

VSL is a continuum of discovery, determination, invention, design, development, validation, deployment, and reflection. It is the never-ending circle of using *imagination* to craft strategies and new methods, discovering *insights* to discern what the true opportunities and expected outcomes are, and developing *innovations* to create the solutions and pathways for realizing positive outcomes. They are supported by the intellectual capital of the organization, the intuition and integrity of the strategic leaders, and the inspiration strategic leaders and managers provide to people. They are tied together through the integration of the entities of the enterprise and the contributors and recipients.

Imagination entails strategic thinking about the business world and beyond and envisioning how to make dramatic and even radical changes. It necessitates thinking outside the box about possibilities and potential outcomes. Imagination requires global perspectives, extraordinary perceptions, and new theoretical constructs, since it is impossible to rely on just strategic analysis given that the information and data about the future does not exist. It is relatively easy to analyze the prevailing situations and circumstances, but how do strategic leaders obtain statistical information and data about what has not occurred or what might occur in the future? For instance, the cost of providing service personnel in a store who assist customers is apparent and readily available, but what is the impact on loss revenue if some employees are eliminated to reduce expenses? It is unknown!

Imagination involves blazing new pathways toward a richer and more vibrant future. It enables strategic leaders who can lead positive change and overcome the limitations and barriers; leaders who have the fortitude and courage to develop and use innovative management constructs that are not dependent upon mainstream thinking. Visionary strategic leaders use imagination to conceive and articulate a vision for the future based on the aspirations for the organization and their knowledge of what is necessary, desirable, reasonable, possible, and distinctive.

Insights provide perspectives about reality and the associated opportunities and challenges. Visionary strategic leaders develop and deploy insights to set strategic direction and determine the corporate agenda that positions the organization on the pathway to success. Insights are gleaned from the market spaces and the business environment that provide a broader understanding of global realities and how to manage the conditions and trends and make proper strategic decisions; ones that are novel, yet realistic. Insights focus on the future possibilities as well as present situations and circumstances. Insights are also determined using scenarios of plausible possibilities and understanding what are the potential opportunities. Scenario planning is discussed in Chapter 4.

Innovations involve creating new solutions, systems, structures, and business models that provide enhanced performance and sophistication in the present and exciting new realities for the future. Strategic innovations focus on strategic developments pertaining to new-to-the-world technologies, products, systems, and processes that enhance the strategic positions of the corporation. They require a different mindset from just developing products and satisfying customer needs. Strategic innovations involve going beyond expectations in situations, in which incremental innovations are insufficient to achieve enduring outcomes and sustainable success. The aim is to create new ways of doing things that create more positives and eliminate the negatives.

Imagination, insights, and innovations are about leading change, setting the stage, creating extraordinary value, and realizing sustainable success. Leading change means developing and deploying new solutions, making paradigm changes, formulating new strategies, and inventing new methods and techniques for developing and implementing the change processes. Creating extraordinary value and achieving sustainable success are the overarching goals of businesses that provide desirable outcomes and good financial performance in the short term and excellent strategic positions and exceptional well-being for the long term. Imagination, insights, and innovations are a triad. Insights go hand in glove with imagination. While imagination can be based on mental models and global perspectives, insights are typically based on assessments of the prevailing situations and circumstances and scenarios pertaining to the realities of the world and plausible possibilities. Innovations are about inventing the future and making it real—creating positive outcomes.

Visionary strategic leaders spend a significant amount of time and effort contemplating what the future holds and how to take advantage of it. VSL is not an "either-or" proposition, but a duality, in which strategic leaders assure success in the present and prepare the organization for the future. Visionary strategic leaders have to understand the timelines for laying the foundation for their businesses and building the systems and structures for future actions. They have to craft the strategies, plan the initiatives, and implement the action programs for creating more sophisticated approaches and realizing the desirable outcomes before the need to do so becomes apparent

The main challenge is that imagination, insights, and innovations and the associated approaches are not always based on proven theories and accepted practices or ones that can be statistically analyzed and validated. Visionary strategic leaders may not be able to provide hard evidence that their strategic thinking, global perspectives, management constructs, and corporate strategies are correct. They have to depend on their intellectual capital, intuition, ingenuity, and inspiration; what they know to be true and appropriate. Moreover, astute strategic leaders generally know that if they wait for the proof, it may be too late to achieve success since others (competitors) may have already usurped the most attractive opportunities.

Visionary strategic leaders who are first movers can gain strategic advantages by preempting peers and competitors in achieving the desirable outcomes. For this reason, visionary strategic leaders create their own pathways to success and have the courage to act on their insights and convictions. Visionary strategic leaders cannot create success alone, they need their entire organizations. They have to use inspiration to get the organization to go along. It is the integration of the whole moving along the pathways to the future that ultimately supports sustainable success. Moreover, visionary strategic leaders lead without depending on their industry participants and peers to agree with them. For instance, Lord John Browne, former Group Chief Executive of BP p.l.c [formerly British Petroleum], highlighted his views on the future of the petroleum industry and his company in a speech at Stanford University in 2002. The following is an excerpt of his comments:[1]

> There is no single solution... but there are many ways forward. What we and others have done shows that there are rich and wide-ranging possibilities... Our aspiration then is to sustain the reduction in emissions we've made. And by doing that contribute to the world's long-term goal of stabilization. Not by abandoning oil and gas, but by improving the ways in which it is used and produced so that our business is aligned with the long-term needs of the world.

Lord Browne broke ranks with other industry leaders by recognizing that climate change is a serious issue requiring concerted attention and actions. He led his company in its quest to create a new vision based on becoming an energy company rather than a company focused on petroleum production and marketing. He wanted his company to move away from a reliance on petroleum and its ultimate constraints on future opportunities to a broader, more exciting and fruitful future based on strategic innovations; ones that focus on cleaner technologies, renewable energy, and more sustainable solutions. However, occasionally, visionary strategic leaders like Browne fail to ensure the dual aspects of VSL; remember VSL is not an "either-or" proposition. It is about doing everything possible to obtain and assure sustainable success. BP experienced several major setbacks in the United States due to an explosion at its Texas City refinery in March 23, 2005 and widespread corrosion problems with the Alaskan pipeline.[2] Subsequently, Browne was criticized for spending too much time on BP's vision and not enough on oversight of BP's operations. Good intentions are not enough.

Contrarians usually ask for proof before they agree to take action. While validation is important in most situations, it may not be necessary if the underpinnings of change are inherently correct. Making dramatic improvements, enhancing the well-being of the organization, seeking out new opportunities, and eliminating risks and vulnerabilities are almost always appropriate. Moreover, focusing on sustainable success is one of the most important critical elements of strategic leadership. These perspectives are akin to the logic behind the development of total quality management (TQM) in the United States three decades ago. The goals of TQM are to build quality into every product and process and to strive for continuous improvement. To do so, TQM depends on a well-honed management system that assures quality during every step of a process and for all processes within the system. It requires managing the whole system rather than just examining quality at the end of a process. It requires everyone in the organization to contribute to quality improvements and to assure that quality is achieved.

W. Edwards Deming, Joseph Juran, Armand Feigenbaum, Kaoru Ishikawa, Philip Crosby, and Genichi Taguchi were some of the principal architects of the quality imperative. These quality management leaders laid the foundation for TQM and its related practices in the US. Deming emphasized that it is management's responsibility to ensure quality and continuous improvement. During the early 1980s, when corporate leaders of many American companies asked Deming for proof that TQM would solve their problems and produce extraordinary results, Deming said just do it because it is inherently correct. He suggested that most quality defects are attributable to poor management and/or the management system, not due to the workers. He said that people want to produce quality products, because their jobs depend on it.[3] Deming believed in taking the appropriate actions before proof, if the theories were sufficiently in line with the requirements and expected outcomes. He indicated:[4]

> Experience alone, without theory, teaches management nothing about what to do to improve quality and competitive position, nor how to do it. If experience alone would be a teacher, then one may well ask why are we in this predicament [huge number of defects experienced by many American producers during the 1980s]? Experience will answer a question, and a question comes from theory. The theory in hand need not be elaborate. It may be only a hunch, or statement of principles.

Deming focused on getting companies out of the quality crisis. His perspectives can be applied to the management crisis of today, which goes beyond quality and the management system. It is a crisis of leadership and strategic management in many of the large companies and small- and medium-size enterprises (SMEs). Deming's thinking pertaining to TQM fits the logic of VSL and CSM perfectly.

Corporate leaders of today must take ownership of the current business crisis and adopt new theories and approaches for achieving successful outcomes across their business enterprises. They have to adhere to Deming's words and become the architects of change and new horizons. They must lead. Ultimately, such leadership involves not just a great vision and strategic direction, but a better understanding of reality and the expectations of the markets and business environment and the future. This includes the use of strategic thinking, the development and implementation of great strategies and solutions, and the proclivity for taking action. While some argue that a vision is the critical element for establishing one's future and others favor actions as the means to success, in today's world, it is not an "either-or" situation. Sustainable outcomes demand great visions, great strategies, real-world solutions, high-level actions, broad-based contributions, and everything in between. VSL incorporates the critical elements across the whole enterprise. It is impossible to say what elements are actually more important than others, especially when strategic leaders are engaged in turbulent times and their situations vary considerably. In his book, *Who Says Elephants Can't Dance?: Inside IBM's Historic Turnaround*, Louis Gerstner Jr. summarized his first press conference after becoming chief executive officer (CEO) of IBM in 1993. He said:[5]

> There has been a lot of speculation as to when I'm going to deliver a vision of IBM, and what I'd like to say to all of you is that the last thing IBM needs right now is a vision... I went on: What IBM needs right now is a series of very tough-minded, market-driven, highly effective strategies for each of its businesses—strategies that deliver performance in the marketplace and shareholder value. And that's what we're working on.

Gerstner's mindset at the time was exactly what was necessary to get IBM back on track. In the long term, many companies may face the need for such turnaround strategies unless they can break the typical pattern of employing successful mainstream approaches to maximize the short term that are followed by less successful approaches in the long term. Often these unfortunate cycles relate to the changes in strategic leadership or the failures of the strategic leaders. For example, Apple was very successful based on its first personal computer under the leadership of Steve Jobs and Steve Wozniak. Then, failure followed. Now, it is back on the road to success based on the leadership of the former CEO Steve Jobs (1955–2011) who redirected Apple and recreated its innovative spirit.

Competitive strategies and actions on a narrow front may sustain a company during the tenure of a given CEO (say ten years), but without proactive strategies designed to ensure the ongoing success, the company may decline after the incumbent leaves. Without a compelling vision and an integrated business framework for sustaining success, corporate leaders may find that they have to continuously solve problems and deal with turbulence in the marketplace. They may risk failure and even bankruptcy. The best strategies are useless unless there is a commitment to action and the willingness and dedication of knowledgeable people to properly execute the action plans and achieve results. Success is realized through execution, not just strategic thinking and planning.

Global Perspectives on VSL Pertaining to the Business Enterprise

The business enterprise is a management construct characterized by broad social, ethical, economic, environmental, technological, and organizational elements that are integrated into a holistic framework for achieving strategic objectives and realizing desired outcomes. It includes the corporation, the business units, the extended enterprise, and the broader aspects of the business environment and market spaces. The extended enterprise includes all of the important contributors to the success and all of the recipients of its solutions. The former includes supply networks, partners, allies, and other value networks. The latter includes customers, stakeholders, and related industries. It also includes competition.

VSL of the business enterprise is characterized by the extensive scope of the entities included and the time frame under consideration. It goes beyond just thinking about customers, markets, and competitors. Such broad-based strategic thinking runs the gamut from defining the business domain and direction of the business enterprise to understanding explicit and implicit realities for determining the needs, expectations, and perceptions of the business environment. It includes strategizing, creating, and implementing solutions and systems.

VSL implies being inclusive and innovative in leading the entire business enterprise, not just the company. As with the concept of a corporation, the business enterprise has multiple definitions and perspectives. The concept includes a new venture, the strategic transitions of existing businesses, the radical transformation of the entire company into a new reality, and high-level strategic innovations that produce enhanced solution(s), systems, and outcomes. While there are many ways to characterize a business enterprise, the following categories are the basic classifications for making strategic changes, improving future prospects, and enhancing the sustainable success:

- **New venture**—Framing the external and internal dimensions for planning, designing, developing, validating, and implementing a new business and/or startup company. VSL in this context involves corporate entrepreneurs who develop and implement business plans, business models, strategic frameworks, and the essentials for creating a new business.
- **Strategic transition**—Improving, developing, expanding, and growing business opportunities in existing businesses through a comprehensive and detailed assessment of the business environment, formulating and implementing hard-to-imitate strategies, and developing unique technologies, products, processes, and capabilities across the value system. VSL in this setting provides the perspective for discovering, detailing, developing, and deploying innovative solutions that exceed the needs and expectations of the market spaces. It focuses on making dramatic improvements, increasing strategic capabilities, and enhancing strategic positions.
- **Strategic transformation**—Redefining the strategic position(s) and direction of the company through quantum improvements and radical innovations that create exceptional new value. VSL provides a comprehensive perspec-

tive for determining and assessing opportunities and obtaining and developing the intellectual capital for achieving exceptional outcomes via social and economic enhancements, technological change, and business model transformations. It focuses on achieving enhancements in management sophistication and in the levels of achievements.
- **Strategic innovation**—Reinventing the vision, mission, and grand strategies of the corporation through radical changes from new technologies to a new business model, i.e., creating a whole new framework. VSL provides a comprehensive perspective for determining and understanding the opportunities for linking with strategic partners and external sources of intellectual capital to redefine the corporation and its businesses.

The business enterprise involves linking of the company and its business units with all of the external entities that are participants in the strategies, actions, transactions, exchanges, and processes for achieving outcomes and success. It also involves making ongoing changes and developments of the company with its direct and indirect relationships, all of its ventures, and innovation programs. The focus shifts from the traditional thinking of "what businesses are we in" to the more critical thinking of "what businesses should we or must we be in."

Regardless of the type and scope of the endeavor, whether it is a new company (a start-up) or a global corporation with enormous resources, the concepts discussed herein apply. The main perspectives are on VSL, value creation, the broad aspects of the internal and external dimensions, the future, and sustainable success. Most of the specifics pertain to companies that have been in business for some time and how their strategic leaders sustain success, i.e., how they make significant transitions and transformations and lead change. Evolving, changing, and making dramatic transitions or transformations are not options in today's business environment; they are absolute necessities. Survival and sustainable success depend on recognizing new requirements, mandates, opportunities, and challenges as soon as possible, and taking advantage of the positives and mitigating the negatives. Change is not an option; it is a relentless driving force.

Figure 1.2 provides a simplified view of the global perspectives of VSL. The perspectives provide visualization of the adage pertaining to out-of-the-box thinking. The "inner box" represents the scope of traditional strategic and operations management. Obviously, it does not include all of the complexities and richness of the real world of managing an organization and the strategic leadership and management thereof. However, some of the detail elements are covered in the subsequent chapters. The inner box represents the familiar landscape and time horizon that most strategic leaders feel comfortable with and where they are usually able to achieve reasonable financial, market, and strategic successes. Most strategic leaders are well trained and experienced in strategic management and the fundamentals of finance, marketing, operations, and the other functional areas. They have an adequate understanding of the prevailing conditions and trends in the served markets and the business environment. They typically have sufficient insights and innovative capabilities to deal with incremental

10 ■ *Visionary Strategic Leadership*

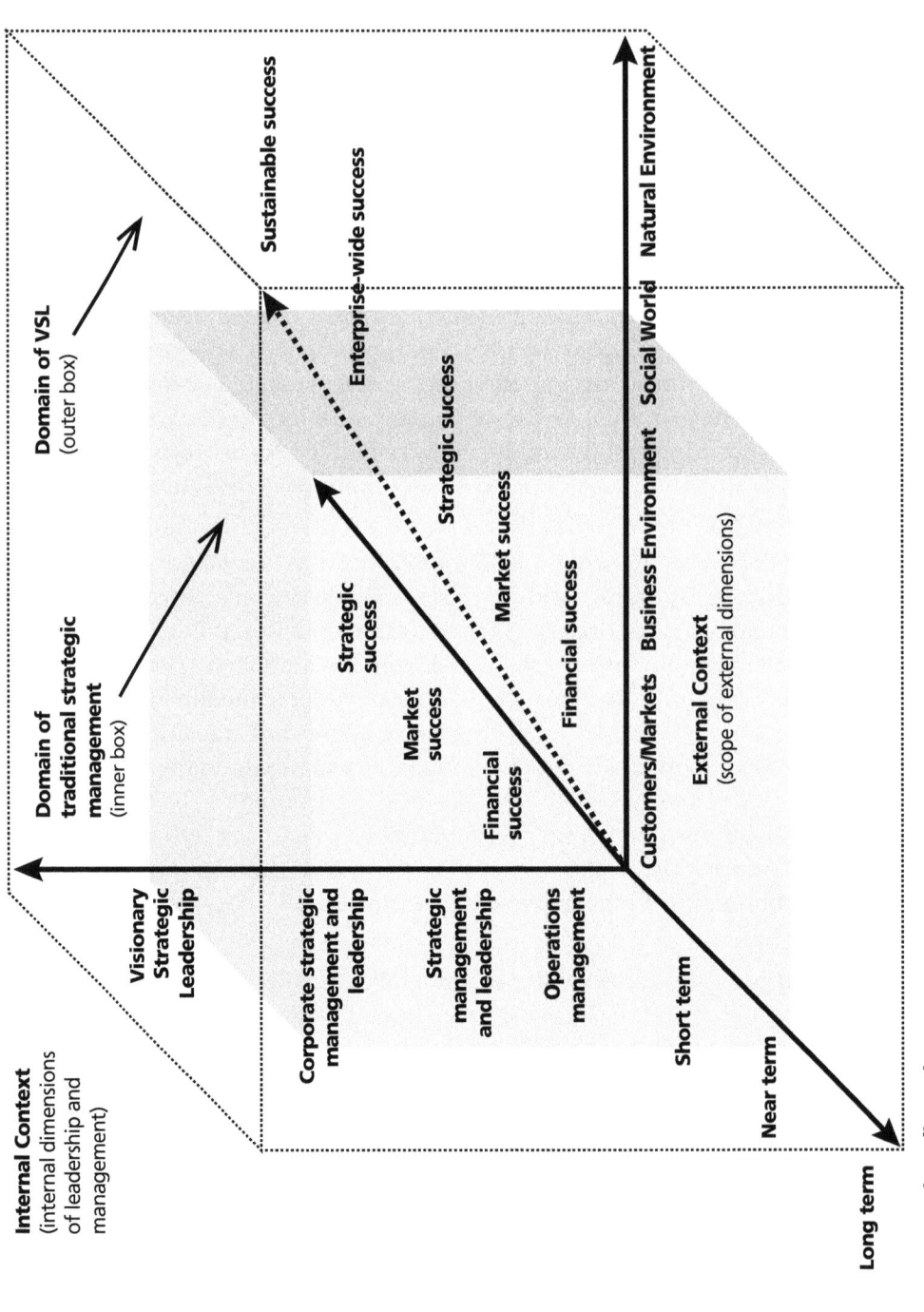

Figure 1.2 Global perspectives of visionary strategic leadership.

improvements in the short term and near term. For operational and functional management, the limited scope of the inner box provides an opportune reality, since functional leaders concentrate on converting inputs into outputs and turning actions and activities into desirable outcomes. They live in the present and near term and have to sustain their well-being through market success and financial performance.

For corporate leaders of most global corporations, the inner box perspectives provide real opportunities, but they are often narrow. There is a bigger world of opportunities as depicted by the "outer box" that may be many times larger than the realities of the prevailing business situations. However, most of the broader, long-term and/or global opportunities therein are often not addressed because strategic leaders have limited perspectives. While corporate leaders may engage in high levels of strategic thinking and explore opportunities outside of their served markets, many strategic leaders lack imagination and insights to discover and develop new markets, determine the new opportunities in the business environment, and understand the realities and possibilities in the broader social world and natural environment.

VSL involves finding new opportunities within the prevailing business situations (the inner box) and exploring the broader possibilities as portrayed in the outer box. While the broader business world is full of new and exciting opportunities and challenges, it takes global (holistic) perspectives to identify new opportunities in markets that are not being served or those in the broader social and natural worlds. Visionary strategic leaders need an inclusive framework for determining the true realities of the world to discover what the possibilities mean over time. For instance, in the developing countries there are approximately four to five billion people who like basic products for their well-being (food, shelter, clothing, health care, etc.), but most of the existing products provided by the global corporations are not suited for their situations. Think about the enormous opportunities in finding solutions for the majority of humankind living in the developing countries; those who are usually not on the radar screens of the multinational corporations.

As the business world changes over the next several decades, resource requirements and human-related activities are expected to increase three to fourfold, yet the sources of raw materials and strategic resources are limited in the natural environment, especially the non-renewable ones. Therefore, there are great opportunities in changing the business world from one based on "production and consumption" to one based on sustainable development, clean technologies, sustainable solutions, and sustainable success. The business world of tomorrow requires visionary strategic leaders who have the imagination and insights to know what the best opportunities and real possibilities are, and how to translate them into exciting realities through intellectual capital, value creation, strategic innovations, value systems, value delivery, and hard work.

Principles, Values, Beliefs, and Ethical Standards

VSL is based on the philosophical underpinnings that include being open and honest, engaging people, building solid relationships, and leading change. Visionary strategic leaders are not superiors who dictate to the organization, but are high-level strategic leaders who have the overarching duty to ensure the survival and long-term success of the organization. They have to envision and articulate the fundamental values, beliefs, and ethical standards for the organization and the enterprise(s). They set the examples and "walk the talk." They do not place themselves at the top and look down upon subordinates; they view themselves as part of the organizational team. They have the awesome obligations to think about the future, to determine the strategic options, and to select the means and mechanisms for achieving success. They ultimately are the ones who make the strategies, solutions, systems, and structures work and integrate people into a seamless business enterprise with solid relationships amongst the people.

VSL necessitates leaders who are trustworthy and have integrity and personal courage. Visionary strategic leaders create an organizational culture that follows these principles and ensures that everyone regardless of positions and status is treated appropriately and with respect. Jim Collins in his bestseller, *Good to Great*, describes exactly what it takes to be a visionary leader. He suggests that the most critical element for developing a great company is to develop great leadership.[6] Collins asserts "Level 5 Leadership" as the highest level of strategic leadership. He describes "Level 5 Leadership" as the starting point in the process to becoming great.[7]

> *Level 5 leaders* channel their ego needs away from themselves and into the larger goal of building a great company. It's not that Level 5 leaders have no ego or self-interest. Indeed they are incredibly ambitious—but their ambition is first and foremost for the institution, not themselves.

Leadership is often an esoteric concept that is difficult for young business leaders and students to fully comprehend. VSL obviously is even more difficult to truly articulate, never mind fully comprehend and practice. While VSL is a complex topic, there are fundamentals that everyone can develop and use. In my book, *The Pursuit of Sustainable Leadership: Becoming a Successful Strategic Leader Through Principles, Perspectives, and Professional Development*, the main precepts of full-spectrum strategic leadership are articulated as follows:[8]

- **Truthfulness, candor, integrity and trust**—Truthfulness and honesty imply telling the whole truth in every situation. Candor involves making full disclosures of the facts and circumstances. Integrity means protecting the whole and ensuring that no one is caused to suffer losses due to inappropriate actions. Integrity results from high standards, ethical practices, impeachable methods, and proper disclosures. Trust binds people together across the enterprise in the knowledge that the proper actions are being taken. Trust is essential for achieving sustainable success. Collectively, truthfulness, candor, integrity and trust enhance the reputations of the strategic leaders and their organizations.
- **Openness and transparency**—Openness is essential in building trust, integrity and awareness across the enterprise. Information and data is shared with all appropriate constituents to ensure that plans, actions, and outcomes have peer review and are generally acceptable both internally and externally. Transparency implies that companies provide pertinent facts and information to customers and stakeholders, and report all of the salient details about products, operations and activities to the public on a reasonable, not confidential, basis and in keeping with regulations.

- **Ethics and responsible behaviors**—Ethical practices are related to trust. It is expected that corporations and their associations will police themselves to ensure that best practices are employed and that individuals, groups, departments, business units and the entire organization act and behave in a responsible, prudent, and safe manner. Ethical practices involve complying with laws and regulations, mitigating problems and negative impacts, and informing constituencies about the full implications of products and operations.
- **Value creation and innovativeness**—Astute leaders ensure that value innovations include incremental improvements to existing technologies, products and processes and radical new inventions and discoveries for exciting solutions through new technologies and new products; ones that meet the needs and wants of customers, stakeholders, and constituents. Innovations include new business models, systems, processes, methods, and techniques for creating sustainable solutions
- **Inclusiveness and connectedness**—Inclusiveness implies that leaders integrate the internal strategic and operating systems with the external entities, partners, allies, supply networks, customers, stakeholders, related industries, infrastructure and other support relationships. It is based on a holistic understanding, analysis, and execution of all of the processes involved from the raw materials to the disposal of the residuals and waste streams. Connectedness involves building solid relationships with people across the enterprise.
- **Dual-sided perspectives and sustainable success**—Leaders must focus on creating sustainable solutions in terms of balanced perspectives of all of the forces and requirements impinging on the enterprise. The overarching objective is to create outstanding value for everyone by improving the positive outcomes, reducing the negative impacts, and ensuring that all contributors and recipients are successful.

Leaders of all persuasions must always engage in the truth and never use deception and deceit. Moreover, telling the whole truth means disclosing all of the relevant (non-confidential) facts and ensuring that people are not disadvantaged or harmed by the organization's leaders, products, processes, etc. In many cases, strategic leaders create their own problems because they operate in the shady areas or they fail to evaluate outcomes on an ongoing basis. It takes courage to be open and lead rather than simply following the norms of selective disclosures, especially when it involves going against the prevailing practices. Visionary strategic leaders have to operate in the real world and in the "sunshine" so that the fuzzy gray areas that often create problems and uncertainties are eliminated. Effective strategic leaders ensure that the company's rhetoric is followed by proper actions across the organization. Openness and transparency involve initiating actions to discover and disclose difficulties and taking corrective actions quickly and decisively.

Visionary strategic leaders have to be the role models for their organizations. They have to exhibit good behaviors and avoid using the old adage "do as I say, not as I do." Great sounding rhetoric without substance quickly becomes readily apparent to people within and outside the organization. Employees, in particular, have a great sense of the realities of their organization. Regardless of what the executives espouse, employees usually understand the realities and the true meanings of the messages. They intuitively know whether leaders are committed to their words or are just using flowery statements to get through some challenges and difficulties.

Being ethical implies that strategic leaders follow generally accepted principles and high standards of personal behavior. Ethical leaders make sound decisions for the greater good of the organization and the enterprise; they do not do so to enrich themselves. They are fair and balanced in their approaches and provide equitable outcomes. Equality encompasses the human side and the social implications of ethical responsibilities. It can be divided into categories: the "must do" (laws and regulations), "should do" (social norms and expectations), "may decide to do" (logic and fit), and "would like to do" (philanthropy). Fairness implies being unbiased and impartial in decision making and strategic action. It also means ensuring that everyone is treated with respect and is rewarded for his or her contributions. Being fair goes a long way in getting people to follow one's lead.

Integrity is one of the most important fundamentals of leadership. Not everyone has charisma and attractive personal characteristics, but every leader can have integrity and high personal values. Leaders can live up to their commitments and honor their word. Integrity is a key ingredient in being a successful leader. It reinforces the trust that people have in the leaders and their willingness to depend on the leader's leadership. Integrity is difficult and time consuming to build, but it is easily damaged, and quickly lost.

The Critical Roles and Responsibilities of Corporate Leaders

Corporate leaders usually have the most complicated and demanding roles and responsibilities of all the decision makers within the ranks of strategic leaders and management. They have countless explicit and implicit requirements, mandates, expectations, actions, and decisions that have to be addressed, assessed, and acted upon in a global context that is often ill-defined and constantly changing. Change is the norm and managing change is one of most critical roles of corporate leaders, i.e., to prepare the company for the future and to assure that it can sustain success. The strategic challenges involving change are often difficult to identify because of the inexact nature of the knowledge, the limited understanding of the external context, and the lack of generally accepted methods for cutting-edge strategic analysis and corporate decision making. In the old world of the early twentieth century, corporate leaders had more time to sort out the strategic alternatives and select the most effective choices. In the more open-ended and fast-paced world of today, time is a critical factor. Corporate leaders generally do not have the luxury of the old "wait and see" approach. They have to act expeditiously based on knowledge, information and data that are often incomplete and fragmented. Taking the time to study and completely assess the external context after an opportunity or threat develops often results in delays in decision making and ineffective results. Thus, one of the most critical roles and responsibilities of corporate leaders and the senior professionals who support them is being fully aware of the global context from the natural environment and social/human world to market spaces, customers, and stakeholders.

Corporate leaders have to develop potential solutions and systems that create better business value and a better business world. But, unlike most strategic management frameworks or processes of the past, the focus is on global perspectives that are holistic and not just on markets and competitors. Indeed, the latter is more of the responsibility of lower level management and not high-level (corporate) strategic leaders whose agenda(s) should focus on considering what has to be done to create a more positive future than just trying to optimize the present and near term.

Corporate leaders are more akin to the innovative leaders who created and directed the space programs, like the Apollo Program and the International Space Station. There were no maps to follow or predecessors to chart the way. Knowledge, intellectual capital, wisdom, and effective decision making were necessary attributes as the leaders navigated the uncharted routes of space exploration. Uncertainty was high, but there were many accomplishments and encouragements through the understanding of the fundamentals of science and technology and the realities of human intellect and learning. Based on searching for knowledge and understanding, constraints and limitations faded away, replaced with imagination, insights, innovations, and confidence. Corporate leaders face the same challenges. They have to think more broadly and have more global perspectives of what is possible and desirable. The two most critical aspects are the available or prospective strategic opportunities and the possible solutions that can be developed and deployed to create sustainable advantages and enduring outcomes. Strategic opportunities include external challenges and threats since, if acted upon correctly, threats can be turned into opportunities. While it is not always easy, a primary role and responsibility of corporate leaders is to discover how to reinvent and expand the corporation's horizons, not just to make continuous improvements. Creating exciting new-to-the-world solutions based on global perspectives is among the most effective ways to transform corporate realities into sustainable success.

A corporate/visionary strategic leader is a planner, an architect, a change agent, and an implementer as well as a fiduciary and an administrator. He or she focuses on the business environment, market spaces, strategies, objectives, systems, and solutions—not just on technologies, products, and processes; and on strategic success—not just making money. Solutions are exactly where the interests of businesses and people converge. People want great solutions and sustainable businesses seek to create, produce, and deliver the best solutions possible.

Figure 1.3 identifies some of the essential roles and responsibilities of corporate leadership and VSL. It is not intended to be comprehensive. It can be modified or adapted to fit the specifics of a given company or the specific situations and circumstances of corporate leaders. It involves broad generalizations, but should not be viewed as normative. While it is intended for corporate leaders, some of the elements are applicable to strategic leaders at lower levels of an organization.

The following include the main segments and the critical elements:

- **Fiduciary roles and responsibilities:** The top segment illustrates some of the high-level roles and responsibilities; those pertaining to corporate leaders' fiduciary requirements to shareholders and stakeholders, such as assuring proper governance, understanding, and managing external context, complying with government mandates, protecting the well-being of humankind,

16 ▪ Visionary Strategic Leadership

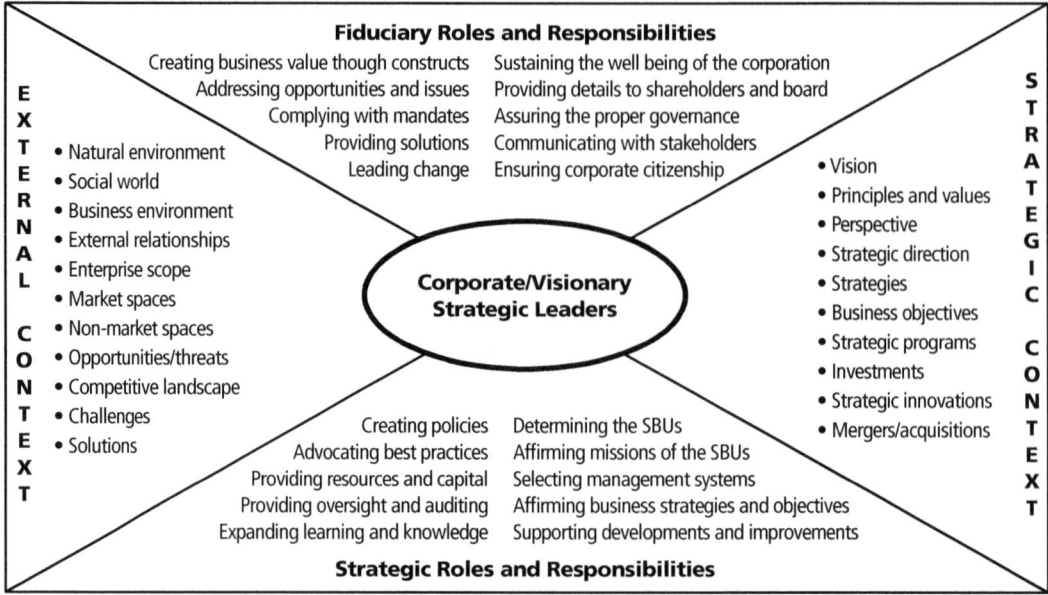

Figure 1.3 Essential roles and responsibilities of visionary corporate leaders.

preserving the natural environment, and leading change. The specific roles and responsibilities depend on the individual's duties and, of course, the realities of the actual business situations.

- **Strategic roles and responsibilities:** The bottom segment illustrates primary internal leadership and strategic management roles and responsibilities; ones pertaining to providing proper strategic direction, strategic management, policies, business strategies and best practices, allocating resources, and making commitments. It includes the systems and structures.
- **External context:** The left segment denotes roles and responsibilities pertaining to all of the dimensions of the external business world. They include the realities and driving forces in the market spaces, business environment, social world, and natural environment. They include all of the global contributors and recipients of the solutions and the related value delivery systems.
- **Strategic context:** The right segment involves the strategic context of the company and its strategic business units (SBUs). The focus is on the strategic leadership and management constructs and how the corporate leaders create a sustainable future. It includes strategic plans and high-level strategic programs for transforming the company into a more effective and successful entity.

In essence, the global perspective is akin to the cardinal directions of the Earth—north, south, east, and west. Corporate leaders are involved with and responsible for the full spectrum of the people involved and of space and time. One is not more critical than the other, and each has its own degrees of importance depending on situations and circumstances.

The fiduciary roles and responsibilities [the north] are generally explicit based on the external context [the west] and the driving forces impinging on the company. The fiduciary roles and responsibilities include those that corporate/visionary strategic leaders have to shareholders, the board of directors, the investment community, government agencies, the external communities and stakeholders, and society. First and foremost, corporate leaders ensure that the well-being of the company is sustained over time. They protect the shareholders' interests and ensure that shareholders receive their due rewards. In this regard, they communicate with shareholders and provide fair and accurate information about the strategies, initiatives, and affairs of the corporation. They report to the board of directors and obtain board approvals for strategic actions like the strategic plans, strategic direction, high-level strategic programs, investments, strategic innovations, and mergers/acquisitions, among many other strategic actions.

Astute corporate leaders encourage the selection of a board of directors that represents the broad interests of the shareholders and communities served by the corporation. While this may be difficult to orchestrate, corporate leaders are better served by an inquiring and dedicated board that reviews everything and reaches concurrence on strategic direction and actions. While boards that tend to "rubber stamp" everything that may appear to support corporate management, such situations are not helpful in the long term and often leave corporate leaders without one of the most valuable contributions from the board-positive oversight, especially from knowledgeable outside directors.[9]

Corporate leaders have to assure the proper governance of the company and the SBUs. In these turbulent days of many corporate transgressions, strategic leaders have to create policies and/or practices to control the affairs; to monitor the ongoing administration, operations, actions, and activities; and to find and resolve discrepancies and difficulties before they become overwhelming. Governance is the duty of all strategic leaders and managers who have assets that they have to protect, operations that they must maintain and control, and people of whom they have to take care. Corporate governance includes many topics some of which are covered in Chapter 2. The in-depth details require additional discussions and assessments that are beyond the scope of this book.[10]

Corporate leaders are the crucial links with the outside world of customers, stakeholders, and society. They function as the corporate citizens. They are the individuals who create and support relationships with all of the high-level connections of the corporation. Moreover, they ensure that everyone within the corporation exhibits the proper responses to the other citizens in the external context, and specifically in the countries and communities where the corporation conducts business. Corporate communications and reporting are critical management constructs that the global corporations and SMEs rely upon to deliver their messages and information to shareholders and stakeholders alike. However, corporate reporting is not a marketing tool to favorably influence outsiders with the corporate leaders' view of reality. It involves fair and honest disclosures of corporate information that help owners and outsiders understand the corporation and what it is trying to accomplish. It also involves the unveiling of non-confidential information and data to convey openness and build trust with the outside entities, communities, and individuals. In doing so, corporate leaders inspire confidence in their strategies and actions and reinforce the faith that people have in the corporation.

Corporate leaders lead change by finding new-to-the-company opportunities and getting the organization to convert them into new-to-the-world solutions. They select the management constructs for guiding and encouraging the organization to make strategic decisions and take actions. While it is usually the whole organization that ensures compliance with laws and regulations, corporate leaders and SBU leaders have the overarching responsibilities to ensure compliance and fulfill ethical considerations.

Strategic roles and responsibilities [the south] are the derived management constructs that embrace strategic context and decision making [the east]. The strategic decisions are based on assessments of the external context and the strategic direction provided by the board of directors and corporate leadership. Strategic decisions provide direction that SBU leaders and managers of the operating systems require to execute their responsibilities, to fulfill their missions, and to achieve their business objectives. Corporate leaders are responsible for the strategic management of the whole, but they typically delegate lower level decision making and actions to strategic leaders and general managers of the SBUs. Corporate leaders determine the organizational design and the configuration of the SBUs and operating systems, but they typically allow the SBU leaders to articulate the missions of their business units. However, corporate leaders generally have the obligations to affirm the strategic decisions and actions, and to assure proper oversight. The same is true for selecting the individual strategic management systems. Corporate leaders may wish to have certain similarities among the business units. Yet, given the importance of flexibility and the dissimilarities that may exist in highly diversified corporations, such decisions are often based on the circumstances and not by hard rules.

Corporate leaders may allow lower level leaders latitude in selecting business strategies and objectives with the provision that they fit the overall corporate strategies and objectives. Again, the approaches are dependent on the context and nature of the company and the business units. The actual approaches are often based on how closely aligned the corporation and the SBUs are and the degree of flexibility that is necessary. While there are many specific roles and responsibilities that corporate leaders have in creating, promoting, supporting, and monitoring the success of the company and its SBUs, some of the most critical are the implementation and the execution of high-level strategic programs. These topics are covered in Chapters 5 and 6.

Sustainable success involves selecting the overall policies and practices that are used. It also involves allocating the appropriate level of resources and ensuring that the organization has the intellectual capital. The former includes money and the required resources and the latter includes people and the talent. A critical factor involves expanding the knowledge and learning within the organization and ensuring that new leaders are developed and given the opportunities to gain experience and insights through real world decision making. Moreover, corporate leaders have the duty to guide lower level decision making and actions. They may execute this responsibility through various forms of performance evaluation.

While many elements can be specified and certain responsibilities are articulated in corporate documents like corporate charters and by-laws, the roles and responsibilities of corporate leaders are difficult to completely identify and fully articulate. Such positions tend to be open-ended and it is impossible to characterize them completely; leaving them open may be the best way to deal with the degree of sophistication necessary and complexities involved. Corporate leaders are critical contributors and are often paid very well because they have the awesome roles and responsibilities to sustain success and to ensure that the undesirable effects and impacts are eliminated or avoided.

As an aside, the board of directors often rewards corporate leaders for increasing profits, improving the share price, and expanding the businesses. They should also find ways to reward corporate leaders for assuring that bad things do not happen and that good things continue to happen well into the future. Think about the shareholder value lost due to explosions at refineries, supertankers spilling their cargo, product defects that result in massive recalls, and environmental liabilities due to negligence.

BOX 1: STRATEGIC LEADERSHIP AT GENERAL ELECTRIC

General Electric (GE) is one of the most complex and successful corporations in the world. It is ranked near the top of the Fortune lists in market capitalization, revenues, and profitability. The sustained growth and success of GE make it among the best of all of the corporations to operate over the last one hundred years. In its 2005 Citizenship Report, GE lists several testaments to its heritage of sustained success.[a]

> In a recent study conducted by the consulting firm Booz Allen Hamilton, GE was named one of the World's 10 Most Enduring Institutions of the last 100 years—putting GE in the company of the U.S. Constitution, Oxford University, the Olympic Games and the Rolling Stones. Criteria included an institution's ability to maintain market leadership over time, an ability to innovate,m and to lead in governance practices. In a poll of global CEOs conducted by the Financial Times and PriceWaterhouseCoopers in November 2004, GE was rated the most respected company in the world for corporate governance and the most respected company overall for the seventh consecutive year. In February 2005, GE was named the "World's Most Admired Company" in a poll of business leaders conducted by Fortune magazine. GE was one of only 34 companies to receive a perfect score of 10.0 from GovernanceMetrics International, an independent service evaluating the quality of a company's corporate governance.

GE's success in achieving growth, customer and stakeholder satisfaction, and financial performance is based on its global perspectives of the business environment and its ability to make investments at the right time. GE's goal is to "increase the range and depth of our engagements with non-governmental organizations and advocacy groups to identify how GE can best perform and deliver products and services that meet the needs of society and the environment."[b] While this goal is not extraordinary in the grand scheme of goals, it does suggest a broad range of global perspectives that include the needs and expectations of society and the natural environment. GE's overarching principles complement the goal; its nine guiding principles include:[c]

- Maintain a culture that makes performance with integrity the bedrock principle of the company
- Set high standards of performance
- Make compliance a core operating principle
- Build exceptional governance with a strong board
- Be open and transparent
- Develop great leaders with the right incentives
- Make a business out of solving the world's toughest problems
- Take ethical actions that are beyond what the rules require and in the long-term interest of stakeholders and the company
- Give back to communities through philanthropy and volunteerism

These principles combine a focus on performance, leadership, good governance, ethics, and social responsibility. They promote the idea of seeking out opportunities to create new solutions to global problems. Working under the guidance of these principles, GE's strategic imperatives are to sustain a strong portfolio organized around markets and customers, develop initiatives that promote organic growth (growth in customer value, innovation, and leadership in technology, commercial excellence and globalization), and to develop people within a strong culture.[d]

Jack Welch focused on financial performance and six-sigma quality among many other initiatives. During his tenure, Welch changed the structure of GE's portfolios, eliminating or selling unprofitable or underperforming businesses. He shifted the portfolio toward service businesses and dramatically increased GE's market capitalization. He created an impressive array of new businesses. Welch decentralized the organization, simplifying its structure and downsizing the management core. During those years, GE enjoyed great financial success, improving from sales of $27.2 billion and profits of $1.6 billion in 1981 to sales of $173.2 billion and profits of $10.7 billion in 2001.[e] However, even with such great accomplishments, there were many areas that received insufficient attention. The most important areas were innovation and environmental management.

In 2001, Jeff Immelt became the CEO and he quickly made fundamental shifts in strategic thinking. He focused on the importance of customer-driven value creation, strategic innovation, and strategic leadership. His goals were to make GE more customer-centric and to make the "customer more efficient, more profitable, and more innovative."[f] Immelt is also an advocate of strategic innovations and new-to-the-world technologies. In a *New York Times* article dated December 26, 2002, Nicholas P. Heymann of Prudential Securities is quoted saying, "Jack Welch won the socket wars, the battle to stay ahead with tangible products. Jeff must now use R&D to win the value-added wars."[g] Immelt is doing just that as GE focuses on customer needs and creates new businesses and technologies to meet those related to water, energy, nanotechnology, and healthcare.

Immelt is transforming the strategic leadership and corporate culture of GE and striving to achieve long-term success through organic growth. To this end, the company has identified five leadership traits that have significantly contributed to its sustainable success to date. The most significant traits of strategic leaders are:[h]

- had *external focus* that defined success in market terms
- were *clear thinkers* who simplified strategy into specific actions, made decisions and communicated priorities
- had *imagination* and courage to take risks on both people and ideas
- were energized by *inclusiveness* and a connection with people which builds loyalty and commitment
- developed *expertise* in a particular function or domain, using depth as a source of confidence to drive change

Indeed, these are some of the most important elements of VSL. Leaders have to use imagination and insights to create solutions and achieve sustainable success. They have to take a holistic view of all of the forces affecting the business environment. They have to be well educated and prepared to deal with issues outside their training and knowledge. With these requirements in mind, Immelt is leading GE's transformation to its next level of success. While the road is never straight and easy to follow, the journey is exciting with great promise. GE is focusing on external context to create an even more sustainable enterprise because its leaders recognize that success is not guaranteed and past performance provides a great legacy, but the future requires courage and strategic innovations to stay on the cutting edge of corporate success.

NOTES

a. GE 2005 Citizen Report, p17.
b. Id, p15.
c. Id.
d. GE 2005 Annual Report, p7.
e. GE Annual Reports
f. GE 2005 Annual Report, p18.
g. www.nytimes.com/2002/12/26/business/26LAB.html?ex=1041945881&ei=1&en=e01a1 6a293c0f497
h. GE 2005 Annual Report, p11.

Reflections

Astute corporate leaders understand that they have to lead the way through imagination, insights, and innovations. They have to inspire their organizations and enterprises to create new solutions based on global perspectives. They have to produce extraordinary value and outcomes that ensure sustainable success. Corporate leaders create the means and mechanisms to identify and evaluate opportunities, challenges, risks, vulnerabilities, and constraints faced by their businesses in determining their strategic direction and mapping out initiatives and strategic actions. The focus is on discovering, developing, and implementing creative strategies and innovative solutions.

Corporate leaders create systems and structures through people and entities in the business environment. They encourage collaboration and achieving mutual success. Likewise, they build solid connections and working relations with strategic and operational management within the organization. They also create a sense of belonging, which turns into welcoming relationships with all the contributors and recipients of the company.

Corporate leaders decide upon the overall framework, the management constructs, and management approaches that apply to the whole organizations and the lower level strategic and operational managers, especially those at the business unit level. The strategic leaders at the lower levels generally have to follow the dictates of the higher level executives and their strategic direction. While there may be latitude within such approaches and processes for handling specific needs based on the differences among business units, most large corporations have frameworks and management constructs that map out the pathways to provide a sense of uniformity and control across the organization.

Notes

1. BP Environmental and Social Review 2002, BP p.l.c., London, p15.
2. http://www.texascityexplosion.com/
3. W. Edwards Deming, *Out of The Crisis* (Cambridge, MA: MIT Press, 2000, pp77–79).
4. Id, p19.
5. Louis Gerstner Jr., *Who Says Elephants Can't Dance?: Inside IBM's Historic Turnaround* (New York, NY: HarperBusiness, 2002, pp68–69).
6. Jim Collins, *Good to Great: Why Some Companies Make the Leap . . . and Others Don't* (New York, NY: Harper Business, 2001, p21).
7. Id. While some of the concept discussed in *Good to Great* fit the constructs of sustainable enterprise management, the premise of success using Collin's methods depended on meeting financial objectives rather than achieving multifaceted outcomes.
8. David L. Rainey, *The Pursuit of Sustainable Leadership: Becoming a Successful Strategic Leader Through Principles, Perspectives, and Professional Development* (Charlotte, NC: Information Age Publishing, 2013, pp6–7).
9. It is not possible to examine the roles and responsibilities of the board of directors in this book given that it a special topic that requires in-depth analysis and discussions. Please refer to *Taking Back the Boardroom: Better directing for the new Millennium*, Phillip Phan, McGraw-Hill Book Company, 2000.
10. John Colley, Jr., Jacqueline Doyle, George Logan, & Wallace Stettinius, *Corporate Governance*, (New York: NY: McGraw-Hill Companies, Inc. 2003).

References

Colley, Jr., John Jacqueline Doyle, George Logan, & Wallace Stettinius (2003) *Corporate Governance.* New York, NY: McGraw-Hill Companies, Inc.

Collins, Jim (2001) *Good to Great: Why Some Companies Make the Leap . . . and Others Don't.* New York, NY: Harper Business.

Deming, W. Edwards (2000) *Out of the Crisis.* Cambridge, MA: MIT Press.

Gerstner Jr., Louis (2002) *Who Says Elephants Can't Dance? : Inside IBM's Historic Turnaround.* New York, NY: HarperBusiness.

Rainey, David L. (2013) *The Pursuit of Sustainable Leadership: Becoming a Successful Strategic Leader Through Principles, Perspectives, and Professional Development.* Charlotte, NC: Information Age Publishing.

2

Corporate Leadership and Management

Introduction

Corporate strategic management (CSM) involves high-level management constructs pertaining to the strategic management of the corporation and its proper governance. CSM entails enriching, protecting, and preserving the short-term and long-term successes and the value of the corporation and all of its knowledge, capabilities, assets, and contributions. It involves assessing, selecting, and developing the frameworks, models, methods, techniques and approaches used for understanding context, formulating and implementing strategies, creating and producing solutions, designing and deploying systems, organizing and managing structures, and delivering positive outcomes. Corporate leadership underpins CSM.

Corporate leadership is broadly used in the context of CSM, but it is difficult to precisely define and it often conveys numerous connotations. It generally implies that high-level strategic leaders develop the vision for the future of their organizations and they translate the vision into strategic direction, actions, and outcomes. Context involves external and internal domains of the corporation and its enterprises. Context includes the global business environment, market spaces, the organization, the businesses, and the extended enterprises. External context involves the broad perspectives about the driving forces, opportunities, challenges, threats, risks, and all of the exciting prospects for discovering or creating new possibilities and realities. Internal context involves strategic leadership, the systems and structures, and all of the resources and capabilities.

Corporate leadership involves determining what needs to be done and developing innovative ways to translate external opportunities and challenges and internal capabilities and resources into positive outcomes and enduring success. Corporate strategic leaders combine information, data, experience, and knowledge with theoretical thinking and practical judgment about how to direct and guide the company and its business enterprises in light of its opportunities, challenges, limitations, and risks.[1] Corporate leaders are responsible for ensuring that the long term is more fruitful than the short term. This implies that the organization and contributors become more capable and sophisticated over time. This necessitates that corporate leaders embrace visionary strategic leadership (VSL) and engage in being the architects of the future.

As discussed in Chapter 1, VSL is about imagining what can be done, determining how to achieve positive outcomes, and realizing successes even though many of the requisite actions are not possible given the existing realities. VSL goes beyond traditional strategic leadership and strategic management. While VSL includes many of the elements of the traditional concepts, it principally involves creating a more desirable future based on imagination, insights, and innovations. It is about creating desirable solutions and achieving sustainable outcomes. It involves awesome duties and responsibilities based on global perspectives and real world needs, wants, and expectations. Visionary strategic leaders embrace change. They invent the future. They craft a vision and set strategic direction just like technologists invent new technologies and products. Inventing the future involves understanding the prevailing context and having a great sense of the expected changes.

A corporate vision is the set of clearly articulated aspirations, desires, and goals. It maps out the big picture of what the corporation/enterprise/organization wants to be at some time in the future, why it is important to realize the desired positions and outcomes, what pathways lead to success, and how to effectively and efficiently move along the pathways to the future. It is generally understood that the vision may take years, even decades, to realize. Moreover, the aspirations and aims are not the terminal points, but the high-level targets that set forth the direction and guide strategic decision making without constraining possibilities and outcomes. The vision should inspire the organization and the whole business enterprise and facilitate the development of the long-term objectives, grand strategies, expected strategic positions, and desired outcomes.

VSL and CSM in the context of this book pertain mostly to high-level strategic leaders of global corporations and small- and medium-size enterprises (SMEs). Strategic leaders are expected to exceed the needs, wants, and expectations of customers, stakeholders, shareholders, all of the internal and external contributors, and the other direct and indirect entities involved in creating and providing fruitful outcomes and success. While the constructs of VSL and CSM may also pertain to many types of leaders including government agencies and not-for-profit organizations, the content herein generally focuses on high-level strategic leaders of complex business organizations.

Conventional leadership perspectives are typically more limited in scope and timeframe than the constructs associated with the discussions herein about VSL and CSM.

The traditional view usually involves only the corporation and its direct contributors and beneficiaries. The time frame is also more limited to the near term, say five years out, rather than ten or more years. Conventional methods focus on the specific elements within the strategic management system(s) and the related operations. Such methods are normally simple and easy to understand because each element is examined separately. In many cases, each part of the construct is developed and optimized as if it is an independent component. However, the strength (simplicity) of more traditional approaches is also the main weakness (limited perspectives). While examining the parts separately facilitates understanding the details of what is required, the big picture and the more elaborate context are often lost. Using such constructs, most strategic leaders have little difficulty orchestrating what is necessary for making incremental improvements, but they often find it difficult, if not impossible, to create the means and mechanisms for achieving significant strategic innovations; ones that transform the organization and dramatically enhance its prospects and realities. For instance, with the growing energy crisis, petroleum industry leaders usually ask the wrong questions; they want to know where to find more oil reserves and how to exploit the existing resources and capabilities. The more important questions are: how to better utilize the petroleum-based fuels?; how to dramatically reduce their negative effects and impacts on the social, political, economic, and environmental well-being of the world?; and, how to develop new solutions that have fewer shortcomings? Finding new solutions like renewable energy technologies would allow the petroleum companies to continue producing their current products for a longer period of time; thus, leveraging existing assets, while at the same time offering more sustainable solutions and better outcomes. The sooner such strategic leaders start tackling the critical questions, the quicker the resolutions are likely to come to fruition.

CSM is also about business integration. Astute corporate leaders integrate the organization and the enterprise together through systems and structures that ensure the whole is more than the sum of the parts. The intent is to create a cohesive entity that is creativity, insightful, innovative, interrelated, collaborative, and moving ahead in unison.

The chapter includes the following main topics:

- Describing the VSL and CSM framework
- Articulating the main elements of VSL and CSM including corporate governance
- Discussing high-level management constructs including sustainable business development (SBD) and corporate social responsibility (CSR)

The Integrated VSL and CSM Framework

At the corporate level (C-level), VSL and CSM tend to merge and it is difficult to truly separate the domain of strategic leadership from the domain of strategic management. Thus, an integrated framework for VSL and CSM (referred to herein as "the integrated framework") includes the primary constructs of leadership, management, innovation, and integration. The integrated framework links the essential elements of the company and its extended enterprise(s) into an integrated system(s). The integrated framework is depicted Figure 2.1. While it is difficult to show all of the elements and interrelationships of a business enterprise, the integrated framework attempts to identify the most critical ones so that corporate leaders can understand how best to address the most important opportunities, challenges, threats, risks, and vulnerabilities. While an integrated framework provides a better understanding of the business world, it is also more difficult to explain the details to leaders, managers, professionals, and practitioners because it is more involved than traditional management constructs.

The integrated framework more accurately represents the proper perspectives of the corporation, its businesses, the business world (external context), and the interrelationships therein. While the intent is to portray the essential elements involved in leading and managing global corporations and SMEs, it is impossible to convey all of the intricacies and interfaces in a single framework or even in a single book. The focus is on the global perspectives of VSL and CSM.

Business scholars using conventional strategic management thinking may argue that the integrated framework is complex; and, they might be right. Nevertheless, today's business world is even more complex. It is much more complicated than just a

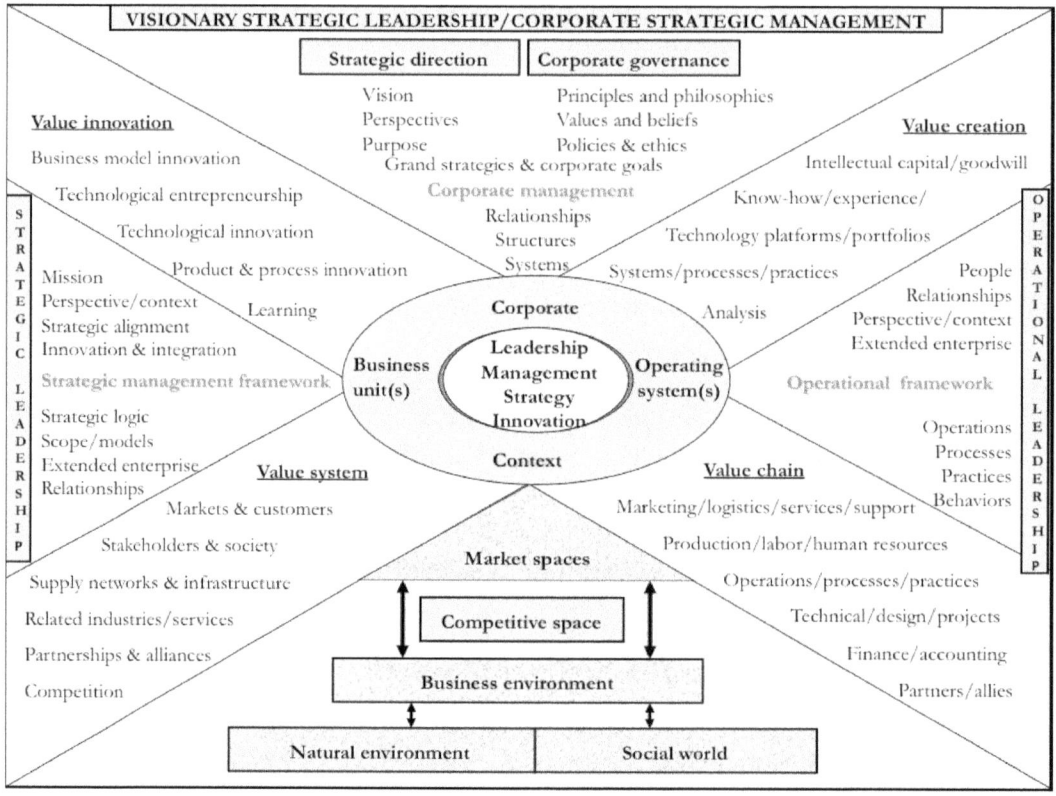

Figure 2.1 The integrated VSL and CSM framework.

generation ago and more so than indicated by conventional management constructs used by many global corporations.

The integrated framework provides a graphical form of the broad perspectives. It shows the embedded corporate management system that includes the CSM of the whole company, the strategic management of the business unit(s), and the operational management at the core levels of the organization. The embedded corporate management system is shown at the center because it is based on the perspectives of the strategic leaders, especially corporate leaders. This is not to suggest that the framework is company-centric, but rather to indicate how decisions flow from the corporate leaders to other strategic leaders, managers, and professionals and what are some of the critical elements for sustainable success. The corporate leaders are the visionary strategic leaders and the architects of the vision, strategic direction, and the future of the corporation. Their grand strategies and strategic initiatives induce change and create value for the company and its enterprise(s).

Leadership is the most crucial aspect of the integrated framework. It must be visionary and focus on the strategic direction of the whole company and strategic innovation for value creation. Visionary strategic leaders examine the market spaces to discover what can and should be done to lead the enterprise, to take advantage of all of the opportunities, and to eliminate or mitigate threats and risks. They inspire people at every level of the organization and extended enterprise(s) to translate the principles, values, aspirations, and aims into actions that support the missions of the strategic business units (SBUs) and to realize high levels of performance and sustainable success.

As discussed above, VSL involves creating a more sustainable future by transforming all that the organization and its enterprise(s) has been in the past and all that they currently are into new capabilities and positions, i.e., more sophisticated and sustainable entities. It is important to recognize the integrated framework pertains to the general elements and aspects, while management constructs and business models focus on the specifics. Moreover, the integrated framework focuses mainly on the elements of strategic formulation, while business models focus on strategic implementation. The integrated framework is intended to map out how the elements of the leadership and strategic management system fit together. Furthermore, leaders and managers at each of the management levels may also form frameworks and/or management constructs that help them make sense of the forces, factors, functions, and requirements in their realities.

Many strategic leaders, managers, and professionals like processes and projects that have starting points and possible ending points that help guide them through the flow. Unfortunately, the integrated framework does not have a simple process to follow. It encompasses a systems perspective. There may be many processes and sub-processes within the framework, but they do not always have a definitive starting point or ending point. For instance, most established companies may find it difficult to stop what is being done and act as if they are starting with a clean sheet. Corporate leaders have to deal with legacies of the past, realities in the present, and commitments to the future. For strategic leaders, governing, strategizing, leading, managing, and executing are based on a continuum. That continuum is represented by the inner circle of the integrated framework. The inner circle shows the corporate, business unit(s), operating systems, and context as the pivotal aspects of the framework. While many strategic leaders and business scholars suggest that the most critical perspective is external context, everything is important from a global perspective.

As discussed above, context is the sum of all of the external and internal forces and dimensions. It includes the natural environment, social world, business environment, market spaces, and the organization and its enterprises. These include the driving forces of change and the reasons for the company to exist. Context provides opportunities, challenges, capabilities, and resources, among others. It is context that drives strategic leadership and management forward. Context also involves competitive space(s). Competition plays an important role in providing alternatives for customers, a frame of reference for identifying the value proposition(s), and a motivation to exceed the needs, wants, and expectations of customers and stakeholders. Existing competitors generally focus on the same markets as the company and its SBUs and offer similar products and services. However, new competitors and substitutes drive change. They provide alternative solutions and attract some of the existing customers of the company's product lines to the new options.

From a strategic perspective, corporate leaders, i.e., C-level executives, in unison with the board of directors and the shareholders, provide the strategic leadership for the corporation and its business units. In a sophisticated, market-centric and future-oriented company, the corporate leaders are visionaries. They set strategic direction and provide the governance of the whole enterprise. They are responsible for everything from the triumphs and tribulations of the present to the aspirations and dreams for the future. Corporate leaders have to ensure that the business units and operating systems are performing according to strategic direction, corporate governance, and company policies, and that they are achieving the desired outcomes. They also provide the proper oversight for managing the company and ensuring that it fulfills its intended purpose(s) and it is staying ahead of changes in the business environment. They establish the principles, values, beliefs, ethics, and policies to guide the corporation and its decision making through the charted and uncharted waters to the future. The underlying purposes, philosophies, and principles of the company guide all strategic leaders as they consider what are the right solutions, what new products and services to design and develop, who should provide those solutions, and how to create extraordinary value. Through the ongoing quest to achieve sustainable success and outstanding performance, corporate leaders focus on increasing shareholder wealth, improving market capitalization, and enhancing the respect, recognition, and reward for all of the contributors.

Corporate leaders determine the grand strategies and how value is created by the company, the business units, and operating systems. They set the overarching goals, ensure that the company meets its fiduciary duties to shareholders and society, and determine the management systems and organizational structure. Value creation depends on intellectual capital, know-how, technologies, systems, and processes, and the contributions of the core capabilities, resources, and functional areas. The details about vision, strategies, goals, and planning are covered in Chapters 3 and 4.

Strategic leadership of the business units concentrates on the mission of the businesses and relationships with the entities in the value system(s). For large global corporations, the business units typically function as semi-independent businesses that have their own strategic management framework and strategic management system(s). Such frameworks and systems include the strategic alignment of the operating systems and the integration of the value system(s). They also include building relationships with customers, stakeholders, partners, allies, and supporting entities. Strategic leaders of the business units (SBU leaders) are also responsible for leading change, innovation, and the strategic integration of the value systems and the extended enterprise. SBU leaders concentrate on achieving total satisfaction across the enterprise and ensuring that customers and stakeholders are successful. They focus on building positive reputations, enriching the capabilities of the enterprise through learning and new knowledge, and achieving extraordinary financial performance. Not only do such approaches, actions, and outcomes contribute to the bottom line, they enhance the strategic and competitive advantages and the long-term prospects of the corporation.

Operational leadership involves the day-to-day operations and process management. It includes a functional framework that provides the connections between the value systems and the value delivery processes. Since operational leaders and managers generally engage the tactical aspects, their roles and responsibilities are not covered in this book.

The incredible growth of the U.S. economy during the twentieth century is an example of the possibilities for creating many winners. While U.S. business history is full of distortions, bad actors, and corporate failures, the general economic development has been positive for most people. The great inventors, entrepreneurs, family-owned companies, and industrial corporations of the nineteenth century, the large stock corporations and financial institutions of the twentieth century, and the global corporations and SMEs of today have provided a rich legacy of knowledge, experience, know-how, intellectual capital, and great contributions to humankind. They imbue future generations with the capabilities and confidence to continue making positive changes so that people can enjoy sustainable social, ethical, economic, technological, and environmental developments.

The Main Elements of VSL and CSM

Strategic Perspectives and Management Systems

Corporate leaders are the prime architects of the organization and the related enterprise(s). They select the management constructs and articulate the solutions. A management construct is a theoretical framework or model used to analyze, design, develop, determine, validate, and deploy strategies, solutions, systems, structures, and business models. It is a relatively new perspective that is intended to be a representation of the dimensions and elements of business situations. A solution is a multifaceted concept that includes the product, the service, the underlying technology(s), and the tangible and intangible elements of the internal system and extended enterprise that accompany it. It has physical, psychological, and temporal factors. Solutions are market-centric, since they are designed, produced, and delivered from the perspectives of customers and stakeholders.

In the context of the integrated framework, the essential tasks of corporate leaders pertaining to strategies, solutions, systems, structures, and relationships are to:

- Articulate the strategic leadership and management constructs.
- Craft the objectives, strategies, and solutions.
- Determine the embedded corporate management system.
- Organize the people and resources into a logical structure(s) that has flexibility and agility.
- Provide good governance and oversight and ensure sustainable success.

Strategies and solutions drive the selection of the systems that then drive the design of the organizational structure. Moreover, the trend for many corporations is to have the organizational structure embedded in the management systems, since organizational design and change are often slow and arduous tasks that retard strategy implementation. In a fast-paced business world, the organizational structure is often obsolete before it gets fully implemented. While there are many perspectives that corporate leaders have to develop pertaining to management systems, establishing the overarching foundation, selecting the management constructs, and designing the organizational structure(s) are among the most important.

Corporate leaders select the frameworks and the management systems to be used by the corporation. Corporate leaders work with lower-level strategic leaders to develop the systems and structures, especially in the cases of diversified global corporations like General Electric (GE) in which a single management system and structure would not fit the needs of all of the sectors in which GE participates. Multiple systems and structures are often desirable when there are wide differences in the contexts, purposes, missions, strategies, and solutions among the various business units. On the other hand, a single management system and structure may be efficient and effective for much smaller single-business companies. For example, Southwest Airlines is a medium-size corporation with a fairly narrow market focus and a corporate management system that is integrated top to bottom with most of the strategic actions centered on a dominant single-product [service] business based in the U.S., i.e., a specialized airline with its platform of support services.

Management systems and organizational structures are supposed to be developed in concert with the business strategies. Alfred Chandler Jr. stated in his book, *Strategy and Structure*, that strategy leads structure as suggested by:[2]

> The comparison [of the companies Chandler studied] emphasizes that a company's strategy in time determined its structure and that the common denominator of structure and strategy has been that application of the enterprise resources of market demand. Structure has been

the design for integrating the enterprise's existing resources to current demand; strategy has been the plan for the allocation of resources to anticipated demand.

...Finally, the rate of growth and the effectiveness in the use of the enterprise's resources rested on the ability and ingenuity of its administrators [leaders] to build, adjust, and apply its personnel and facilities to broad population, technological, and income changes. Although an enterprise undoubtedly has a life of its own above and beyond that of its individual executives, although technological and market requirements certainly set boundaries and limits growth, nevertheless, its health and effectiveness in carrying out its basic economic functions depended almost entirely on the talents of its administrators.

Chandler's views still resonant today. However, rather than strategy simply preceding structure, strategy begets the selection of the strategic management system and the management constructs for formulating and implementing the strategies. Structure is the organizational design that facilitates implementation and follows the selection of the management system(s). Corporate leaders set the stage by determining corporate strategies and objectives and then determine how the people and resources of the corporation (money, assets, facilities, etc.) are integrated into a cohesive framework for realizing the strategic direction and achieving the missions of the business units, i.e., the management systems that involve design, flow, processes, activities, and deployment.

The Embedded Corporate Management System

The embedded corporate management system with its business units and operating systems is an essential element of the integrated framework. Most of the cutting-edge corporate management systems are based on the full integration of the strategic management of the corporation from the top to the bottom with effective linkages between the people within the organization and all of the external parties. The concepts of management systems and systems integration have been evolving for more than 150 years in the U.S. They emerged from the halcyon days of the American System for the manufacturing of interchangeable parts in the 1850s and the practical innovations of Henry Ford's mass production and assembly during the 1900s. From an internal (company) management perspective, it became a mainstream management construct with Michael Porter's concepts of the value chain and the value system and the more recent views on the extended enterprise.[3] While the concept of systems integration was an important factor in the success of many companies over the course of the last century, the degree and level of integration was minuscule in comparison to the requirements for business integration in the more complex business world of today. Yet, with the current levels of management sophistication, there are still difficulties integrating all of the necessary operations, processes, and contributions from the initial suppliers of suppliers to the internal operations and customer applications.

The present business world is more demanding, turbulent, and exciting, and it is expected to become even more so over the next decade. The latitude and time frame that corporate leaders have in crafting strategies, making decisions, implementing action plans, and recovering their investments continues to shrink as entities in the business environment, especially customers and competitors, become more informed and more sophisticated. This means that as the margin for error decreases, even a few problems and difficulties can cause significant negative impacts. Merck's handling of the side effects of the Vioxx during 2004, Toyota's slowness to respond to customer complaints about brakes in 2010, and BP's inability to quickly stop the Gulf of Mexico oil spill in 2010 are indicative of such challenges. The full story of Vioxx will play out over time, but it is clear that a philosophy of candor can mitigate or reduce the consequences of many of the problems plaguing corporations, especially those involving hidden defects and burdens.[4] The demonstrations against corporate greed that rocked Wall Street and many other locations throughout the U.S. are also indications that corporate leaders have to pay more attention to the concerns and voices of stakeholders. Such demonstrations are much easier to orchestrate using Facebook and Twitter. Small events protests may eventually have big impacts on the economic, political, and market realities.

To be effective and responsive in a fast-paced business environment, companies have to have an embedded corporate management system that involves the rapid design, development, and deployment of strategies and action plans to take advantage of changes in the market spaces and to mitigate the challenges, threats, and risks. Companies have to have the ability to make rapid changes whenever necessary. Time is precious and corporate leaders cannot afford to have time-consuming, ill-coordinated exchanges between the various management systems of the corporation and slow decision making. It is essential that all levels of strategic management be in concert with each other, so that strategies and actions can be developed and implemented before they became imperatives driven by external forces or they are rendered obsolete by a rapidly changing business world.

The embedded corporate management system is not an updated version of the old hierarchical organizational structure with better communications and more responsiveness; it involves a well-honed, holistic system of participants, subsystems, processes, practices, and actions. It involves strategic leaders at all levels who know their roles and responsibilities and can perform them well without time-consuming command and control techniques. The old notion of superior-subordinate is superseded by more flexible interactive relationships that are based on mutual respect and recognition of the knowledge, competencies, and contributions that people make at each level.

Large business organizations typically have many levels of strategic leaders and a broad array of key contributors. Philosophically, the embedded corporate management system is like a symphony orchestra and choir. An orchestra has a conductor, aka the strategic leader, and there are unit leaders in the orchestra like the head of the musicians and head of the choir, and functional leaders like the first violinists, etc. There are the players, singers, and administrators. The former are analogous to the SBU leaders and operational managers and the latter are analogous to the key contributors and support staff in business organizations. While an organization consisting of an orchestra and a choir is fairly simple in comparison to the organizational complexities of many global corporations, it typifies the roles, responsibilities, and relationships that are critical for success in a demanding world. The conductor has the overall responsibilities for determining what concert is selected and arranged and for ensuring that the organization achieves the highest standards. The conductor also ensures that the performance is of the kind and quality that exceeds the audience's expectations. As the strategic leader of the symphony, the conductor fully understands and appreciates his or her roles and responsibilities, and that success depends on the other leaders and professionals to do the same. The conductor empowers the head of the musicians and head of the choir to do their jobs. He or she does not usurp their roles and responsibilities nor does the conductor assume that he or she knows more about playing the violin than the first violinist knows and does. Likewise the other leaders fulfill their responsibilities without infringing on the performance of the other players. A symphony orchestra operates as an integrated team of leaders, professionals, contributors and administrators who are well prepared to develop and implement the game plan based on the direction of the conductor and the supporting services of the staff. While the analogy is not an exact fit to the corporate world, it does shed light on how an embedded management system works and the roles and responsibilities of the strategic leaders, professionals, and participants.

Business models are specific strategic management frameworks/constructs that link the management systems with the external business world, depicting how the company or business unit translates strategies into actions. Depending on the size and nature of the company, there may be a single business model for the whole company, specific business models for each SBU, or individual business models for each value delivery system. For instance, an integrated petroleum company like ExxonMobil could have a single model tying together its various SBUs that are engaged in the exploration, refining, distribution, and delivery of petroleum products. However, it may have separate business models for its SBU dealing with non-petroleum related businesses. On the other hand, United Technologies Corporation (UTC) has many individual SBUs. Its SBUs include Pratt & Whitney; Sikorsky Aircraft; UTC Climate, Controls and Security; Otis; UTC Aerospace; UTC Power Fuel Cells; and United Technologies Research Center. They are significantly different from each other and are in different business portfolios. Each SBU has a strategic management system with its given mission, strategies, objectives, action plans, and business model(s)/constructs.

The business model is the management approach for implementing programs and actions, executing tactics and activities, and achieving results. The embedded corporate management system with its various levels can be a business model that is directly linked to the extended enterprise and fully capable realizing objectives and sustaining results. The determination of the framework and scope of a company's or SBU's business model is becoming increasing important for the proper execution of corporate and business strategies. While the strategic logic of the corporation as manifested through the vision, grand strategies, and goals explains the why and the what, the business model relates to who and how. It is intended to bridge the gap between crafting strategies and implementing them. It provides a mapping of the essential connections, important relationships, and expected actions across the extended enterprises that assist strategic leaders, professionals, and practitioners to understand their roles and responsibilities, know what has to be accomplished, and how to achieve the goals.

Creating a Logical Organizational Structure

Creating a logical and dynamic organizational structure is a critical challenge for corporate leaders and SBU leaders. The establishment of the embedded corporate management system has taken away some of the pressure for trying to optimize the organizational structure. Today, most corporations implement strategies and actions plans through the various management systems and the related processes that have been identified at each level. Still, management systems depend on having organizational structures that support the actions, inform employees how they fit into the overall organization, and establish the reporting relationships.

People within the organization need a sense of how they fit and relate to each other. They also need direction, feedback, communications, respect, recognition, and rewards. The organizational structure provides an understanding of how people are linked to the whole and with whom they relate. Developing an organizational structure is still one of the most difficult corporate management responsibilities to master, especially in a fast-paced business world. Organizational design that leads to a new structure often takes considerable time to develop and implement and usually involves debates and disappointments as people's professional and personal lives are affected. Not only is there a tendency for disruptive situations to occur, but in many cases the redesigned structure is ineffective because organizational structures tend to be static rather than dynamic.

Organizational design is a joint responsibility between corporate leaders, SBU leaders, and senior professionals. Each leader should organize people based on the management systems and the requirements for realizing the strategic direction and the objectives. Rigid structures should be avoided, if possible; flexibility and agility should be encouraged. Of course, there are exceptions. For instance, corporations or business units engaged in operating aircraft safety systems, nuclear power plants, or similarly demanding or regulated businesses have to ensure very strict operational reliability, safety codes, performance standards, and compliance with regulations. There is no tolerance for errors. In such situations, very robust and highly stringent organizational structures are necessary to insure that execution is flawless. Nuclear power plants are examples of base-loaded operations with very few changes on a day-to-day or even month-to-month basis. On the other hand, in fast-paced businesses like electronics, flexibility and agility are absolutely necessary. Change is the norm. Rigid organizational structures often impede the corporation's or business unit's ability to respond to the changing business environment. Team-based structures are more commonplace in such situations. They provide the organization the ability to change quickly by changing team players or by creating new teams that are more in concert with the requirements and expectations. Apple, Inc., under the leadership of former chief executive officer (CEO) Steve Jobs, who died on October 5, 2011, is an example of a highly innovative and adaptive organization that was able to orchestrate new product development programs in fields ranging from computers and cell phones to music and software.

Organizational design and structure include some of the following areas that corporate leaders have to ensure are provided either by the CSM or by strategic leaders at the lower levels:

- Developing strategic and operational leaders who have the mindset, knowledge, skills, and talents to lead change and manage their assigned roles and responsibilities; ensuring that the next generation of corporate and strategic leaders are educated, trained, and prepared to assume the higher, senior-level positions
- Building the competencies, capabilities, and skills sets within the organization so that people are able to fulfill their roles and responsibilities; educating the professionals and practitioners with new skills and capabilities so that transitions and transformations can occur seamlessly
- Linking resource requirements with resource availability and prioritizing the allocation of resources among the SBUs; ensuring the whole organization has the means and mechanisms to implement the strategic direction, and if adequate resources are not available, making adjustments before the disconnections lead to difficulties and failures
- Establishing the governance, policies, and operating procedures for guiding people and performance, including ethical principles and acceptable behaviors; guiding the development of best practices for whole organization and the SBUs
- Ensuring the there is mutual respect and recognition of the achievements by individuals and groups; creating positive incentives for achieving sustainable success and rewarding those who make significant contributions
- Being open and honest with the organization so that information and data are shared equitably across the organization and everyone is empowered and no one is disadvantaged because they are not part of inner circle

Corporate leaders have a fiduciary responsibility to ensure that employees are treated properly and that everyone has opportunities to realize their professional goals. Good implementation requires capable leaders and a proficient organization. Sustainable success is achieved though dedicated strategic leaders who encourage and support highly capable people with the knowledge and resources to perform at the highest levels. The intellectual capital of the organization is most critical strategic asset in most cases.

Underpinnings of Corporate Governance

Corporate governance involves the smooth sailing of the corporation and ensuring that the intellectual property, wealth, and well being of the company and the people are protected and enhanced. It involves preserving the assets and know-how and assuring that the company continues to be successful. The concept of corporate governance and the notion of sustainable success are inexorably linked. They are clearly interrelated and are critical VSL and CSM elements. Governance is also the most important duty of the board of directors.

First and foremost, corporate leaders and the board of directors have to fulfill their legal obligations in accordance with the laws of the state, province, or nation in which the company is incorporated. They are responsible for governing the affairs of the company, representing and protecting the shareholders, and conducting business according to the articles of incorporation, bylaws, any shareholder agreements, and other legal instruments pertaining to the company that apply. Corporate executives are usually officers of the company who have the authority to act on behalf of the corporation as its agents in conducting official business, making decisions, approving agreements, meeting legal requirements, and reporting on the financial and business affairs of the company. Corporate officers can bind the corporation to arrangements and contracts with outside entities. They have the formal authority and responsibilities to assess and approve such instruments and ensure that the company and the outside parties execute them in accordance with provisions and/or specifications. Corporate officers also have the duty to ensure that the company and all of its business units, subsidiaries, ventures, and formal partnerships are in compliance with the laws, regulations, and directives in the political units and countries in which the company operates and/or conducts business. This includes complying with the provisions set forth in the laws and regulations of the company's home country as well as meeting all legal mandates from financial reporting and paying taxes to protecting the well being of people and the natural environment. Many of these responsibilities can be delegated to other strategic leaders, managers, and professionals within the company, but corporate officers have the duty to provide oversight and ensure compliance. Delegation empowers others in the company to perform, but it never lessens the corporate executives' duties and responsibilities to the board of directors and shareholders.

Financial reporting has always been one of the most important responsibilities of the corporate officers. As companies have grown in size and complexity, financial reporting has also become more complicated and difficult for ensuring full compliance with the laws, regulations, and codes. This is especially critical as companies have to deal with global business, international trade, currency exchange, the different financial rules and interpretations between countries, and the numerous ways in which financial valuations and determinations are made. While the financial aspects are critical duties of corporate leaders, the specific details are beyond the scope of this book. The intent herein is to highlight the broad aspects and their implications. Financial management and reporting are extensive topics that are covered in many books.

Additionally, corporate leaders have to address many strategic decisions, organizational tasks, and administrative aspects on an ongoing basis, most of which can be delegated to other strategic leaders but still require the oversight and scrutiny of the

CEO and officers of the corporation. Some of the most important strategic roles and responsibilities of corporate leaders pertaining to governance include the following:

- Establishing the overarching principles, values, beliefs, ethical standards, and codes of conduct pertaining to the practices and behaviors of the people within the organization and with outside entities (suppliers, partners, allies, etc.)
- Crafting the vision, grand strategies, and overarching goals of the corporation and ensuring that the missions, business strategies, and objectives of the business units resonate with the strategic direction and are achieved in a timely manner
- Managing the financial affairs and the company and ensure the proper accounting and reporting of the financial aspects
- Discovering broad-based opportunities for new businesses and enhancements to existing businesses and operations; managing and mitigating threats and challenges
- Establishing the decision-making criteria for all levels of management that incorporate the values, beliefs, principles, and strategic direction so that good decisions are made; ones based on integrity, honesty, and sustainable success[5]
- Determining and promulgating the formal rules and guidelines of the company, especially those pertaining to employees, health, safety, and the environment, dealing with external entities, complying with laws and regulations, and safeguarding the well being of the corporation and the people it touches
- Providing the leadership, necessary resources, and intellectual capital so that the business units and operating systems have the means and mechanisms to sustain success and create extraordinary value
- Developing new strategic leaders who are capable of assuming the roles and responsibilities of leadership in the future and ensuring an orderly transition of leadership over time
- Making transformations and transitions across the company to realize sustainable outcomes and position the corporation for the future; leading change through corporate strategic plans and initiatives, especially through directing high-level strategic programs, managing mergers and acquisitions, forming partnerships and alliances, and creating joint ventures
- Eliminating or mitigating risks and vulnerabilities to the corporation, its business units, operations, technologies, and products; especially those affecting people and the environment, and ensuring that strategic leaders across the organization and enterprises do the same
- Evaluating proper performance across the company; reporting the successes and failures and taking corrective actions to mitigate the problems, defects, burdens, and impacts; reporting on prevailing financial conditions and significant outcomes

The list is open-ended. It is virtually impossible to specify all of the roles and responsibilities of corporate leaders. As the business environment becomes more complex and challenging, governance is expected to continue to expand and play an even more important role in maintaining stability.

Overarching Management Constructs

Select Management Constructs

The selection of the key management constructs is among the most important corporate decisions following the determination of values and principles, the creation of a vision and grand strategy, and the establishment of governance. They are the mechanisms for integrating the corporation into a comprehensive management system(s) and for achieving results. They involve the design/redesign of the strategic management systems, and updating of the management philosophies of the corporation to provide an umbrella for decision-making. It is imperative that such management constructs are tailored to the context of the corporation and they are enduring, i.e., they are not just the latest version of "looking for the magic formula." They require the commitment of the whole organization and substantial investments of time and money to realize. Some of the most widely accepted and deployed include:

- Six-sigma quality management and design for six-sigma (DfSS);
- Lean business philosophies and practices;
- Business process reengineering (BPR);
- Sustainable business development (SBD);
- Corporate social responsibility (CSR).

The drive for improved quality and the competitive pressures for product differentiation made six-sigma quality management and design for six-sigma among the most touted management constructs of the 1990s. While GE's former CEO, Jack Welch, was among the leading architects of DfSS, many corporations established their own versions of high-level quality management that embraced all aspects of the corporation including the manufacturing operations and marketing methods. For example, UTC developed its Achieving Competitive Excellence (ACE) program with assistance from Yuzuro Ito, a Japanese quality guru, and illuminates like James Womack. ACE focuses on producing 100% defect-free products and services, partnering with customers to ensure that they are delighted, and creating a great place for UTC employees to work. ACE evolved to include the percepts of DfSS, BPR, and lean business practices. While the initial goals of ACE targeted operations, it transitioned into a more comprehensive management system that includes most of the processes used by the company.

Lean business philosophies and practices were developed by Toyota in the late 1940s and early 1950s, allowing the company to produce a wider variety of products having low volumes, while at the same time achieving good quality and cost-effectiveness. It focused on the value stream and sought to add value during every step of a process and to eliminate all wastes. Lean was adapted during the 1980s by many global corporations in their quest to become more competitive and to provide customer-driven solutions in contrast to producing company-centric products. James Womack and Daniel Jones, in their book,

Lean Solutions, outline the transitions from production-consumption thinking to "win–win–win" perspectives, enabling producers, employees, and customers to jointly create lean solutions using lean thinking, process integration, and the pursuit of perfection.[6]

BPR was one of the leading management constructs of early 1990s that changed the focus from internal functions to systems and processes. It also focused on benchmarking best practices and thinking about what the process meant to customers and how it could be dramatically improved to eliminate costs and wastes. It incorporated many of the tenets of total quality management and laid the foundation for achieving customer satisfaction. Michael Hammer and James Champy were among the leading business scholars who championed the constructs of BPR. They highlighted the transformations toward process management and the radical redesign of processes to achieve dramatic improvements in performance and outcomes, especially in costs, quality, speed, and service.[7] However, Hammer and Champy were disappointed by how large corporations actually implemented BPR because many of the strategic leaders reverted to managing in terms of the organizational structure and used BPR as a reason for downsizing the organization to theoretically reduce costs. The true underpinnings of BPR are regaining some attention as strategic leaders again think more in terms of management systems and process management. On an operating level, modern theories about management systems combine the constructs of process management, lean thinking, six-sigma quality, and environmental management.

SBD and CSR and their various forms have gained significant inroads into mainstream corporate management over the last ten years. SBD involves creating innovative solutions to the social, economic, ethical, technological, environmental, and business challenges in today's turbulent business environment, leading profound change, and sustaining success. It means taking responsibility for the decisions and actions of the enterprise, not just those of the corporation. CSR implies that corporations have a fiduciary duty to address the social aspects, meet the needs and wants of customers and stakeholders, and protect the well-being of humankind.

While there are others that could be discussed, the general themes of most of the cutting-edge management constructs include creating high-quality products and services; invoking lean business practices; eliminating economic and environmental wastes; providing market-driven solutions; optimizing processes and using process management; extending the management systems to include all of the value systems from cradle to grave; and adapting SBD and CSR to obtain customer- and stakeholder-driven outcomes and sustainable success. The trend is toward an integrated management framework that includes the elements of the management system(s).

The Crucial Role of Sustainable Business Development

Sustainable development (SD) involves creating a future that enhances the positives aspects of social, economic, ethical, technological, and environmental considerations, reduces or eliminates the impacts of pollution and wastes, and minimizes the depletion of resources and the negative impacts on the natural environment. The concept of SD originated in the 1987 based on the Brundtland Report, *Our Common Future*, prepared by The World Commission Environment and Development for the General Assembly of the United Nations. The report defined SD as growth and development that "meets the needs of the present without compromising the ability of future generations to meet their needs."[8]

SBD is a holistic management construct that includes the embedded corporate management system and the extended enterprise from the origins of the raw materials and production processes to the customer applications and the end-of-life considerations. SBD involves making dramatic improvements and positive changes to the full scope of the processes, activities, relationships, and linkages of the supply networks, customers, stakeholders, and support providers for creating positive outcomes and managing and mitigating wastes, residuals, and impacts. It also involves life-cycle assessment and management of the effects and impacts from cradle to grave. SBD implies designing, producing, and delivering sustainable solutions that are economically sound, socially responsible, and environmentally conscious. These have huge implications.

The principles, concepts, and resolutions of the philosophical debates pertaining to SBD are more urgent today than in prior times, especially due to globalization and outsourcing. In the past, governments in most of the developed countries defined much of what businesses were obligated to do through laws and regulations and often specified how they were required to do so. While most corporations did not welcome the potential limitations imposed by laws and regulations, such government mandates often eliminated the difficulties involved in making determinations about external obligations, requirements, and expectations as they might negatively impact internal objectives like profitability and return of investments. They leveled the competitive landscape and made it easier for strategic decision-makers to know what was expected and what they had to do. For instance, if a regulatory agency mandates certain requirements that make it more costly to produce and market products and services because of restrictions, covenants, product specifications, certifications, permits, audits, and reporting requirements, such mandates may have little overall effect on the competitive landscape since everyone has to comply. Laws and regulations impose the new conditions on every entity affected by the mandates. Strategic decision-making based solely on complying with government mandates is seemingly a straightforward business paradigm; the mandates define the obligations and the required actions, and corporate leaders do what is required. Until recently, many corporate leaders believed that their scope of the social and environmental responsibilities was mainly concerned with complying with the associated laws and regulations.

In today's complex business environment, determining a company's direct and indirect responsibilities is not as simple. Many corporate leaders have had a change of philosophies. Instead of thinking in terms of the limits of corporate responsibilities or just following the established mandates, visionary strategic leaders are adapting more inclusive perspectives. Astute strategic decision-makers who influence the internal practitioners and external entities are shouldering more of the social, environmental, and ethical obligations to mitigate the impacts of defects, burdens, and harms for which their company is directly or indirectly responsible. Moreover, if the company is linked to issues and problems through its relationships, transactions, and decisions, astute strategic leaders take an implicit, if not explicit, responsibility to ensure that the social, economic, ethical, technological, environmental, and market implications of the company's choices are appropriate and sustainable. In doing so, such strategic leaders are careful not to infringe on the legitimate rights of other entities like national governments, social organizations, or individuals. While the scope of direct corporate responsibilities may be specific, the implied or indirect responsibilities are less definitive and often vary according to the involvement and the degree of influence that the corporation has on the situation. The good news is: the more inclusive strategic management philosophy often provides strategic leaders with new opportunities to create additional value, to have positive influences on situations, and to develop more beneficial outcomes. The more inclusive scope means that responsibilities include relative factors as well as absolute ones, especially when examining the broader context. For instance, outsourcing certain activities may eliminate direct corporate responsibilities for managing certain wastes and environmental impacts by seemingly transferring responsibilities to suppliers. Its regulatory responsibilities may be diminished by such decisions and actions as well. However, in the broader sense, outsourcing does not necessarily lessen the impacts of the wastes nor does it eliminate the social, economic, ethical, technological, and environmental responsibilities of the company with respect to addressing the negative aspects of the operations of suppliers or the suppliers of suppliers. The impacts and consequences are still related to the decisions and actions of the company. The company and its leaders are the ones who approved the design of the products and the selection of the suppliers. Therefore, they are still responsible for managing and controlling the activities that lead to the impacts. Thus, they have an implied obligation to remedy any problems.

In many such situations, outsourcing can make the scope of the corporate management system and extended enterprise more complex and more difficult to manage because the company must assume some of the responsibilities for the impacts of its suppliers, agents, partners, etc. and take appropriate actions, if the outcomes are not sustainable or not in line with the principles, strategies, objectives, and social and environmental responsibilities of the company. The company also has an implied responsibility to ensure that actions of its suppliers, agents, and others are in compliance with laws and regulations. Failure to track such compliance may leave the company vulnerable to political, social, and economic problems.

The logic for a more inclusive view of corporate roles and responsibilities as discussed above is driven by the realization that corporations are social and economic constructs that operate to fulfill the expectations of customers, stakeholders, and society as well as achieve the strategic and financial objectives of shareholders. Contemporary thinking is illustrated in John Elkington's *Cannibals with forks: the triple bottom line of 21st century business*. Elkington states that businesses should think in terms of a "triple bottom line," focusing on economic prosperity, environmental quality, and social justice.[9] The triple bottom line suggests a convergence of thinking about what corporations have to achieve, i.e., balanced outcomes.

George Molenkamp, Partner at KPMG Global Sustainability Services in The Hague, provides a sense of this convergence in objectives in the following: "For a variety of reasons, sustainability, CSR, triple bottom line and/or triple P (people, planet, and profit) are receiving attention in the business community."[10] Those reasons include pressure from stakeholders for corporations to reduce their impacts on society, new mandates from governments in response to social and political pressures to monitor and control corporate behaviors, and most critically, pressure from the investment communities to monitor performance and reduce shareholder risks.

Philosophical Aspects of Corporate Social Responsibility

CSR is a management construct that implies that corporations have a fiduciary duty to meet the needs and wants of customers, stakeholders, and other direct and indirect constituents in a socially responsible manner, to protect the health and safety of people, and to prevent negative impacts and their consequences. Though CSR has been debated for decades, it remains a nebulous construct. Definitions vary from narrow perspectives of fulfilling the direct contractual and legal obligations to customers, suppliers, distributors, and employees to the broad perspectives of assuming responsibilities for the direct and indirect effects and impacts of the decisions and activities of the corporation and its extended enterprise and protecting the well-being of people and society. They include the duties to protect human rights and ensure balanced outcomes.

The narrow view assumes that the primary social responsibility of business is to make sufficient profits to cover all expenses and provide an appropriate return on shareholders' investments. Corporate leadership, it contends, is rightly guided by the "economic self-interest" of capitalism; the purpose and primary objectives of corporations are to maximize profits and shareholder wealth.[11] In the 1960s, Milton Friedman, Nobel laureate in economics, characterized traditional thinking as follows:[12]

> The view [social responsibility of business and labor] has been gaining widespread acceptance that corporate officials and labor leaders have a "social responsibility" that goes beyond serving the interest of their stockholders or their members. This view shows a fundamental misconception of the character and nature of a free economy. In such a economy, there is one and only one responsibility of business-to use its resources and engage in activities designed to increase its profits so long as it stays within the rules of the game, which is to say engages in free and open competition, without deception or fraud...
>
> Few trends could so thoroughly undermine the very foundations of a free society as the acceptance by corporate officials as a social responsibility other than to make as much money for their stockholders as possible.

Friedman's perception was widely endorsed and may have been reasonable within the context of his time and the prevailing view of free market capitalism. However, it is narrow and company-centric. First, it is difficult to articulate exactly what is required to maximize profits. Generally, profit maximization is based on short-term financial results. Historically, many corporations have maximized their profits in the short term by failing to make the proper investments for the long term; thus, becoming more vulnerable in the future. Maximizing profits in the short term often results in transferring current expenses into long-term liabilities or failing to manage problems and challenges within a reasonable time frame. For example, many corporations have unfunded pension and health care liabilities because past leaders did not properly accrue the expenses for the retirement commitments made to employees. While many governments in the developed countries now require companies to fund such future benefits, it may take many years for such companies to pay down those liabilities. As an aside, many governments face the same challenges and contemporary political leaders struggle with finding the money to pay for the pensions that their predecessors committed to during more affluent times.

Corporations have many other objectives beyond the financial ones that they must meet to ensure their success. Protecting the assets of corporation is one of the most important responsibilities. Corporate leaders have to ensure that customers are successful and that customers remain loyal. The social, economic, and ethical imperatives are broad, and strategic leaders are expected to fulfill all of their obligations including ones to customers, stakeholders, employees, and shareholders. In the 1980s, Peter Drucker reiterated the importance for ensuring the survival of the corporation and sustaining its economic benefits to employees, customers, shareholders, and external communities. He refined Friedman's theory to include developing new opportunities and creating wealth through social initiatives. Drucker articulated a broader view:[13]

> The first "social responsibility" of business is then to make enough profit to cover the costs of the future. If this "social responsibility" is not met, no other "social responsibility" can be met. Decaying businesses in a decaying economy are unlikely to be good neighbors, good employers, or "socially responsible" in any way...
>
> But the proper "social responsibility" of business is to tame the dragon that is to turn a social problem into economic opportunity and economic benefit, into productive capacity, into human competence, into well-paid jobs, and into wealth.

Drucker's views reinforce the responsibilities of strategic leaders to serve markets and customers effectively and to find new opportunities for ensuring the enduring success of the corporation. He believed that a corporation's expenditures must include the investments to make and facilitate economic, social, and technical changes and to prepare for the future. He viewed profits as capital for investments and sustaining economic activities. To Drucker, maximizing profits and the implicit social responsibilities hinged on the inclusion of both short-term performance and outcomes and long-term objectives and investments. His ideas go beyond Friedman's narrow definition of the simple purpose and business objective (responsibility to shareholders), but not as far as the still broader views that have evolved over the last twenty years. In this regard, he may have been an early advocate that social responsibility is not an "either–or" proposition, but one that involves balanced perspectives on the social, economic, and ethical imperatives.

The broader view pertaining to CSR goes even further and implies that corporations have implicit obligations to be ethical corporate citizens and to ensure that their strategies, actions, and solutions are viable and appropriate. Moreover, modern CSR implies that a corporation's social responsibilities are more than statements of ethics or codes of conduct; they represent real initiatives and actions that extend beyond the boundaries of its facilities and operations to include both the direct and indirect effects and impacts of the supply networks, customer applications, and linkages with other entities. CSR has become a combination of stated ethics, standards of behaviors, compliance with laws and regulations, stewardship to protect employees, customers, stakeholders, workers, society, and the natural environment, and deliberate actions to create a better world. CSR includes philanthropy (supporting charities), contributing to public policymaking, and promoting the common good and well-being of humankind. Indeed, these perspectives tie CSR with the principles of SBD. Actually, CSR is a subset of SBD, since it focuses mainly on the social rather than the broader and more inclusive aspects of the social, ethical, economic, technological, and environmental considerations.

Shifting Mindsets Pertaining to SBD and CSR

SBD and CSR have increased in importance for many reasons. A more global economy is a primary one, especially for global corporations. Needs, wants and expectations vary from country to country and region to region and, while it is often possible to customize products and services to accommodate local specifications, it is much more difficult to customize the corporation and its principles, philosophies, and management systems to selectively meet the mandates and requirements of the wide array markets. For instance, American consumers may be primarily interested in obtaining low-cost products, while their European counterparts might be driven by social considerations first, environmental concerns second, and then economic outcomes. Moreover, it is impossible to be socially responsible and environmentally friendly in European markets and have no such considerations in China and India or in rest of Asia, Africa, and South America. There are many possibilities and variations. However, most people want great solutions and expect the best outcomes without suffering ill effects due to negative impacts and burdens. People want to be treated equally from the global perspectives of human rights and well-being, and they expect corporations to respect their local traditions, beliefs, and cultures. It is important to meet the cultural aspects of each market and country. The solution to such variations is to simply do the best in every situation and have an inclusive management system.

Broad management constructs like SBD and CSR are more universal than the limited views of Friedman and others. Many global corporations are adopting management constructs like SBD and CSR to offset the negative implications of the failures of companies like Enron and WorldCom. Governments in the developed countries have introduced more stringent reporting requirements like those imposed in the United States under the Sarbanes-Oxley Act of 2002 (SOA), which mandates annual evaluations of the effectiveness of anti-fraud programs and financial controls. SOA brings the force of law to ensure that ethical behavior and compliance are critical considerations in corporate governance, especially in financial reporting. SOA requires that boards of directors and corporate leaders take proactive steps to ensure compliance and are legally responsible for the accuracy of the financial reports. Enhancing SBD, CSR and ethical behaviors provides opportunities to improve corporate reputation, obtain competitive advantages, and save money by avoiding costly product failures, operational disruptions, accidents, and other types of business disasters. Still, most financial models consider catastrophes and problems like the Exxon Valdez accident, the disaster at Bhopal, and the Firestone tire failures to be isolated events rather than system-related failures. The prevailing economic models usually do not include the costs to rectify these kinds of situations in their financial calculations.

Business for Social Responsibility (BSR), a global non-profit business association that promotes CSR, believes that CSR improves financial performance, increases sales, enhances brands, improves workforce retention, and helps mitigate risks.[14] BSR proposes that socially responsible business practices contribute to productivity and profitability. The premises are:[15]

> The solution lies in business practices that reflect and respect the competing claims of all stakeholder groups. No longer simply a matter of publicity or philanthropy, socially responsible business practices affect all aspects of business operations and contribute significantly to corporate productivity and profitability. A company must regard corporate social responsibility as an essential and integral part of mission, strategy and operations.

A study conducted by Marc Orlitzky of University of Sydney and Frank Schmidt and Sara Rynes of University of Iowa indicated that there was a statistically significant association between corporate social and financial performance.[16] Their report, "Corporate Social and Financial Performance," offers evidence that CSR is a good indicator of good management.[17]

Stakeholders and investment groups tend to view CSR as the compelling perspective, while business leaders may consider SBD to be broader and more relevant. In reality, they both incorporate some of the same principles and constructs and have many overlapping concepts and considerations. The key difference is that SBD involves extensive social, ethical, economic, technological, and environmental considerations, and CSR is often viewed from social and economic terms. Jim Gustafson, noted expert on CSR, believes that CSR is the convergence of global citizenship and environmental stewardship. He believes that CSR implies that leaders have to:[18]

- Be sensitive to the issues that affect the lives of the people they live and work with.
- Possess an understanding of the conditions in society on which they could have a positive influence.
- Consider the social impact that their financial and business decisions have on a wide range of constituencies, stakeholders, and the environment.
- Be conservative about not only what the company produces, but how it is produced.

However, Gustafson's suggestions are somewhat passive in the sense that they call for business leaders to become aware of how their companies affect people and the environment, but he does not compel corporations to take actions. By speaking about non-economic entities and individuals, Gustafson asserts that corporations need a more inclusive construct than what CSR alone provides.

Strategic management constructs over the last quarter century have included ethical principles and codes of behaviors as fundamental social responsibilities of businesses. Enhancing environmental protection and promoting employee health and safety also became important elements of strategic management during the 1980s. However, these elements were principally driven by laws and regulations and were really must-do (mandates) requirements rather than corporate-selected initiatives. Many traditional models of CSR involved passive perspectives or tangential actions like philanthropy. While such actions are good, they often attempt to buy social responsibility rather than live it. This statement is not to undermine the tremendous good done by great philanthropists. For instance, Bill Gates and his wife, through the Bill and Malinda Gates Foundation, have given billions to numerous charities around the world. Moreover, many corporations, their leaders, and shareholders have excelled at charitable works and have provided significant improvements in the quality of people's lives through financial resources and good works.

SBD and CSR together fit the prescription of what is necessary. During the late 20th century, strategic thinking evolved from the narrow, more linear philosophies of focusing on selling products and making profits to improving the strategic underpinnings of the corporation and discovering opportunities for enhancing business performance and improving financial success. More recently, it includes global perspectives about creating a more sustainable future with more opportunities and better outcomes for corporations, customers, stakeholders, constituencies, and society. Many strategic leaders have changed their overarching philosophy from Friedman's static views based on profit maximization to a more inclusive perspective of value maximization that includes social, economic, environmental, ethical, and legal responsibilities to shareholders, government mandates, customers, stakeholders, employees, key contributors, and other constituents. Many leading global corporations have adapted the principles and constructs of SBD and CSR.

Corporate self-interest, extended enterprise thinking about sustainable success, or a combination of the two drive today's SBD/CSR perspectives. The most compelling considerations are the ones that involve enhancing and sustaining the corporation, its assets, people, and performance. These are in the corporation's self-interest, and if the corporation is meeting societal needs and expectations in beneficial ways, it is usually being socially, economically, and financially responsible as well. Today, the business and management paradigm is shifting toward more inclusive approaches. Table 2.1 depicts a simplified view of the changing perspectives.

The focus of SBD and CSR is on creating sustainable solutions and protecting the well-being and assets of the corporation. Having a solid corporate reputation is one of the most critical factors for sustainable success. Enhancing one's reputation through

TABLE 2.1 Selected Perspectives Involving Paradigm Shifts in Management Thinking[19]

Consideration	Mid 20th century	Late 20th century	Early 21st century
Economic	Create shareholder wealth	Invest in future opportunities	Create value & wealth across the enterprise
Social	Focus on economic outcomes	Be ethical and charitable	Integrate social responsibility into strategic management constructs
Environmental	Comply with regulatory mandates	Prevent pollution and eliminate wastes	Eliminate defects, wastes, and impacts and move toward ideal outcomes
Finance	Maximize profits	Maximize cash flow and returns	Maximize value creation and business performance; mitigate risks
Customers	Meet needs and demand	Satisfy customers	Exceed needs, expectations, and mandates; enhance and sustain success
Products	Produce acceptable goods	Improve quality, reliability and affordability	Provide sustainable solutions; achieve zero defects and zero burdens
Imperative	Economic Perspectives (Friedman's model)	Strategic Perspectives (Drucker's model)	Global Perspectives (VSL/SBD/CSR)

CSR and SBD is often a low cost, high-return investment that has long-term implications and benefits. For instance, mitigating risks lowers costs and future liabilities and a stable, well-satisfied workforce with high morale results in higher quality transactions with customers and in lower employment costs.

Understanding the full scope of social, ethical, economic, technological, and environmental opportunities enriches the prospects for innovation and leads to greater capabilities, knowledge, and learning. Being more responsible gives customers the confidence that their needs will be fulfilled. Greater customer confidence and satisfaction enhance competitiveness. Eliminating mistakes and problems makes the management system more efficient, effective, leaner, and more productive. In many developed countries, especially in the European Union, there is the perception that society grants corporations a license to operate. Corporations are registered and sanctioned by each of the countries, states and/or provinces in which they do business; they are recognized as legal entities that have been granted, in effect, a license to operate.

There are numerous views on the purposes and duties of corporations. While the prevailing views may still hold that the most important objectives are to generate profits and cash flow for shareholders, maximizing corporate value and satisfying the needs, wants, and expectations of customers, stakeholders, employees, and society are critical outcomes. SBD and CSR recognize that corporations are social entities that create outcomes through people and for people. These broader perspectives are often critical for achieving profit objectives as well. Customers and stakeholders can quickly lose faith in businesses and corporate leaders who are only self-interested and self-serving.

48 ▪ *Visionary Strategic Leadership*

The broader the perspective, the greater is the opportunity to discover new prospects for generating successful business outcomes and to sustain the future. Those who fail to integrate the whole business enterprise may miss extraordinary opportunities; ones that others are certain to exploit.

BOX 2: CANON'S CORPORATE LEADERSHIP, GOVERNANCE AND ITS *"KYOSEI"* PHILOSOPHY

Canon is a leading high-tech company with outstanding corporate philosophies, governance, and business plans. It is driven by its *"kyosei"* (living and working together for the common good), a corporate philosophy that aspires "to a society in which all people, regardless of culture, custom, language, or ethnicity, harmoniously live and work together into the future.[a] Canon is devoted to developing its businesses in ways that support, protect, and develop the people involved, the surrounding environment, and the broader communities around the world. The *kyosei* philosophy was developed in 1996 along with Canon's "Excellent Global Corporation Plan (The Plan)." The Plan is a mid-to-long-term strategic plan for achieving social, economic, and environmental outcomes, extraordinary business success, and sustainability. The goal is to make Canon one of the most respected and successful corporations in the world. According to Chairman and CEO Fujio Mitarai, The Plan is:[b]

> Over the past 10 years, all members of the Canon Group have been working together to carry out innovations and reforms, aiming to be a corporation worthy of admiration and respect worldwide. Broadly speaking, during Phase I we sought to close out the 20th century by strengthening our financial health with an emphasis on cash flow under the themes of "Total Optimization" and "Focus on Profit." In Phase II we sought to establish a solid foothold for continued advancement in the 21st century with an emphasis on product competitiveness, aiming to become No. 1 in the world in all major areas of our business.

Canon's corporate leadership sets the stage for corporate expansion through diversification and globalization. Diversification focuses on proprietary technologies and business ventures leveraging Canon's solid reputation and respected brands. It also involves developing new businesses at headquarters and enhancing basic research and development. The *kyosei* philosophy means balancing business growth and activities with the pursuit of sustainability and CSR. Sustainability and SBD are top priorities as well as promoting communications with diverse groups of stakeholders to build relationships of trust and cooperation.[c] They involve engaging all of the key contributors and providing benefits to them and all of the intended recipients. Canon's leadership believes that being a truly excellent corporation requires a strong commitment to promoting environmental assurance initiatives based on maximizing resource efficiency and harmonious relationships with stakeholders and society. Figure 2A.1 is Canon's stakeholder model.[d]

Corporate management structure and governance are the high-level means and mechanisms that assure corporate success. Corporate leadership supports the product

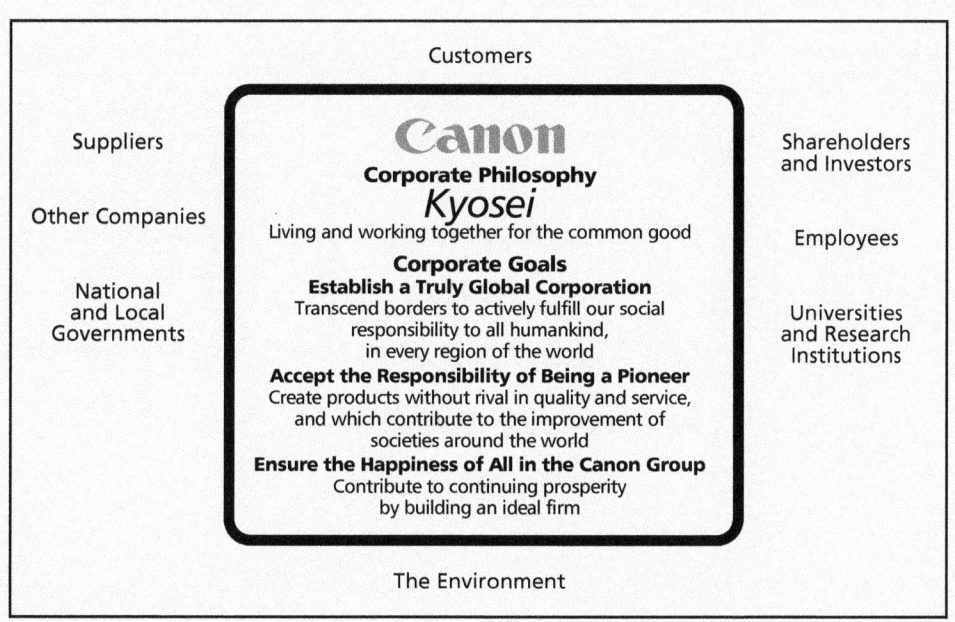

Figure 2A.1 Canon's stakeholder model.

groups that are Canon's SBUs. The governance structure consists of an executive committee, in which all executive officers participate, special management committees for special issues, the Board of Directors, and the Board of Corporate Auditors.[e] Headquarters also has Administrative Divisions that provide special support and control for such affairs as corporate ethics and compliance, planning, human resources management, finance, communication systems, procurement, quality, and engineering.

The audit functions are a joint responsibility of the executive committee and the Board of Directors. The Board of Corporate Auditors has five members, three of which are external members. It provides the external audit functions which include prior approvals for external contract, policies, and procedures related to auditing and other important areas. Internal audits are performed by the Corporate Audit Center. It monitors compliance, risk management, and internal controls; it also works with headquarters administrative divisions to assure that responsibilities are fulfilled for quality assurance, environmental conservations, information protection, security, and compliance. The product groups are the business units and operations. Figure 2A.2 provides a more complete listing of the corporate structure.

Canon's management structure combines decentralized operations and centralized high-level or critical functions like planning, finance, and new business development. Canon's executive leaders are aggressive in their pursuit of making dramatic improvements and realizing significant achievements in their quest toward a more sustainable future. Corporate leadership recognizes the importance of balance, and knows how to lead change.

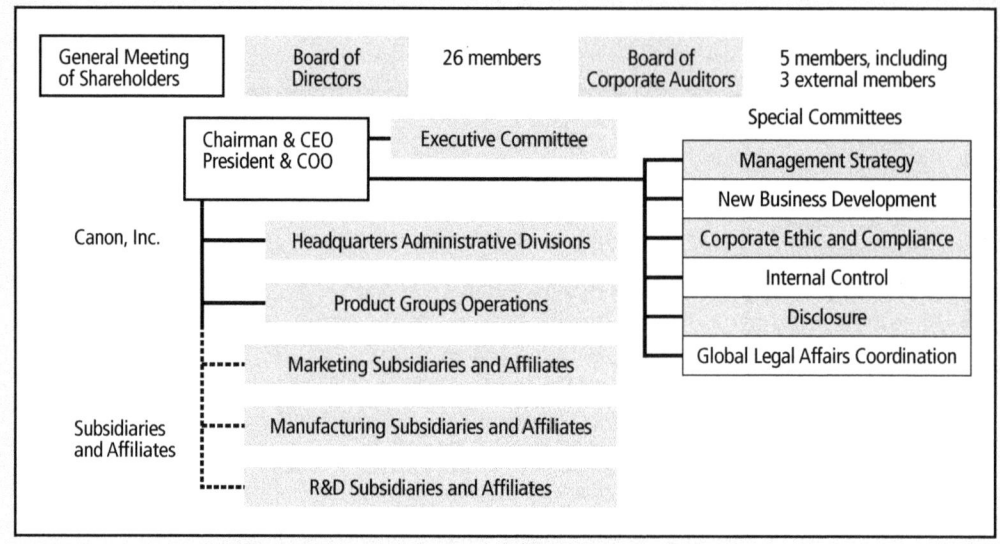

Figure 2A.2 Canon's corporate governance structure (June 1, 2006)[f]

NOTES

a. Canon Sustainability Report 2006, p3.
b. Id, p4; Canon Annual Report 2005, pp7–8.
c. Canon Sustainability Report 2006, p13.
d. Id.
e. Id, p23.
f. Id.

Reflections

CSM and VSL constructs involve cutting-edge frameworks, approaches, methods, techniques, and practices used to understand context, determine strategies, design and deliver solutions, develop systems, design structures, and achieve sustainable success. They are intended to shed light on the business dimensions (space and time) and the elements (entities) of business situations. Strategic leaders must assess their leadership and management constructs for strategic fit and alignment, appropriateness in terms of the business context, and their potential to support strategizing, decision-making, and implementation.

The forms of the strategic management and leadership constructs depend on the company's positions, circumstances, scope, and time horizons. They may take global perspectives about the whole business environment and global markets or they might take a narrower view of the operating system and the critical dimensions of customers, stakeholders, suppliers, and competitors. They also depend on the related dimensions of time, speed, and rate of change. Many corporations have well-defined strategic management constructs and models that are used for developing and realizing the desired strategic direction. These constructs are based on how the corporation manages its business landscapes, and how it plans to improve performance. The constructs and frameworks provided in this chapter pertain to just some of what senior executives focus on in leading change at the corporate level and in fulfilling their responsibilities to the whole corporation.

The underlying purposes of the discussions on the theories and practices throughout this book are to encourage corporate leaders, strategic leaders, senior professionals, and future leaders to reflect on the theoretical underpinnings and practical aspects of VSL and CSM and to think about how to change and improve those constructs given the global perspectives, expectations, and realities. The underlying intention is to invoke thoughts, debates, and reflections about how to lead, innovate, integrate, and create positive changes for a more sustainable future.

Notes

1. Corporate strategic leaders are hereinafter called simply corporate leaders since most corporate leaders are strategic leaders.
2. Alfred Chandler Jr., *Strategy and Structure: Chapters in the History of the American Industrial Enterprise* (Cambridge, MA: The M.I.T. Press, 1962, p383).
3. Michael Porter did not use the term "extended enterprise" but his notion of the value system is a limited version of the extended enterprise. His value system involves just the direct relationships with supply networks and customers.
4. Alex Berenson, *"For Merck Chief, Credibility at the Capitol",* New York Times, November 19, 2004, www.nytimes.com/2004/11/19/business/19merck.html. On November 18, 2004, Raymond V. Gilmartin, Merck's Chairman and CEO, had to testify before Congress to explain Merck's failure to disclose information about Vioxx.
5. Good decisions are based on the whole context of the business and critical elements associated with the decision process. They include all necessary considerations, are balanced from social, economic, and environmental perspectives, do not put anyone at risk, and endure for a reasonably long time so that the investments are recovered and rewarded, and people are successful. Good decisions do not always turn out to be correct because there may be unforeseen events and changes in the business environment.
6. James Womack and Daniel Jones, *Lean Solutions: How Companies and Customers can Create Value and Wealth Together* (New York, NY: Free Press, 2005, p9-17).
7. Michael Hammer and James Champy, *Reengineering the Corporation: A Manifesto for Business Revolution* (New York, NY: HarperCollins Publishers, 1993, p46).
8. World Commission on Environment and Development, *Our Common Future* (Oxford, UK: Oxford University Press, 1987).
9. John Elkington, *Cannibal's with forks: the triple bottom line of 21st century business* (Gabriola Island, BC: New Society Publishing, 1998, p2)
10. *KPMG International Survey of Corporate Sustainability Reporting 2002* (Amsterdam, The Netherlands, 2002, p6).
11. Milton Friedman, *Capitalism and Freedom* (Chicago, IL: University of Chicago Press, 1962, 2002, p133)
12. Id.
13. Peter Drucker, "The New Meaning of Corporate Social Responsibility," California Management Review, Vol. XXVVI No. 2 Winter 1984, p62.
14. Business for Social Responsibility: Advancing Leadership in Responsible Business, www.bsr.org.
15. Id.

16. http://www.business-ethics.com/current_issue/winter_2005
17. Id.
18. Daniel Goleman, *Business: The Ultimate Resource* (Cambridge MA: Perseus Publishing, 2002, p291).
19. David L. Rainey, *Sustainable Business Development: Inventing the Future through Strategy, Innovation and Leadership* (Cambridge, UK: Cambridge University Press, 2006, p660).

References

Goleman, Daniel (2002) *Business: The Ultimate Resource.* Cambridge MA: Perseus Publishing.

Chandler Jr., Alfred (1962) *Strategy and Structure: Chapters in the History of the American Industrial Enterprise.* Cambridge, MA: The M.I.T. Press.

Elkington, John (1998) *Cannibal's with forks: the triple bottom line of 21st century business.* Gabriola Island, BC: New Society Publishing.

Friedman, Milton (1962, 2002) *Capitalism and Freedom.* Chicago, IL: University of Chicago Press.

Hammer, Michael and James Champy (1993) *Reengineering the Corporation: A Manifesto for Business Revolution.* New York, NY: HarperCollins Publishers.

Rainey, David L. (2006) *Sustainable Business Development: Inventing the Future through Strategy, Innovation and Leadership.* Cambridge, UK: Cambridge University Press.

Womack James and Daniel Jones (2005) *Lean Solutions: How Companies and Customers can Create Value and Wealth Together.* New York, NY: Free Press.

World Commission on Environment and Development (1987) *Our Common Future.* Oxford, UK: Oxford University Press.

3

Vision, Strategies, and Goals

Introduction

Visionary strategic leadership (VSL) and corporate strategic management (CSM) transcend all of the management constructs of the corporation. Corporate leaders provide the high-level direction and guidance for integrating the business enterprise with the natural environment, social world, and business environment, ensuring that all elements are strategically aligned for realizing exceptional outcomes and outstanding performance. They engage in crafting and implementing high-level strategies, systems, structures, innovations, programs, and concomitant actions required for leading change. They bring to bear the appropriate capabilities and resources to implement the strategies and objectives. They include transforming the capabilities, resources, and knowledge into more powerful realities. VSL and CSM are shaped by all of the external and internal forces from the broadest in the business environment to the narrowest internal process. While it is difficult to articulate all of the complex and far-reaching elements of VSL and CSM, it is imperative that corporate leaders act as the fiduciaries for shareholders, employees, customers, stakeholders, society, and all of the constituents who rely on their leadership, judgment, and sound decision-making as discussed in the previous chapters.

VSL and CSM are necessary for illuminating uncharted pathways and making the corporation, its business units, and their extended enterprises more successful and sustainable. They require proactive thinking and interactive action. They are not process-oriented or prescriptive. Rather, they are open-ended, requiring a great deal of intellectual capital and wisdom on the part of corporate leaders to determine the implications and how to manage them. VSL and CSM necessitate a broad knowledge of the business world so that the strategic leaders can ascertain what needs to be done and how to do it. Too often good strategic leaders are unsuccessful because they fail to pay attention to the seemingly mundane, yet crucial, factors like the well-being of employees, the proper functioning of operations, and regulatory compliance. Nothing is unimportant.

VSL and CSM involve the creation or reaffirmation of the vision and strategic direction of the organization, making them understandable and attainable in the hearts and minds of the people. The founders and early leaders of most companies generally had clearly established purposes, aspirations, and aims for leading and directing their enterprises. They provided the logic and focus for the organization and encouraged people to achieve extraordinary outcomes. Subsequent corporate leaders have the awesome responsibility to enhance the vision and strategic direction over time and keep all facets alive and relevant as time marches on. Strategic leaders at every level have the responsibility for translating the vision and strategic direction into exciting possibilities and operational realities so that everyone knows why the vision and goals are important, what is expected, what actions are appropriate and necessary, and how to make good decisions.

Just as important as creating the vision, corporate leaders have to articulate an overarching strategic perspective (OSP) that provides a road map to guide the business enterprise(s) successfully into the future. While the construct of vision is inherently understandable, the pathways to the visions are often fuzzy and difficult to maneuver. The notion of an OSP is a new construct that is intended to bridge the chasm between the esoteric aspects of the vision and the realities of crafting and implementing corporate strategies and action plans. It lays out the philosophical and pragmatic meanings that define why the strategic direction is desirable, what has to be done to invent the future, and how people have to participate in achieving the results.

The OSP provides a profound sense of what the strategic direction is and how to make it real. It provides understanding, guidance, and connection. It is intended to keep people within the corporation and across the whole business enterprise on track and on target. It is the virtual link between the external and internal, the present and the future, and the corporation and its enterprise. It describes the most critical aspects of creating the future and identifies some of the most critical strategic factors for realizing the vision. These include why the vision and strategic direction are appropriate, where to find opportunities, with whom to establish relationships, what management systems and business models to adapt, and how to measure effectiveness and achievements. In simple terms, corporate leaders can use OSP to provide a sense of continuity from the vision to sustainable success without prescribing all of actions or usurping the roles and responsibilities of lower levels of strategic leadership.

Corporate leaders guide the corporation in its realization of a more desirable future. Innovative companies and enterprises position themselves to orchestrate their own destinies. Corporate leaders provide the means and mechanisms to guide people within the organization and enterprise(s) to achieve strategic objectives and implement strategies and action plans. While they provide the overarching aspects, they generally have a cadre of other strategic leaders who engage in a multitude of the actual strategic decisions and actions. As an aside to make the point using a historical example, Henry the Navigator of Portugal (1394–1460) was a great patron of global exploration and navigation, but he used surrogates to go on most of the actual journeys. Yet, he was considered to be a great explorer. He used his imagination and insights about expanding trade based on circumventing Africa instead of using the well-established land routes. He provided the means (ships and cargo) to realize the outcomes. Eventually, great explorers like Bartolomeu Dias and Vasco De Gama realized his aspirations of sailing around the tip of Africa (The Cape of Good Hope) twenty-eight years after his death.

VSL and CSM are difficult to precisely articulate because they are broad, open-ended, and viewed in terms of the context of the business world. It is impossible to map out the definitive processes for engaging in all of the actions and for achieving success. They often involve doing the opposite of what the mainstream views and approaches are at a given point in time. For example, 3M is focusing on "Made in America" in times when competitors are outsourcing production to developing countries. In today's context, there are millions of opportunities, yet it takes astute corporate leaders to set the stage for their organizations, to articulate what the opportunities are and what they mean, and how to allocate the intellectual capital and resources necessary to successfully realize the desired outcomes. While good luck does play a role, realizing the vision, achieving strategies, goals and action plans, and tracking sustainable success require exceptional visionary strategic leaders who have steady hands at the helm.

Successful corporate leaders are the theoretical strategists who develop the vision, the OSP, and the game plans for achieving sustainable success. They kick-off new-to-the-world endeavors and high-level strategic programs that are difficult to prescribe and often have to be embraced before precise road maps are available. They are the pioneers of their organizations. They lead change and are responsible for achieving the implicit and explicit goals. Their leadership roles and agendas are akin to those of famous explorers like Lewis and Clark and the interdisciplinary teams that successfully completed the Apollo missions to the moon and created the International Space Station. They are also like the great social leaders like Mohandas Gandhi and Martin Luther King Jr. Those leaders had the vision and understanding of what had to be done, and they did it, even though the pathways to success were uncharted and froth with challenges and risks.

The main topics discussed in the chapter are:

- Articulating the corporate vision.
- Describing the OSP that links the desired future with the present.
- Defining corporate strategies and goals that guide people toward targeted outcomes and sustainable success.
- Measuring corporate performance.

Corporate Vision

Corporate vision is the high-level strategic aspiration that encapsulates the strategic direction and the requisite transformation of the company. It involves how a business entity intends to exceed the needs and expectations of the present, realize its goals and desires for the future, and achieve sustainable success without compromising the short term or the long term. It is what the company wants or expects to become. To be effective, it has to be logical, aggressive, farsighted and innovative, yet realistic and understandable. It should include dramatic, if not radical, developments and improvements and transformations with more positive aspects and significantly fewer negatives.

The vision should light the way and serve as a beacon for the people within the organization as well as for customers, stakeholders, shareholders, and other constituents. It must clearly articulate for them why the corporation exists, what it seeks to do to create value in an improved future, and how everyone can participate and benefit. The vision imparts foresight, provides a sense of the organization's pursuit for excellence, and embraces a never-ending zeal for sustainable success. A vision must be an enduring challenge with practical implications for the people involved. While the vision may take years or even decades to realize, the short-term gains and near-term successes must be apparent to foster the willingness on the part of people to remain steadfast in their quest. Nevertheless, even before the prevailing vision is realized, most corporate leaders conceive of an even more compelling new vision for going forward, and the cycle repeats itself over time.

Visionary strategic leaders craft a vision based on the current reality, the needs, requirements, demands, and expectations of the business environment, the broader aspects of the social world and the natural environment, and the necessary changes over time. The vision includes the desired developments that are expected within a specified time frame and how the corporation intends to lead change over the long term. It is a moving target that may have a number of intermediate stages in the quest toward the endless pursuit of excellence and greatness. For example, Shell Oil has a vision to become an energy company instead of just being a petroleum company. Its vision is subdivided into distinct stages as the company transforms its strategic direction, assets, resources, capabilities, and operations from petroleum-based ones to those pertaining to renewable energy technologies. It may take fifty years to become an energy company that is not dependent on petroleum. The challenges are great and the future will tell how well its corporate leaders are able to carry out the vision. Words are easy; actions are more difficult. Moreover, staying the course is even more difficult as new leaders often change the vision or fail to keep the momentum moving forward. It is all too easy to focus on the present and reap short-term rewards.

The vision should inspire people within the organization and across the whole enterprise and enjoin them to take action and achieve extraordinary results. It should be an exciting departure from the prevailing situations and possibly the boring realities. It should reflect the positive forces that create opportunities to excel. It should extend to the markets, customers, stakeholders, and networks of external entities that provide opportunities for the organization to achieve its goals and to satisfy its constituents and make them successful as well. The vision should also embrace the long-term challenges in the business environment, the social world, and the natural environment. The broader the reach and perspectives, the more opportunities there are to excel.

The vision should unify strategic thinking within the organization and the enterprise and across space and time so that everyone understands what is desirable and necessary for achieving success. For instance, marketing people often do everything possible to convey positive messages about the products and services without much consideration about the negative side or the associated social, economic, and environmental challenges. Many environmental management professionals, in turn, address the negative environmental aspects without thinking about how to turn negatives into positives. While this statement may be an oversimplification, an essential requirement of a vision is to have everyone thinking and acting in terms of the whole and ensuring that there are consistent plans, accurate messages about reality, and appropriate actions and programs to realize the desired outcomes, especially the hopes and dreams for the future. For instance, sales executives have implicit and explicit responsibilities to assure that the products are sold to people who can enjoy the benefits and not to those who have limitations with respect to the use of such products; products must not be sold to people who might be at risks to unacceptable or unwanted outcomes. Think about Merck's problems stemming from the sale of Vioxx.

Vision statements are often used to articulate the desired vision. They should be comprehensive and innovative. They specify the content and details of the vision in words that people can relate to and understand. Visionary strategic leaders should eschew traditional vision statements that assert flowery concepts about high-quality products, satisfying customers, being the best and other often substance-less claims. Instead, their vision statements should involve commitments to make dramatic improvements to the solutions and systems by focusing on all of the critical factors for success. They should reflect on the positive perspectives of realizing the economic goals of the company, mitigating negative aspects, and curing and/or eliminating difficulties, problems, and vulnerabilities wherever they may be in the extended enterprises.

Visions and vision statements are not intended to be part of marketing campaigns. Unfortunately, many vision statements are really feel-good marketing messages intended to impress potential customers, stakeholders, and/or investors. Yet, they often fail to convince customers and stakeholders how wonderful the brands, products, and operations really are unless there is a reality to the statements. The messages are often out of context with reality. The messages that customers hear from the company often exclude any discussions about difficulties or challenges. People quickly understand the underlying flaws in the flowery single-sided messages. With the Internet and other sources of information, people easily find out about various problems, issues, etc. Ultimately, such vision statements fail to inspire people within the enterprise to reach out and transform the present situation into a richer reality or to cure existing problems and difficulties. They may even damage the corporation or its brands as customers and stakeholders pierce through the shallowness of the statements and question the integrity and honesty of the company. This is especially important with the post-Enron challenges of believability and accountability. Perceiving misleading information or even deception, people may doubt the authenticity of the messages and even the veracity of the company and its strategic leaders. In addition, there are many non-governmental organizations (NGOs) that follow every aspect of what corporations do and say. They try to ascertain the truthfulness of corporate statements and reports. For instance, several of the major petroleum companies are constantly challenged by NGOs through web sites and their own marketing campaigns suggesting that many of the environmental initiatives are "greenwash", i.e., marketing campaigns to put a positive spin on problems.

A vision should include potential solutions to the difficulties and problems associated with the waste streams, defects, and impacts of today and the actions required to overcome the negative legacies of the past. Moreover, the vision should address the business challenges and the poor practices within company and in the extended enterprise and the constraints that limit opportunities in the business environment. It should describe how to turn disadvantages into advantages, problems into solutions, and resources and capabilities into achievements and sustainable outcomes. While such visions are seemingly almost impossible to contemplate, never mind to formulate, think about the incredible changes that have occurred over the last two decades and how seemingly impossible technologies, products, and processes have become realities. For instance, new technologies like digital cameras have eliminated the costs associated with poor-quality pictures and photo storage and significantly reduced the use of toxic photographic chemicals that generate incredible quantities of hazardous wastes. There are multiple benefits including allowing users to simply delete what they do not want and try again and again—no costs, no wastes, and no residuals.

Figure 3.1 outlines the elements of a vision depicting the main elements, interconnections, and interrelationships for corporate and enterprise transformations.

Built on corporate values and business excellence, a vision is a complex abstraction of the desired reality. It is intended to invoke belief, desire, and actions. While it can be argued that simplicity is beautiful, it is imperative that the vision and vision statements convey a balanced and fuller perspective. Too many companies fail to capitalize on the power of what a great vision statement can accomplish. A vision statement should not be a simple statement of nebulous perspectives or desires. For instance, General Motors (GM) enunciated in 2004 the following as its vision statement:[1]

> GM's vision is to be the world's leader in transportation products and related services. We will earn our customer's enthusiasm through continuous improvement driven by the integrity, teamwork, and innovation of GM people.
>
> Becoming the best is an unending journey, a constantly changing destination. But that's where we've determined to drive-one car, one truck, one customer at a time.

While there are many business leaders and scholars who would like GM's 2004 vision because it is simple, straightforward and easy to remember, it seemingly fails to explain how GM planned to operate differently in the future to achieve its goals. People

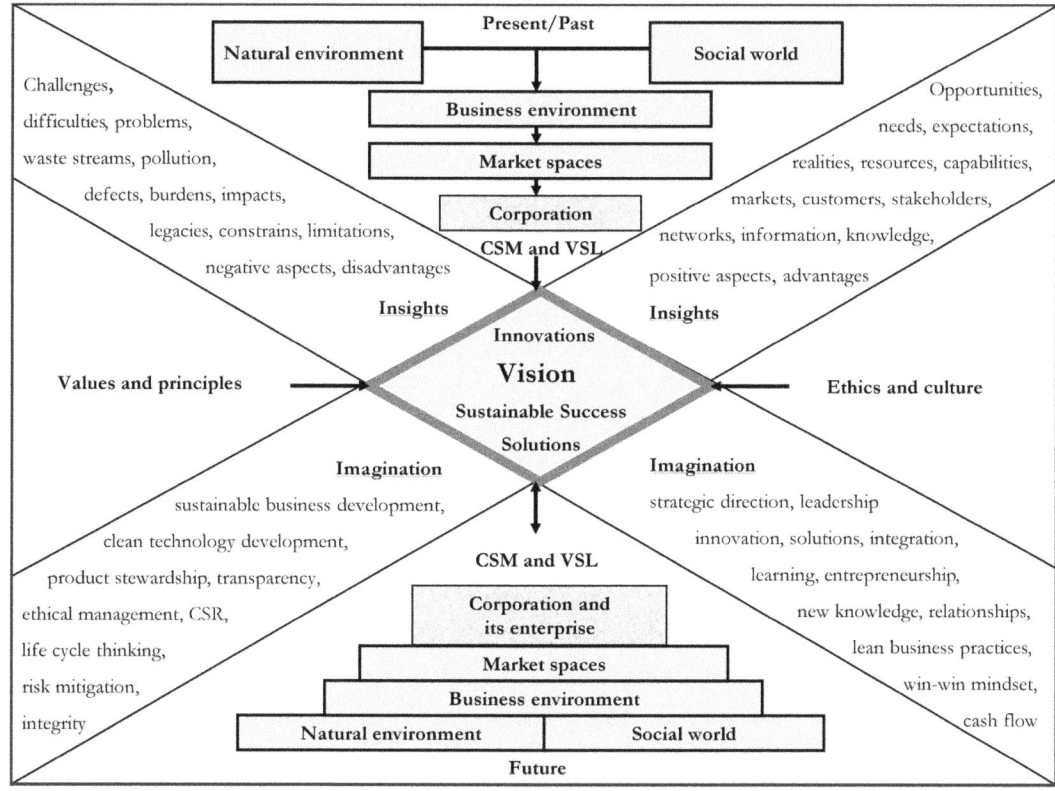

Figure 3.1 The vision construct for company and enterprise transformations.

may have been left wondering just what this language means and whether the intent was to inspire people within the enterprise to excel or just to promote the marketing objectives. GM's older vision statement focused too much on just quality, customer satisfaction, and performance. Indeed, history suggests that GM's vision statement was not very effective given the collapse of the company several years later. However, it had plenty of company; many other companies had put forth similar statements. In today's turbulent and complex business world, such vision statements are simply too limited. They focus more on today than tomorrow, and more on products and customers than on the broader social, economic, ethical, environmental, technological, and market considerations of the business environment.

Corporate leaders have to create and be committed to a vision to which they can rally the organization. The vision has to articulate the strategic direction to people inside the organization and outside it as well. The strategic direction must guide them in understanding what has to be done and what is critical for success. This understanding drives innovation. Developments, improvements, growth, solutions, positive gains, and successes are achieved through leadership, innovation, entrepreneurship, knowledge, learning, and hard work. They are also created by building positive relationships across the enterprise and developing lean business practices that promote efficiency and effectiveness and eliminate wastes and losses.

Strategic leaders have to envision win-win outcomes. They have to overcome the traditional mindset of concentrating on rivalry amongst the competitors rather than focusing on creating value for the contributors and recipients. Shareholders want and expect sustained positive cash flow and profitability. They want corporate leaders to reduce vulnerabilities and risks as well. Such outcomes propel the organization toward sustainable success.

Sustainable business development (SBD) and corporate social responsibility (CSR) as discussed in Chapter 2 provide management constructs for solving many of the existing problems. Other approaches like creating clean technologies and innovative products that are free of the defects, burdens, and impacts of their predecessors also provide exciting possibilities for a brighter future. Clean technology development is part of eliminating environmental problems, especially those associated waste streams. Product stewardship obligates producers and others to ensure that products and processes are safe, effective, and used properly. Transparency allows outsiders access to information and data so that they are informed and can contribute. Ethical management, customer and stakeholder satisfaction, and life cycle management examine the inputs and outputs of every process to determine the strengths and weaknesses and identify the actions required to create sustainable solutions. A key to such assessments is risk mitigation which is the inherent responsibility of every decision maker.

Ultimately, corporations may have even longer vision statements, if they include most elements suggested in Figure 3.1. While in certain situations some of the elements may not apply, it is the job of corporate leaders to reflect on how they are going to get everyone engaged and working in concert with each other. Everyone must understand the vision and work in unison to realize it. Enhanced respect for the company is one of the most important outcomes; one that can be realized fairly quickly (within a few years) even though it may take decades to actually realize the vision.

The Overarching Strategic Perspective

Linking the Overarching Strategic Perspective with the Corporate Vision

Most companies have an established vision statement. However, as discussed, many vision statements are typically weak and fail to inspire. They lack a sense of what the corporate leaders are actually trying to accomplish or fail to convey the future possibilities. Such failures make it difficult for people in the organization to understand how to take actions based on the vision. Even in those cases when the vision is clearly stated, it may be difficult for lower-level leaders, managers, and professionals to translate the vision into reality. For example, it may be difficult for employees at Shell Oil to understand how to change from a petroleum company to an energy company, especially when they are just engaged in petroleum. It takes more than just words to convey what is the vision.

The OSP provides a sense of reality to the vision, if the vision statements are esoteric and difficult to interpret. It links the present business realities and strategic logic with the future expectations and desired strategic positions. It translates the rhetoric of strategic language into meaningful dialogue for everyone from leaders to employees. For instance, during the American Revolutionary War, George Washington realized after suffering defeats in several battles during early stages of the War that he did not have to win; he had to avoid losing, especially losing the Continental Army. General Washington kept the army together and continued the struggle, even though he and his soldiers were fighting a well-trained and well-equipped professional army. Most importantly, Washington had to translate the wonderful vision of independence and freedom as stated in the Declaration of Independence into language that his soldiers could understand and relate to, given their harsh living conditions and the historic reality of being ruled by agents of the King. The new vision was difficult for most of them to understand, because they had never enjoyed a sense of political freedom and personal liberty. Washington was successful because he translated the vision of the American Revolution into an overarching perspective that every soldier could understand and use in contributing to the war effort. Washington gave them the courage to persevere knowing that time was on their side as the British would grow weary of costs of war. The vision was esoteric with many intangibles; yet the overarching perspective was relatively simple: keep the army together and support the efforts on a day-to-day basis. Washington believed that the Americans would ultimately prevail, if they did not capitulate.

In the business world, the grander the vision, the more difficult it might be for people to understand and relate to it. Imagine the founding fathers of the U.S. trying to articulate a vision of building a strong and powerful country, one equivalent to the leading economic powers in Europe. It would have been viewed as an impossible dream. Grand visions require translations into more popular and understandable terms. It is the OSP that provides a sense of reality and how to translate the vision into strategies and actions. It answers the why and what questions. It is based on the purposes, principles, philosophies, values, ethics, behaviors, and practices of the organization. The OSP is intended to offer a grounded sense of the strategic logic of the organization, especially if circumstances force major modifications in the prevailing vision and strategic direction because of the realities of a dynamic world. It gives a sense of continuity across time.

The OSP can be a statement(s) of deeply held values and principles, ethics and corporate culture. For example, Johnson & Johnson (J&J) has a powerful Credo that provides guidance as strategic leaders and practitioners make strategic decisions about their businesses. The OSP can take the form of a business model for strategic decision-making. For example, Toyota established a lean business management model as its OSP. It gives employees an understanding of where they fit in the corporation and what are the expectations. Another form of the OSP is a strategic management framework or management constructs like SBD and CSR. They offer guidance and support with flexibility, using well-defined set(s) of principles and acceptable beliefs and behaviors. People know what is desirable within the context of the business environment, yet have the ability to adapt and be creative. The OSP and the related management constructs make it far easier for people to understand and appreciate the logic of the strategic direction and what is expected. At a minimum, the philosophies, principles, and practices provide a foundation upon which strategic leaders can embellish. For example,

Siemens, A.G., the high-tech producer of sophisticated technologies, focuses on complex requirements and enjoys dealing with complexities. Dealing with complexities has become a strategic advantage. In doing so, Siemens is becoming a sustainable enterprise using SBD constructs that simplify its CSM approaches and decision-making.

The Importance of an Overarching Strategic Perspective

One of the most significant challenges facing strategic leaders is to make the vision real and provide the organization with a sense of how to realize the vision. There is often a chasm between the vision and the strategic direction that has been articulated through the strategies and goals. Even in the cases in which the vision is clear, concise, and people fully understand what is expected, it is often difficult to connect the vision with strategic direction.

The OSP is often an implicit or even a historical construct that is well-understood in many organizations, but usually absent from formal strategic logic and direction. The OSP provides decision-makers with a sense of stability and confidence in their actions. For instance, German automobile companies, especially BMW and Mercedes-Benz, rely on the robust quality of their "German engineering" and their performance driven solutions as strategic links between various business units, product platforms, and strategic innovations. Their visions and grand strategies for translating what they do into who they want to be are linked by the ever-present notion of what made these companies great and what sustains their strategic positions in the business world, i.e., "German engineering." These companies link the present capabilities and operations to their future success using their values, beliefs, and capabilities. Figure 3.2 depicts the theoretical view of OSP.

The greater the expected rate of change the more likely there is a huge gap between what the vision implies and the prevailing strategic positions and strategic direction of the corporation. While the notion is theoretical, the logic is based on common

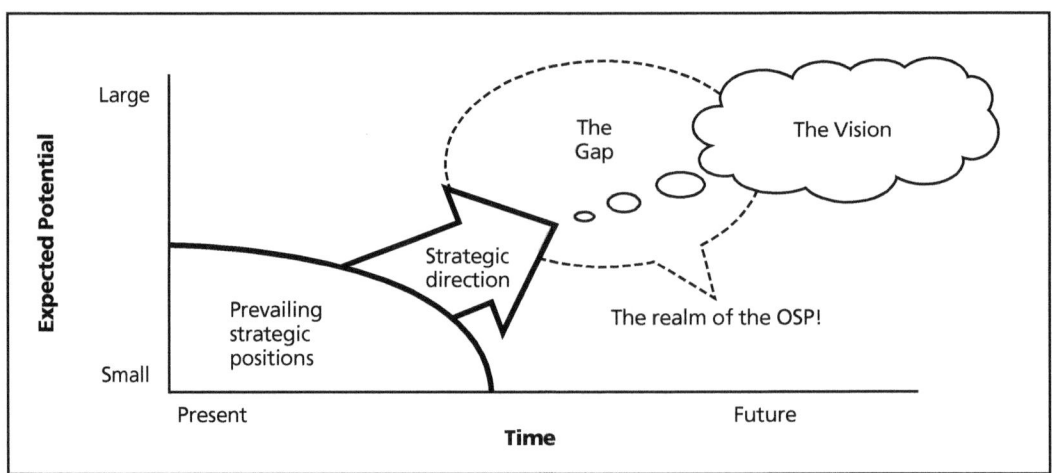

Figure 3.2 The connections between the vision, the strategic direction, and the OSP.

sense and the practical implications of change. If the vision requires only modest changes through incremental improvements and small investments, then the gap between what is and what is expected is small and easy to overcome. People can easily relate to the strategies and objectives and achieve desired results. On the other hand, if the vision requires revolutionary changes through radical innovations, large investments, and new learning, knowledge, and capabilities, the chasm is often significant and requires intense corporate leadership, i.e., VSL, to overcome the challenges. As new technologies and economic developments have accelerated over the last several decades, expectations have dramatically increased, and it is becoming more and more difficult to succeed with modest visions and incremental improvements. The business environment is in a constant state of flux that demands significant changes. If a corporation fails to maintain the expected rate of change, it is actually falling behind despite the fact that it is making continuous improvements. The actual improvements must exceed the rate of change in the business environment to realize true gains.

In the comparatively slow pace of the twentieth century, most corporations kept astride with change, although thousands of innovative companies like RCA and Digital Equipment Corporation ultimately did not and failed to survive as independent entities. Today, there is little choice other than to stay well ahead of change in the markets and business environment, if one wants to succeed. This phenomenon explains why many large corporations of the past had little understanding of an OSP and why they must be cognizant of it today. Failure to keep pace with change creates even greater difficulties in trying to make up lost ground and catch up with the pack.

Relatively new management constructs like six-sigma thinking, lean business practices, SBD, and CSR give substance to the connections between the vision, the strategic direction, and the OSP. For instance, corporate leaders of companies like Siemens and General Electric (GE) provide guidance and direction to their organization by subscribing to the constructs of SBD and CSR. The beauty of such approaches is that the principles, processes, and practices are spelled out through the SBD and CSR constructs—corporate leaders do not have to reinvent them. They simply have to articulate and apply them.

The Fundamental Aspects of the Overarching Strategic Perspective

The fundamental aspects of the OSP involve the strategic aims and aspirations of the company; what is it now and what does it want to become? OSP relates to the desired "ends" that extend well beyond products and services or customers and stakeholders. They are the precursors to the strategic goals and the grand strategies. They include positive changes that involve moving from the present state to a more desirable one. The most crucial "ends" include not just specific targets, but goals that are often diverse and intangible. For instance, the notion of sustainable success is a never-ending perspective and an overarching goal. It is easily understood, but it is difficult to contemplate how a company would actually reach an end point that cannot truly be defined and never really achieved.

An OSP tells people what they have to seek, and what is important. For instance, human beings generally seek health and safety, economic success, and meaningful lives with an inner feeling of happiness. What do companies seek? Although an organization does not necessarily become "happy," one of the main goals might be to realize its full potential—to strive for excellence in everything it does, and to become more capable and successful over time. This is similar to the beliefs of ancient Greeks who sought "arête" or the pursuit of excellence and virtue for its own sake.

The well-being of the company is a primary aim. Corporate well-being focuses on the long term, the reasons why the company exists, and the ultimate good that it creates. Companies exist for many reasons, including serving society, promoting human development, creating wealth for shareholders, satisfying customers, and realizing a fair return on invested capital. While there are many other reasons that include providing employment for people and serving other constituencies, it is imperative that corporate leaders think broadly about what are the aims and reasons for being, and how they create the means and mechanisms to achieve them.

Historically, the focus of corporate leaders was on financial capital and maximizing the return on the capital. While such thinking is not inappropriate, it is narrow and often leads to difficulties in the long term because equally important aims related to value creation and sustainable success were not realized, leading to potential problems. For instance, charging more than a fair price for products and services may produce excellent profits in the short term, but often infuriates customers who seek alternatives in the long term; thus, such approaches may maximize profits today, but often threaten sustainable success. One of the most important functions of the company is to produce good solutions for others and itself. Such functions are done well when they are developed and executed at the highest levels of achievement and within the highest standards of excellence. Moreover, business is not a game based on the notion of winner takes all, as is the case in sports or winning a ball game. The overarching purpose of business is to excel and to create extraordinary value that leads to broad-based successes across the full spectrum of customers, stakeholders, employees, and shareholders. Sustainable success requires harmony and well-being, not conflicts and a win-lose mentality among the participants.

Corporate leaders create success that permeates the corporation. Some of the main aims that can bridge the gap between vision and reality using OSP include:

- **The well-being of the company.** The organization and its enterprise(s) must survive and prosper if it is to create value across space and time. This relates to the overarching goals of survival and sustainable success.
- **Positive outcomes for the social world and the natural environment.** The company must use resources wisely and minimize degradation, depletion, disruption, and/or destruction of the social world and the natural environment. Companies have a right to achieve their ends, but not at the expense of the greater good.
- **Value creation.** Success is based on providing the best solutions possible. It is about creating positive value and benefits for people and eliminating negative burdens and impacts.

- **Customer and stakeholder satisfaction and success.** Customers have to be satisfied and successful with their decisions and outcomes. Stakeholders have to be likewise satisfied. It is imperative that the decisions and actions of the company support external entities and people, and lead to their success. Failure to provide success leads to discontinuities and dissatisfaction.
- **Positive relationships through value networks.** The interactive business world requires many connections to accomplish the desired outcomes. Success depends on having positive relationships with customers, supply networks, stakeholders, and a myriad of other constituents.
- **The wealth of the company and shareholders.** Success is more than surviving and prospering. It involves increasing shareholder equity and realizing the strategic goals. It also involves enhancing intangibles like the corporate reputation.

There are many other elements that could be listed. The well-being of the company is preeminent, because if the company fails, all of what it could accomplish fades with it. While the business world would still exist, corporate failure ultimately means that the vision and potential contributions are not realized. Therefore, the foremost responsibility of corporate leaders is to protect, preserve, develop, and improve the well-being of the company and its people, not just for the sake of existence, but for the benefits and good that it provides.

The protection of the social world and natural environment is a shared obligation by corporations, governments, NGOs, and people in general. Corporate leaders have the duty to ensure that their organizations are contributing to the public good and they are not doing harm. While such matters are not always high on the list of priorities in many enterprises, corporate leaders have to ensure that their internal organizations and external partners from the top to the bottom are mindful of their obligations. These include complying with the laws and regulations and ensuring ethical and best practices, if the laws and regulations are lax. Attention to the negative impacts on the social/human world and natural environment provides a parallel track for achieving corporate success. The proof for such contentions lies in the operations of global corporations in the developed countries. Generally, their success is a function of the overall well-being of the people, markets, and societies that they serve. Successful businesses are dependent upon the stability and the growth of the associated national and regional economies. Corporate success generally necessitates having stable, secure, and successful social, political, economic, and environmental structures that make commercial and financial activities possible and sustainable. When stability is lost through political intrigue, social unrest or economic upheavals, turbulence and failure may follow. Even great businesses may fail under such conditions.

Value creation is the heart of business. Perceptions often play roles in what people believe to be valuable in the short term, but in the long term people seek real solutions for their needs and desire positive and enduring outcomes. Peter Schwartz, a noted futurist and President, Global Business Networks, suggests in his book, *The Art of the Long View: Planning for the Future in an Uncertain World* that the long view requires business leaders to think about plausible scenarios of the future.[3] Schwartz depicts the process for how to think about the future:[4]

> [M]anagers [strategic leader] invent and then consider, in depth, several varied stories of equally plausible futures. The stories are carefully researched, full of relevant detail, oriented toward real-life decisions, and designed (one hopes) to bring forward surprises and unexpected leaps of understanding. Together, the scenarios [pertaining to plausible future possibilities] comprise a tool for ordering one's perceptions. The point is not to "pick one preferred future," and hope for it to come to pass (or, even work to create it-though there are some situations where acting to create a better future is a useful function of scenarios). Nor is the point to find the most probable future and adapt to it or "bet the company" on it. Rather the point is to make strategic decisions that will be sound for all plausible futures. No matter what future takes place, you are much more likely to be ready for it—and influential in it— if you have thought seriously about scenarios.

The OSP is based on plausible future scenarios. It is a combination of fitting into "all plausible scenarios" and being adaptive and developing the preferred future. It is based on understanding value creation and creating solutions that realize valuable contributions.[5] OSP involves corporate leaders who think about "what is," "what could be," and "what should be." It involves out-of-the-box thinking about the possibilities and the pathways to realize the value derived, if the possibilities become realities. It is important to note that the process should be ongoing, per Schwartz's comments about permanent strategic conversation. The OSP is reinforced, reinvigorated, and reexamined every day. Chapter 4 provides additional discussions about scenario planning.

Building theoretical bridges from the present to future that enrich value creation is the essence of OSP. They facilitate understanding and creativity. In the Harvard Business Review article, "Value Innovation," the authors, W. Chan Kim and Renee Mauborgne, suggest that value innovators "think in terms of the total solution customers seek, and they try to overcome the chief compromises their industry forces customers to make."[6] They do this even if it takes the company beyond its industry's traditional offering.[7] OSP reaches beyond the obvious and examines how to create value for everyone in innovative ways.

Value creation is dependent on context, the needs and expectations of the people involved, and the conditions and trends in the business environment. For instance, most global corporations generally focus their attention on less than twenty percent of the world's population, those living in the developed countries. Their attention is on people who have the financial resources to buy the products and services that were designed and developed to fit the lifestyles of the affluent. Yet, there are enormous opportunities to create solutions for improving their lives of billions people who don't have the means or mechanisms to buy the typical products sold in the developed countries. People in developing countries need affordable products designed for their condition and lifestyle and there are incredible opportunities to provide the right solutions for such people.

Business enterprises are about the relationships among people who have shared interests in achieving positive outcomes. Each party wants to succeed and become more fruitful in its own way. Business people, customers, and stakeholders enter into relationships to realize their objectives of which they, theoretically, would be less successful if the relationships did not exist. If relationships are critical to success, then corporate leaders have to orchestrate the best possible connections. Relationship building involves a higher level of thinking about value creation and value networks. They include all corporate relationships from government entities and community officials to customers and strategic partners. At the core levels of the corporation, the focus is usually on value networks which support and promote commercial exchanges. Building solid relationships involves people-to-people interchanges that take a considerable amount of time to realize, but are usually much more enduring than the typical commercial exchanges that often have start and end points.

Companies that have achieved great financial rewards usually did so because they made other people successful, not just satisfied, since business success is generally dependent on making others successful. The story of Chester Carlson, the inventor of the copier, and Joe Wilson, the strategic leader at Haloid Corporation, illustrates the concept. Carlson developed a solution for making copies of documents and Wilson invested the money to implement the solution. Wilson bet the future of his company because he believed in the promise of Carlson's copier technology and its potential to create value for customers. The solution was extremely successful and made Haloid, renamed Xerox Corporation, a very wealthy enterprise. The great financial success of Xerox during its early years (1959 thru 1979) was due to the benefits derived by its customers. The ease of copying documents allowed customers to grow their businesses and enjoy financial rewards. Customers' success led others to make Xerox a name synonymous with making copies. Great success and achievements result in a multiplier effect benefiting contributing parties and recipients.

Sustainable success requires ongoing investments in the resources, capabilities, relationships, and the leadership and management of the company. It involves creating and sustaining wealth over the long term. Great achievements can be leveraged into even more powerful positions that can be used to produce more positive outcomes. It is the multiplier effect of the ongoing investments and achievements that leads to great wealth.

Corporate Strategies and Goals

The Notion of Grand Corporate Strategy

Corporate strategy involves high-level strategy formulation and implementation impacting the whole corporation. It involves translating the vision and the OSP into a strategic direction and provides the strategic logic for the business units and the operating systems. Corporate strategies include the patterns of strategic decisions and actions that map out what the corporation wants to be, through a realization of its vision. Arnoldo C. Hax of the Massachusetts Institute of Technology (MIT) and Nicolas S. Majluf of the Catholic University of Chile provide a comprehensive view of corporate strategy. In their book, *The Strategy Concept and Process: A Pragmatic Approach*, Hax and Majluf identified the elements corporate strategy:[8]

1. a coherent, unifying, and integrative pattern of decisions;
2. determines and reveals the organizations purpose in terms of long-term objectives, action programs, and resource allocation priorities;
3. selects the businesses the organization is in or is to be in;
4. attempts to achieve long-term sustainable advantage in each of the businesses, by responding properly to the opportunities and threats in the firm's environment, and the strengths and weaknesses of the organization;
5. engages all of the hierarchical levels of the firm that include corporate, strategic business units (SBUs) and functional/operational; and,
6. defines the nature of the economic and non-economic contributions it intends to make to its stakeholders.

While Hax and Majluf discuss strategy in general, their perspectives fit the notion of corporate strategy that pertains to CSM. Corporate strategy provides a dynamic strategic map that extends across space and time. It embodies the overarching objectives, the programmatic (transitional and transformational) approaches to achieve sustainable success, and allocation of resources and intellectual capital for achieving the desired goals. It includes the identification, analysis, and selection of opportunities and challenges that the corporation views as crucial for realizing the vision and achieving sustainable success. The focus is on high-level imperatives that shape the corporation's future. Corporate strategy provides direction for the development of lower-level strategies—business units and operational. Most importantly, it defines and determines what contributions the corporation expects to make for all of its constituencies from customers and stakeholders to shareholders and employees. Corporate strategy is distinct from business and functional strategies, which typically focus on markets, competition, and business processes. The latter often addresses how the business units serve customers and stakeholders with products and services—how those products and services are designed, produced, and delivered with respect to needs and expectations of customers and stakeholders and how competitive responses play out.

The chief executive officer (CEO), the corporate leadership team, and the board of directors usually craft the grand corporate strategy. They establish the central focus and the integrating perspectives that guide the organization toward the vision and the realization of the corporate aims and purposes. They set the stage for what the corporation wants to pursue, and how it plans to serve its constituents. Corporate leaders establish the grand strategy(s) and take proactive actions to occupy the high ground and/or exploit new territories that give them competitive advantages. Keep in mind that the biggest opportunities may be derived from the most significant risks and the negative aspects. Think about what Kodak could have done with the digital camera technology that it invented. The grand strategies involve translating the vision and strategic direction into business strategies and action plans that can be implemented. Some of the corporate strategic options include:

- Growing the existing businesses (organic growth).
- Gaining new knowledge and capabilities through learning.

- Developing more sophisticated capabilities, resources, technologies, products, and processes.
- Transitioning existing businesses through improvements to realize more fruitful positions in space and time.
- Transforming businesses through leading change and strategic innovations.
- Developing new ventures, new-to-the-world technologies, and products.
- Acquiring or merging with other companies that fit the vision.
- Acquiring new product lines and/or complementary assets.
- Divesting businesses or product portfolios that no longer fit.

Selected strategic actions are discussed in Chapter 4.

The notion of grand corporate strategy may vary considerably from corporation to corporation. Grand strategies should be balanced and go beyond existing markets and customers, which are more appropriate topics for business strategy. They include opportunities to extend the scope of the corporation to new heights, new horizons, and new landscapes. They should identify what the corporation expects to be or wants to be in a given time horizon. Most importantly, it should describe how corporate leaders plan to transition and transform the corporation into a more sustainable enterprise.

Overarching Corporate Goals

Categories of Corporate Goals

Corporate goals are the broad overarching aims that involve the entire corporation. They typically define what the strategic direction expects to achieve over a given time horizon, although for certain companies, corporate goals may have an extended or even open-ended time frame. Corporate goals provide a balanced set of ambitious targets that define what the shareholders, board of directors, and strategic leaders want to achieve. They provide a global view that inspires people across business domains to achieve the social and economic objectives and to move toward a more powerful destiny.

Corporate goals have to compel the organization to reach beyond its normal capabilities and achieve extraordinary outcomes. The selected goals have to be tied to the vision, philosophies, principles, values, and beliefs of the corporation. Corporate goals include internal and external aspects including financial rewards, customer success, organizational development, and enterprise improvements. Consistency is an important consideration. Corporate goals help delineate the pathway toward the future. It is the journey that is important and not just the destination. Corporate goals may also be open-ended statements that communicate the underlying strategic intent and provide a sense of long-term purpose and consistence of action. However, such goals are difficult to articulate, since they have to be meaningful to everyone. Ambitious goals are meant to stretch the capabilities of the organization, but corporate goals have to be realistic, achievable, and measurable. Inconsistency adds to complexity and slowness in mapping out strategies and action plans. Without consistency, lower-level management has to contemplate what is the real intent, and how to achieve it. This makes translating strategic direction more difficult, which may lead to misinterpretations and skewing of the outcomes. In many situations, such confusion forces lower-level leaders to focus on the short term rather than the more balanced approaches. Skewing actions toward the near term usually results when lower-level leaders have a better sense of what is expected in the short term than what is desired for the long term.

The most common goals like maximizing profits are usually fatally flawed, because they pertain to a single dimension, the financial one. Optimization of one dimension usually results in the suboptimization of the other dimensions. For instance, companies can exploit their supply networks through excessive demands in the short term to maximize the revenues and the margins of the principal, but in the long term suppliers and distributors may find alternates that are fairer and better balanced. It is simplistic to think that companies can succeed by achieving financial or economic objectives only, especially ones limited to profits and financial return.

Peter Drucker suggested that organizations should have diverse goals. According to Drucker, "Objectives are needed in every area where performance and results directly affect the survival and prosperity of the business (his key result areas for selecting objectives)."[9] Drucker's eight key result areas (KRAs) are:[10] (1) market standing; (2) innovation; (3) productivity; (4) physical and financial resources; (5) profitability; (6) manager performance and development; (7) worker performance and attitude, and; (8) public responsibility. Robert Kaplan and David Norton build upon Drucker's views with their construct, "Balanced Scorecard." Kaplan and Norton frame key areas in terms of: (1) financial; (2) customer; (3) learning and growth; and (4) internal business process.[11]

The two constructs are related and share some common elements. While debates continue about what the KRAs are, corporate goals should cover a balanced approach and embrace the complexities of the business world and the multiplicity of driving forces, mandates, requirements, and expectations. Indeed, the logic of Drucker and Kaplan and Norton argues in favor of a broader depiction of corporate goals. The approach includes internal goals pertaining to shareholders, management, the management systems, the people, and financial aspects; and external goals that pertain to market spaces, the business environment, the social world, and natural environment.

Figure 3.3 diagrams the main categories of corporate goals as they relate to the total spectrum of goals that support sustaining success. Clearly, these categories and elements of corporate goals are more extensive than generally suggested by scholars and business practitioners. However, corporate goals have to fit the realities of the company and the business environment.

The categories contain traditional areas such as those listed under the category of "grand strategic." They also contain categories that are not usually included in the typical listing of corporate goals, such as those related to the business environment, social world, and natural environment. The intent of the listing is not to be prescriptive, but to highlight areas that might be considered when selecting corporate goals. The more comprehensive choices provide the strategic leaders, managers, and professionals of the organization with guidance that pertains to proper direction and the achievement of expected results. Some of the goals can be stated in quantitative terms, while others can be stated in qualitative terms. While this construct may be viewed as going beyond

Vision, Strategies, and Goals ▪ 71

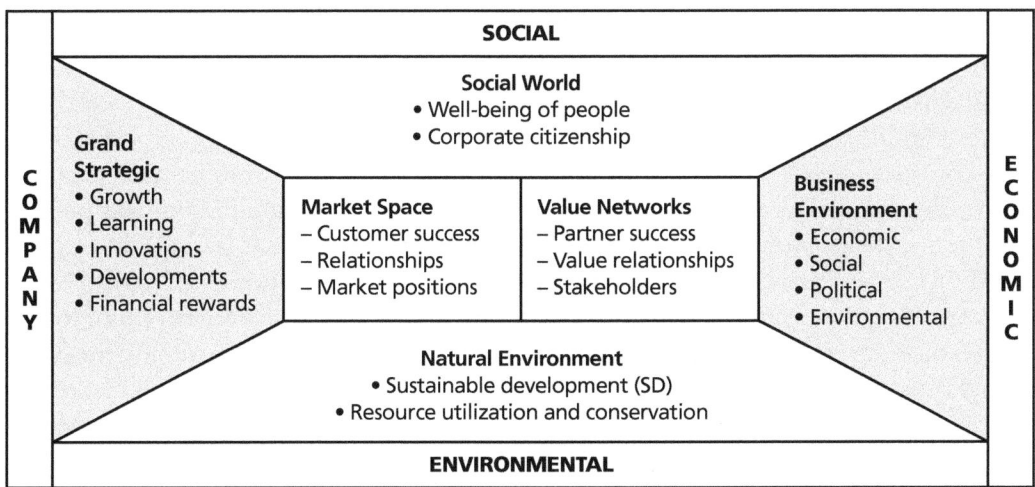

Figure 3.3 Corporate goals: categories and connections.

traditional thinking, it can also be viewed as an expansion of classical thought, especially that of Drucker.

Grand Strategic Goals

The "grand strategic" goals pertain to the company, its leaders, management, employees, and shareholders. They are the primary internal drivers for the economic, financial, and management underpinnings of the whole company. The objectives of the business units and operating systems are subsets of these goals and they should be consistent with them and support their achievement.

The "growth" goals are the easiest to understand and the most difficult to properly determine. Typically, growth goals pertain to the desired rate of increases in revenues and profits, typically in financial terms. However, growth goals may also pertain to expansion of the business units, the investments of the corporation, the corporate transformations via new business ventures, and many other non-financial aspects including the growth of intellectual capital. Growth in revenue goals can be difficult to achieve as the corporation expands and becomes more successful over time. While growing at a given rate may be achievable when the revenue streams are relatively small, the growth rate becomes more and more challenging as the corporation increases in size. For example, Walmart was able to maintain an average annual compound rate of approximately 20% in increased revenues during the 12-year tenure of former CEO David Glass ending in 2000. Scott Lee, his successor, expanded revenues from $165 billion to over $312 billion during 2000-2006, but the rate of growth declined to about 12%.[12] As the base gets larger, the absolute value may increase, but the growth rate usually decreases. Great care must be used when determining the expected growth rate. Many corporations often try to grow beyond their means or the potential of the business environment to support the growth. Such goals may be achievable for a few years, but eventually they may overstretch the business potential. Overreaching and growing beyond one's means and capabilities or the capacities of the markets are some of the main reasons why many companies fail.

According to Kaplan and Norton, "learning" is one of the most important goals. While it is difficult to precisely identify what the learning goal is, it can be stated in terms of the increase in the knowledge of the organization (its intellectual property) or in terms of the expansion of the intellectual capital (capabilities of the people). During the 1990s, many large corporations downsized their organizations as they refocused on core competencies, cost savings, and profitability. In doing so, many of them lost a significant amount of intrinsic knowledge that would have allowed them to grow and be more prosperous. Many such corporations achieved short-term improvements in their cost structures and financial results, yet suffered long-term problems because they lacked the intellectual capital and capabilities to continue to expand. Some companies suffer during recovery periods after an economic recession because they fail to maintain and/or develop the intellectual capabilities due to "downsizing." Short-term cost reductions can lead to long-term disasters.

The learning goal should focus on the intellectual capital required for what the company wants to become. Learning can be measured based on the investments made to improve the knowledge base, the financial resources devoted to developing intellectual property (IP), and the support for management and professional development programs used to enrich the human capital of the organization. Like the technological underpinnings and the investments required for technology, product and process developments, corporate leaders have to appreciate that investments are necessary to develop new knowledge and enhanced organizational capabilities. The rate of obsolescence and the inherent changes in the knowledge base of an organization are important considerations that often go unnoticed until it is too late. For instance, as more companies outsource the fabrication and even production and assembly of their products, the competencies and education and training requirements shifts from executing internal manufacturing processes to managing external supply networks using project management methodologies and other management techniques. Often there is a management failure to develop and implement the necessary learning paradigms in advance of implementing the new approaches. Learning goals can be measured in terms of the types of programs initiated, the numbers of people educated, the level of new capabilities acquired, the sophistication of the learning, and knowledge gained.

Grand strategic goals include strategic innovations that transcend the whole company. They include research and development of new-to-the-world technologies, and applied development programs for making improvements to existing products and processes. However, innovation goals typically address high-level strategic developments that have the potential for changing the strategic direction, enhancing the viability, and ensuring the success of the corporation.

Corporate and/or strategic innovation goals involve the investments, action plans, and related programs for realizing the vision and achieving the grand strategy and for transforming the organization into a more sustainable and successful entity. The goals involve specifying the portfolio of desired programs and how it fits the strategic logic and direction of the corporation. The grand strategic goals also involve identifying the requisite requirements for technology and product-development programs. For instance, criteria pertaining to the goals might require the development of clean, affordable, safe, and effective technological solutions to the social, economic, and environmental problems in the business environment. They may include requirements for new technologies that create opportunities that are not presently available through the existing SBUs.

Development goals involve dramatic improvements to the existing businesses, solutions, systems, processes, competences, and capabilities of the company. There are critical differences between growth and development goals. While development goals are often seen as related to or a subset of growth goals, they may actually be at a higher level. They may support the growth of the company by increasing the company's ability to perform and realize positive outcomes. Development goals focus on advancing the underpinnings of the company to make it more capable of achieving success. On the other hand, many growth goals simply focus on exploiting the prevailing situations without furthering developments in capabilities and long-term potential. For example, McDonalds grew through linear expansion during the second half of the twentieth century. It built more and more of the same types of restaurants. It did make some enhancements like the addition of play lands, but the basic scheme remained fairly consistent. Its revenues increased because it could serve more customers geographically. However, the business model stayed much the same over time. The small improvements focused on the prevailing approaches. Recently corporate leaders changed the goals to focus more on making dramatic new developments to reinvent the business model. Development goals typically address the quality, capability, viability, and sophistication of the means and mechanisms to achieve sustainable success. GE invested heavily into developing its capabilities during the 1990s. While such investments helped GE grow its revenues, the underlying development goal was to make GE's businesses more sophisticated and technological advanced, thus more competitive and sustainable in the future.

Corporate financial goals often take the form of the growth of revenues, net income, the return on investment, and the value of the corporation itself. The growth of revenues is usually stated in terms of percent increase on an annual basis. Net income goals are often stipulated in both absolute and relative basis. They typically involve the profits that are generated annually and the rate of increases in profitability. They may also involve profits and cash flow over a number of years in the future on a cumulative basis. They may be couched in ways to recognize the variability that may exist due to fluctuations in the business environment. For instance, the profit goals might be average profits over a five-year period. Financial rewards are important traditional goals. Financial return takes many forms including return on equity (ROE) reflecting the owners' invested capital, return on assets (ROA) reflecting the total financial investment, and return on investments (ROI) in new programs reflecting the performance of recent investments. Corporate financial goals also include increase in the share price of the corporation's stocks and in the market capitalization. These goals provide strategic direction and a sense of the expectations of the owners of capital and the directors of the corporation. While the appropriateness of such goals is obvious, they should involve more than just making money and maximizing profits. They are the incentives and rewards for taking risks and achieving success. Without financial rewards, it would be difficult to sustain success.

Corporate leaders have to decide which of the corporate strategic goals are the most appropriate for their situation. Moreover, they have to select the specificity of the goals. For instance, if they wish to articulate growth goals, what should the goals be? For example, GE is seeking new areas to sustain its growth goals. Table 3.1 lists the main categories of grand strategic goals and some of the advantages and disadvantages associated with each.

Each of the goals would be established, periodically reviewed, and modified to keep current with the realities of the business environment. The financial performance is one of the corporate priorities, especially if its survival is threatened. This perspective is in keeping with management's duty to shareholders to protect their investments.

Corporate Goals Pertaining to Market Space

Market space goals involve exploring for new and improved ways to address markets, latent market potential, and customer needs and expectations. They relate to the new opportunities in the market spaces that may be attractive for investments. This includes markets that are not served by the corporation's business units and those market segments and customers that the business units are currently serving, but require enhancements. The goals focus on how the company relates to its served and un-served markets and how corporate strategic leaders can enhance customer and stakeholder relationships, improve customer satisfaction, and most importantly ensure customer and stakeholder success. While corporate leaders often play critical roles in acquiring new businesses and supporting the business strategies of the lower levels of the organization, the primary corporate-related market-space goals involve ensuring that market opportunities and challenges are being assessed and confronted and that the organization's focus is on sustainable success.

Market-space goals are very broad, stretching across many market sectors and geographical areas. An integrated perspective explores how well the company is serving its

TABLE 3.1 Selected Grand Strategic Goals and Their Advantages and Disadvantages

Type of goal	Purpose	Advantages	Disadvantages
Growth	Exploiting opportunities to create more value and sustain viability; one of the main goals used by investors.	Simple to understand and measure; provides a sense of expectations; can be linked to opportunities in the markets.	Becomes more difficult to maintain the growth rate as the base expands; does not measure the value of the growth.
Learning	Knowledge rate requiring organizations to keep pace with the new requirements.	Corporate success is based on its intellectual capital and capabilities to perform and its ability to meet new challenges.	The amount and rate of learning is difficult to measure; requires a stable workforce to maintain the benefits.

(continued)

TABLE 3.1 Selected Grand Strategic Goals and Their Advantages and Disadvantages

Type of goal	Purpose	Advantages	Disadvantages
Innovation	Provides a sense of the creativity of the organization to meet the needs of the business and exceed the expectations.	Provides an indicator of how well positioned the corporation is to lead change and outperform expectations; innovations are linked to new value creation.	Innovations are usually complex and require time to determine their value and the long-term effects and benefits; innovations are often copied.
Developments	Developments focus on transformations and transitions; they reinforce the foundation and create solid systems.	Provide means and mechanisms to make improvements that are usually based on established capabilities and resources; provide short- and long-term benefits.	The gains may be insufficient to realize strategic benefits; there is little advantage in improving obsolete items; it is difficult to measure long-term outcomes.
Financial rewards – Profitability – Cash flow	Profits are one of the primary purposes of making investments; they encourage investors to continue to supply capital; cash flow is the lifeblood of businesses.	Strategies and action plans require money and internal investment; use cash flow to sustain outcomes; profits and cash flow are used by investment community to measure success.	Determining what the profits are is complicated for most global corporations; it is easy to manipulate the calculations; one may obtain short-term profits at the expense of the long term.
Return on assets	Return on equity is the net income per period based on the total assets including debt.	ROA gives a measure of how effectively assets are used and whether it is worth having the selected assets.	ROA can be improved by reducing assets; selling off the means to produce solutions may result in negative impacts.
Share price	Share price represents the perceived value of the corporation; it represents the present value of the future earnings and the assets.	Share price is a fundamental that investors follow to determine the value of their investment; it is easy to track and provide feedback from the markets.	Share price is also influenced by many external factors of which management has little control; share price can be manipulated in the short term.
Market capitalization	The total perceived value of the corporation by the stock markets.	Market capitalization provides a measure of how much leverage there is in acquiring capital.	Market capitalization can fluctuate widely because of external factors.
Return on equity	ROE is the net income per period based on the shareholders' equity-invested capital and retained earnings.	Capital investments are made based on the investor's ability to realize a gain on the investment.	ROE can be improved by reducing the equity. Leaders can buy back shares to reduce equity draining the capital.

customers and how those customers enjoy the benefits of the transactions and relationships. It also includes latent customers. The corporate view examines the big picture that extends from the present to the long term. For instance, corporate leaders at Kodak and Fiji during the 1990s could have established goals for the digital photography market segments instead of primarily focusing on protecting market shares in conventional film-based photography. The corporate perspective should have been broader and focused more on the strategic implications. Time passes quickly and the long term soon becomes the present. Moreover, corporate goals related to markets and customers go beyond the prevailing conditions pertaining to demand, volume, sales, market share, competitive positions, and the like. They should identify and deal with what customers perceive as success and establish what customers really want in terms of their solutions. For example, during 1950s and 1960s most Americans bought their cars from the "Big Three" (GM, Ford, and Chrysler) automobile companies. While sales, profits, and market shares were great, customer satisfaction and success were questionable. The products were costly, had many defects, were often unreliable, and had relatively short life cycles. When customer choices were limited and the American competitors were comparable, customers continued to buy products that failed to fully meet their expectations. However, in the 1970s and 1980s, as European and Japanese companies made significant forays into the American automobile market with more benefits like improved fuel efficiency and reliability, customers sought out the products that not only satisfied their immediate needs, but provided better long-term solutions. At the upper-end, German manufacturers like Mercedes-Benz and BMW concentrated on mechanical performance, high-quality materials, and engineered superiority. Japanese companies, like Toyota and Honda, focused on three primary factors: overall quality, reliability, and affordability. The international competitors took more of a customers' perspectives and provided products that gave customers better solutions. As customer satisfaction increased due to higher quality and better reliability, customers did not have to buy a new car every three to five years, since the value of their purchase did not depreciate as quickly. While it is difficult to cite the perfect example and discussions about customer successes are usually based on relative aspects, market-space goals must be derived from what markets and customers seek, and not just what is seemingly best for the profitability of the corporation or other internal objectives.

In a hypercompetitive world with new competitors emerging in China, India, Brazil, and elsewhere, corporate leaders and other strategic leaders must pay attention to customers in the broadest sense to ensure they are successful. Moreover, companies have to build new relationships that sustain corporate success and ensure that existing relationships are reinvigorated and enhanced over the long term. It is too easy to take loyal customers for granted and assume that they will continue to do business with you. Customer success and customer perceptions are typically transient. In today's world of six-sigma quality products and sophisticated technologies, customers continuously upgrade their wants, needs, and expectations. Indeed, expectations play critical roles in customer decision-making. Customers desire everything and their expectations evolve. They are no longer willing to make tradeoffs. They want the best outcomes and expect them to be affordable.

In a world of constant change, change becomes the norm. Solid market positions can quickly evaporate as new technologies, new products, and new ways of doing things emerge. In the fast-paced markets of electronics and telecommunications, customers exhibit little loyalty for producers and providers and often switch their preferences each time they have an opportunity to change. For instance, in the TV business, LCD, LED and 3-D technologies opened the door for new competitors like Vizio, LG and Samsung. Market positions are costly to build and erode quickly when there is not a concerted effort to reinforce customer relationships. From a corporate perspective, the strategic goals pertain to relationship building and customer success, not marketing.

Market positions are often solidified when there is trust and honesty. People establish and maintain relationships with those who have mutual interests with supportive and complementary objectives. Customers are not only served by corporations, they depend on the relationships to ensure their own success.

Corporate Goals Pertaining to Value Networks

Corporations and their SBUs are increasing becoming more and more dependent on their external relationships with partners, supply networks, and the other support entities. While this view was discussed earlier under the banner of the extended enterprise, it is critical that corporate leaders establish strategic goals pertaining to the corporate roles and responsibilities related to the value networks. Value networks are all of the interrelated entities in the enterprise(s) that contribute to value creation and the sustainable success. They include all of the partners, alliances, supply networks, and stakeholder relationships used to create value. While each of the entities is generally an independent corporation or organization that is responsible for its own affairs, it is imperative that corporations ensure that fairness and truthfulness underpin the dialogues and communications when dealing with such entities. While one or more of the entities including the corporation or its business units can exploit external relationships in the short term, such actions usually destabilize the situation and lead to less than satisfactory results. For instance, powerful retailers can use their enormous purchasing power to dictate terms to many of their suppliers to the point where the suppliers may become marginalized. In the short term, such suppliers may not have many options other than to continue to meet the demands and dictates. In the long term, they may seek relationships with other retailers who offer better margins and improved prospects for success. Suppliers may merge or form alliances to gain more power, like the merger between Proctor & Gamble and Gillette.

The specific goals related to value networks have to be determined based on the context of the situation. Corporate leaders should focus on ensuring that external contributors are fulfilling their responsibilities and are achieving appropriate or related success. This includes validating all mandates and requirements. For example, several companies had to recall toys because their suppliers in China had used lead paint in the manufacture of certain products. Such potential liabilities might be avoided, if there were better goals pertaining to the use of supply networks. Such goals should reinforce relationships and provide corporate leaders with the assurance that such relationships and the outcomes will be successful and endure as long as there are mutual benefits.

Corporate Goals Pertaining to the Business Environment

Corporations are generally in the business of creating value; value that extends to customers, partners, related entities, and shareholders. They are also have to ensure that stakeholders and members of society receive an appropriate share of the benefits derived in value creation, and are not disadvantaged or harmed in the conduct of business, or during the execution of strategies, action plans, and operations. From every perspective—social, ethical, economic, technological, and environmental—corporate leaders have obligations to ensure that positive aspects are enhanced and the negative impacts and burdens are eliminated within the business environment.

From a business environment perspective, corporations have additional economic goals that go beyond the typical company, enterprise, or industry-based objectives. For instance, corporations and small- and medium-size enterprises (SMEs) have an interest in supporting, if not enhancing, overall economic development and stability. Everyone benefits from low inflation, reasonable interest rates, the availability of credit, and favorable macroeconomic conditions and trends. Moreover, corporate leaders may want to encourage economic developments in the selected communities, regions, or countries and support the development of trade and growth opportunities. Such goals may relate to the fair, safe, and proper treatment of industry participants including the appropriate compensation for labor, subcontractors, and vendors, and other inputs and outputs in economic exchanges. They may also collectively have goals pertaining to correcting market imperfections and competitive abuses that may exist.

Broad economic goals may include protecting IP rights, eliminating unfair labor practices and unsafe working conditions, increasing foreign investments in developing countries, and enhancing many other related developments. Such goals may include the elimination of trade restrictions, the free and efficient exchange of money, and the fair allocation of externalities across industry participants. Corporate leaders have to carefully select what goals are in their best interests and determine how they can participate in processes that promote the common good. Companies may have to form alliances or join industry groups to accomplish the broader social, economic, ethical, and environmental goals. Usually, such broad goals are established and exercised in conjunction with others that include government agencies and NGOs. While many of the broader economic goals relate to the primary goals of the corporation, some involve conditions and trends that are beyond one's direct control. For instance, it may be desirable to have the means and mechanisms to provide end-of-life solutions for customers, but the cost of providing a facility limited to only one company's products may be prohibitively expensive. Partnerships with government agencies, NGOs, and other corporations may provide attractive approaches to create solutions that no single entity could afford to develop by itself. Moreover, everyone has an interest in protecting the fundamental resources that are used across industries, commercial activities, agriculture, and residential communities. For instance, improving the quantity and quality of water and air in a community or region fits the broad economic and environmental goals.

A corporation may institute goals pertaining to social aspects. For instance, many large corporations get involved in supporting the public education of the school-aged population. These goals are in the best interest of society and at the same time contribute in meeting the long-term employment and training needs of the corporation. This is particularly critical for those corporations using advanced technologies that require knowledgeable and technologically sophisticated workforces. For example, GM established objectives to help primary and secondary schools; the goals are:[13]

> Few things in life are more satisfying than watching a child revel in excitement when learning something new. This is especially true when the subject of their delight is math and science. That's right, math and science.
>
> GM strongly believes in supporting a comprehensive, diverse base of education programs for children in grades K–12 (Kindergarten through 12th grade). These include hands-on, experience-based education activities, math and science mentoring programs, technology curriculum dissemination to schools, and an educational web site for families...
>
> Our goal is to foster enthusiasm for science, environment and energy issues with a combination of innovation, technology and partnerships that support the following principles:
>
> - Enlightenment: Help students develop an awareness of science, math and technology issues
> - Knowledge: Reinforce awareness with solid concepts and real-world applications
> - Attitudes: Help students personalize their relationship with the global environment.
> - Action: Help students make a difference.

Companies may promote human development in specific countries to enrich the opportunities for people and business activities. Impoverished societies have difficulties sustaining their well-being and are usually unable to enjoy the broader benefits of the global economy. Improving living conditions in developing countries and in poorer sections of the major cities in developed countries is an important social goal for corporations. Such improvements may lead to more opportunities for everyone and for business activities. This includes having more potential customers who have the means to buy products and services. Likewise, companies may have goals related to political processes for eliminating illegal or unfair practices such as government corruption, institutional bribery, and political favoritism. One such goal might be to have corporate leaders use peer pressure to force their colleagues to stop making inappropriate or illegal contributions to political campaigns. While it is noteworthy when a corporation pledges to refrain from direct political contributions, it may take a consensus among corporations to affect real change. In the short term, the corporations that take such initiatives may become disadvantaged in the political process until a majority of corporate leaders follow. Corporate leaders may have goals on providing input for new laws and regulations.

Companies may have goals related to ethical considerations. They should encourage fair treatment and equal opportunity for all people throughout the world, especially in locations where they operate. They may encourage businesses and non-economic organizations to use ethical standards and best practices regardless of the lack of stringent laws and regulations, especially in less developed countries and regions.

Corporate leaders have to think about their roles and responsibilities in dealing with and solving the numerous environmental problems. Such thinking extends beyond the domain of laws and regulations and covers the broader, non-specific challenges facing people and the natural environment. Some of the goals relate to subjects such as sustainable development, resource utilization and conservation, and preservation of the natural environment. They might also include specific subjects such as climate change, habitat protection, water quality and availability, clean air, and the elimination of toxic substances. For example, Alcan, a unit of Rio Tinto, has broad goals for the protection and appropriate uses of water resources. It addresses its goals and approaches in the Alcan Sustainability Report: *Taking The Next Step* per the following:[14]

> Our use of water for power and in our processes has a range of impacts on the quality of the water, natural water cycles and its availability for other uses. We expect the local, regional and global significance of water issues to increase. Currently, 2.3 billion people live in water-stressed areas. This number is projected to increase by more than one billion people by 2025. We have a responsibility to manage water and other natural resources with care. Sound stewardship of these resources is a form of public trust, and how well we meet our responsibilities affects our license to operate and our corporate reputation.

The selection of broader corporate goals is not yet a mainstream view. While there are examples of corporations with nontraditional goals, each corporation has to select the areas of specific interest and subsequent targets for making improvements.

Evaluating Corporate Performance and Communicating Outcomes

Corporate leaders have a duty to ensure that the company and all of its related business enterprises, and the strategic leaders and managers, are fulfilling their roles and responsibilities, are complying with legal requirements, are meeting ethical standards, and are performing according to corporate policies, strategies, and objectives. CSM examines performance based on the broad perspectives of long-term corporate goals, and the more specific criteria pertaining to near-term objectives and expectations. They include the more qualitative aspects such as:

- Achieving sustainable success;
- Enhancing value creation;
- Improving corporate reputation;
- Building high-level relationships;
- Mitigating problems, difficulties, and impacts;
- Discovering new opportunities and creating innovative solutions;
- Developing new leadership and improving organizational capabilities;
- Integrating the organization and the enterprises into a cohesive system;
- Achieving positive outcomes that are balanced.

Given the open-ended nature of these broad aspects, it is difficult to map out exactly how they can be monitored and evaluated. Corporate leaders can translate each of the areas into specific objectives at the SBU and operating system levels that contribute to the total level of achievement.

Corporate performance evaluation involves the periodic examinations of the strategic outcomes and achievements related to the grand strategy(s) and overarching goals. It requires fairly simple mechanisms used by corporate leaders to determine the corporation's progress. Corporate performance evaluation is intended to measure performance against goals and targets relative to peers, competitors, and stakeholder expectations. It is quick and inexpensive to take a snapshot of the overall picture of corporate performance pertaining to selected goals and targets. Its strength is its main limitation. It provides an overview, but lacks detail. It usually does not provide corporate leaders with the reasons for the lack of achievement, nor does it provide a sense of how to cure the problems. However, it can signal concerns and the need for more thorough analyses, i.e., leading to audits and other methods for discovering and correcting poor performance and outcomes.

Auditing is one of the more powerful mechanisms for determining how well the organization is performing and meeting the goals. Auditing approaches have grown more popular over the last several decades. They vary from financial auditing to a wide variety of audit types and mechanisms. Financial audits are commonplace. Additional types include health and safety, environmental, operational, product safety, and due diligence audits. Most corporations, especially publicly owned and traded ones, are required to have externally performed financial audits by independent, certified accounting firms. The purposes are to ensure the accuracy of financial reporting and to promote confidence in the financial affairs of the corporation. Similarly, the other types of audits provide mechanisms for strategic leaders at every level to understand their performance and take corrective actions expeditiously, if discrepancies are found. Corrective actions are particularly critical when compliance with government mandates are involved since government agencies also conduct various types of audits that range from compliance with financial reporting and tax laws to environmental regulations.

Audits allow corporate leaders to have an invisible hand in managing performance across the corporation without actually controlling the day-to-day decision-making and operations. It gives them and others the knowledge that actions will be scrutinized, and that proper behaviors are expected. People within the organization realize that good behavior and compliance will be rewarded, and that poor performance, misdeeds, and deception will be discovered and dealt with. In most cases, auditing should be viewed as a positive; it gives people the opportunity to obtain evidence about their contributions and to be recognized for their work.

Effective corporate reporting is a critical requirement. Annual and quarterly reporting of financial results are essential disclosures. Financial reports are mandated by the government for publicly traded corporations. Reports are intended to inform shareholders about the past results, reflect on positive achievements, and cite difficulties and liabilities. Although corporate leaders try to present favorable results, they must ensure that the reports are accurate and a fair portrayal of the strategic and financial positions. The reports are audited and certified by an outside accounting firm.

Formal reporting includes disclosures pertaining to such areas as environmental management, social responsibility, corporate citizenship, and SBD. Expanding the reporting mechanisms is crucial for global corporations that have many watchdogs who seemingly follow every move that the corporation makes. Reports provide information on the corporation's activities on an ongoing basis. One way to mitigate the negative comments that may be made by outside organizations is to fully disclose such related information in advance. Openness and transparency involve disclosures of positive contributions and negative effects and impacts. They build trust with shareholders, customers, stakeholders, and employees. "No surprises" may even be part of the corporate culture. They include making available to others the information needed for making decisions about the corporation. In today's complex business world, people can obtain the information they seek about any corporation using numerous mechanisms, especially the Internet. It may take a concerted effort, but outsiders usually can obtain the data and information. The best philosophy is to provide accurate and timely information and data before judgments are formed based on someone else's view of reality.

BOX 3: SAM WALTON'S MARKET AND FINANCIAL SUCCESSES

Wal-Mart (the original form) is one of the great stories of entrepreneurial leadership in business history. In the early 1950s, Sam Walton recognized the emerging opportunity for a non-traditional retail store to serve the needs of an expanding population living outside of center cities. While Sears was one of the early innovators of the suburban mall stores and K-Mart opened discount stores in 1962, Wal-Mart was the most successful in establishing a business model for exploiting retail opportunities in a changing business environment.

During the Depression, the U.S. Congress passed the Miller-Tydings Act of 1937 that established fair trade prices for many products. Retailers were required to sell certain products at a fixed price regardless of their situation, volume considerations, or competitive factors. Rather than moderating the effects of the Depression, the regulations on profits and competition caused prices to remain higher than a competitive environment would have provided and made it more difficult for poor people to buy the products they needed beyond the basics. However, during the early 1960s, many states began eliminating the restrictions on fair-trade pricing. This was one of the critical changes that led to the development of discount stores and the opportunity for Walton to create Wal-Mart in 1962.

Walton recognized that there was enormous market space for retailers that could operate somewhere between the giant department stores like Macy's and Bloomingdale's and the general stores throughout the cities and small towns of America. He also realized the implications of the Baby Boom, the growing prosperity of the post-World War II U.S. economy, and the rapidly increasing number of households, improved lifestyles, and the needs for good quality (branded) consumer products.

Walton and the early leaders of Wal-Mart successfully developed stores in the smaller communities around the Midwest United States and sought out customers with modest incomes. Walton took the counterintuitive approach and focused on providing cost-effective solutions to the bottom segment of the retail market. Wall-Mart's corporate leaders clearly understood that poor people needed affordable products that could be purchased in small quantities. Walton realized that the whole operating system from suppliers, logistics, distribution, and retail operations had to be cost-effective and efficient, if Wal-Mart was going to meet customer expectations for low prices. He also realized that every aspect of the system was critical and every part of the value system had to provide opportunities for achieving market and financial successes. Wal-Mart sacrificed higher profit margins to expand its enterprise and market reach. Walton had most products marked up with a thirty percent margin. He was satisfied to make a relatively small margin on each product so that Wal-Mart could make profits on the whole enterprise. Low prices and small margins allowed customers to share in the benefits of his enterprise and allowed Wal-Mart to leverage the goodwill it created from store to store across the expanse of its value system. Wal-Mart used customer word-of-mouth instead of expensive advertising to promote its advantages and attract customers.

Walton's strategy was to price products low, sell them quickly, and induce large volumes. He had the wisdom to understand the value and power of rapid turnover before it became a major retail philosophy during the 1990s. He successfully integrated the personal style and friendliness of the old general stores with the modern efficiencies of computerized inventory management, cost-effective logistics and distribution, and innovative information technologies among many other business strategies and technological initiatives. Not only did customers benefit, but suppliers were enriched as well, at least during the early years. Wal-Mart presented suppliers with opportunities to improve their efficiencies and effectiveness through its highly concentrated distribution system. It focused on making its entire system as cost-effective as possible and delivering great results to the participants and the shareholders.

Wal-Mart's first generation business model was a great success, and it allowed the company to grow dramatically during its first three decades from 1962 to 1992, the year Walton passed away. Walton successfully used the concepts of CSM, VSL, business integration, and strategic innovation to create extraordinary value and corporate financial success as well as a great personal fortune. His initial business model might be viewed as one focusing on market and financial successes, since it created multifaceted outcomes. Walton outlined his secret formula for success in ten rules which are summarized in Table 3A.1 with further details in the footnote.[a]

TABLE 3A.1   SAM WALTON'S RULES FOR BUILDING A BUSINESS

Sam's Rules	Connection to Sustainable Success
Rule 1—Commit to your business	Success requires dedication and commitment to the long term.
Rule 2—Share your profits with all your associates and treat them as partners	Value creation depends on the successes of the company and its employees, customers, stakeholders, supply networks and constituencies.

(continued)

TABLE 3A.1 SAM WALTON'S RULES FOR BUILDING A BUSINESS

Sam's Rules	Connection to Sustainable Success
Rule 3—Motivate your partners	Success depends on inspiring partners to embrace value creation and value delivery processes and ensuring that everyone is successful.
Rule 4—Communicate everything you possibly can to your partners	Enterprise-wide management requires openness and sharing across the value system.
Rule 5—Appreciate everything your associates do for the business	Respect, recognition, and reward are essential for ensuring that all participants realize their potential.
Rule 6—Celebrate your successes	A key to sustainable success is building on previous successes and inspiring people to further success. Celebrating allows success to motivate further success.
Rule 7—Listen to everyone in your company	Enterprise thinking involves engaging everyone from the top of the organization to the bottom.
Rule 8—Exceed your customers' expectations	Exceeding customer and stakeholder expectations are the essence of sustainable success.
Rule 9—Control your expenses better than your competition	Cost effectiveness contributes to affordability and customer success.
Rule 10—Swim upstream	Counter-intuitive approaches or leading-edge concepts can lead to incredible opportunities.

During Walton's tenure as the prime corporate leader of Wal-Mart, the company used many of the tenets of VSL. The scope of the company's business model was broad, including respect for individuals and service to customers. Its ethical principles included:[b]

1. Follow the law at all times.
2. Be honest and fair.
3. Never manipulate, misrepresent, abuse or conceal information.
4. Avoid conflicts of interest between work and personal affairs.
5. Never discriminate against anyone.
6. Never act unethically—even if someone else instructs you to do so.
7. Never ask someone to act unethically.
8. Seek assistance if you have questions about the Statement of Ethics or if you face an ethical dilemma.
9. Cooperate with any investigation of a possible ethics violation.
10. Report ethics violations or suspected violations.

Wal-Mart was able to grow dramatically and at the same time provide extraordinary benefits to suppliers and customers. For instance, it shared its sales data with suppliers so that they had first-hand information on what was actually being sold to end customers. While it is always risky to characterize complex stories and business models in simple terms, it can be argued that Walton's success was based on his principles, philosophies, and vision. Walton was a simple man who lived modestly. He was driven by his vision to create extraordinary results that benefited employees, customers, suppliers, and society. He was a master at holistic thinking and thinking outside-the-box. He believed in sharing success and treating people fairly, which contributed to Wal-Mart's incredible growth. However, not all of the views at the time were positive; even during Walton's stewardship many of the retailers in the small towns with Wal-Mart stores found fault with Wal-Mart. Walton believed that it was customer decisions that affected those retailers and not Wal-Mart.

After Walton retired in 1988, Wal-Mart's corporate leaders tightened their control on the supply networks. As the company expanded under the corporate leadership of Walton's successor, David Glass, who was CEO from 1988 to 2000, dramatic growth was achieved through improving same-store sales and increasing the number of stores on a national and international basis. Company revenues increased from $20.6 billion in 1988 to $165 billion in 2000.[c] Sales growth was approximately 20 percent per year with the expansion being attributed to the increases in revenues of the traditional Wal-Mart stores, the development of super-centers, the expansion of Sam's Clubs, and the addition of international stores.[d]

In January 2000, H. Lee Scott became the third CEO of Wal-Mart. Under his leadership net sales have increased by more than two times to $373.8 billion with net income of $12.9 billion in 2008.[e] In January 2009, Michael Duke became President and CEO of Walmart. (Wal-Mart changed its name to Walmart in 2009.) In 2010 revenues were $405 billion with a net income of $14.4 billion.[f] Growth slowed to approximately seven percent per year in 2009 with only one percent in 2010; return on investment was 19.3 percent.[g]

Walmart has been very successful and has enjoyed great financial rewards, making its principal owners, members of the Walton family, among the wealthiest people in the world. However, there are growing concerns about labor problems that could affect Walmart's ongoing success. If unchecked, public confidence could erode and Walmart's customer base might decline as consumers seek other options to buy their goods. The intent of these points is not to criticize Walmart, nor is it to provide an in-depth assessment of the positive and negative aspects of Walmart's strategies, operations, or practices, but to identify areas that Walmart could make fundamental shifts in its corporate leadership and business model.

Notes

a. File://K:\Wal_martRules.htm, Wal-Mart Stores—Sam's Rules for Building Business were:
   Rule 1—Commit to your business.
   Believe in it more than anybody else. I think I overcame every single one of my personal shortcomings by the sheer passion I brought to my work. I don't know if you're born with this kind of passion, or if you can learn it. But I do know you need it. If you love your work, you'll be out there every day trying to do it the best you possibly can, and pretty soon everybody around will catch the passion from you—like a fever.

Rule 2—Share your profits with all your associates, and treat them as partners.
In turn, they will treat you as a partner, and together you will all perform beyond your wildest expectations. Remain a corporation and retain control if you like, but behave as a servant leader in a partnership. Encourage your associates to hold a stake in the company. Offer discounted stock, and grant them stock for their retirement. It's the single best thing we ever did.

Rule 3—Motivate your partners.
Money and ownership alone aren't enough. Constantly, day-by-day, think of new and more interesting ways to motivate and challenge your partners. Set high goals, encourage competition, and then keep score. Make bets with outrageous payoffs. If things get stale, cross-pollinate; have managers switch jobs with one another to stay challenged. Keep everybody guessing as to what your next trick is going to be. Don't become too predictable.

Rule 4—Communicate everything you possibly can to your partners.
The more they know, the more they'll understand. The more they understand, the more they'll care. Once they care, there's no stopping them. If you don't trust your associates to know what's going on, they'll know you don't really consider them partners. Information is power, and the gain you get from empowering your associates more than offsets the risk of informing your competitors.

Rule 5—Appreciate everything your associates do for the business.
A paycheck and a stock option will buy one kind of loyalty. But all of us like to be told how much somebody appreciates what we do for them. We like to hear it often, and especially when we have done something we're really proud of. Nothing else can quite substitute for a few well-chosen, well-timed, sincere words of praise. They're absolutely free—and worth a fortune.

Rule 6—Celebrate your successes.
Find some humor in your failures. Don't take yourself so seriously. Loosen up, and everybody around you will loosen up. Have fun. Show enthusiasm–always. When all else fails, put on a costume and sing a silly song. Then make everybody else sing with you. Don't do a hula on Wall Street. It's been done. Think up your own stunt. All of this is more important, and more fun, than you think, and it really fools the competition. "Why should we take those cornballs at Wal-Mart seriously?"

Rule 7—Listen to everyone in your company.
And figure out ways to get them talking. The folks on the front lines—the ones who actually talk to the customer—are the only ones who really know what's going on out there. You'd better find out what they know. This really is what total quality is all about. To push responsibility down in your organization, and to force good ideas to bubble up within it, you must listen to what your associates are trying to tell you.

Rule 8—Exceed your customers' expectations.
If you do, they'll come back over and over. Give them what they want—and a little more. Let them know you appreciate them. Make good on all your mistakes, and don't make excuses...apologize. Stand behind everything you do. The two most important words I ever wrote were on that first Wal-Mart sign, "Satisfaction Guaranteed." They're still up there, and they have made all the difference.

Rule 9—Control your expenses better than your competition.
This is where you can always find the competitive advantage. For 25 years running—long before Wal-Mart was known as the nation's largest retailer—we ranked No. 1 in our industry for the lowest ratio of expenses to sales. You can make a lot of different mistakes and still recover if you run an efficient operation. Or you can be brilliant and still go out of business if you're too inefficient.

Rule 10—Swim upstream.
Go the other way. Ignore the conventional wisdom. If everybody else is doing it one way, there's a good chance you can find your niche by going in exactly the opposite direction. But be prepared for a lot of folks to wave you down and tell you you're headed the wrong way. I guess in all my years, what I heard more often than anything was: A town of less than 50,000 population cannot support a discount store for very long.

b. File://K:\Wal_martEthics.htm, Wal-Mart Stores-Global Ethics Office.
c. Wal-Mart Annual Reports.
d. Super-centers ranged in size from 100,000 to 250,000 square feet, while the typical discount stores were in the range of 40,000 to 100,000 square feet.
e. Walmart 2010 Annual Report, p15.
f. Id
g. Id, p19.

Reflections

Corporate leaders develop the vision, frameworks, models, concepts, techniques, and methods for analyzing, formulating, and implementing strategies and objectives. The vision guides the organization in creating the strategies, objectives, capabilities, innovations, and initiatives necessary for leading change—instead of reacting to it. VSL and CSM provide the guiding force for directing the organization along its pathway to the future. They also provide the overarching insights for creating innovative and sustainable advantages.

Corporate leaders take global perspectives on leading change. They examine the theoretical and practical principles, methods, and techniques involved in exploring, creating, assessing, selecting, and implementing strategies and management constructs. They develop new business opportunities through insights on changes in the business environment, especially in the market spaces, and by combining capabilities and resources in innovative ways to create value.

The preceding discussions focused on the key roles and responsibilities of corporate leaders and provided a sense of the most important elements. The intent is to guide strategic leaders and management professionals through the strategic management aspects of CSM. However, the discussions should not be considered comprehensive or a perfect fit for all corporations. Corporate leaders have to tailor their situations to fit their context and reality. The diversity of the strategic positions of global corporations makes establishing a generic framework with a common format very difficult, if not impossible.

Notes

1. General Motors 2004 Corporate Responsibility Report (Detroit, MI: General Motors, 2004, p32).
2. Johnson & Johnson's Credo is its stakeholder strategy. The Credo is as follows:

   We believe our first responsibility is to the doctors and nurse, and patients, to mothers and all others who use our products and services. In meeting their needs everything we do must be of high quality. We must constantly strive to reduce our costs in order to maintain reasonable prices. Customers' orders must be serviced promptly and accurately. Our suppliers and distributors must have an opportunity to make a fair profit.

We are responsible to or employees: the men and women who work with us throughout the world. Everyone must be considered as an individual. We must respect their dignity and recognize their merit. They must have a sense of security in their jobs. Compensation must be fair and adequate, and working conditions clean, orderly and safe. Employees must feel free to make suggestions and complaints. There must be equal opportunity for employment, development, and advancement for those qualified. We must provide competent management and their actions must be just and ethical.

We are responsible to the communities in which we live and work and to the world community as well.

We must be good citizens –support good works and charities and bear our fair share of taxes. We must encourage civic improvements and better health and education.

We must maintain in good order the property we are privileged to use, protecting the environment and natural resources.

Our final responsibility is to our shareholders. Business must make a sound profit. We must experiment with new ideas. Research must be carried on, innovative programs developed, and mistakes paid for. New equipment must be purchased, new facilities provided, and new products launched. Reserves must be created to provide for adverse times.

When operate according to these principles, the stockholders should realize a fair return.

3. Peter Schwartz, The Art of the Long View: Planning for the Future in an Uncertain World (New York, NY: Currency Doubleday, 1991, pxiii).
4. Id, pxiii-xiv.
5. Id, p227-236.
6. W. Chan Kim and Renee Mauborgne, "Value Innovation," Harvard Business Review, January-February 1997, p 107.
7. Id.
8. Arnoldo C. Hax and Nicolas S. Majluf, The Strategy Concept and Process: A Pragmatic Approach (Englewood Cliffs, NJ: Prentice Hall, 1991, p6).
9. Peter Drucker, The Practice of Management (New York, NY: Harper & Brothers Publishers, 1954, p63).
10. Id.
11. Robert Kaplan and David Norton, The Balanced Scorecard: Translating Strategy into Action (Boston, MA: Harvard Business School Press, 1996, p9).
12. Wal-Mart 2006 Annual Report: Building Smiles
13. General Motors Corporate Responsibility Report 2004, p154.
14. Alcan Sustainability Report 2004: Taking the next step, p11. Alcan has prepared a 64-page position paper in recognition of the international year of freshwater. Published in December 2003, "Committed to the Sustainable Management of Water, One of our Most

References

Drucker, Peter (1954) *The Practice of Management.* New York, NY: Harper & Brothers Publishers.

Hax, Arnoldo C. and Nicolas S. Majluf (1991) *The Strategy Concept and Process: A Pragmatic Approach.* Englewood Cliffs, NJ: Prentice Hall.

Kaplan, Robert and David Norton (1996) *The Balanced Scorecard: Translating Strategy into Action.* Boston, MA: Harvard Business School Press.

Schwartz, Peter (1991) *The Art of the Long View: Planning for the Future in an Uncertain World.* New York, NY: Currency Doubleday.

4

Corporate Plans, Actions, and Relationships

Introduction

Corporate leaders typically have the authority to commit the organization to make changes based on approvals from the board of directors. They can make dramatic, even radical, changes that are major transformations to the embedded corporate management system, its elements, the portfolio of business units, the organizational structure, and high-level programs. Such transformations are usually top-down strategic initiatives and actions that require significant investments and may take many years of planning, developments, and actions.

Corporate leaders can also take less ambitious approaches and make steady transitions through unending improvements to the critical elements at rates that outpace expectations and changes in the business environment. Transitions involve making positive changes to the strategic positions, solutions, subsystems, processes, operations, capabilities, and resources of the organizations and enterprise(s). Both transformations and transitions are typically based on the broad economic, social, ethical, technological, environmental, market, and financial realities and long-term opportunities and challenges. Moreover, there are numerous other options. Regardless, visionary strategic leadership (VSL) is the crucial aspect that drives change and success.

An understanding of the realities and possibilities is obtained through broad-based assessments of market spaces, the business environment, the social world, and the natural environment. While such assessments are not easy, there is usually information and data available to obtain insights, to ascertain what is happening, and to make determinations. However, discovering the long-term opportunities and challenges and the related possibilities is much more difficult. There is limited information available about the long term. Therefore, one of the key mechanisms used by corporate leaders and their professional staffs is scenario planning.

Scenario planning is a strategic management tool used to shed light on the realities and possibilities in the external context and their implications, to reflect on the potential effects and impacts, and to understand what options corporate leaders have. It provides a mechanism for a diverse group of strategic leaders and planners to think about the future in an organized and unbiased way. Scenarios do not prescribe what the actual decisions should be or what is expected to actually occur. They simply help to facilitate strategic leaders in making the best strategic decisions in light of the possibilities.

The most critical of these perspectives are the high-level options or potential action plans and initiatives; ones that are the domain of visionary strategic leaders, especially those related to the vision, grand strategy(s), and corporate objectives. They include investing into corporate research and development (R&D), developing new ventures, orchestrating mergers and acquisitions, managing strategic innovations, and forming strategic alliances and joint ventures. While there are numerous other alternatives, the focus herein is on options, corporate actions, and high-level strategic programs that lead to significant transformations and/or transitions of the company. Incremental innovations to the operating systems and functional areas are usually the domain of the lower-level strategic leaders, operation managers, and project managers who engage in implementation and execution.

Sustainable success depends on building and having solid business-related relationships. Business relationships exist in a continuum from the top of the company and enterprise with linkages to partners, allies, peers, stakeholders, constituents, and shareholders to business-unit level with interactions and interconnections that include customers, stakeholders, supply networks, all constituents, and society in general. Corporate leaders have the overall responsibility for establishing corporate (high-level) relationships with outside entities; they generally focus on relationships with the board of directors and shareholders, the entities of the business environment, and the broader connections with the social world and the natural environment. Such requirements also include relationships within the organization and the key external contributors.

The main topics discussed in the chapter are:

- Employing scenario planning to shed light on the opportunities and challenges.
- Developing corporate plans and actions to enhance transformations and transitions.
- Building relationships with strategic partners and critical constituents to enrich the capabilities of the enterprise to realize its goals.

Scenario Planning

Definition and Purpose

Scenario planning in a business setting is a strategic planning methodology for developing an understanding of the underlying driving forces in the business environment, especially their significance and impacts over time and for determining the long-term implications related to the company's strategic direction. It involves linking the possible scenarios with the company's strategic options for strategy formation and execution. It is an important mechanism because it involves:

- Preparing multiple scenarios about possible outcomes in the business environment and market spaces that provide insights and implications about the future and the associated possibilities.
- Assessing the possibilities and their potential consequences and contemplating one's strategic options when crafting and implementing strategies.
- Reducing the risks and vulnerabilities to adverse consequences of unfavorable scenarios.
- Selecting the option(s) that provide the potential for positive outcomes.

While the number of alternative scenarios to be examined could be endless, most strategists select between four and six scenarios that cover the most important strategic aspects. Even numbers of scenarios help leaders to avoid thinking that the middle one is the most likely scenario. A two-by-two matrix of four scenarios provides a mechanism for assessing variations of significant driving forces like two that are positive and two that are negative. Alternatively, if the desired approach is to present a base case with more extreme possibilities on its flanks, then odd numbers are desirable.

Scenario planning involves thinking about what might happen in the future based on plausible premises and mapping out the resultant implications for strategic decisions and actions in the present. Scenario planning also involves using solid information and data (evidence) about the conditions and trends in the business environment and examining how they might play out over time. The former builds upon key assumptions and variables that are linked into perspectives about the future based on postulates and/or mental models. While mental models provide great latitude, there are enormous uncertainties involved, which become more difficult to deal with as one contemplates possibilities further out into the future. Regardless, it is important to make reasonable assumptions and to ensure that implications of the variables are plausible so that the scenarios are credible and serve a useful purpose. The latter is based on the logical extensions of prevailing situations and what might be expected to occur over a reasonable time frame. The logical extensions should be based on predetermined elements that are the same in each scenario.

Predetermined elements are the known facts, factors, and underlying aspects that are generally stable and somewhat predictable over time; ones that change very slowly. A good example is the predictability of demographics. For instance, the demographics of the populations in most of the developed countries like Japan are mirroring a uniform distribution; the number of people in each of the age categories is approximately the same. Demographics tend to be predetermined elements because the underlying aspects are reliable and the changes are generally predictable. For instance, people who are forty years old today will be fifty years old in ten years, if they are still living. Moreover, the number of people who are forty years old is fixed (at least on a global basis); there cannot be any new people who are forty years old. While there is always the potential for catastrophic events like wars, natural catastrophes, and pandemics, demographics provide reasonable and plausible views about the future, especially those pertaining to the implications of the global population. Most projections using predetermined elements are based on quantitative analysis of existing information and data. It is easy and scientifically sound to make certain estimates and extrapolations about the expected conditions and their implications, say ten to twenty years out.

The purpose of scenario planning is not to predict the future or to suggest that certain trends will lead to distinct or preordained outcomes, but to perceive credible insights from the set of plausible outcomes and to obtain an understanding about the potential impacts and consequences. The business environment is a dynamic system in which the number of possible outcomes dramatically expands as time marches forward; therefore, scenarios tend to be more reliable in the near or intermediate term. For instance, it would have been impossible to predict the expansion of the Internet and the changes from an analog to a digital world twenty-five years ago, but it would have been much easier to make such determinations five years ago. Like trying to predict the weather, there are real limitations in the ability to understand all of the variables involved, especially in the longer term in which unforeseen driving forces and new variables enter the possible situations. Moreover, the range of outcomes for each variable tends to increase with time as the interactions between forces and variables increase as well.

Scenario planning is not a form of forecasting. Forecasting methods usually involve using historical data and trends to make predictions about the near term. Forecasting is typically used to make estimations about some of the salient aspects of the business environment and market spaces and provide quantitative views of the implications. It usually involves projections using statistical methods based on a time series of existing conditions and on insights from cause and effect analysis and various other methods. Forecasting is most useful for market and economic aspects, like trying to understand the demand for a specific product over the next three years. Some examples include the expected revenues from the sale of cars, computers, and cell phones and the production requirements for products. Forecasting is a good tool for the functional or operational aspects of a business. It usually gives reasonable results about short-term expectations. The general time frame is three to five years (or less) based on the assumption that the business world remains relatively stable during that period. Such assumptions are usually reasonable and more accurate during the early years and may give acceptable results for the short term, especially if the rate of change is low. However, forecasting usually does not provide very good indications about the changing conditions and expectations in the long term, in which major shifts in the underlying social and economic conditions may degrade or confound the results. The compounding effects of change make it extremely difficult to forecast five to ten years or more out into the future. The development of the Internet is a good example of profound changes; ones that impact the forecasts for most products and services. Think about the new Internet technologies that have been created over the last five years and how even newer technologies may impact the Internet five years from now. For example, Facebook and Twitter were inconsequential just a few years ago, but they are now major factors for social networking and in communicating.

Scenarios should be internally consistent, but they do not have to follow the rigors of scientific methods. They can be mental models of what might happen. However, it is important to have structure in scenario planning since without structure scenario planning would be an open-ended approach about "guessing," in which anyone's guess is as good as the others, but most "guesses" are unhelpful in contributing to insights and strategic thinking. Furthermore, guessing is a trial-and-error approach, while scenario planning attempts to build a logical framework about the future implications. It is not an attempt to accurately determine what is expected to happen, but to better understand the effects, impacts, consequences, and implications for strategic decision making.

Visionary strategic leaders make decisions today that determine the success of their businesses tomorrow. They have to decide on what direction to pursue, what investments to make, how to develop their organizations, and the many other aspects in creating more productive and successful positions and situations. Scenarios are based on the art and science and the intellectual capacity of strategic leaders to contemplate the "what ifs," and how selected change mechanisms might influence the future. For instance, most strategic leaders might have foreseen the increased potential for terrorism, but it would have been impossible for them to predict the attacks on 9/11 or the subsequent wars in Iraq and Afghanistan. An intuitive sense of what might take place uses insights about prevailing conditions and trends and imagination about what the consequences might be and how to prepare for the implications.

Each scenario has relevance within itself, i.e., it is plausible and it is linked to the other scenarios in some way that provides decision-makers with a sense of the range of possibilities and their meanings to the company. A comprehensive scenario should include the periods covered, say the next ten to fifteen years, and provide a sense of what the general conditions are expected to be, and why they are expected to occur.

Brief Historical Background Pertaining to Scenario Planning

Scenario planning as a management technique is attributed to Herman Kahn who developed the basic elements, circa 1967. Kahn worked on the potential impacts and consequences of nuclear war. He developed scenarios about the interactions and possible outcomes to understand the potential devastation. He realized that there was no way to use forecasting as a technique for determining the consequences of nuclear war because there was no historical data. Given the absence of data, Kahn made judgments based on broad knowledge and scientific underpinnings about the possible impacts and aftermath of a nuclear conflagration.

Scenario planning was developed to envision the implications of future situations where forecasting is not possible. Most of the forecasting techniques like time series are based on statistical analysis, which is rooted in scientific methods generally accepted by the business and academic communities. Statistical analysis was developed by numerous scholars and practitioners over the last century. Much of the early work was done at AT&T in the 1930s. Statistical analysis and forecasting were important tools for AT&T's strategic leaders, providing them with an understanding of the future requirements for its services and systems well ahead of actual demand. AT&T's senior leaders used forecasting to understand the needs for installing the necessary equipment and having the appropriate capacity to handle the wide range of demand situations well before the implications became critical factors. They also determined details about customer usage like frequency of customer usage of the telephone at key hours of the day and days of the year. For instance, on Mother's Day many adult children call their mothers, greatly increasing the numbers of telephone calls in the system. This could place high stress on the system, if the company was unprepared for the spike in demand. At AT&T, forecasting worked well because the conditions were stable and predictable. Moreover, the statistical variations were understood and within normal limits. Most importantly, the implications were most profound on near-term decision making.

Scenario planning, on the other hand, is more subjective and typically lacks the rigor necessary to gain broad scientific acceptance. It is based on judgments, not statistical analysis or scientific principles. The development of scenario planning in the business community is attributed to business leaders at Royal Dutch/Shell (Shell) during the early 1970s. Pierre Wack and Andre Benard at Shell were among the early advocates for scenario planning. Wack suggests that scenario planning was more effective than forecasting. In a Harvard Business Review article, he noted that:[1]

> Most mangers know the [through] experience how inaccurate forecasts can be. On this point, there is probably a large consensus.
>
> My thesis—on which agreement may be less general—is this: The way to solve this problem is not to look for better forecast by perfecting techniques or hiring more forecasters. Too many forces work against the possibility of getting the right forecast. The future is no longer stable; it has become a moving target. No single "right" projection can be deduced from past behavior.
>
> The better approach, I believe, is to accept uncertainty, try to understand it, and make it part of our reasoning. Uncertainty today is not just an occasional, temporary deviation from a reasonable predictability; it is a basic structural feature of the business environment. The method used to think about and plan for the future must be made appropriate to a changed business environment.
>
> Royal Dutch/Shell believes that decision scenarios are such a method.

Shell used scenario planning as a tool for understanding the dynamics of the oil business with all of the fluctuations in crude oil exploration, production, demand, pricing, etc. Peter Scwartz is one of the leading futurists today and President of Global Business Networks; he was a Shell planner during the 1980s. He wrote *The Art of the Long View* articulating how scenario planning can help strategic leaders think about the future. He states that "scenario planning is about making choices today with an understanding of how they may turn out."[2] He suggests that scenarios are not predictions, but ways of examining future possibilities and the company's strategic choices. Without a link to decision making, scenarios are interesting exercises about what the future might look like.

Strategic Implications of Scenarios

Scenarios can form the basis for translating opportunities into options (choices) and for developing and implementing strategies and action plans that convert possibilities into realities. They provide snapshots of possible future states, allowing the strategic leaders a better understanding of what they need to know about the potential implications and consequences of the plausible possibilities. They also provide ways to ascertain the learning and knowledge that must be obtained to function and succeed in such future states. Scenario planning involves the blending of the following:[3]

- What is known (knowledge and experiences)?
- What is happening (observations, insights, and reflections)?
- What is theoretically possible (plausible outcomes)?
- What makes sense (rational and feasible) to convey in a model of conceivable sequences of future events or situations?

The business environment is full of uncertainties and risks that are ever changing. The more uncertainty there is, the more important it is to discover the true variables of change. Over the last several decades, new technologies and innovative products have expanded the reach of global corporations. Globalization has opened up opportunities to produce products anyplace in the world. Today, most products are more affordable, have higher quality, and provide numerous benefits.

In scenario planning, one contemplates the underpinnings and linkages that drive change and create new possibilities. It can be argued that one of the common treads is the digital world, typified by how easy it is to send incredible amounts of information and data anywhere in the world at low costs, to produce millions of copies of software, music, and movies, and to communicate with millions of people.

The overarching variables that shape the business world are the key elements for trying to understand uncertainty and reality. They are the "predetermineds" according to Kees van der Heijden, author of *Scenarios: The Art of Strategic Conversation* and a founder of the Global Business Network.[4] Predetermineds or predetermined elements are the known key variables. They are the essential factors that are well understood and stable in the short and intermediate terms. They provide a sense of stability and indicators of what can be expected to some extent in the future. Predetermined elements provide structure and common linkages between the scenarios that can be articulated because they remain essentially the same, regardless of what scenario is contemplated. Predetermined elements do change over time and become less reliable over time as indicators of the ultimate direction that change takes. Thus, they provide guidance that is common to all scenarios, but there is a limit as to how long upon which they can be relied.

Figure 4.1 depicts the time frames for forecasting and for scenarios. Van der Heijden suggests that the further one looks into the future, predictability goes down and uncertainty goes up. His graph on the balance between predictability and uncertainty is helpful in getting sense of the time frame in which scenarios may be useful. "F" represents forecasting and indicates the domain (time frame) in which forecasting provides reasonable results. "S" represents scenario planning and indicates the domain in which scenario planning is useful for obtaining a sense of what the possible future states might be like. "H" represents hope and is the domain of the long term that is outside of the realm of effective strategic planning. It is the domain in which uncertainty is very high and the ability to use predetermined elements or understand variability is very low. There are few established techniques that can be used to provide a sense of what to expect in the "H" domain and how to plan for the possibilities or management of the potential changes.

The domain of forecasting is generally less than five years and the domain of scenario planning is generally less than twenty years; however, the actual time horizons depend on the rapidity of change in the business environment. In some business sectors like consumer electronics, telecommunications, computers, and information technologies, the time horizon of a domain is significantly less for both. Moreover, as the rate of change accelerates, uncertainty is expected to increase more quickly, shifting the theoretical boundaries between the domains to the left. It is clear that most forecasting techniques have become less effective and the results more questionable, because the domain for forecasting has shrunk considerably over the last decade. Strategic leaders in the 1950s might have been able the forecast demand for their products for more than five and even ten years into the future. The ability to forecast or the use forecasting techniques today is possibly less than half of what it was fifty years ago. Worse yet, there are possibilities like those of the financial meltdown of 2007–2009

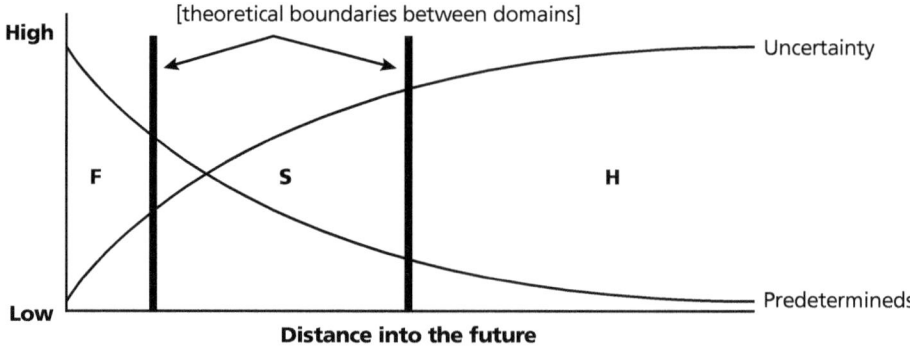

Figure 4.1 van der Heijden's model pertaining to predictability and uncertainty.[5]

in which the changes in the variables exceed the range of deviations of the past. For instance, the demand for automobiles dropped thirty percent, which would not have been predicted using conventional forecasting techniques.

Scenario planning can be developed within the organization or it may be subcontracted to consultants who specialize in it. The former may require more time and effort than what external professionals would take, but it does have advantage of capturing the organizational learning about the intricacies of the business environment. The internal approach may make strategic sense even though it may cost more time and money, because strategic leaders and the organization can obtain additional outcomes from scenario planning activities like learning, capturing information about markets, and enhancing internal capabilities and competencies. Moreover, if scenario planning occurs within the organization, the people involved have a better understanding of the implicit aspects and are better equipped to interpret and respond to changes as they unfold. The main advantage of subcontracting is the leveraging of information, data, and analyses available to external consultants who may have performed numerous scenario planning events over the course of time. Moreover, the time required to complete the scenarios may be significantly less because of the expertise of the individuals and the support structures that specialty groups have. The latter is also more beneficial and appropriate when the topics under considerations are more general or ones that pertain to many companies within a business sector or industry. These include climate change concerns, social conditions and trends, and the implications of political systems and structures. There are numerous groups like the Stockholm Environment Institute that prepare scenarios on topics like sustainability and sustainable development.[6]

The main purpose of scenario planning in the context of VSL and corporate strategic management (CSM) is to support the decision-making process and facilitate a broader understanding of the strategic options pertaining to specific decisions of the company or business units. Scenario planning is about exploring the possibilities and making sense out of the implications.

Scenario Planning Process

Scenario planning may be developed and implemented using a stepwise process. The steps taken before the start of scenario planning process include deciding whether scenarios should be developed by the organization or outsiders and establishing the time horizon and scope of the scenarios.

If the organization plans to do scenario planning itself, an interdisciplinary team should be selected to ensure broad perspectives and unbiased developments. The team(s) should include people who are open-minded with multifaceted experiences. Strategic leaders should assure that views of the selected participants are not skewed toward any specific agenda or discipline; especially ones that support traditional thinking and the status quo. Strategic leaders should also avoid selecting team members who are dependent on certain outcomes for their personal or professional success. For instance, a product manager who relies upon the continuation of certain product lines may be biased toward the prevailing business situations, resulting in a business-as-usual mindset; he or she may favor shaping scenarios that are more inclined to show high market demand related to his or her areas of responsibilities.

The time horizon should be in van der Heijden's "S" domain. This is typically five to fifteen or twenty years with a midpoint of eight to ten years. If the time horizon is not long enough, then certain profound implications may be missed and the organization may be unprepared for the longer term. For instance, if the selected time horizon is six years, the dominant technologies may remain viable during the period, thus indicating that no significant changes are seemingly necessary. Yet, there may be a possibility that within ten years radical new technologies may overtake the company's existing product lines and make them obsolete. Again, think about what happened to Kodak; the 1990s were relatively stable and the 2000s were extremely turbulent. On the other hand, as suggested by van der Heijden's "H" domain, if the time horizon is too long, then the scenarios are just hopeful guesses because the uncertainties are so great, and the predetermined elements become so weak that anything is possible. However, scenario planning is not normally done just once in a decade, but examined periodically to obtain a better understanding of reality and changes.

As discussed, Shell was one of the originators and main developers of scenario planning in the 1980s. It is still one of the leading companies on the subject and continues to provide insights into the applications. While there are numerous suggested processes for developing scenarios, Schwartz's eight-step process for scenario planning captures the essential aspects of most of the others and is indicative of the how-to-create scenarios. His eight steps are:[7]

- Step 1: Identify[ing] issue[s] or decision[s]
- Step 2: [Determining] the key forces in the local environment [and obtaining information]
- Step 3: [Identifying] the driving forces
- Step 4: Rank[ing] by importance and uncertainty
- Step 5: Selecting scenario logics
- Step 6: Fleshing out the scenarios
- Step 7: [Analyzing] the implications
- Step 8: Selection of leading indicators and signposts

Schwartz's approach indicates that certain strategic decisions have to be made before one engages in scenario planning. The logic of this is obvious; it reduces the number of possibilities that have to be examined. It makes scenario planning an easier tool to use for understanding the implications of changes on the strategic options and facilitates strategic decision making. Scenario planning involves dealing with subjective perspectives that are reasonable, but it is not based on evidence, existing situations, or provable constructs. Schwartz's model can be divided into three levels for a better appreciation of the linkages between the steps and the intended outcomes. Figure 4.2 indicates the levels and the steps contained in each one.

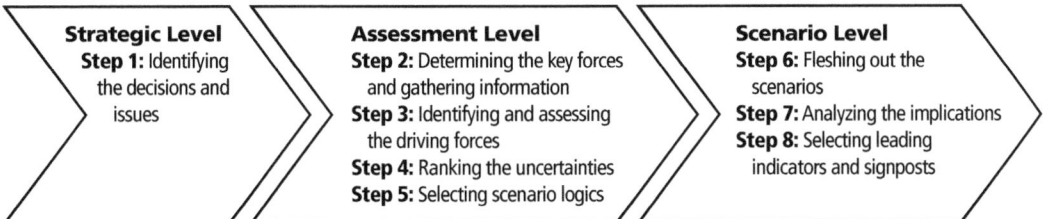

Figure 4.2 Schwartz's scenario planning process.

The first step involves understanding the strategic direction of the organization and the strategic leaders' perspectives on opportunities, challenges, threats, and risks. It involves the underlying strategic logic of the businesses and reasons for existing. While such perspectives are reframed during strategic formulation (especially with business unit strategies), strategic leaders usually have a general sense of what is critical, since CSM involves dynamic thinking, not sequential processing. Regardless of the situation, it is critical for strategic leaders to frame the situation so that the people involved know what futures to uncover and what are the key issues and concerns as well. Schwartz suggests that step 1 includes key questions about the organization's future—its vision and strategic direction; what it wants to become. This might include what businesses it is in or wants to be in, what it expects to change, and how it can shape the future to obtain sustainable advantages and outcomes. It includes examining the possibilities and circumstances for achieving success. It also includes determining the business risks and how they can be mitigated.

The second step involves obtaining information and gleaning insights about current customers, markets, suppliers, and competitors. This includes information and data on all facets of the business environment, especially those areas that might involve significant changes such as technological developments, new scientific knowledge, and innovative breakthroughs. The progression should begin with the simplest, fastest, and least costly research methods and proceed to more sophisticated approaches until the requisite information and data are obtained. In most situations, a well-tailored approach starts with obtaining appropriate information that is already available. This leads to getting most of the results in a timely and cost-effective way. In the developed countries, there is usually an enormous amount of information and data in the public domain. Government agencies like the U.S. Department of Commerce and U.S. Department of Labor publish documents on industry activities with market data and relevant information about the conditions and trends in most business sectors and industries. Trade associations and research organizations are rich sources of information and data about markets and industries and may usually be obtained at a low cost. Many such organizations publish almanacs covering developments during the previous year along with statistical information and details about the solutions and structures of the industry. Typical information includes market size, growth rate, competitors, buyer behavior and patterns, technologies, etc. Trade journals tend to follow industry conditions and trends and provide rich sources of information on activities, processes, and events. They often disclose full market data including market structures, statistics, and performance. University-based research is a substantial source of information and analysis as well, especially on new-to-the-world technologies, products, and processes. Academic scholars and researchers conduct surveys, analyses, and studies of companies, industries, and economies to facilitate the broader understanding of the research phenomena and their implications. Research costs tend to increase as the sophistication of the research methodology increases. The more expensive, customized sources and approaches can be engaged to fill in the gaps after the obtaining all of the possible publically available information and data. Market research companies typically prepare market analysis for selected sectors that may cost more than $100,000, but it depends on the scope of work.

The third step involves identifying and assessing the driving forces of change and the critical dimensions of the business environment. The dynamics of changes must be framed in the context of overall economic, social, political, legal, ecological, and technological realities. The most important aims of the assessments are the identification of the essential driving forces and a determination of their influences and impacts on the potential strategies of the company. The market conditions and business trends provide the context for identifying new opportunities, challenges, risks, and vulnerabilities before they become apparent. Such assessments provide profound mechanisms for understanding the future implications. For instance, the potential impacts of climate change could affect everything from weather patterns, the availability of water, and energy consumption to food production, human habitat, and the underlying demand for products and services. The assessment process includes identifying, understanding, and selecting the most critical driving forces that might be expected to have a profound influence on the future.

The fourth step is the key point. It focuses on understanding critical uncertainties and ranking their importance in preparing scenarios. The critical uncertainties are the seeds of the scenarios. These are the factors that are expected vary considerably over time. For instance, Shell spent a lot of time thinking about the availability and costs of petroleum. In today's world, the supply of petroleum products and crude oil reserves are fairly well known, but the expected demand and pricing have a high degree of uncertainty. While the usage of petroleum is expected to increase dramatically as economies in rapidly industrializing countries like China and India expand, such views are based on continuing favorable global economics, market stability, and reasonable crude oil prices. The high degrees of uncertainty and the economic turbulence make it difficult to predict the course of possible outcomes. Another critical factor is humankind's ability to control disease. The effects of diseases and controlling them may be predetermined elements today, but concerns continue to be raised about potential pandemics that could significantly affect everyone and alter lifestyles and living conditions in the developed countries as well as in the developing ones. Often there are precursors to big changes that manifest themselves as small disruptions; they are referred to as weak signals. They often provide indications that things are changing. Weak signals pertain to the possibilities of having more serious problems in the future. For instance, the 2003 SARS scare in China may be an indicator about how quickly new diseases can spread across the planet; the global concerns about Swine Flu (H1N1) during 2009 show how disruptive these concerns can be.

The fifth step involves selecting the most critical driving forces and areas of uncertainty and using them in developing scenarios. The most difficult aspect is making the right selections from the broad array of variables and uncertainties. Some of the most important uncertainties involve the growth and development of the global economy, political stability, security from terrorism, wars and conflicts, climate change, resource depletion, environmental degradation, the availability and cost of energy supplies, and potential for global epidemics. These are some of the most challenging uncertainties, and each could have catastrophic effects on humankind and the natural world. Step 5 also involves discovering the predetermined elements that usually undergo little change. Again, the notion of a predetermined element is that its effects are predictable. As discussed, the demographics of the population are usually relatively stable for long periods of time. For instance, the large numbers of baby boomers in the United States (those born between 1946 and 1964) who are expected to retire over the next decade are well known and it is unlikely to vary considerably from the current estimates. Their effects on the Social Security System and other retirement programs are expected to be significant, causing many financial concerns about the viability of such programs.

The sixth step involves the construction of a framework for the possible scenarios—weaving together the critical factors for plausible scenarios and developing externally and internally consistent versions. Scenarios are built around selected driving forces and related uncertainties, and how they might change over time. It is helpful if an overarching logic can be developed to provide a sense of how the scenarios are related. There are many ways to map out scenarios. One approach is to use a two dimensional perspective mapping out how the driving forces might relate to each other. For instance, how are the concerns over environmental considerations like degradation and depletion and economic growth interrelated? A strategic leader has to consider how such scenarios play out across many sectors of the global economy and social and political structures.

Figure 4.3 depicts four scenarios that present a range of outcomes based on driving forces and the possible actions that could be taken. The *"business as usual"* scenario presents the base case, in which businesses around the world continue to expand without concerns about their environmental impacts and the related consequences. It assumes that companies comply with the existing laws and regulations (predetermined elements), but they are not compelled to go beyond such mandates. It is the base case since it accurately depicts the current global business situation. The scenario is positive from an economic perspective, but negative from an environmental one. If the time horizon is relatively short, say five years, such a scenario may indicate that the prospects are reasonable and stable. The difficulties may lie in the out years. For instance, if the effects of oil depletion are the most profound in latter stages of the life cycle of petroleum, then the next ten years may be relatively stable in terms of energy, but more chaotic thereafter. Many strategic leaders assume that such phenomena are

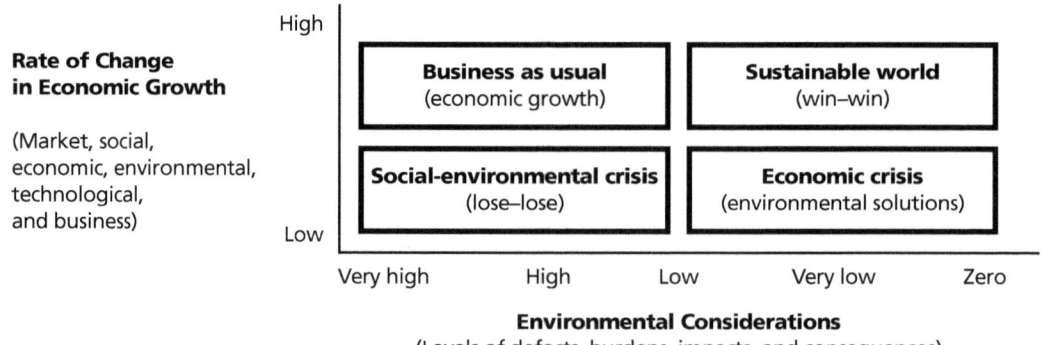

Figure 4.3 Scenarios pertaining to economic growth/environmental concerns.

continuous functions rather than step functions, but such phenomena and changes are likely to be non-linear in the long term.

The *"social-environmental crisis"* scenario presents the case in which environmental factors have negative effects on the social and economic well-being of the human population. This may be due to such phenomena as climate change making products more expensive as conditions become less favorable. For instance, climate change may make food production more costly and less successful. Historically, a stable food supply has been one of the key determinants for economic and social stability. One could argue that the economic success of the United States over the last two centuries has been underpinned by the phenomenal success of American agriculture. It takes less than two percent of the U.S. population to produce the food resources to support the rest of the population. What would happen to economic success in the United States and elsewhere, if the farming yields were cut in half or worse? What would happen if numerous forests and woodlands are destroyed; farmlands lay to waste; and diseases run amuck, among other potential disasters? The effects and impacts on businesses would be profound and most likely catastrophic. Many businesses, if not all, might find it difficult to grow significantly and be profitable. Survival might be questionable. This extreme scenario is based on most of the factors being unfavorable. It is the scenario in which companies, even entire countries, try to grow without the due considerations about underlying environmental and social forces and run into adverse impacts from every perspective. While it is difficult for most leaders to envision such prospects, such a scenario may not be so far-fetched. Consider China. China may have many serious environmental problems within a decade, causing its stellar economic growth to slow down or even come to a halt due to poor ambient air quality, the lack of clean water, electric power disruptions, and uncontrolled waste generation. The precursors to such potential consequences are on the horizon today. Not only has ambient air quality declined in China, but its air pollution is now affecting the west coast of the United States. About twenty five percent of the poor ambient air quality in California is said to be caused by industrial processes, energy generation, and environmental problems in China. The growing number of coal-fired power plants producing electricity for the escalating power demand in China is one of the main causes of air pollution.

The *"economic crisis"* scenario presents the case in which the needs and desires to solve environmental difficulties around the world have severe negative effects on economic stability and growth. In this scenario, people are willing or have to reduce their economic rewards to improve environmental conditions and outcomes. It may also be the case, in which environmental factors were not adequately considered and managed until the associated impacts went well beyond the crisis point, after which drastic actions are required to obtain the necessary solutions. Such conditions may be forced upon businesses and consumers by social pressures or the political establishments, i.e., society is willing to forego improvements in economic well-being to enjoy more important improvements in environmental conditions. Such willingness is more likely to be the situation in countries with high levels of discretionary consumption as in the United States, Japan, Canada, and Western Europe. Within such countries, people already enjoy higher standards of living and can more easily improve environmental factors at the expense of economic growth and relatively modest changes in lifestyle. This scenario may be one of "satisficing," which means that one is satisfied with a little less, sacrificing to achieve a more balanced set of outcomes. The results of this scenario might significantly reduce business opportunities, especially in the growth dependent sectors of the economies. The lack of growth may lead to a decline in the market value of many companies, since economic and financial growth are key determinants in market valuation. Imagine what the market capitalization of most global corporations would be, if there were little or no growth opportunities for an extended period of time. Using conventional management constructs like discounted cash flow, the market value of many corporations would simply be the sum of its discounted cash flows based on the existing results, plus other relevant factors like the value of certain assets, such as cash and securities. The share price-to-earnings ratio of most companies would be similar to the companies of today that are viewed as low-growth companies. The typical multiples might be in the range of three to five; not very exciting and a lot less than what high growth companies enjoy.

The *"sustainable world"* scenario presents the case in which companies in both developed and developing countries start immediately on developing and commercializing clean technologies green products, and sustainable solutions, thus generating significantly lower impacts. It involves balancing the social, economic, and environmental perspectives and creating sustainable enterprises. It includes using social and environmental factors to gain economic advantages and financial rewards. It represents a "win-win-win" approach, and may be viewed as the extreme case that is positive from many perspectives. The notion of a sustainable world does not necessarily mean making outrageous sacrifices or lowering one's lifestyle to sufficiency levels; it simply means using resources more wisely, avoiding the generation of wastes and pollution, and ensuring a balance between the social, economic, environmental, ethical, and technological requirements and expectations. It involves developing clean technologies and products that accomplish the same or more than the old ones with fewer impacts and problems. It is akin to working smarter, not harder.

Scenarios may also be presented using a matrix. The simplest may be the two-by-two matrix, in which two main uncertainties are presented. This may be suitable for a

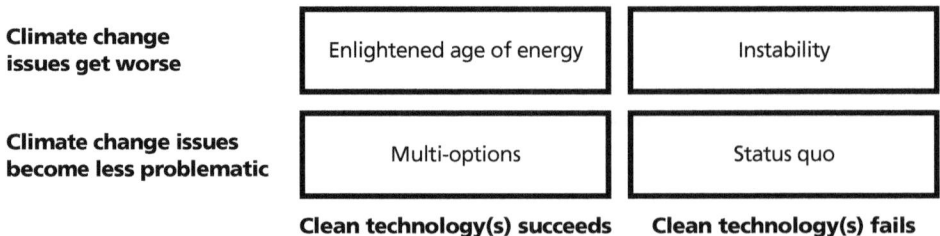

Figure 4.4 Matrix form for depicting scenarios.

business unit or even for technological considerations. Figure 4.4 shows that layout for how the uncertainties might play out.

The matrix may take the form of four scenarios based on the implications of two major uncertainties. For example, the development of clean technologies like more fuel-efficient motor vehicles is dependent on many factors including petroleum prices and fuel availability, the impacts of climate change, and the political mandates. The layout might examine the positive and negative aspects of the uncertainties. The extremes do not have to be the best- or worst-case scenarios. The scenarios are intended to map out possible outcomes in a way that helps strategic leaders envision what the future business world might be like and how they can explore strategic options to optimize their situations and long-term positions. Each of the uncertainties is examined from positive and negative perspectives in the form of "what-if" statements. If the technology development(s) succeed and the driving forces require change, then it may result in an enlightened age of cleaner energy sources and new business realities as aggressive businesses continue to invest in related innovative solutions. If the technology development(s) fail and the driving forces require change, it may result in economic instability, especially in markets related to energy production and use. Such instability may destabilize other markets and negatively affect other social and economic considerations as well. On the other hand, if the driving forces become weaker, then clean technologies may assume an appropriate share of the overall energy sector that has multiple options. This is especially the case if they are successful; there are incremental improvements, but the prevailing situation is not radically altered. If the new technology(s) fails in a business environment in which climate change issues are less important for whatever reasons, then the status quo is maintained at least for some period of time. The matrix approach is usually simpler and most useful for direct comparisons.

The seventh step involves understanding the implications of the scenarios. Finding opportunities for making improvements and developments or other strategic options is the objective. The implications provide insights for developing strategic options. Indeed, scenarios provide strategic leaders with a sense of the potential implications of a given scenario, and how to examine the options and select most appropriate strategies that would lead to most favorable results, regardless of which scenario actually occurs. Such strategies should also be the most relevant even if there are slight deviations from the scenarios that were developed and analyzed.

Global corporations have little control over most of the external driving forces and uncertainties, but having a sense of what might happen is of great value in strategic formulation and implementation. The strategist's job is not only to improve strategic, market, and financial performance, but also to avoid failures and disasters. Strategic leaders have to craft strategies that create the best possible outcomes, regardless of what occurs in the market spaces or business environment. For instance, despite the fact that recessions are reoccurring aspects of economic realities, many corporate leaders in the past blamed a given recession for their failures and poor decision making. Such strategic leaders often rationalized their plight by explaining that everything would have been great if only the recession did not occur. But strategic leaders have to prepare and be favorably positioned for multiple scenarios.

The eighth step involves selecting leading indicators that show the direction that driving forces are moving. Establishing the indicators is always a difficult and crucial step. Indicators give early warning about how the scenarios and the subsets thereof are unfolding and provide feedback to strategic leaders who have to make decisions and manage their businesses based on uncertainties and risks. The increasing concentration of carbon dioxide in the atmosphere provides a tracking mechanism that the concerns about climate change are intensifying and that people are getting more exasperated about the potential repercussions. Gross domestic product reports provide a sense of the change in the economy, which signals the potential economic viability of certain strategic options. For instance, building a new production facility in a down market may lead to more excess capacity and less economic success. Such indicators may also provide a sense of what has to be adapted to be consistent with the driving forces of change. Their primary purpose is to provide a means to determine whether the strategic direction and the corporate strategies are appropriate in the external context and moving toward success.

Scenarios are not critical in themselves. They are not created to wager which scenario is most likely to play out. Most successful companies might hope for the "business as usual" scenario, if such a thing exists. For example, petroleum companies have invested billions of dollars into renewable technologies, but most of them would be quite happy if their current market positions and product lines in petroleum prevail for decades in the future. Scenarios help strategic leaders understand current realities and future possibilities to guide their decision making. Even with great imagination and insights and well-mapped-out scenarios, there are no guarantees that any of the scenarios depict what will eventually happen. The future may involve numerous wildcards that are impossible to imagine.

Gap Analysis Between Scenarios and Strategic Options

A gap analysis between the scenarios and strategic options is a relatively simple technique, yet it may provide a critical understanding about the related decisions and their implications. Scenario planning and strategic options provide insights on what might be done. A gap analysis is one of the most important aspects for using scenarios in the process of strategic formulation and/or implementation. The basic approach is to compare each of the strategic options with the scenarios and determine whether the strategic options result in favorable outcomes or not.

The underlying perspective suggests that the best strategic options are the ones that are mostly favorable regardless of how the scenarios play out or what the future conditions are. It is important to recognize that only a few of the many possible scenarios are actually prepared and scrutinized. Numerous other scenarios might unfold. Moreover, there is always the small chance for a wildcard or two to occur, and that such situations may have unforeseen implications. For instance, the discovery of new locations with vast quantities of crude oil that doubles the known reserves would change the business environment significantly, but it is an extremely unlikely situation given the fact that most of the Earth has been explored for oil and most of the regions that have oil deposits are known and are being exploited. The known deposits that are not being exploited today are not significant enough to change the overall dynamics of oil production and usage.

Gap analysis involves a quantitative or qualitative view of the strategic options in light of the scenarios. It provides an understanding of the value and use of the strategic options. Table 4.1 provides a relative view of gap analysis using the scenarios identified in Figure 4.3. While it can be argued that the perspective shown is subjective, the purpose is to illustrate the linkage between scenarios and strategic options. The gap analysis discussed herein is hypothetical since explaining all of the potential implications would require many pages of explanation. In the example, the options are as follows: (Please note that there may be many more options than just four.)

- Option 1 (traditional growth and expansion) is favorable only if the business environment continues along the positive lines without significant changes or surprises.
- Option 2 (strategic innovations based on clean technologies) is favorable regardless of whatever scenario plays out. For example, Toyota's technological innovations have led to development of lean-burn combustions engines and hybrid drive systems for vehicles; and fuel cell technology for automobiles.

TABLE 4.1 Theoretical Relationships Between Scenarios and Strategic Options

Gap analysis	Scenario 1 Business as usual	Scenario 2 Social-environmental crisis	Scenario 3 Economic crisis	Scenario 4 Sustainable world
Option 1 Growth/expansion	Favorable +++	Not very favorable – – –	Not very favorable – – –	Not favorable –
Option 2 Innovations	Very favorable +++	Favorable ++	Favorable ++	Very favorable +++
Option 3 Acquisitions	Favorable ++	Not favorable –	Not favorable –	Favorable ++
Option 4 Alliances	Very favorable +++	Favorable +	Favorable +	Very favorable +++

These are expected to be favorable regardless of the expected scenarios for energy availability and pricing.
- Option 3 (acquisition of existing old-line businesses) is favorable under scenario one, but may not be favorable if radical changes occur and the acquisitions pertain to the outmode methods.
- Option 4 (strategic alliances with sustainable enterprises) is also favorable under all of the scenarios depending on the actual alliances and partnerships.

While strategic leaders have little or no influence to make the preferred scenario become the prevailing situation, they do have options and choices. The strategic perspective is to choose one or more strategic options that favorably fit all or most of the of the scenarios, if possible, so that success is obtained regardless of what scenario occurs, or if that is not possible, there is a very high probability of being successful. Per the example, there may be two strategic options that cover most possible scenarios. In general, there does not have to be even one strategic option that is favorable with respect to the defined scenarios.

Gap analysis in this context may also involve creating new options, if all of the known options are poor. This might include examining new-to-the-world technologies or working with other corporations to find new options to fill in the gaps. This might include exploring whole new business arenas or developing new ways to overcome the constraints or weaknesses that limit the development of new opportunities. It may necessitate building new capabilities to realize the future possibilities. Beginning early not only provides a head start over others, but allows for a more deliberate process to explore opportunities and find new ways to create value. Moreover, recognizing the implications of change and being on the cutting edge of change often provide strategic leaders with the ability to gracefully transition out of the old and transform their companies into the new. If the evidence is clear that the driving forces necessitate change, then visionary strategic leaders take bold moves to transform their businesses immediately into the new paradigm; not wasting time, money, or efforts on existing positions or old methods. Developing new sustainable solutions before others are prepared to follow provides the means and mechanisms to obtain competitive advantages. This is exactly what Toyota and Honda did with hybrid-drive technology. They started their development programs for more fuel-efficient automobiles when crude oil was ten dollars a barrel. They realized that within a decade or so fuel prices would be significantly higher. Being proactive involves taking moves to preempt the situations, both enhancing the old and/or creating the new.

High-Level Corporate Plans and Actions

Corporate Strategic Plans

Corporate strategic plans involve high-level planning and decision making that map out the company's strategic formulation and implementation over the planning horizon. Strategic formulation involves developing new or revised vision statements and crafting new corporate objectives, strategies, action plans, and initiatives that set the stage for strategic implementation. Strategic implementation involves converting corporate strategies and objectives into actionable programs; designing and developing systems and organizational structure; taking actions and initiatives; and allocating resources.

Corporate strategic plans are based on a broad strategic analysis of the business environment and the market spaces served by the corporate and business units. Corporate leaders often depend on the strategic business unit (SBU) leaders to prepare their strategic business plans that are then incorporated in the corporate strategic plan. While there are many ways, in which corporate leaders can prepare high-level strategic plans, the simplest and most empowering way is to first develop the vision statements, the corporate objectives, and grand strategies as discussed in the previous chapter and do scenario planning per the section above, and then submit the results to the SBU leaders for inclusion in their strategic plans. The SBU leaders then prepare comprehensive strategic plans for their businesses and submit them to the corporate leaders. The corporate leaders then assess the pluses and minuses of their portfolios of SBUs and their operations and determine the gaps and actions necessary to ensure that the corporation as a whole can exceed the corporate goals and have the means and mechanisms to achieve the vision and aspirations. Since there are many avenues that corporate leaders can travel toward the desired ends, the strategic management process at the corporate level is less definitive than at the business unit level. For an understanding of strategic management of business units, read my book, *Enterprise-Wide Strategic Management: Achieving Sustainable Success through Leadership, Strategies and Value Creation* (2010, ISBN: 978-0-521-76980-8).

After evaluating the business unit strategic plans, corporate leaders and their professional staffs examine the overall strategic position of the corporation and determine what strategies, solutions, actions, initiatives, and strategic innovations are necessary to assure success. Essentially, they explore what has to be added to, changed, or eliminated from the business portfolios to realize the corporate goals. While there are numerous options, the main corporate approaches are mergers and acquisitions (M&As), strategic alliances and joint ventures (external), strategic innovations, and high-level strategic programs (HSPs). External actions and initiatives have the allure of high-profile, concrete assets, known attractiveness (positions), and tangible substance. However, there are many potential difficulties that may offset the advantages. The main concerns are hidden problems that may impact the business value obtained in the transactions. For instance, the company may be buying liabilities instead of assets. The external entity may have environmental problems that require extensive remediation projects or the merged corporation may be difficult, if not impossible, to assimilate and manage. There are numerous examples of mergers like Time Warner-America Online (AOL) and Daimler-Benz-Chrysler that resulted in losses, not gains.

Strategic innovations and HSPs are the broad categories of internal initiatives and development programs taken by the corporation to plug the gaps or develop new businesses. There are a myriad of strategic innovations and HSPs from new business ventures involving new-to-the-world technologies to developing new business units in new lines of business or in new market spaces. They also include high-level initiatives to transform the corporation into a significantly more capable and sophisticated entity. For instance, becoming a six sigma company or a sustainable enterprise is a profound undertaking that may take a decade or two to achieve.

The discussions herein outline some of the most often used high-level actions and initiatives. It is virtually impossible in a single book to highlight all of the possible variations. HSPs are discussed in the next two chapters.

Corporate Mergers and Acquisitions

Corporate M&As are typically the high-level business combinations, additions, and integrations that affect the whole corporation and have considerable influence on strategic positions, the portfolios of businesses, corporate governance, and market capitalization. While there are numerous types of mergers and acquisitions, some of the most common corporate types are:

- *Consolidation*—usually involves the combination of two similar corporations for the purpose of increasing the size and adding strengths to the resultant entity. These are often based on specific objectives like improving economies of scale or increasing overall market share(s). The combination of Exxon and Mobil is an example of two of the largest petroleum companies in the world trying to leverage their resources and capabilities and to continue to grow.
- *Geographic expansion*—typically focuses on the addition of strategic positions in new market spaces to improve global reach in related businesses. Such approaches are often used by large corporations that have regional strengths, but limited global reach. BP's acquisition in 1998 of Amoco, one of the original Standard Oil companies with a strong presence in the Midwest United States is an example of a global corporation increasing its strategic position in a national market (the U.S.).
- *Horizontal integration*—involves the joining of two corporations that have product and market positions in different segments of the same industry. The objectives usually include sharing knowledge, leveraging marketing, and increasing power. The failed merger of Daimler Benz and Chrysler Corporation is an example of well-positioned producers in their home and regional markets, but ones that lacked a full range of product-market offerings that would allow them to compete effectively against the global competitors in their industry. The theory was that they would complement each other; Mercedes in the luxury segments and Chrysler in the economy segments.
- *Vertical integration*—involves buying or merging with suppliers, distributors, and/or customers that theoretically increase the business value and scope of the product-market offerings and positions. Such approaches are complicated and often focus on strategic resources that are pivotal for long-term success. For example, General Electric (GE) acquired a number of water companies to bolster its long-term objective of being a premier provider of

water resources and innovative technologies for the production and distribution of water.

- ***Technology and knowledge acquisition***—focuses on obtaining the intellectual properties (patents, trade secrets, and know-how), innovative technologies, proprietary assets, and creative people that represent opportunities for enhancing the strategic positions of the corporation and/or the business units. Buying proven technologies and product-market positions and acquiring new competencies and capabilities are often more cost effective than developing them in-house from an investment perspective. Such approaches are believed to have low business risk, since it is easier to determine the value of proven technologies, market positions, and critical competencies than it is to understand the strategic, technological, market, and financial implications of establishing a new R&D program and starting a new venture. For example, Cisco Systems uses such acquisitions to grow its technological strengths and product-market positions.
- ***Diversification***—involves strategic moves into businesses that are not directly related to the core positions of the corporation; ones that are in significantly different business domains. While corporate leaders involved in diversifications often have a tendency to justify the strategic logic of the potential fit or linkages between the companies, unrelated combinations are usually difficult to manage and it is often likewise difficult to create additional value and enduring success. For example, the merger of AOL and Time Warner was touted as having enormous synergies, but history has proven otherwise.

While the corporate types identified above are just the tip of the iceberg, they provide an overview of the strategic intents and actions for making dramatic changes to the complexion of the company. At the corporate level, the purposes of M&As are to enhance the potential value creation, to discover new ways to realize the corporate goals, and to enhance the long-term value and viability of the corporation. While the main goals usually are to enhance market capitalization and to find new ways for making money, many M&As are just the opposites. Not only are there failures, but in certain business situations M&As result in liabilities that often exceed the original investments. Some of reasons for failures include paying more than the M&As are worth, the lack of long-term strategic fit, unexpected changes in the business environment, the underlying opportunities are not realized, hidden liabilities arise, and poor pre- and post-M&A management difficulties. For example, Daimler-Chrysler struggled from the onset. It can be argued that the served markets and the corporate cultures of the two original companies were distinctively different and the fit was not easy to orchestrate. Such problems eventually led to the disintegration. It is often difficult to combine two companies that may be at the extremes of the market spaces and have distinct cultures; Mercedes at the high end and Chrysler at the low end. It was difficult to manage the merger of companies with long histories and powerful corporate cultures that are dissimilar.

In many M&As, corporate leaders often focus on the financial, legal, market, and operational aspects, but do not think in sufficient detail about the effects on the people involved, which are among the most important considerations. Difficulties with people and/or the social aspects often arise because of the differences in the cultural underpinnings and the fact that the dissimilarities between the companies were not given adequate considerations. Moreover, it is often assumed that the time required to assimilate will be short and the requirements for learning and understanding of the new reality will be minimal. In reality, changing people's views and the corporate cultures are among the most difficult aspects to change and obtain positive results.

Corporate leaders may fail to actively seek out the concerns and issues before the M&As, because they wish to maintain secrecy or want to move ahead quickly. Moreover, the lack of sufficient research and the limited depth of understanding of the challenges often lead to hidden problems that surface after the M&As are completed. Such problems fester into barriers for success or worse. Buying liabilities and unsolvable problems are among the flawed actions taken by corporate leaders. They not only cost money, but they take attention away from other more fruitful opportunities to create value and expand corporate fortunes.

M&A processes and actions usually are comprised of three phases: pre-M&A research and discovery; formal negotiations and agreements; and, the post-M&A integration. The first phase is the most critical for building a solid foundation for long-term success. It includes performing due diligence and preparing an in-depth assessment of inherent value and fit and the underlying challenges. Due diligence consists of formal and informal audits, reviews, discoveries, and validations. It is impossible in a short section in this text to map out all of the critical requirements; however, it is imperative that due diligence include a full assessment of compliance-related issues, especially those pertaining to environmental laws and regulations, labor laws, tax payments, and product liabilities. As part of the due diligence process, audits should be conducted to validate the value or worth of resources, intellectual property, and other assets, especially for real estate, capital equipment, inventories, know-how, and patents, and core competencies. Moreover, special considerations should be given to hidden problems, defects, and liabilities pertaining to assets, products and operations, and health and safety issues pertaining to employees, contractors, customers, stakeholders, and partners. The most significant concerns with property and operations generally involve environmental, health and safety problems, especially those associated with hazardous wastes, contaminations, remediation requirements, and hidden liabilities. The biggest concerns pertaining to people are potential for litigation, under-funded benefits programs, and dissatisfied business unit leaders, functional leaders, managers, professionals, and key employees who are likely to leave due to unresolved difficulties like poor remuneration and high stress levels. People often represent the intangible strengths and value of an organization, yet they are often not fully considered or are assumed to part of the package. Moreover, people are not the property of the company and the assumed strengths of the acquired firm may eventually evaporate as key contributors quit and move to other opportunities including working for competitors.

Cultural compatibility with the new situation is an essential consideration. Often people employed in more entrepreneurial companies do not like the formalities and rigidities of large global corporations. They like being key players at the center of the attention. They typically dislike being just one of the tens of thousands of people who work for a multinational corporation, especially if there are stringent policies and tight controls effecting how people perform their duties and functions. Such people may quickly begin exploring other options that better suit their lifestyles and work behaviors. Moreover, they often have an entrepreneurial mindset to act expeditiously in decision making situations. They may become frustrated when they are required to go through an elaborate process of dealing with high-level management reviews and obtaining approvals.

The requirements and activities associated with the formal M&A negotiations and agreements typically involve many provisions that require specialized professional skills and know-how of lawyers and financial analysts. Such provisions and protocols are usually spelled out in detail by the sanctioning governmental agencies such as the Securities and Exchange Commission (SEC) in the United States and the specific regulations pertaining to products, processes, and operations promulgated by the responsible governmental body.

The post-M&A actions are even more varied and difficult to stipulate. Business integration touches the business units and operational levels. Strategic decision making becomes a bigger challenge with even more severe effects and consequences. Corporate leaders of the resultant corporate structure have to ensure that the parties can be assimilated into an entity that can become sustainable, and that the business unit leaders and managers have the understanding, willingness, and capabilities to achieve sustainable success.

Poor integration and a lack of understanding about the resultant company are two of the most serious challenges. They are very important when the resultant corporation is significantly larger than the predecessors. For instance, Daimler-Chrysler as a $162 billion corporation was a significantly more complex business proposition than managing two separate $80 billion corporations. Post-merger integration is often stymied because corporate leaders fail to appreciate the cultural and managerial differences within the new entity they created. Moreover, most of the strategic underpinnings and strategic direction usually change based on the requirements of the new entity. In such cases, senior management is often slow to understand what has to be done and the urgency of getting it done. Depending on who is in control, CSM may become skewed toward one of the predecessor companies. While this may facilitate the transition, it may also disadvantage the people of the acquired company that have to learn the new policies, systems, processes, and practices. Worst yet, none of the old strategies, policies, and approaches may fit the new realities.

Strategic Alliances and Joint Ventures

Strategic alliances are increasingly popular arrangements between two or more companies. They provide a flexible structure for meeting the needs and objectives of business situations without being encumbered by ownership, rigid structures, and/or huge upfront investments. While such relationships are usually expected to function for a reasonable period of time, i.e., they are ongoing, they are usually not considered to be permanent. They endure as long as they make strategic sense and the parties receive concomitant rewards.

A strategic alliance allows the parties to share capabilities and resources and/or participate in actions and activities that might be beyond the individual company's reach, capabilities, or willingness to take on certain risks. The reasons for establishing strategic alliances are numerous and take many forms. The typical reasons are to complement each other's resources and capabilities (based on strengths and weaknesses) and to share the costs and investments in technology, product, and market developments that are perceived to be risky or have significant degree of uncertainty. Strategic alliances may also allow the parties to build critical mass when each of the parties is too small or too weak to engage in the business opportunities separately. There are several main types of strategic alliances: coalitions, co-specializations, and long-term agreements (LTAs).

Coalitions involve special forms of strategic alliances in which competitors, producers, suppliers, and distributors in related endeavors share their capabilities and resources to develop or market products and services in a more cost-effective or more successful way. Coalitions are often used to develop and/or market new technologies and products. For example, GE and Pratt & Whitney teamed up to develop a new jet engine for the Airbus 380, since neither one was willing to invest its resources on such a large, expensive and risky project.

Co-specialization is a form of strategic alliance that involves complementing each other's specialized capabilities where each of the parties is not fully capable or confident of going it alone. Co-specialization is typically used to create a broader network of relationships, to expand the reach for existing products and services, to split the responsibility for producing and marketing products, to create more powerful competitive positions against giant competitors, and/or to form a network of related or complementary services, and a plethora of many other specific reasons. For instance, the airline industry has numerous alliances among the international companies that try to provide the full range of global locations through the network. The Star Alliance is an example of informally linked airlines that compete in certain situations and complement each other in other in order to better serve customers, especially those going to international destinations.

Strategic alliances also run the gamut from limited arrangements between companies in a local area for managing certain problems, issues, and concerns to global alliances for solving large-scale concerns like climate change. In most cases, the approach is to take on agendas that may be impossible for single entities to deal with. Some alliances are simply research oriented to gain more information and knowledge about a subject so that better solutions can be developed in the future.

Other types of alliances include equity participation in the ownership and capital of the partner corporations and LTAs between producers, suppliers, and customers. Renault-Nissan equity participation and management arrangement is an example of the former. Renault owns 45 percent of Nissan, and Nissan owns 30 percent of Renault. Boeing has a ,LTA with Mitsubishi Heavy Industries of Japan for the production of the fuselages for Boeing 777s and 787s.

Joint ventures (JV) are formal arrangements between parties that establish a legal entity for conducting business and pursuing special objectives. The typical legal structure is a duly-organized corporation owned by the parties and managed by its own board of directors and executives. Typically, a JV would have its own shares, assets, financial control, and reporting, products and services, strategic management, and business relationships. A JV separates the purpose, activities, and risks of the new entity from the owners, but the owners have to be careful to avoid commingling roles, responsibilities, and decision making. If they are not careful they might eliminate the protection under the limited-liability provisions of the corporate statutes that shield the owners from the risks and liabilities of the JV. JVs function like any corporation and have to be managed accordingly. Agreement among the owners is one of the main difficulties, especially if the owners have a 50–50 ownership arrangement. In such arrangements, decisions by the board of directors and management are usually 100 percent in agreement or there is no agreement at all.

While the expressed purpose of this book is not to assess all of the aspects and implications of strategic alliances and JVs, corporate leaders must ensure that they fulfill their responsibilities in managing the JVs as they do for their corporations.

Strategic Innovations

Corporate Research and Development and Corporate Entrepreneurship

R&D in most large corporations is typically divided into the fundamental areas being explored and developed. Corporate R&D usually involves centralized programs that pertain to new-to-the-world technologies, significant technological developments, and dramatic improvements to technology platforms. Typically, such programs involve the technology or product domains that go beyond the existing missions or operations of the business units; or they represent revolutionary changes that are outside of the current capabilities of the existing businesses and their product portfolios. Such R&D programs often result in new business ventures. R&D programs that focus on the existing product lines are usually the domain of the business units.

R&D programs require large investments of time and money that usually do not produce near-term rewards. Funding them involves huge financial risks. Corporate leaders often have difficulty justifying the investments in R&D programs, especially during the early phases, since it often takes five to ten years or more to obtain positive cash flows. Moreover, high-level R&D programs usually involve developing and commercializing new-to-the-world technologies, products, and businesses that are disruptive to the current portfolios of the technologies and products at the business unit levels. Lower-level management may not be inclined to embrace such R&D programs knowing that they may cause stresses within their organizations and may even cause their current operations to become less important, and in some cases, to be closed or sold off. SBU leaders often prefer exploiting current products rather than seeking better alternatives, especially when they have specific missions for which they are responsible and are compensated based on the short-term performance. The easiest way to determine what fits into high-level R&D and what is in the domain of the business units is to examine what strategic perspectives and whose goals are driving the decision making processes. For corporate R&D, the focus should be on the vision and strategic direction of the corporation and not the missions of the existing business units. The most crucial corporate R&D programs involve advanced development programs for new-to-the-world technologies and products; ones that may require new business ventures and/or new business models. They necessitate acquiring new capabilities and resources that are usually beyond those of the business units. Moreover, in the context of sustainable business development (SBD), the radical new technologies should embrace the criteria for clean technologies that eliminate the negative aspects of the prevailing technologies. While the development of new technologies involves corporate R&D management, the development of the new business venture requires creating the technology, then translating it into a commercial reality via corporate technological entrepreneurship (CTE).

CTE focuses on the mindset, skills, know-how, concepts, information, and processes that are relevant for entrepreneurs and strategic leaders who are starting new corporate ventures based on new-to-the-world technologies. It involves developing complex new business units within a large global corporation from its corporate R&D or acquired technologies. CTE includes establishing a strategic framework for developing new ventures, screening strategic options, and selecting the most viable approaches. It requires developing a business plan, analyzing and determining valuation, securing sources of financing, structuring the arrangement, and obtaining the resources and capabilities for deployment. It may also involve developing the business model, determining the methods and techniques for solving difficulties, and implementing the business plan.

The creation, development, and deployment of radical and clean technologies often change the entire nature of the business practices, the management systems, and processes. The relationships in the organization may all require innovative changes or enhancements. They may require improving the effectiveness and applications of knowledge, and making the transformation to richer levels of technological sophistication and organizational learning. Corporate leaders and CTE leaders have to provide the means and mechanisms for commercializing the aspects related to the new technologies: create the business; prepare a business plan; develop new business model(s); establish the management system(s); and institute the support structures.

Radical Innovation

Radical innovation requires an open-ended strategic management mindset. The approach should be entrepreneurial and creative. The strategic leaders involved in radical innovations have to be aggressive and tolerate failures as well as demanding successes. They have to conceive, discover, and analyze opportunities through the intellectual capital of the organization and turn opportunities into realities through R&D efforts. The critical leadership perspective involves determining why certain opportunities are important; analyzing the advantages and disadvantages pertaining to the alternatives; developing the means and mechanisms to exploit the most advantageous options; designing and developing the technologies, products and processes (the solutions); determining how to measure success; validating outcomes; and implementing programs.

The most crucial consideration is usually the people. How does the organization acquire the talent and knowledge necessary to engage in radical innovations, especially participants who have the mindset and inclination to engage in complex and open-ended ventures? The critical part is identifying the essential qualities and characteristics required. Managing radical innovations incorporates multiple disciplines within the organization and relies on a strategic management framework for mapping the way from inception to completion. For the more involved and complicated new-to-the-world technology and new product development programs, corporate leaders typically use high-level program management, project management methodologies, or a combination of the two. The project management approach is often used for the less complicated programs, especially ones that are similar to successful programs of the past.

Radical innovations are highly dependent on the nature of the business environment. Again, context is critical. The starting point is assessing the business environment and the market spaces as they relate to changes and determine how the core capabilities and resources of the organization and enterprise fit the needs and requirements for the future. Visionary strategic leaders have to exhibit due care not to base decisions on just the internal dimension (core competencies and strengths) but on both the external ones (opportunities and challenges) and the internal. The external forces are usually the primary drivers of strategic innovations. Some of the key drivers are:

- Changes in the business environment and market spaces.
- New customer and stakeholder needs, wants, and expectations.
- Intense competitive pressures from world-class companies or emerging competitors.
- New mandates from governments and other stakeholder organizations.
- Dynamic technological changes and/or innovations.
- Enhanced capabilities and offerings from suppliers and related industries.

Strategic leaders use radical innovations to transition and/or transform their corporations. They convince people across the organization and extended enterprise that the vision and strategic direction necessitate new initiatives and actions to realize the aspirations. Visionary strategic leaders generally do not manage the radical innovation programs themselves. They set the tone. They set the agenda, the policies, and the aims, and provide the means and mechanisms. They allow for risk taking and even failures to occur. Strategic leaders link the development programs with the corporate strategies, objectives, and action plans.

Effective strategic leaders persuade people that the radical (strategic) innovations are imperative and that the notion of maintaining the status quo is illusionary, since the external business world is changing dramatically; accelerating forward with new opportunities and challenges. While radical innovations are perceived to be risky, trying to retard change is often more risky and even fool hardy. Many strategic leaders in many different industries lost their preemptive positions over time simply because they failed to keep pace with or ahead of change. For example, AT&T was the premier telephone service provider in the world for most of the twentieth century. Within two decades (1980s and 1990s) corporate leaders lost AT&T's incredible strategic positions as they tried to understand and deal with the enormous changes occurring in the industry. Those changes included deregulation, new (wireless) technologies, the emergence of new market segments, and the evolving competitive scene.

Most importantly, strategic leaders establish the front-end framework for radical innovations to assure the requisite programs are developed and implemented. The framework provides a clear mapping pertaining to how new technology and products programs are initiated by the corporation. Radical innovations involve revolutionary changes. The requisite strategies and actions necessitate creating new realities that are superior to the prevailing ones. Figure 4.5 provides a sense of the essential elements of the framework.

Radical innovations invoke the new world of the tomorrow. Since radical innovations usually take considerable time to identify, define, assess, select, verify, and develop, the focus is on creating new value and achieving long-term success. Based on the strategic direction, the strategic leaders use their imagination and insights to understand context. While this is similar to perspective discussed in previous chapters, the key to success is the full integration of the external aspects like opportunities, challenges, human capital, and know-how that is in the public domain with the internal capabilities, resources, intellectual capital, learning, and principles. The approach is dynamic, involving many iterations. For instance, if the new opportunities are outside of the realm of the capabilities, then the strategic leaders have to determine how to

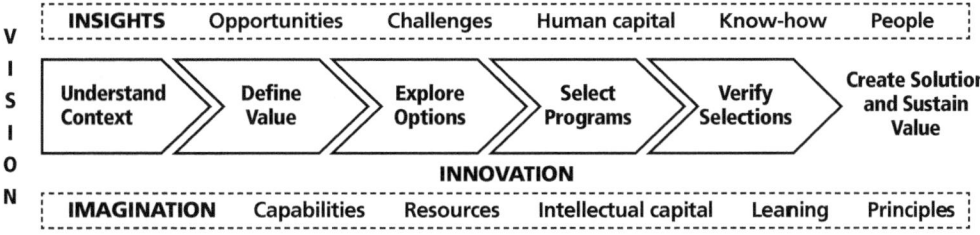

Figure 4.5 The front-end of the radical innovation framework.

acquire the knowledge and affect the learning necessary to proceed when the opportunities are beyond the current competencies and capabilities.

Understanding context allows strategic leaders to define what business value can be created and what are the requisite value propositions. It is crucial to determine what creates value before options are considered. People expect the best value possible. Any proposed solutions must be capable of exceeding customer expectations, achieving the world-class standards, meeting government mandates, and achieving corporate goals. The required specifications include superior performance, high quality, reliability, affordability, exceptional customer benefits, high value, low unit cost, and rapid development time and/or speed to commercialization. Providing exceptional customer benefits means providing an entire package of benefits; customers want solutions, not just products. Performance is a fundamental requirement. It is the ability to deliver what the customers and stakeholders want, need, and expect. However, performance is also relative. It is measured in terms of the cost (the investment) to the customer. Total quality is a fundamental as well that relates to the perceived value provided by the solution. Total perceived quality is the customer's view of the experienced quality. Providing high value is a key to success.

Strategic leaders must explore many options when determining what radical innovations they plan to invest in, if any. The more options strategic leaders have, the more power they have in selecting the right programs. A significant challenge during the development aspects is to ensure that selections and designs have been validated using real-world information and data. During each step of the process, present and future customer and stakeholder needs and wants must be understood and articulated and used as the basis for making key decisions about product features and benefits. The strategic innovation process begins and ends with a strategic perspective of the organization's vision, mission, objectives, and strategies and covers the all of the technical, marketing, production, and financial decisions that have to be made to be successful.

The tools, techniques, and methods allow management to establish the information and data necessary to make informed decisions and to validate the decisions and outcomes. Success depends on people and their abilities and skills. Building a knowledge-based, adaptive, and creative organization is the crux for achieving superior results. Please note that the intent of this chapter is to highlight the strategic aspects. The details of program management are discussed in the next chapter.

Building Relationships with Partners, Customers, and Employees

The Theoretical Underpinnings for Building Corporate Relationships

Companies depend on people and relationships to achieve their goals. People are the contributors and recipients of the solutions and the success of the company. Success means higher stock prices and greater wealth for shareholders, superior solutions for customers and stakeholders, enhanced recognition and rewards for leaders and employees, and better outcomes for society. One of the most important ways for making dramatic strategic improvements is to develop positive relationships with all of essential people related to the company. This includes the direct and indirect relationships with employees and labor unions; customers and stakeholders; suppliers and distributors; partners and allies; government officials and politicians; non-governmental organizations (NGOs) and issue leaders; local and regional communities; financial groups and investors; media organizations and reporters; and the long list of people who touch the corporation and are touched by it.

Corporate leaders have very critical roles and responsibilities in building enduring relationships with all of the contributors and recipients. Corporate leaders have to think about how to create, build, and integrate the complex set of strategic relationships into cohesive value networks and long-term interactions that support each other and contribute to the sustainable success of the whole. While lower-level strategic leaders and operations managers concentrate on the operational, transactional, and financial affairs of business relationships with people and organizations, corporate leaders focus on the strategic linkages and communications, especially those pertaining to the vision, strategic direction, and strategies of the whole corporation. Corporate leaders have the overarching duties to protect corporate goodwill and reputation and to ensure that all of the business connections are in harmony with the vision, grand strategy(s), goals, and values: those that are legal, ethical, and economically and financially sound.

The reputation and goodwill of the company are among its most significant intangibles. Corporate and strategic leaders within the embedded corporate management system have the primary obligations to protect, enhance, and expand these most valuable assets. Such intangibles include the most critical factors in the determination of value of the corporation; they make up a majority of the perceived value of the share price and market capitalization. Perceived value is really based on what people think and believe, especially those in the investment communities and the market spaces around the world. Moreover, corporate value is often based on the perceived risks of the company by investors. Low risks generally means higher value; conversely, high perceived risks translate into lower market valuation. Managing risks is discussed in Chapter 7.

Corporate leaders have to think about creating an enduring and successful company based on the totality of its relationships and positive contributions of all of the value networks. They are driven by making the whole more successful and sustainable, not just by selling products and services, satisfying customers, or obtaining revenues, cash flow, and profits. The latter aspects are important, but they are the usual domain of the general managers of the business units and the managers of the operations and value-delivery systems. Corporate leaders are the purveyors of truths, integrity, factual evidence, and CSR. They have to be the most enthusiastic proponents of honesty, fair dealing, and sustainable outcomes, since they are directly linked with the people who have a significant role in determining market capitalization and are the front line for ensuring that shareholder value is sustained.

Corporate leaders have to be diligent in building and preserving trust and ensuring that corporate and personal ambitions and achievements are holistic, positive, and balanced. Despite recent changes in business philosophies, especially the adoption of SBD and CSR and the related initiatives toward more openness and inclusiveness in overall corporate decision making, actions, and communications, there are still criticisms and skepticisms across many markets, communities, governments, NGOs, other stakeholders, and investors. Great words and good intentions do not necessarily resonant with people unless they are supported by great strategies, actions, and outcomes. It is imperative that corporate leaders provide compelling evidence that the intentions are followed by commitments and compelling actions. Positive actions are much more deterministic than philosophical perspectives, visions, and strategies; people measure success on the basis of solutions and outcomes that are beneficial and sustainable.

People conduct business and accept outcomes (products and services) that they trust. Trustworthiness is the pivotal quality of great companies and VSL. Growth and making money are the result of investments, strategic developments, and VSL, not just because they are the main strategic objectives. Corporate leaders have to prove their integrity through positive actions and ongoing results, not just expressing grandiose visions, platitudes, or wonderful-sounding marketing messages. In a world full of information and millions of skeptics, reality is more easily determined and the lack of integrity is more quickly discovered. Trust is the glue that links the company with all of its contributors and recipients.

Building High-Level Mutually Beneficial External Relationships

Corporate leaders build external connections deemed crucial for the long-term development and growth of the company. They foster and promote mutually beneficial strategic relationships with strategic leaders in other companies, industries, governments, NGOs, and the public, among many others. Strategic relationships are usually long-term associations between entities and organizations that have broad agendas and expectations, such as solving industry-wide problems, dealing with global issues, establishing common standards, helping to develop public policy, and enhancing the common good. Strategic relationships address the well-being of the whole, the overall corporate responsibility to be good citizens, and the desire to achieve sustainable success. Strategic relationships take considerable time and effort to build and often depend on the personal integrity and goodwill of the people involved. It is difficult to articulate how to develop such relationships, and most often they are based on the personalities and amiability of those involved. Moreover, strategic relationships are solidified by the credibility of the individuals and the trust established amongst the participants. They take time and considerable efforts to obtain and maintain, but are always fragile and easily lost, especially if strategic leaders are not honest and forthright.

Corporate leaders form high-level relationships for numerous reasons from simply ensuring good governance to enhancing long-term success. There may be altruistic reasons as well as more materialistic ones. Some of the broader, nonspecific reasons include:[8]

- Preserving the social, economic, and environmental stability of the business world; enhancing social and political life; and protecting the natural environment.
- Understanding the context of the business environment and knowing what is expected before it is required.
- Participating in the development of public policy decisions, global management methods, and industry standards.
- Identifying opportunities for new-to-the-world innovations that promote sustainable success.
- Increasing connectedness to reduce the vulnerabilities associated with uncertainties, globalization, and change, and to improve capabilities and knowledge required to strategically build for the future.
- Promoting ethical behaviors across the spectrum of business, government, NGOs, and social interactions, and engaging in SBD and CSR.
- Providing direct and indirect mechanisms to enhance linkages with shareholders and organizations that provide information, analysis, and control over corporate ownership.

Stability is among the most crucial requirements for sustainable success. Stability in the context of the business world does not mean resisting change, but the maintenance of equilibrium and the avoidance of turbulence, chaos, and catastrophes. Corporate leaders have shared responsibilities with leaders from other endeavors to ensure that harm is avoided, that progress is achieved in all segments of society, and that the natural environment is protected and preserved. Corporate leaders have to collaborate with social, political, economic, and environmental leaders to work on initiatives that improve the quality of life for everyone.

From these broad-based relationships, corporate leaders often have a better understanding of reality and can make better contributions to the common good while promoting the strategies and objectives of their organizations. Corporate leaders can gain significant insights about what is truly happening in the business environment by working and collaborating with a multiplicity of business and non-business leaders who can provide additional information and knowledge about the conditions and trends that shape the future. These interactions allow the company to foresee certain changes before others are even aware of the trends. For example, companies may volunteer some of their executives to work on trade policies such as the new United Nations treaty on electronic trade and commerce.[9] Such strategic leaders gain incredible insights about the provisions of new treaties and have a potential advantage over others who failed to take on such efforts.

Relationships have to be open and honest, and if there are agendas they should be explicitly identified. While altruism may be at the foundation for many of the activities associated with these high-level involvements such as supporting the development of international accords and industry standards, such involvements give corporate leaders insights and new ways to view the business world. Building relationships reinforces corporate leaders' knowledge and understanding of the business environment.

Creative corporate leaders do not craft strategies and action plans in a vacuum. Ideas are taken from all kinds of suggestions and translated into actionable programs with positive strategic outcomes.

Corporate leaders manage high-level contacts with national and international government officials and politicians who influence public policy and the enactment of new laws and directives. These relationships should be based on the broad agendas that are important to both businesses and governments, and not just on specific issues related to producing and selling products. The connections and discussions might set the stage for the development of better approaches for the conduct of business. Corporate leaders should take the high ground and think about the common good that is the shared responsibility of both government officials and business leaders. This is not to say that positive lobbying is inappropriate; it suggests that most of those kinds of activities should be carried out by specialists and lower-level management.

Broad participation in the affairs of business, government, and society allows strategic leaders to help set the agendas rather than being subject to agendas established by others. Such approaches are extremely critical in the development of the acceptable standards of behaviors pertaining to business practices. While some corporate leaders prefer to have governments set the standards through regulations under the assumption that they level the playing field, smart corporate leaders realize that it is in the best interests of their companies to collaborate in establishing the standards for ethical behaviors and acceptable practices. Astute strategic leaders understand the needs for standards and that standards reduce the probability of deviant behaviors. Moreover, they know that deviant behaviors by a few of their peers or competitors, whether criminal or not, affect all businesses and put pressure on government officials to take corrective actions.

Corporate leaders have to stay abreast of changes occurring in other industries, diverse markets, and other countries that are generally not part of the company's primary strategic focus. This is based on the theory that changes anywhere may have repercussions elsewhere, and the consequences may spread across space and time, i.e., global perspectives. With globalization, there are very few isolated events or situations. For instance, the growth of the economic power of China and the low wages paid to people in that country are putting pressures on wages and benefits in the developed countries. Moreover, corporate leaders have to consider the impacts and consequences of outsourcing jobs to China and India as they search the means and mechanisms to lower the costs of their products and services. While there may be immediate advantages by making one's products more affordable, there are also risks associated with such actions in the long term. What happens if emerging companies in developing countries usurp the full production of the end products, making the current providers irrelevant? Will people in the developed countries have the disposable income to be able to buy those more cost-effective products five to ten years from now, if their incomes lag? Too many corporate leaders simply follow the pack; they do what their competitors appear to be doing. In the process, they may be giving away their strategic positions and competitive advantages or failing to understand the implications of the changing business environment.

Visionary strategic leaders obtain answers to such questions from every source they can get; from government officials who track economic trends and from their peers in other industries who may have a shorter time horizon between events, effects, and their consequences. Early warnings and intelligent reflections on the impacts of social, economic, environmental, technological, and market changes across the whole spectrum of the business environment provide corporate leaders with the insights necessary to reduce uncertainties and risks, and to take advantage of such changes rather than be threatened by them. Again, if corporate leaders cast a broader net, they increase their ability to acquire the knowledge and capabilities to manage the changes.

Developing and maintaining effective communications are also prime responsibilities of the corporate leaders. While communications and official disclosures are seemingly straightforward obligations, they are becoming more complicated as the ownership of the global corporations expands and becomes more diverse and transitory. While corporate leaders usually know who owns the shares of their corporation, there may be millions of virtual shareholders including those owning mutual and pension funds. The latter involves large group holdings that can be traded within a short time with new owners replacing the interests of the previous ones. Today, it is more difficult for corporate leaders to know and understand what the shareholders really want. Do they want growth? Do they expect better profitability? Do they understand and value concepts like SBD, CSR, and sustainable success? Meeting the expectations of individual and institutional investors is daunting. The simplest approach is to be open and honest and provide all appropriate information using systematic reporting mechanisms. Astute corporate leaders engender enduring relationships with their contemporaries in government, business, and society and ensure that there is commensurate success.

Reinforcing Internal Relationships

Corporate leaders are ultimately responsible for all of the people within the organization. While most of the internal relationships are structured through the embedded corporate management system, corporate leaders have an overarching responsibility to the whole organization that only they can exercise. Such responsibilities include setting the moral tone,; establishing or reinforcing the principles and corporate values; determining strategic direction; promulgating corporate policies, standards and decision criteria; and recognizing and rewarding achievements. While this list is not comprehensive, it does highlight some of the most crucial elements in developing an effective and dynamic organization. Corporate leaders lead the organization; they do not just manage it. They are all responsible for the proper functioning of the administrative affairs and details.

As previously discussed, corporate leaders have the fiduciary responsibility to protect the assets and well-being of the corporation. Unlike many of the prevailing views about corporate leadership that focus on executive power, pay, and perks, corporate leaders are not the authorities vested with supreme power to reign over their organizations; they are really fiduciaries with the awesome obligations and responsibilities to ensure that the internal relationships are robust with everyone supporting the vision, grand strategies, and goals of the company and all of its relationships with external entities and individuals.

Bill George, former Chairman and Chief Executive Officer (CEO) of Medtronic, advocates the concept of authentic leadership in his book on that subject. George suggests that:[10]

> Authentic leaders genuinely desire to serve others through their leadership. They are more interested in empowering the people they lead to make a difference than in power, money or prestige for themselves. They are guided by qualities of the heart, by passion and compassion, as they are by qualities of the mind.

Corporate leaders may have special roles, but they are not a special caste that deserves privileged status and extraordinary rewards and recognition. To the contrary, they have the duty to build an organization and the relationships within it so that everyone is respected and those who deserve rewards and recognition are acknowledged.

The embedded corporate management system is intended to be an integrated system with everyone in concert with the strategic direction and playing his or her part in achieving sustainable success. People desire dialogue and seek empowerment. They want to be linked to the whole strategic management process, not just part of execution. Similar to the successes achieved with "integrated product development" as articulated in my book, *Product Innovation: Leading Change through Integrated Product Development*, in which participants are concurrently engaged from the first phase of the new product development (NPD) process to commercialization and the end of the NPD program, corporate leaders need to engage the entire organization in the whole experience.[11] Corporate leaders must allow people to participate through open dialogues that solicit input and share information. They have to explain and discuss the opportunities and challenges to be addressed and the logic of the choices available. However, there is no end point; building relationships is a continuum. While many corporate leaders believe that they do not have the time to engage the people, such efforts are often timesavers, since the organization becomes engaged and execution is enhanced.

Many strategic leaders and business scholars state that the implementation and execution of strategic plans are the most difficult and troublesome phases of the strategic management process. Such difficulties are understandable since strategy formulation is often done by a relatively small number of strategic leaders and professionals. There are usually solid relationships among the participants. On the other hand, implementation and execution within the organization are often full of difficulties and failures because the strategic leaders do not create positive relationships with the

BOX 4: KEN IVERSON AND THE TRANSFORMATION OF NUCOR STEEL THROUGH CORPORATE ACTIONS

Ken Iverson (1925–2002) was the president and CEO of Nucor (from 1955 to 1971). It was called Nuclear Corporation of America from 1965 to 1995. He was one of the most exciting, innovative, and successful strategic leaders of the 20th century. Iverson focused on making his company successful using technological innovations and action plans that created positive outcomes using capabilities and resources in the most effective and efficient ways possible. He invested most of the company's assets into productive capital and making and selling the best products using the most productive processes. He also focused on people and built solid relationships with employees and customers in his quest to make Nucor a leader in the steel industry.

Nucor Steel was an automobile manufacturer in the early 1900s. As the R. E. Olds Motor Car Company or REO Motor Car Company, it competed with the hundreds of other automobile companies. REO was founded by Ransom E. Olds, the creator of the Oldsmobile.[a] While REO produced some innovative automobiles, it stopped making automobiles in 1936.[b] Thereafter, its main niche was specialty trucks and buses. It remained in business during the depression and World War II, but its strategic positions were usually tenuous. In 1955, it acquired Nuclear Consultants, Inc., and renamed the combined company Nuclear Corporation of America, Inc. In 1962, the company acquired Vulcraft, a manufacturer of steel joints and girders. It hired Iverson to run Vulcraft. Iverson quickly sold off unproductive businesses and concentrated his efforts on making the remaining steel-making businesses profitable. In 1972, the company was renamed Nucor. In 1980, Nucor became a Fortune 500 company.

Iverson transformed the company using innovative steel manufacturing technologies like electric arc furnaces. He optimized the cost of production using scrap metal as the main ingredients and having highly efficient work practices. Iverson believed that making steel efficiently and profitably was the key to sustainable success. He relentlessly pursued inventing or acquiring innovative ways to make the operations more productive. While Iverson articulated numerous principles and philosophies and had a great sense for crafting business strategies, most of the upfront aspects of CSM was informal. He clearly understood that strategies were worthless without dedicated leadership and strategic implementation. The following are a few of Iverson's insights on leadership and management:[c]

- "When is laying people off a practical or sensible thing to do? Can we expected employees to be loyal or motivated if we lay them off every dip of the economy, while we go on padding our own pockets?
- The people at Nucor stand in sharp, even deviant, contrast, to the status quo [mainstream thinking]. We are big on safety, informality, caring, freedom, respect, equality, and the simple truth. We have little tolerance for politics, pettiness, the fixation on rank and status, and the insensitivity to employees' legitimate needs that people in most big companies endure as a matter of course.
- To my eyes, two of the most fascinating sights to behold are hot metal in motion and a group of people in headlong pursuit of shared purpose. Those images are the essence of NUCOR. They convey how we turned a confused, tired old company on the

brink of bankruptcy into a star player in the resurgence of American steel.
- I believe in long-term survival over short-term profitability. I believe in sharing the pain among all managers and employees. I believe in pushing decision making as far down as it can go. I believe in minimizing distinctions between managers and employees. I believe in paying people for their productivity.
- I believe in keeping things simple.
- Along the way, we did something that is probably more consequential for you: We showed that many of the so-called "necessary evils" of life in corporate America are, in fact, not necessary."
- I've said often that it's not enough to attack hierarchy-you have to destroy it."

These principles were not prescriptions, but fundamental ways of thinking and acting that guided the whole company. As indicated above, they were not policies just for the employees, but ones that applied to management as well. In simple language and common-sense terms, it was clear what Iverson intended. Some of the key aspects are: treat people fairly; be honest and truthful; empower employees; be practical and focus on outcomes; and be straightforward, i.e., don't engage in politics. Iverson expected employees, especially managers, to follow these principles in their everyday actions and decisions and he undauntedly followed them himself. Iverson encouraged employees to follow ethical standards and always do what is proper and correct.

Iverson was a great strategic leader, an innovator, and a business architect. His concept of paying employees based on their productivity and company performance was cutting-edge thinking. He instituted his concept of "sharing the pain" by paying for performance as well as providing hourly wages. His approach allowed Nucor to weather the storms during recessions without employee layoffs or closing facilities. Moreover, Iverson ensured that such approaches were balanced and fair. He established a "pay for performance" plan in which each member of a production team would get a bonus if the team exceeded production standards for the period. He was astute to realize that if he wanted teamwork he had to encourage it through pay for performance. The whole team received the additional compensation or no one did. Moreover, the concept encouraged productivity, but excellent health and safety measures were implemented to assure that employees would not take risks as they tried to increase productivity. Employees were confident that their jobs were secure if they did the work properly and productively. Generally, Nucor's facilities outperformed the integrated mills by a factor of two or three based on labor hours per ton of steel. While Nucor's base pay was less than the typical steel industry worker's, its employees more than made up the difference in compensation through the bonuses. The fundamental basis for the compensation system was to ensure that everyone had a stake in the business. The most brilliant part of the system was to pay employees their bonuses every pay period. While most profit-sharing (bonus) schemes paid employees at end of the year, Iverson wanted employees to have a direct connection between their performance and the pay, hence every pay period. The short-term "win" would encourage employees to achieve even more the next period; or, if they were not successful they would get the feedback and try hard the next time.

Iverson was a technological leader and a great innovator. He was always willing to be at the forefront of cutting-edge technologies. He introduced the mini-mill technology in 1969 based on his belief that success was obtained by having holistic solutions. Electric arc furnaces provided customers in a region with low-cost products at the same time Nucor obtained low-cost raw materials in the form of scrap steel. Nucor was providing environmental benefits through recycling. With his great successes, he was never satisfied with the achievements. Over the course of the 1970s and 1980s, Iverson continuously improved Nucor's strategic positions as it transformed itself from a low-end commodity provider of steel shapes like joists and angles to higher-end products like flat roll coil steel used by the automobile and appliance industries, among many others. Iverson moved Nucor from a seemingly insignificant competitor to a major force in the steel industry. By the time the integrated producers like U.S. Steel and Nippon Steel of Japan recognized Nucor's power, Iverson had already achieved significant competitive advantages that sustained the company for decades in the future.

The development and implementation of thin-slab, continuous flow technology was one of Iverson's and Nucor's greatest achievements. In 1987, Nucor announced that it would build a thin-slab casting facility in Crawfordsville, Indiana. The technology would dramatically change the production of steel by reducing the size of the slab from ten inches to two inches. Conventional casting technology required many processing steps in a roughing mill to reduce the size of the slab to one and one-half inches before the slab could be processed in the finishing mill.[d] Nucor's innovative technology saved energy, time, processing, and costs. The Crawfordsville plant started production in 1989 and it quickly became one of the most competitive U.S. mills in the world.

Iverson had the confidence and courage to take on the giants in his industry. He created a new landscape for producing great solutions and making his customers successful. His attention was geared toward ensuring the most beneficial outcomes possible for all of the contributors and recipients. He deployed corporate assets and resources toward the strategic objectives of the company. During his tenure, the executive office was small with about 19 employees. There were no company planes or big perks for the corporate officers. Iverson focused on creating powerful, value-added positions and future capabilities. These included learning new knowledge and capabilities, creating new businesses, training employees, and developing the future leaders of the company. He knew that developing new solutions, technologies, products, and capabilities would result in powerful means and mechanisms to enhance value for customers and stakeholders, to sustain the success and well-being of the organization and the employees, and to support positive cash flow for future investments and shareholder wealth.

As an aside, Iverson may have been one of the best and most effective strategic leaders in the United States during the second half of the twentieth century. Many of his strategic perspectives and management practices are now used by strategic leaders of cutting-edge companies today. Iverson recognized that everything was important and that solutions had to be holistic, encompassing the social, economic, ethical, technological, and environmental aspects. He made his employees successful as he produced successful outcomes for customers, stakeholders, and shareholders. Most importantly, Iverson put the company first and his own personal goals secondary.

NOTES

a. http://www.nucor.com/story/chapter2/
b. http://www.nps.gov/nhl/DOE_dedesignations/Reo.htm
c. http://www.nucor.com/story/chapter2/
d. http://www.nucor.com/story/chapter5/

people. Implementation and execution depend on people who have the knowledge, commitment, and incentives to engage in achieving the desired outcomes. These elements must be incorporated from the start of formulation, not just at the beginning of the implementation. People want to be part of the solution, but they often realize that they are viewed as tangential, rather than pivotal.

Reflections

Corporate leaders create the strategic framework and systematic approaches to identify and evaluate opportunities, challenges, and constraints faced by businesses in determining their strategic direction and mapping out initiatives and strategic actions. The focus is on discovering, developing, and implementing creative strategies, solutions, and action plans. For most companies, other than start-ups or unsophisticated small companies, crafting corporate strategies within the overall embedded management system is part of ongoing efforts to improve, to transition, and/or to transform the strategic position(s) and future of the company and its business units in light of the business environment, market spaces, and competitive realities. Being proactive in this context implies engaging in positive actions to create value across the whole business enterprise. It also infers mitigating the negative impacts and risks associated with strategies and actions. This ensures that success is distributed fairly and appropriately among contributors and is sustained across time as well. Such a view does not imply that competition is unimportant, but rather involves making competitors less relevant in the pursuit of sustainable success.

Most corporations have well-defined strategic planning constructs and models. These constructs are based on how the corporation manages its business landscapes, and how corporate leaders plan to improve outcomes and performance. The constructs and techniques provided in this chapter pertain to just some of what corporate leaders do in leading change at the corporate level and in fulfilling their responsibilities to the whole corporation.

Corporate leaders build external relationships with critical people and entities in the business environment. They encourage collaboration in achieving mutual success. Likewise, they build solid connections and working relations with leaders, managers, and employees within the corporation. They create a sense of belonging, which turns into a welcoming relationship with all the employees.

Notes

1. Cynthia Montgomery and Michael Porter, *Strategy: Seeking and Securing Competitive Advantage* (Boston, MA: Harvard Business School Press, 1991, p347). The article was by Pierre Wack, entitled, "Scenarios: Uncharted Waters Ahead." It was taken from Harvard Business Review, September–October 1985.
2. Peter Schwartz, *The Art of the Long View* (New York, NY: Currency Paperback, 1996, p4).
3. Id. Based on insights from Schwartz.
4. Kees Van Der Heijden, *Scenarios: The Art of Strategic Conversation* (Hoboken, NJ: John Wiley & Sons, 2005, pp97–98).
5. Id.
6. Paul Raskin, Tariq Banuri, Gilberto Gallopin, Pablo Gutman, Al Hammond, Robert Kates, and Rob Swart, *Great Transition: The Promise and Lure of the Times Ahead* (Boston, MA: Stockholm Environment Institute, 2002)
7. Peter Schwartz, *The Art of the Long View*, (New York, NY: Currency Doubleday, 1991, 1996, pp241-247).
8. David L. Rainey, *Enterprise-wide Strategic Management: Achieving Sustainable Success through Leadership, Strategies and Value Creation* (Cambridge, UK: Cambridge University Press, 2010, p473).
9. UNCITRAL was established by the UN General Assembly and is the core legal body of the United Nations in the field of international trade law. Its mandate is to further the progressive harmonization and unification of the law of international trade. Perhaps its best known is the "UN Convention on Contracts for the International Sale of Goods" (The Vienna Convention.).
10. Bill George, *Authentic Leadership: Rediscovering the Secrets to Creating Lasting Value* (San Francisco, CA: Jossey-Bass, 2003, p12).
11. David L. Rainey, *Product Innovation: Leading Change through Integrated Product Development* (Cambridge, UK: Cambridge University Press, 2005, pp22–27).

References

George, Bill (2003) *Authentic Leadership: Rediscovering the Secrets to Creating Lasting Value.* San Francisco, CA: Jossey-Bass.

Montgomery, Cynthia and Michael Porter (1991) *Strategy: Seeking and Securing Competitive Advantage.* Boston, MA: Harvard Business School Press.

Rainey, David L. (2010) *Enterprise-wide Strategic Management: Achieving Sustainable Success through Leadership, Strategies and Value Creation.* Cambridge, UK: Cambridge University Press.

Rainey, David L. (2005) *Product Innovation: Leading Change through Integrated Product Development.* Cambridge, UK: Cambridge University Press.

Raskin, Paul Tariq Banuri, Gilberto Gallopin, Pablo Gutman, Al Hammond, Robert Kates, and Rob Swart (1996) *Great Transition: The Promise and Lure of the Times Ahead.* Boston, MA: Stockholm Environment Institute.

Schwartz, Peter (1996) *The Art of the Long View.* New York, NY: Currency Paperback.

Van Der Heijden, Kees (2005) *Scenarios: The Art of Strategic Conversation.* Hoboken, NJ: John Wiley & Sons.

5

High-Level Strategic Programs

Management and Implementation

Introduction

High-level strategic programs (HSPs) relate to the implementation and execution of corporate strategies, action plans, and initiatives. HSPs involve the downstream side of corporate strategic management (CSM). They translate the vision, strategic direction, and aspirations of the corporation into desired outcomes through the execution of action plans and the strategic initiatives. Some of the most important HSPs focus on transitions and transformations in leadership and management constructs, systems and structures, business models, innovative technologies, critical new-product developments, enterprise capabilities and resources, and levels of sophistication. While there are many ways to define and develop HSPs, the main purposes are to address and implement the corporate strategies and objectives and make them real through program management, strategic innovations, and high-level actions. Such programs are formulated, implemented, and governed at the corporate level and they are executed and managed by program managers and professionals across the organization, the business units, and their enterprises. Such programs may also be called high-level development programs.

The scope of most HSPs is broad and generally involves dramatically changing the underpinnings, competencies, business portfolios, and management constructs of the corporation. The time horizon is often based on the corporate vision and usually involves many years, if not decades, to reach full maturity and obtain the desired outcomes. Generally, such programs require visionary strategic leadership (VSL) and

CSM with significant commitment and personal direction from corporate executives and the board of directors. Moreover, they require large investments of time, money, and efforts, and there are usually concomitant levels of uncertainties and risks. While most transitional or incremental-type programs are based on business objectives that are generally known to be doable and achievable, HSPs, especially transformational ones, may not be viewed to be achievable when they are conceived and even after they have been initiated by the corporate leaders. They are usually based on audacious objectives and requirements that are deemed to be necessary for positioning the corporation in light of its vision and strategic direction and for assuring it can achieve and sustain the corporate objectives and success.

Transformational programs in the context of CSM generally involve outside-the-box endeavors with great possibilities for changing the strategic positions and competitive advantages of the company. They are often based on broad, occasionally ill-defined aspirations for new-to-the-corporation or even new-to-the-world means and mechanisms for radically enhancing the prospects, the outcomes, and the successes of the corporation and its business units. One of the most famous examples in the political arena is President John F. Kennedy's vision about going to the moon by the end of the 1960s and the U.S. Space Program. Kennedy addressed Congress on May 25, 1961 and articulated the "urgent national needs." In that address, Kennedy made the following comment:[1]

> "I believe this nation should commit itself to achieving the goal, before this decade is out, of landing a man on the Moon and returning him safely to Earth. No single space project [program] in this period will be more impressive to mankind, or more important in the long-range exploration of space; and none will be so difficult or expensive to accomplish."

While President Kennedy surely realized that the United States did not have the means and mechanisms to get to the moon in 1961, the purpose of the address was to reinvigorate a sense of pride in the country and to change political debates from negative perspectives to positive ones. Clearly, the vision of going to the moon was seemingly an impossible dream in 1961. The United States did not have the rockets, the guidance systems, and the technologies to land on the moon and return. Thousands of technologies would have to be developed in order to transform Kennedy's dream into a reality. Based on VSL by President Kennedy, the Congress, and numerous high-level National Aeronautics and Space Administration (NASA) officials, the Apollo Program received the strategic direction and investments it needed to achieve the desired outcomes by the end of the decade. However, the Apollo program was actually a program within a program. It was the third phase of a multiphase space program that was initiated by NASA since its inception in 1958. The U.S. Space Program included three major subprograms and thousands of individual projects to develop all of the technologies, know-how, and capabilities to realize the vision. It took about fifteen years to complete. The Apollo Program was estimated to cost about $20 billion in order to realize its targeted outcomes.[2] Figure 5.1 provides a simple depiction of the early U.S. Space Program subprograms for going to the moon.[3]

The US Space Program—1958 through 1972														
1958	1959	1960	1961	1962	1963	1964	1965	1966	1967	1968	1969	1970	1971	1972
1st Program: Mercury Initiated in 1958 and completed in 1963, Mercury put the first U.S. man in space.														
				2nd Program: Gemini Announced in January 1962, [ended 1966], Gemini involved 12 flights; two unmanned flight tests.										
			3rd Program: Apollo The Apollo Program [1961 through 1972] included a large number of un-crewed test missions and 11 crewed missions. The 11 crewed missions include two Earth-orbiting missions, two lunar-orbiting missions, a lunar swing-by and six Moon-landing missions.												

Figure 5.1 US Space program outline.

The framework for HSPs includes strategic logic, program implementation, and program execution. It also includes program management and program evaluation over the entire scope of the program. Such programs are intended to be multifaceted and have long-term durations. They may include many subprograms or projects within a general charter or theme and across many business units. HSPs focus on the strategic logic of the vision and corporate strategies and are generally how corporate leaders engage in the implementation and execution of their corporate strategic plans and initiatives. For instance, initiating a sustainable business development (SBD) program and transforming a company to higher levels of sophistication are examples of HSPs that take considerable time to define, design, develop, implement, execute, and manage; ones that usually affect the whole company. Such strategic action plans and/or initiatives may unfold over twenty years as the corporation reinvents itself and reaches out to higher and higher strategic positions and capabilities. The more complicated and challenging the requirements are, the more likely corporate leaders have to use HSPs as the vehicles for obtaining the desired outcomes and performance.

Imagine what strategic leaders at a company with poor quality have to do to develop and implement a six-sigma quality (3.4 defects per million) program. If the company is producing ten thousand defects per million opportunities for defects (1 in 100), it would be a big leap forward to obtain six sigma quality (more than a thousand-fold improvement) in a single step. Motorola's and General Electric's (GE) "Design for Six Sigma" programs are examples of HSPs that took more than a decade to realize and required several logical subprograms that each involved 10X improvements. For instance, if corporation is presently at one defect per hundred opportunities for defects and the organization can be expected to make 10X improvements over five years, then it will require three subprograms to achieve a quality level of about ten defects per million. If each subprogram takes five years to reach the 10X improvements, then the overall program requires fifteen years to realize the desired outcome(s). There are significant benefits to dividing the overall program into subprograms. One of the most important considerations is that people generally respond better to well-defined targets that are closer to the present realities. Moreover, most people need to be periodically recognized and rewarded based on achieving their goals and objectives. Many participants have significant difficulties contemplating what has to be done to make huge improvements and even quantum or radical leaps over an extended period of time during which they have little sense whether they can ultimately accomplish the requisite requirements and obtain the strategic objectives. Therefore, subprograms within the overarching program make strategic sense.

This chapter examines the elements and subelements associated with program management and implementation, while the next chapter includes elements and subelements pertaining to program execution and program evaluation. This chapter includes the following main topics:

- Defining the underpinnings and framework of program management
- Developing the means and mechanisms for program selection, definition, and design.

Program Management

General Perspectives on Program Management

A HSP is one that is intended to transition or transform the company or some significant strategic position(s) within it to realize the vision, to affect positively the strategic direction, and/or to develop and initiate high-level/cutting-edge organizational capabilities and management constructs that provide sustainable competitive advantages. Such a program results in a transformation to higher levels of sophistication, allowing the corporation to outperform its peers and competitors across the external dimensions and/or with respect to critical positions or strategic areas.

Corporations initiate a HSP to create new value and cutting-edge solutions for customers, stakeholders, shareholders, and others the corporation affects and impacts. A solution is a multifaceted construct that includes the product, the service, the underlying technology(s), and all of the tangible and intangible elements of the system(s) and methods that accompany it. It is temporal as well as physical and psychological. A solution requires the full integration with all of the complementary products, supporting entities, and external support systems. It also includes all of the means and mechanisms of the corporation and its business units to exceed the needs and expectations of the business environment and market spaces.

The underlying intent of a HSP is to expand opportunities and to find new means and mechanisms for obtaining unique positions, for realizing the social, economic, ethical, technological, environmental, and market space opportunities and for overcoming or eliminating the challenges, limitations, and constraints. It is about sustaining success among other highly desirable outcomes.

Program management requires an entrepreneurial spirit and cooperation among all participants. It is typically based on the corporate leadership, the knowledge, and capabilities of the participants, and the contributions of the entire business enterprise, i.e., the internal capabilities and resources and those of the key external contributors and recipients. Even in those cases where the corporation is able to implement, execute, and manage the whole program on its own, it may still need the cooperation and contributions of its partners, allies, and others in the value networks to fulfill the requirements of the external dimensions—especially in providing complementary products and services and in ensuring that the infrastructure is sound and suitable.

HSPs are huge undertakings that are intended to provide incredible positive effects and outcomes for supporting and realizing sustainable success. Table 5.1 provides some examples.

The types of programs listed are actually only a small representation of the numerous ways in which high-level corporate/strategic programs can be categorized. It is important that such programs involve major transformations or significant transitions to more sophisticated capabilities and realities and are not just incremental improvements to the existing products, processes, positions, or management constructs; those are the domains of lower-level strategic management and operations.

HSPs are usually very broad with long time horizons requiring substantial investments and large numbers of participants. They often consist of several subprograms and/or many individual projects that may be part of the phases of the overall program. In certain situations, a HSP may be initiated before all of the plans, methods, and resources are fully articulated and mapped out. There may be significant uncertainties about many of the details pertaining to what has to be done and how to accomplish all of the tasks and activities. Furthermore, strategic leaders may be unsure about whether the program is even feasible and what it will take to complete all of the actions and activities during the later phases, stages, projects, or elements. The basis for determining what has to be done during the "out years" often depends on the outcomes (the successes and failures) of earlier efforts.

Program management and implementation are based on future requirements and expectations, not just on the prevailing situations and circumstances. Insights are necessary to determine what the business environment is likely to be at some time in the future as well as what it is today. Given that the business world is changing rapidly, strategic leaders have to contemplate what changes they expect to occur over the course of a program. For instance, strategic leaders might decide to initiate a SBD program and they determine that they want their program to mirror what the leading companies in the Dow Jones Sustainability Index (DJSI) like Unilever and BMW have done. According to the DJSI, Unilever and BMW were the super-sector leaders in food and beverage and automobiles, respectively, in 2010/2011. While such program specifications seem to make sense, if such a program requires ten years to achieve the transformation and desired outcomes, the resulting position(s) may be far less than what is necessary to succeed in 2024 assuming the other companies like Unilever and BMW continue to make significant progress in their pursuit of SBD and sustainability. The business world does not stand still and the requirements and expectations continue to change over

TABLE 5.1 Examples of Types of High-Level Strategic Programs

Focus	Corporate	Business Units/Enterprises
Strategic Positions	• Creating a new-to-the-world business venture for providing solutions to people in emerging markets, i.e., addressing new market spaces. • Becoming a global corporation by expanding out of the home (national) markets to include strategic positions in international markets. • Building powerful and enduring strategic relationships with customers, stakeholders, partners, allies, and all contributors. • Instituting a framework that integrates all elements into a holistic value system that integrates all strategies, actions, decisions, and activities, i.e., fully integrated.	• Expanding the scope of existing business units to include the whole of their extended enterprises from the origins of the raw materials to end-of-life considerations. • Preempting competition by creating new-to-the-world solutions that provide exceptional value propositions and value delivery. • Integrating the entities of the extended enterprise into the business models. • Instituting a "cradle-to-grave" approach and establishing life cycle assessment as a prelude to strategic decision making and value creation; reducing the potential for defects and difficulties.
Management Constructs	• Integrating SBD and sustainability as the philosophical and practical underpinning for leading change and managing the corporation. • Transforming the corporation into a more sophisticated and sustainable entity. • Adopting the principles and methods of corporate social responsibility for the management of the corporation. • Integrating a risk management system across the corporate to mitigate risks and vulnerabilities. • Creating corporate-wide new constructs for quality management, environment, health and safety management, and energy management. • Developing a customer relationship management system across the corporation.	• Providing leadership and management development training and education to dramatically enhance the intellectual capital, talent, and capabilities of the organization. • Creating a framework for improving resource efficiency and utilization. • Establishing a formal supply chain management system to improve outcomes and impact the challenges associated with outsourcing. • Incorporating the highest standards of ethics and social responsibility across the enterprise. • Instituting performance and evaluation and auditing systems to track the business units. • Establishing systems to track regulatory compliance by the extended enterprise.
Strategic Innovations	• Using corporate research and development to develop new technologies that provide opportunities to create new businesses. • Providing solutions for people in developing countries and ensuring proper treatment.	• Creating new-to-the world products that eliminate the negative aspects of existing products and process. • Creating clean technology systems that eliminate the negative aspects of existing technologies.

time. However, while the pathway to the ultimate success is uncertain and circuitous, the ultimate results are somewhat predictable since they are based on the strategic objectives and aspirations set forth during strategic formulation.

The body of knowledge required to execute such programs often has to be developed concurrently with the actions and activities of the actual implementation. While this may be disconcerting for many leaders, managers, and practitioners, it is often impossible to have all of the specifications spelled out at the beginning, especially if one is engaged in developing new-to-the-world outcomes. Thus, leading change and learning are two critical aspects of the overall program. In the current business world, internal and external conditions and requirements change quickly. This is what distinguishes program management from project management. Generally, project management necessitates a precise mapping of the flow of the activities from beginning to completion. However, for HSPs, such perspectives may not be possible. Strategic leaders have to deal with uncertainties and the lack of knowledge. Care must be taken to provide the flexibility to meet unexpected situations or changes.

Project Management Versus Program Management

Project management is a well-established and full-articulated management construct for developing and managing non-repetitive, temporary endeavors that produce one-of-a-kind or unique outcomes. Projects usually have defined starting and ending points, i.e., there is an established time frame. Projects produce outcomes in which the actions, activities, and execution have to be determined for each project. Such desired outcomes include designing a new product or service; constructing a building or a large device like a ship; developing a new-to-the world technology; reorganizing a business unit; starting a new business venture, etc.

Project management involves the practical and managerial aspects of how to define, plan, develop, analyze, manage, implement, and control projects and obtain the desired results in today's turbulent business environment. It includes principles, philosophies, concepts, know-how, skills, techniques, and processes. It also includes all of the qualitative and quantitative methods, techniques, and management constructs for assuring successful outcomes. Project management provides: (1) a comprehensive framework for selecting, defining, organizing, designing, developing, managing, and evaluating projects; (2) a clear view of the roles and responsibilities of the key participants and connections and interrelationships among them; and, (3) systematic pathways for achieving and measuring results on a timely basis. The concept of a framework was articulated by Steven Wheelwright and Kim Clark in their book, *Revolutionizing Product Development*.[4]

> Our research on and experience with firms that have superior development capabilities suggest that a much more comprehensive framework for a development strategy [project] provides a far more secure foundation for an individual project. This framework addresses the four main purposes:

- Creating, defining, and selecting a set of development projects that will provide superior products and processes.
- Integrating and coordinating functional tasks, technical tasks, and organizational units involved in development activities over time.
- Managing development efforts so they converge to achieve business purposes as effectively and efficiently as possible.
- Creating and improving the capabilities needed to make development a competitive advantage over the long term.

Project management methods answer the "why, what, when, who, where, and how" questions when planning, organizing, directing, scheduling, controlling, and monitoring projects. They provide an overview of the strategic aspects, the work elements and tasks, the planning methods, the estimating tools, and the implementation processes. The strategic and organizational aspects of project management focus on the development and execution of the project. Project management involves a planned and disciplined approach for managing the transition from project selection and definition to execution and completion. Project planning and development require effective intellectual capital from project leaders and practitioners to systematically think through the whole scope and time frame of a project from start to finish.

Project Management Institute's (PMI) *A Guide to the Project Management Body of Knowledge* is an excellent source on project management techniques. PMI's body of knowledge articulates the main elements of project management. While the intention herein is not to elucidate all of the elements and subelements of project management, the purpose is to indicate some of the similarities and differences between project management and HSP management.

According to PMI, project management includes five main processes: initiating, planning, executing, monitoring, controlling and closing.[5] Each of the processes runs over some period of time, but the activities involved usually depend on the phases of the project. For instance, most of the planning is done fairly early in a project and closing is at the end, while controlling runs throughout. Table 5.2 provides a summary of the elements and subelements:[6] Project integration is basically the defining and organizing element that includes determining project plans and structuring the organization and participants. Project integration also includes the stated purposes, philosophies, guidelines, policies, and practices. The philosophies specify the values and cultural aspects, senior management's expectations, the project's fit into the overall strategic context, and the compliance with laws and regulations and government and industry standards.

Project scope is a critical element that lies at the heart of project management. Unlike repetitive work using process management in which the activities and the flow thereof are well established and predetermined, the scope of a project has to be meticulously determined, defined, mapped out, and validated to ensure that all requisite requirements and the related tasks are identified and structured. Along with determining the scope, scheduling the activities is one of the most critical elements.

TABLE 5.2 PMI's Elements and Subelements of Project Management

Project Management				
4. Project Integration Management	**5. Project Scope Management**	**6. Project Time Management**	**7. Project Cost Management**	**8. Project Quality Management**
4.1 Develop Project Charter 4.2 Develop Project Management Plan 4.3 Direct and Manage Project Execution 4.4 Monitor and Control Project Work 4.5 Perform Integrated Change Control 4.6 Close Project or Phase	5.1 Collect Requirements 5.2 Define Scope 5.3 Create WBS [work breakdown structure] 5.4 Verify Scope 5.5 Control Scope	6.1 Define Activities 6.2 Sequence Activities 6.3 Estimate Activity Resources 6.4 Estimate Activity Durations 6.5 Develop Schedule 6.6 Control Schedule	7.1 Estimate Costs 7.2 Determine Budget 7.3 Control Costs	8.1 Plan Quality 8.2 Perform Quality Assurance 8.3 Perform Quality Control
9. Project Human Resource Management	**10. Project Communications Management**	**11. Project Risk Management**	**12. Project Procurement Management**	
9.1 Develop Human Resource Plan 9.2 Acquire Project Team 9.3 Develop Project Team 9.4 Manage Project Team	10.1 Identify Stakeholders 10.2 Plan Communications 10.3 Distribute Information 10.4 Manage Stakeholder Expectations 10.5 Report Performance	11.1 Plan Risk Management 11.2 Identify Risks 11.3 Perform Qualitative Risk Analysis 11.4 Perform Quantitative Risk Analysis 11.5 Plan Risk Responses 11.6 Monitor and Control Risks	12.1 Plan Procurements 12.2 Conduct Procurements 12.3 Administer Procurements 12.4 Close Procurements	

Determining the project time line, especially the expected start and finish dates, is a critical decision. Project scheduling involves identifying and characterizing the statement of work, project specifications, and work breakdown structure. It includes approaches and practices such as critical path method (CPM) and project evaluation review technique (PERT). The following are some of the key subelements: [7]

- *Activity definition*—identifying the specific activities that must be performed to produce the various project deliverables
- *Activity sequencing*—identifying and documenting interactivity dependencies
- *Activity duration estimating*—estimating the number of work periods required for completing individual activities
- *Schedule development*—analyzing activity sequencing, activity duration, and resource requirements to create the schedule

The activity definition step requires input from all of the participants playing significant roles in the project or program. With a clear understanding of the activities, the next step is to properly sequence the activities within each phase and throughout the project. The general approach is to maximize the number of concurrent activities to speed up the project. However, there are real limitations to the number of activities that can be performed on a concurrent basis, since some tasks cannot be started until predecessor activities have been completed. For example, testing or validation steps have to follow the design and development steps. The identification of the activities and the sequencing of activities necessitate estimating the time required for performing the activities. By starting as many activities as early as possible, the total time to complete the program can be theoretically minimized. Once the activities are sequenced and the time required for completing the activities have been estimated, the entire schedule of all activities is available. The next step is the determination of the required resources and the assignment of participants to ensure that the activities are performed and the deliverables are obtained. Resource planning includes determining the required resources (people, money, equipment, and materials) and the quantities of each necessary to perform the activities. Cost estimates and budgets are then prepared for the activities and the whole project, respectively. Thus, the project is mapped out in terms of scope, activities, sequencing, time estimation, schedule development, resource planning, and budgets. Assigning participants and developing the actual calendar schedule are often the most crucial aspects. The intent is to provide a clear understanding of the flow of required elements and subelements of the requisite processes for the participants and to ensure that the organization has or can obtain the appropriate resources to execute and complete the project.

Project management includes project planning and specifies how to execute the project. It takes a comprehensive view of all of the participants and their needs, interrelationships, and contributions. This includes managing the participants, the supply chain contributions, quality, communications, and risks. Project management also includes the principles, philosophies, decision-making authority, and responsibilities of the project manager(s) and senior professionals. Such elements specify the values and cultural aspects, the expectations of strategic leaders, the fit of the project into the overall strategic context, and the fundamental expectations in terms of compliance with laws and regulations, government standards, and continuous improvement. Project management requires tracking results on a continuous basis using performance measures to evaluate achieving the proper the balance required between costs, timing, quality, and resources requirements.

Program management is generally more aligned with the strategic direction of the corporation and the corporate objectives and strategies. HSPs are among the highest level of importance for ensuring that the corporate strategies and objectives are put into effect, are managed and controlled properly, and the desired outcomes are realized. Corporate leaders are the champions, the sponsors, and the chief architects of HSPs, providing leadership, guidance, investments, direction, and oversight. They are among the most important contributors, especially through the strategic logic phase. HSPs involve the critical elements of planning, organizing, directing, designing, developing, demonstrating, and deploying. They require incredible insights, imagination, creativity, and thoroughness.

Gary Hamel, in his book, *Leading the Revolution*, suggests several design rules for programs involving transformations and/or strategic innovations:[8] (1) unreasonable expectations; (2) elastic business definition; (3) a cause, not a business; (4) new voices; (5) an open market for ideas; (6) an open market for capital; (7) an open market for talent; (8) low-risk experimentation; (9) cellular division; and, (10) personal wealth accumulation. While Hamel has his own interpretations of what the design rules mean, they fit and are appropriate for HSPs. Unreasonable expectations imply that out-of-the-box achievements can be realized and that the strategic objectives may not be doable or achievable at inception, but nevertheless reasonable from a long-term perspective. Strategic leaders and visionaries can often contemplate what the future might look like even though some aspects may not be possible in today's business world. An elastic definition of the business supports out-of-the-box thinking. While out-of-the-box thinking necessitates VSL, the broader horizons in both scope and time provide opportunities to create new realities to achieve success. HSPs may involve reinventing the foundations and structures of the corporation to become more capable and sophisticated and to reach new levels of success. Most importantly, they involve the opening of new venues for all contributors and recipients to voice their global perspectives and offer new ways of achieving success. Bringing in new voices enriches creativity, even if most suggestions are not viable or possible given the realities. Breaking out of the old way of thinking is a fundamental ingredient in managing strategic innovation, developing new programs, and even creating new paradigms. Engaging in low-risk experiments involving smaller portions of the whole program allows innovation to surface without risking everything. The inherent risks of taking on HSPs can be moderated by subdividing the efforts into smaller subprograms or projects that can be implemented, tested, and validated before proceeding to the next elements or subelements.

Table 5.3 provides a comparison between some of the aspects of project management and program management. The table is not intended to be comprehensive and

TABLE 5.3 Comparison Between Project Management and Program Management

	Project Management	Program Management
Leadership	Projects are managed by well-educated and knowledgeable project managers who have multidisciplinary skills and capabilities. Project managers report to program managers or strategic leaders. They often have limited authority within the scope of their projects. Their flexibility is constrained by the budgets and requisite control mechanisms.	Programs are usually led by high-level strategic leaders of the company who have broad capabilities and knowledge across many disciplines and the business environment. They have the authority and flexibility to make strategic decisions for proceeding in new directions. Broad changes are based on approvals of the company officials and/or board of directors.
Objectives	The objectives are usually stipulated based on the specifications of the projects and the expected outcomes. They are relatively easy to determine and most contributors can understand the meaning of the objectives.	The objectives are high-level strategic goals of the company that are intended to make significant contributions to the vision and strategic direction. They tend to be more open-ended with flexibility to accommodate new aspects as the program develops.
Scope	The scope is determined based on the objectives and expected outcomes and the resources committed to the project. The scope is usually well-defined and controlled to avoid "scope creep," adding requirements as time proceeds.	The expected scope is very difficult to precisely determine and it often takes certain achievements and/or failures to map out the scope, at least for the front-end elements. Programs may be started before the scope and expected outcomes are fully articulated.
Duration	Time frame is generally within well-specified start dates and end dates. Time is usually of the essence. Time overruns are viewed as negatives that often cost money and result in less advantageous positions in the future. Duration is usually five years or so.	Time frame is less crucial with flexibility in the start date. The right timing is more important than specific dates. Likewise the completion of the program is less definitive and in certain cases the program goes on well beyond the expected duration. Duration may be ten to fifteen years or longer.
Investment	The investment or cost of the project is usually estimated within a reasonable degree of accuracy and is controlled during execution. Cost overruns are to be avoided and often lead to significant problems. Budgets are used as control mechanisms.	The investments and resources required to define, design, and execute the program are extremely difficult to estimate. Programs are often started without having a definitive understanding of the total costs. Budgets may be prepared on an annual or periodic basis rather than on a program basis.
Expected Outcomes	The expected outcomes are based on the objectives and are fairly well known within the context of the business environment and the company. Outcomes may be improvements upon the prevailing norms, but it is rare when they exceed all expectations and lead to a higher level of sophistication. They are usually in line with the concept of continuous improvement.	The expected outcomes are often uncertain with a high degree of variability. Expected outcomes are based on making transitions or transformations to richer realities. There is the potential for achieving extraordinary outcomes that are exciting and ones that exceed all expectations. On the other hand, outcomes may be less than what is desirable and may even result in great failures.

there are many actual differences in the real world. Moreover, modest strategic program management may be just high-level projects as discussed.

HSPs provide the means and mechanisms to break out of extremely competitive situations. As time marches on and the mainstream of business entities become more capable, the prevailing methods and management constructs become generic approaches that may also be obsolete. Using generic methods may cause a company's strategic position(s) to decline and, in some cases, such positions may become untenable. Failing to innovate and make transformations at a level sufficient to exceed the dictates of the business environment and the market spaces is often a prescription for disaster. One of the most frequent strategic mistakes is just to rely on continuous improvements, incremental innovations, and simple transitions.

Generally, the most critical reasons and requirements for HSPs are mapped out during strategic formulation. Strategic formulation provides: (1) why the programs are important; (2) what has to be done; (3) what the objectives are; (4) who is responsible for implementation; (5) what are the expected outcomes; and, (6) what the investment is expected to be. As stated above, the details are often open-ended and much of the definitive decision making is done during program implementation. One of the most critical responsibilities of the strategic leaders is to ensure that the program organization and the participants have the necessary and appropriate capabilities and resources to perform. In particular, resource allocation is a major responsibility of senior management that is often ill-defined and poorly managed. Without resources and capable people, strategic plans and program implementation are useless. Many strategic leaders want exceptional results, extraordinary performance, and great success, but fail to do their part in providing the necessary ingredients to realize those outcomes.

The Linkages Between Strategy Formulation and Program Management

Strategic leaders are ultimately responsible for the selection, definition, design, development, deployment, and management of HSPs. Strategic programs bridge the gap between strategy formulation and strategy implementation, especially for strategic innovations and transformations. Strategic leaders ensure that the selected programs fit the strategic logic and strategic direction and that the expected outcomes that are expected years into the future are in concert with the corporate aspirations and objectives. However, such expectations are not simple or easy to contemplate, never mind to actually achieve. It is exceptionally challenging to foresee all of the possible changes that might occur over an extended time frame. Moreover, it is difficult to determine all of the implications of the potential changes and to manage all of the program elements and subelements that have to be executed to achieve the desired results.

HSPs can be framed in four main parts of which there are many subprograms, subelements, and subparts; some may be individual projects. The four parts include the upfront strategy formulation involving strategic direction; overall program management involving leadership, organizational structure, and evaluation; program implementation involving program selection, definition, and design; and program execution involving program development, demonstration, and deployment. Each is essential for achieving the right outcomes and directing the organization toward the realization of superior and sustainable positions at higher levels of sophistication. Figure 5.2 depicts the linkages between the four parts.

Strategic formulation and strategic logic are usually determined whether or not there are HSPs. They include all of the leadership and management constructs discussed in the first four chapters of this book, including determining the vision, selecting objectives, crafting strategies, and preparing strategic plans, among numerous others. Strategic implementation may include selecting and detailing one or more HSPs. It may also include other action plans and lower-level programs and projects. Strategic leaders often delegate most of the actual execution of the latter-type programs to functional and project managers. They are responsible for obtaining the near-term objectives and strategies pertaining to the business units.

Program selection, definition, and design are the critical elements for establishing HSPs and determining the critical subelements and projects thereof. Unlike simple incremental innovations and processes related to ongoing operations, it may take a considerable amount of time and effort to reach an understanding and consensus of what the options and potential candidates are. While time is always crucial in CSM and for VSL, sufficient time must be available to ensure that the best decisions are made. In many cases, elaborate research and benchmarking have to be done to determine the state-of-the-art and the best practices pertaining to the principal subject matters involving the options or candidates for HSPs. It is important that strategic leaders and the participants learn as much and as quickly as possible before they get involved in the selecting, designing, and developing HSPs. While program selection, definition, and design involve mostly intellectual and conceptual actions and decisions, it may take many months and even years to come to a full determination of what are the best options, what is the logic of each, and what is necessary in terms of

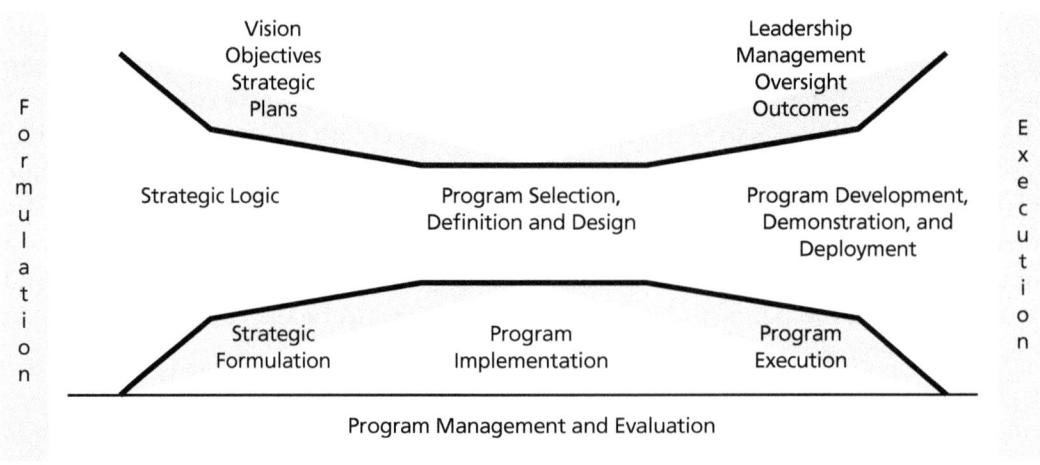

Figure 5.2 Linkages between strategy formulation and program management.[9]

actions, activities, and outcomes to obtain the objectives. The main tensions include knowing what is required and becoming knowledgeable through learning what may be required, executing with speed and being thorough, obtaining short-term results and ensuring long-term success, making money and investing into the future, focusing on core competencies and inventing new ones, and satisfying customers and stakeholders and finding solutions for potential customers. In every instance, it is not an "either-or" proposition; great outcomes depend on achieving all facets of the requirements and objectives, i.e., speed and thoroughness, short-term and long-term results, etc.

Program implementation and program execution are multifaceted. They involve complicated management constructs that have to be developed and learned along the pathways to achievements and successes. The former involves selection, definition, and design. It usually involves near-term actions and decisions. The program execution involves development, demonstration/incubation, and deployment. Both include having the methods, techniques, and tools that may have to be developed along the ways as strategic leaders, program managers, and participants proceed toward their often fuzzy destinations. Program implementation is discussed in more detail in the next section and its elements and main subelements are shown in Figure 5.3. Program execution is covered in the next chapter with the main elements and subelements shown in Figure 6.1.

Program management and evaluation are the crux for leading HSPs and making the essential decisions, especially by the strategic leaders and the program managers. Strategic leaders have the ongoing responsibility to ensure that programs are properly established, managed, and controlled and that results are evaluated to provide feedback and take corrective actions, if necessary. HSPs involve high risks and require ongoing leadership and innovations to keep pace or even stay ahead of changes in the business environment. Most importantly, strategic leaders cannot delegate their responsibilities for providing leadership, direction, guidance, and oversight to program managers and project managers. They have to be directly involved in program implementation and execution to inspire the participants year after year, to engage in organization learning, change management, risk mitigation, and program evaluation, and to assure success. Program management is embedded within the means and mechanisms to implement and execute the program.

Program Implementation

Framework for Selecting, Defining, and Designing High-Level Strategic Programs

Based on the strategic formulation and strategic direction, strategic leaders often have to choose one or more HSPs, if the corporation plans to achieve the desired transitions and transformations in its businesses, strategic positions, organizational capabilities, and corporate performance. Usually, there are many options available to make dramatic improvements and quantum leaps forward to become more sophisticated with higher-level competencies, solutions, systems, structures, and relationships.

One of the keys to success is to select the right HSPs that will lead to highly-rewarding outcomes in the future; ones based on the corporation's aspirations, objectives, capabilities, and resources. However, great care has to be exhibited in selecting, defining, and designing the appropriate program(s) that are both stretches for the organization and achievable in the long term. This means that the right HSPs may not be doable in the present, but given learning, new knowledge, enhanced organizational capabilities, and determination, the desired outcomes can be realized in the future. This also involves some of the aforementioned tensions. If strategic leaders are too timid, they may tend to choose strategic programs based on conventional perspectives that advocate what the objectives and criteria should be: specific, measurable, achievable, realistic, and time-based (often called SMART). While such objectives and/or criteria may facilitate do-ability, they may actually limit the levels of sophistication and achievements necessary to realize sustainable success that propels the corporation successfully in the future. In *Built to Last: Successful Habits of Visionary Companies,* James C. Collins and Jerry I. Porras suggest that corporations have to use "Big Hairy Audacious Goals" (BHAG).[10] Collins and Porras believe that BHAG are "tangible, energizing and highly focused."[11] Such goals and the related criteria not only set the stage for what has to be accomplished, but serve as the means and mechanisms to inspire people to achieve great outcomes that were viewed to be impossible at the inception of the program. The modern business world is full of examples of strategic outcomes that were once thought to be impossible like video over the telephone, small computers (i.e., personal computers), the Internet, and the European Union—history has shown otherwise.

Program implementation is based on the underpinning of strategic logic and consists of three main elements with numerous subelements. The main elements are: selection, definition and design. Figure 5.3 provides a simplified framework identifying the key elements and subelements of program implementation. They are the precursors to program execution: development, demonstration/incubation, and deployment. While the upfront elements can be accomplished in a relatively short time frame, they require incredible intellectual capital and leadership from strategic leaders, program managers, and participants.

The discussions in this section focus on only some of the main subelements of program selection, definition, and design. It would take a book on program management to discuss all of the subelements and their implications. While program selection and definition can be integrated into one element, there are benefits for having separate elements, especially if selection includes many candidates, most of which are expected to be eliminated during a screening process. It is not very efficient and effective to fully define all of the candidates, if only a relatively small number of them might become viable programs. Furthermore, certain candidates may take a considerable amount of time and effort to fully articulate. While other candidates might be easier to construct and articulate, possibly delaying decision making for all of the candidates, if the screening process is based on a comparative assessment of all of the candidates. This is especially a concern if strategic leaders desire to weigh all of the potential programs at a specific point of time rather than the more flexible approach of screening and selecting candidates on an ongoing basis, somewhat independent of the other candidates.

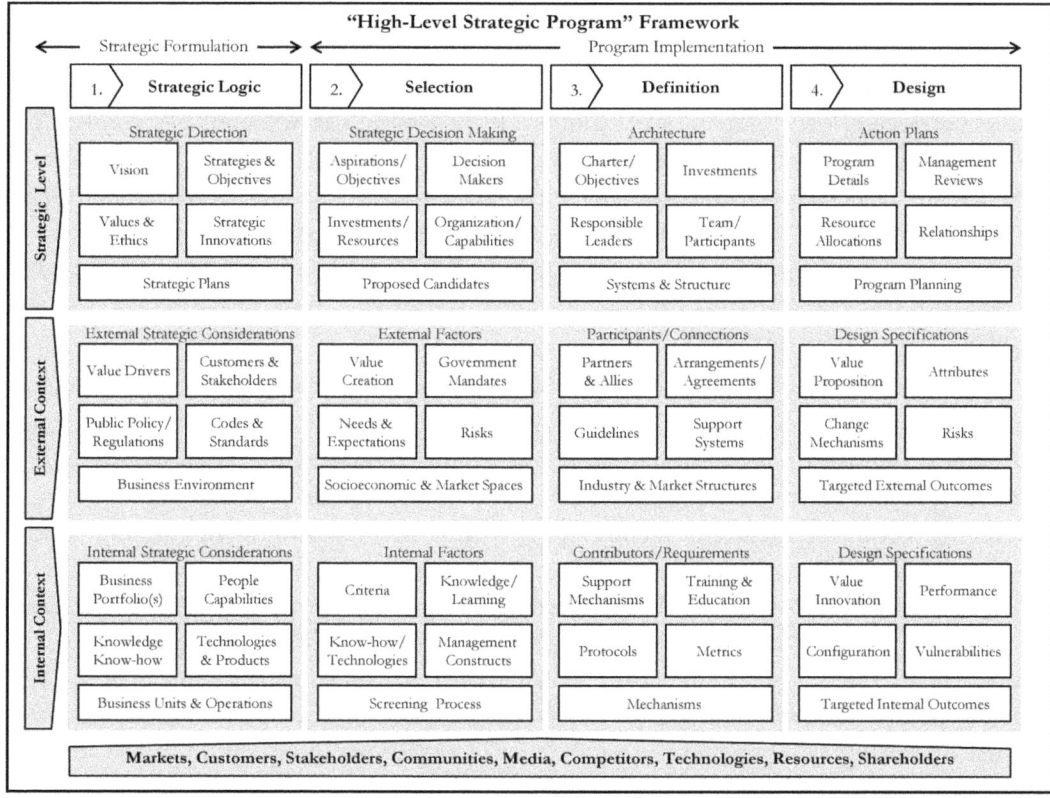

Figure 5.3 Key elements and subelements of program implementation.

While there may not be a normative approach, large global corporations that are well endowed with significant capabilities, resources, and money may tend to select all viable and worthwhile candidates independently. Small- and medium-size enterprises (SMEs) may tend to screen all candidates at one time, since they may only be able to select one or two potential programs. Moreover, the size, investment, complexity, and speed of the potential program(s) also play significant roles in the actual decision making. Even the most well-endowed corporations have constraints and limitations in terms of what is reasonable to undertake.

Definition involves mapping out the essentials of the systems and structures and the means and mechanisms necessary for implementing the specific program. Design includes program planning, determining the targeted external and internal outcomes, and how the actions and activities are expected to flow. It includes the program plans and specifications.

Screening and Selecting the Most Attractive Candidates

Program selection is an art form that involves high-level strategic decision making and good and wise judgment. The ultimate selection decisions are usually made by corporate leaders with input and insights from other strategic leaders and professionals in the organization. It is desirable to obtain consensus among the leaders and contributors, but ultimate decisions have to be rendered. Occasionally the corporate leaders have to have the courage to select the appropriate program(s) and move forward. While corporate leaders may have to make the choices, the selected program(s) are rarely locked in concrete, especially during the selection, definition, and design elements. If the choice(s) proves to be untenable or less valuable as the program(s) proceed toward program execution, changes can be made, including redesigning or terminating the program(s). However, the intent of program selection is to assure that all facets of the external and internal contexts have been explored and assessed and that the best choices are made.

Generally, strategic leaders and program managers, with the assistance of senior professionals, prepare a list of potential candidates. In many cases, the potential candidates are directly related to the strategic logic and the corporate strategic plan developed during strategic formulation. If additional discussions and assessments are required, strategic leaders review how the candidates fit the aspirations and corporate objectives and what the expected investment is for each candidate. The organizational aspects and the prevailing capabilities of the potential program participants are also reviewed to ascertain how they might fit the requirements of the candidates. While these efforts may involve arduous tasks since there are usually only cursory details available during the early going, the actual efforts can be simplified by just obtaining the big picture views or global perspectives rather than a precise determination of the positive and negative aspects and implications of each of the candidates. Moreover, there does not have to be a perfect fit; nor do all of the requisite capabilities and resources have to be available, since strategic leaders usually realize that certain changes and learning might be necessary to make the candidates viable from strategic and organizational perspectives. The essential outcome is to create a list of good candidates that can be screened to select the right programs for further development.

The selection(s) is based on the external and internal contexts of the corporation and its business units. The external view usually precedes the internal aspects, since the latter is dependent on the former. For instance, a corporation's core capabilities are only valuable if they contribute to the socioeconomic aspects and positive outcomes in the market spaces and business environment. Viable candidates have to contribute to the corporation's value propositions and fulfill the needs and expectations of customers, stakeholders, and shareholders, among others like employees. Moreover, candidates have to have the potential to be in compliance with the government mandates; the laws and regulations of the political entities in which the corporation does or plans to do business. Good candidates have to have acceptable risks in the context of the prevailing and expected business and market conditions and trends. While risks are inherent in business and there are no risk-free candidates, the underlying risks associated with each candidate have to be reasonable and manageable; ones that can be mitigated to an acceptable level. Risk management and risk mitigation are discussed in detail in Chapter 7.

The screening process is one of the most important subelements of selection. It is based on criteria set forth by strategic leaders that are related to the strategic logic. The criteria often focus on time, money, performance, and risks aspects.[12] Time is one of the most important considerations. The faster the program is developed and implemented, the less vulnerable the program is to the changes in the business environment. Time also relates to the other critical aspects. For instance, adding time to a program often means adding money. If the duration is extended, competitors may capture the desired first-mover advantages. Economics plays a significant part in determining success. If investment is higher than expected, the desired outcomes(s) and the customer-derived value may change dramatically. Value drives customers and the solutions they seek. Higher investments and higher costs negatively affect the value proposition(s). The performance criteria include the critical benefits that are absolutely required by markets and customers. The expectations include higher quality, enhanced reliability, and improved longevity. The risks include the capabilities of the organization to successfully design and develop the program and deploy the outcomes. The criteria are also based on expectation pertaining to financial objectives. Most of such criteria are well known in terms of financial aspects as discussed in previous chapters. Additional criteria are provided in Table 5.4.

TABLE 5.4 Selected Criteria for Screening Candidates[13]

	Criteria
Philosophy	The guiding philosophy focuses on the corporation's values, culture, character, and vision. The philosophy provides direction, guidance, and focus. Building quality and reliability into products and processes are critical requirements.
Value Creation/ Value Proposition	Value creation is one of the underlying reasons for engaging in strategic programs. Growth and success are achieved by creating superior value and great solutions for all constituencies. Improving the value proposition enhances the capabilities of the corporation to compete in diverse settings.
Market and Customer Satisfaction	Customer satisfaction is critical for the viability of the candidates. If the program fails to meet the needs of potential customers and market spaces, time, money, and efforts are wasted. Failed efforts cost money and consume valuable resources that could have been used more productively.
Stakeholder Satisfaction	Stakeholder satisfaction is often just as critical as customer satisfaction. Stakeholders can be strong proponents or opponents of businesses, their technologies, products, and the related strategic programs. Understanding stakeholder needs helps define requirements and specifications.
Sustainable Development	Solutions have to be balanced in terms of current and future generations and across economic and social groups. They should also be balanced across the geographic and demographic dimensions with many positives and few negatives.
Efficiency Effectiveness	Efficiency and effectiveness involve only using what is necessary to achieve the outcomes and ensuring that outcomes are enduring.
Stability	Stability allows the benefits of the change mechanisms to be enjoyed.

150 ▪ Visionary Strategic Leadership

Screening also depends on the know-how and technologies of the corporation and its prevailing management constructs. While it is expected that HSPs stretch the capabilities of the organization, strategic leaders have to be realistic in what actually can be learned and what new knowledge can be realized within a given time frame. Understanding the prevailing and expected external and internal realities provides a sense of what kinds of programs have to be selected. If the corporation's management constructs are outmoded, then making dramatic changes to the way business is conducted and the business models used by the corporations and its business units may be an imperative. The same is true of market positions, stakeholder engagements, business portfolios, and strategic management constructs. Figure 5.4 portrays the general flow of a standard screening process.

The intent of the screening process is to efficiently and effectively determine what candidates make sense and which ones clearly don't. Often the first step is to eliminate the candidates that obviously do not fit so that more time can be devoted to ascertaining what are the right choices. In reality, the screens may be applied in any order. However, the flow that makes the most sense is one that starts with a strategic fit followed by an assessment of the external forces, and then the internal considerations, with final screens for financial aspects and overall risks. For instance, there is little point in determining the corporation's capabilities for developing and managing a potential program if the candidate is not aligned with the strategic logic or the demands of the business environment and market spaces are moving in a different direction.

The selected programs are then defined and specified during the subsequent elements. While there are always the possibilities of changes in the business environment and market spaces or internal factors that might warrant new considerations, the presumption is that the selected candidates have merit and they should be developed. Some of the candidates that were not selected might be saved until some future time

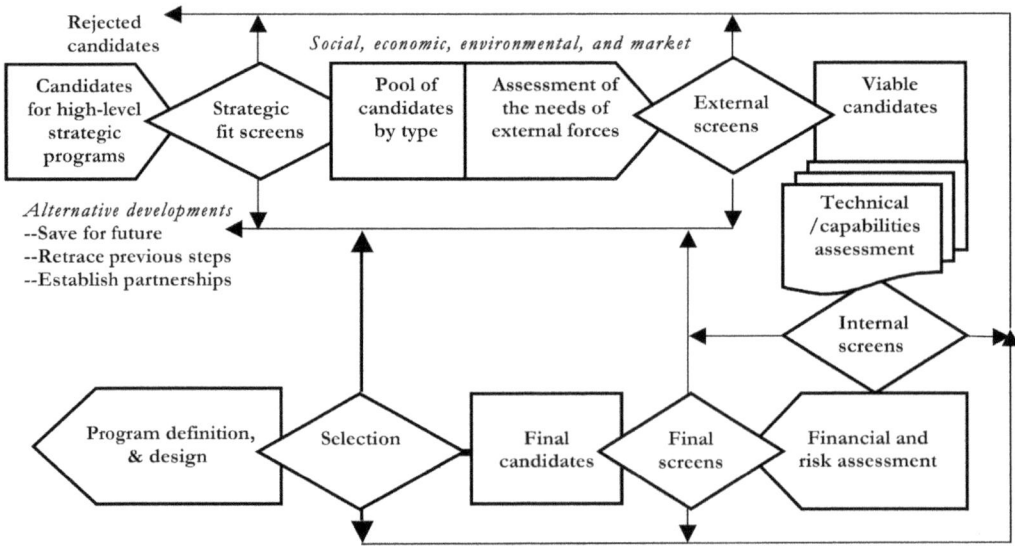

Figure 5.4 Program screening process.[14]

when conditions are more favorable and some might be developed with partners. It is important to note that in some situations, selection is the third or fourth element after the program is defined, or defined and designed. This may be the case when there are only two or three possible candidates and the strategic leaders want to ensure that they select the best one. This is especially important when only one program can be selected from a small number of candidates because of insufficient capabilities and limited resources. However, if there are many possible candidates and there are adequate capabilities and resources to do multiple programs, it is generally advantageous to engage in selection relatively soon so that time and money are not wasted. Moreover, there may be a tendency to hold off making such big decisions since the selection of HSPs tends to be pivotal in the grand scheme of what is going to be done or not done. Not only does it take courage to make such decisions, but there may be side effects that have to be resolved like certain leaders, managers, and participants being unhappy about the choices.

Defining the Architecture of the Selected Programs

Defining the architecture, the subelements, and the flow of the program is an essential element that focuses on the actions, systems, and structures of the program. Definition describes "the what" and "the who," while design involves "the how," "the when," and "the where." The purpose of definition is to establish the critical factors that set the stage for the design of the program and the subsequent program execution. Please note that the discussions herein pertain to HSPs, since each selected program is unique, and strategic leaders and participants have to make such determinations for each one.

Articulating a charter for the program is a crucial, initial subelement that high-level strategic leaders often prepare to establish the parameters for the scope, uniqueness, systems, structures, and the speed of the program. The aim is to provide guidance and specific goals that help program decision makers to know what is acceptable within the realm of the program. A charter is akin to the mission of a business unit except it is more definitive. The charter identifies the key parameters that establish the reach of the program based on geographic, market, technological aspects, and the social, economic, environmental, and financial perspectives. It provides clarity regarding the strategic direction and the intent of the program. The charter might include the following:

- Articulate the main elements and subelements of the high-level strategic framework
- Identify challenges in the business environment (difficulties, concerns, barriers, etc.) and map out the how the program relates to strategic direction and the strategic logic
- Define the critical requirements that have to be met like international standards and compliance with laws and regulations
- Map out the requisite systems and structures of the organization

- Identify the program goals and criteria so that strategic leaders, program managers, and participants understand what has to be accomplished

The charter may also stipulate policies or constraints that may limit the discretion of decision makers in certain areas. The intent is not to reduce flexibility, but to ensure that certain negative implications and impacts are avoided. For instance, the charter might specify what is acceptable from business or ethical perspectives such as all innovations have to be thoroughly tested and validated before they are introduced to customers or the public, i.e., the company will not risk harm to any person.

Based on the charter and the preliminary program constructs used during the screening process, strategic leaders prepare an estimate of the overall investment required to fund the program. While it is typically too early in the design or development of a program to make an accurate estimate, it is imperative that strategic leaders have a sense of what is an expected investment. The estimate can take several forms from a comprehensive view of the whole program to a more limited scope of just the early phases or projects that result in definitive and acceptable outcomes that justify the investment to that point(s). Regardless, the estimate of the expected investment has to be revisited many times during the implementation and execution of the program. Strategic leaders might recalculate the investment requirements at the beginning of each element, do it periodically (say every six months), or both. This is especially important for programs with very long durations. Many factors may change over the course of time like cost escalation and inflation that may substantially change the underpinnings of the program, shifting the requirements and potential outcomes from feasible and desirable to unreasonable and unacceptable.

Determining the organizational architecture is obviously a critical step that has profound implications since positive outcomes and long-term success depend on the people involved. While there are many facets to the organizational structure, the selection and empowerment of the strategic leadership, the program management, and the participants are among the most important decisions. Strategic leadership is usually manifested in a high-level team of strategic leaders, program managers, and senior professionals. There are numerous ways in which the strategic leadership can be established. In simpler programs a single executive may provide the essential direction and oversight. In more complicated programs, it is advisable to have a steering committee of high-level strategic leaders, managers, and professionals to provide the direction, overall management, and oversight. This is particularly critical when the program involves many different disciplines, subjects, and far-reaching perspectives and implications in which few individuals would have sufficient knowledge and experience to manage all of the ramifications. For the most crucial and significant HSPs, it is advisable to have both certain corporate leaders and a steering committee continuously involved.

The critical actions include:

1. *Senior management commitment*—Senior management must be committed to providing direction, guidance, and oversight. Company officers typically

select a strategic leader (a corporate officer) to lead the program or they establish a steering committee of strategic leaders and senior professionals to provide the overall direction. They may also do both.
2. *Steering committee structure*—If established, the steering committee members are directly responsible for program management, evaluation, and oversight. The steering committee guides the program, its implementation, and execution and provides high-level management. It provides the leadership necessary for determining who is responsible for the specific elements of the program and it evaluates ongoing reviews of outcomes and performance. It assigns the program manager(s) and key project managers who are directly responsible for designing, developing, executing, and evaluating the program.
3. *Program leadership*—Depending on the scope and complexity of the program, one or more senior program managers are assigned to be responsible for the whole program. While it is preferable that the program managers are involved from the first day to the last one for continuity, new program managers may be assigned as the program expands during execution or as time moves along. If the program duration is a decade or more, there may be several changes in program managers over time.
4. *Program teams*—Participants have to be selected to engage in the implementation and execution. While it is also preferable to have everyone involved from the early phases, it is not always efficient or feasible to do so, since most programs are relatively tight knit during program implementation and only expand dramatically during program execution. External participants of the extended enterprise may also be included on the team.
5. *Program systems and structures*—Before starting specific actions to initiate and design the program, the specific parts of the systems have to be mapped out and individuals assigned to manage certain parts and processes of the overall system.
6. *Education and training*—It is critical that the steering committee members, the program manager(s), and participants understand the required elements for instituting, implementing and executing the program. There should be education and training sessions to ensure everyone has the capabilities, skills, and knowledge.

Program managers and participants have to be well suited for engaging in HSPs that are large, complex endeavors, especially ones involving new technologies, systems and/or management constructs with significant uncertainties and risks. Moreover, given a rapidly changing and turbulent business world and the necessity to realize the corporate objectives as quickly as possible, the pace of program implementation and execution is usually daunting. Program managers and participants have to be open-minded and willing to proceed along uncharted pathways. They have to enjoy out-of-the-box thinking and taking actions without having proven management constructs and processes. They have to be innovative with the talents to discover new means and mechanisms for achieving results and create the requisite systems and structures.

Management constructs are theoretical and/or practical models, methods, and techniques. Strategic leaders and program managers provide direction and support through the selection and application of appropriate management constructs that combine the organization's knowledge and experience with the theoretical thinking and learning pertaining to the opportunities, challenges, constraints, and uncertainties pertaining to the requirements of the program. With the broader and more complex scope of HSPs, it is much more difficult to map out all of the networks, interrelationships, and dependences. While there has always been a tension between having management constructs that are cutting edge and comprehensive and having ones that are simple and easy to understand, strategic leaders and program managers have to ensure that the management constructs used are appropriate and provide the right means and mechanisms to support decision making and the proper flow of the program. The more complicated approaches and global perspectives are usually needed today because of globalization, the rapidity of change, the increased intensity of competition, the shortened product life cycles, and numerous other changes in today's business environment and market spaces. Industry and market structures are changing at incredible rates, especially due to emerging companies in China, India, and Brazil. It is becoming more and more difficult to predict the needs, wants, and expectations. Since the demands in the market spaces are great and complex, management constructs must measure up to the requirements and fulfill the expectations of the situations.

A key question involves what the overarching approaches should be. Figure 5.5 provides a relative sense of whether project management or program management is best suited for the situation in terms of the business environment and market spaces when making decisions about program definition and design. The graphic is not intended to be definitive, but to provide guidance for decision making. While such determinations may be made prior to program selection or during program design, it is appropriate to identify the mechanisms for the program as soon as possible. If the program duration is short and the business environment is predictable, then project management may suffice. However, such conditions and trends may not endure for very long. They may never exist for HSPs, especially ones that are expected to last for many years or decades. Moreover, if the business environment is turbulent and there are radical changes in the technologies, social, political, and economic conditions and

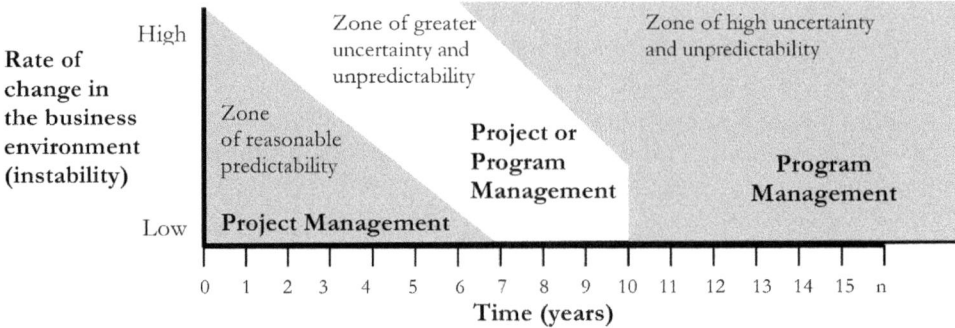

Figure 5.5 A relative sense of project management versus program management.[15]

trends, and there are enormous changes in many of the other variables, then program management constructs should be used.

While this is a theoretical perspective not based on provable constructs, it does provide some guidance about what types of management constructs should be used. It can be argued that the current business environment is somewhere between stable and turbulent, i.e., a mid-range situation that has some sense of stability, but relatively high levels of technological and political uncertainties.

Program management constructs are more inclusive, and drill back to the social world and natural environment, if necessary, to examine the underpinnings of change. Again, they tend to take global perspectives. In such cases, more sophisticated management constructs have to be used to understand the forces of change and to adequately consider the implications of what is happening or expected to happen in the external context. It is imperative that the industry and market structures therein be fully explored to ensure that all of the mandates and requirements are known and understood. Remember that HSPs are implemented to make dramatic transformations or major transitions in the company's abilities to achieve extraordinary outcomes and sustainable success in the business environment and market spaces. Regardless of the intent and objectives of the program, there have to be real connections with the ultimate recipients of the desired outcomes. For instance, "design for six-sigma" programs are often intended to improve the company's quality and to reduce the costs of defects, especially due to failures. While such objectives may be viewed as internal, the eventual beneficiaries are the customers and stakeholders and the business value derived from success in the external context.

The systems and structures must include all of the key contributors in the extended enterprise including partners and allies. Their roles and responsibilities have to be determined as well and mapped out like those of the internal participants. The arrangements with such entities have to be formalized and clearly defined through written agreements so that everything is clear and concise. The agreements must spell out the lines of authority, responsibilities, and expected actions and activities. While some of the details are precursors to formal program design using project management techniques, it is imperative that the foundation and ground rules for the relationships among all of the critical external entities be fully and even legally established. If confidentiality is required, then the agreements must include provisions for maintaining secrecy and protecting vital information and data. Protocols for the working relationships should be devised and guidelines for the actual work should be articulated to all of the internal and external contributors. Most importantly, there must be defined support systems for the contributors and recipients.

From an internal perspective, defining, revamping, and/or selecting the internal systems and structures as they pertain to the program are critical steps in defining the program. This is related to actions at the strategic level as discussed above except they focus on the operating aspects. The critical actions include:

1. *Develop or select a formal operating system*—A formal operating management system has to be fully articulated and functioning so that everyone, including external participants, understands the underlying basis for engaging in the program and how activities and tasks are expected to flow. The existing systems may be suitable, but a review of them may be necessary and appropriate.
2. *Operating requirements*—Program managers and participants have to identify the critical elements and subelements and how they fit into the system. In particular, these include marketing campaigns, production plans, environment, health and safety plans, human resource plans, and formal resource allocation plans.
3. *Develop program teams*—Participants have to be organized into effective teams or organizational structures. It is necessary to have mechanisms by which the operating management system and structures can be integrated and the momentum established to execute the various elements of the program.
4. *Educate and train managers and key participants*—It is essential that key managers and participants comprehend all facets of the program and the key requirements of the operating system.

The operating system(s) includes the selected mechanisms and protocols for management and control. The means and mechanisms provide the managers and participants with the knowledge, capabilities, and resources to carry out the strategies and action plans. It is essential to define the key parameters so that positives are achieved and negatives are avoided or mitigated. While performance within the operating aspects is normally viewed as tactical, operations can become a major consideration if the consequences of actions or inactions result in severe negative situations. Most importantly, defining the metrics used to evaluate performance and success is critical for providing guidelines and support mechanisms. Metrics are senior management's tools for ensuring that program management and the participants perform in accordance with the charter, meet the objectives, and function within sound protocols and generally accepted practices. This includes ensuring compliance with all laws and regulations and providing requisite information to the steering committee and minimizing and mitigating risks. The related subelements are actually part of the mechanisms used for program management.

Training and education of internal and external participants are critical for success. They can begin as soon as the essential people have been selected. While it is important to have participants trained before they engage in design and development, education and training are never-ending requirements, especially for programs with long durations. Again, strategic leaders have to avoid the mindset that such necessities are just subelements that can be done at a given point in time and that once they have been completed there are no further requirements. They are part of the continuum of program management with subelements that are revisited periodically.

The steering committee and program management monitor progress and the outcomes along the way by selecting and using performance criteria and measures. The performance criteria and measures provide ongoing feedback about how well the organization is performing via management reports. Management reports often focus on financial results, but they should include all critical measures so that a balanced perspective is provided and so that corrective actions, if necessary, can be affected immediately. Certain criteria provide early warning about whether the program is tracking properly. The criteria should be linked to strategic objectives and they should monitor the most crucial variables with respect to market spaces, value creation, uniqueness of the program, and financial viability. Numerous measures can be used. The broad categories include:

- *Value creation and sustainable success:* Value creation is a broad, but powerful measure. It relates to the ultimate purpose of the program. If the program creates a high degree of value for customers, stakeholders, the organization, its enterprise, and the shareholders, it has a higher probability of being successful. Value drives customers and customer success translates into program success.
- *Timeliness and the time horizon:* Time is one of the most important measures. The quicker the organization can design, develop, and execute the program, the more likely it is to realize desired outcomes. In turbulent times, the faster programs can be implemented the less likely that changes in the business environment may distort the outcomes or make them irrelevant. Many organizations have the means and mechanisms to get results, but they are simply too slow during implementation and execution, and they are often trumped by peers and competitors.
- *Money and rewards:* Finance and economics are significant factors in determining success or failure. If the investments and cost structures are higher than expected, the expected or desired competitive position(s), customer-derived value, and competitive advantages may be affected. Reductions in these factors will have negative effects on the return on the investment and the financial well-being of the company. For instance, higher investments often translate into lower sales volume and revenues.
- *Risk and uncertainty:* Risk management deals with uncertainty and the probabilities and severities of the negatives. While there are always risks associated with capabilities of the organization and uncertainties of the business environment, they generally have to be within the company's capabilities and tolerance to manage and mitigate them.

Such mechanisms are used to ascertain whether implementation and execution are tracking on course. If the actual values are in line with the expected outcomes, then it may be assumed that there is a high probability that implementation and execution are within an acceptable range. However, if one or more of the criteria and/or objectives are trending toward an extreme point, it indicates that the variance to the established plan is drifting out of control. Criteria are intended to provide instantaneous feedback, while evaluation is used to make determinations about expected outcomes.

Designing the Program Elements and the Specifications

Program design involves the concepts, techniques, and methods used to plan and specify the program. The main subelements pertain to the action plans and specifications. Planning requires systematic thinking by program managers and participants to contemplate the best ways to design the program and how to engage the people and integrate the requirements into a comprehensive flow of actions. Program integration requires a framework for the interactions among all of the participants over time. The intent is to consider design choices in light of customer and stakeholders needs and the with capabilities, resources, and expectations of the company.

Programs can be designed in terms of elements and subelements and/or projects that run sequentially (in series), concurrently (in parallel), or in some combination of the two (herein called variants or hybrids). Sequential programs have subelements that run consecutively. Hybrid forms usually have some subelements that run in series and others that run in parallel or overlap each other. For instance, the early U.S. Space Program had several subprograms within the program, in which some of them overlapped. Figure 5.6 provides a few examples of sequential forms.

Sequential programs usually have subelements or projects that have to be arranged in series because the outcomes of the subsequent subelements/projects are dependent on the outcomes of the predecessors. Such programs usually have long durations with

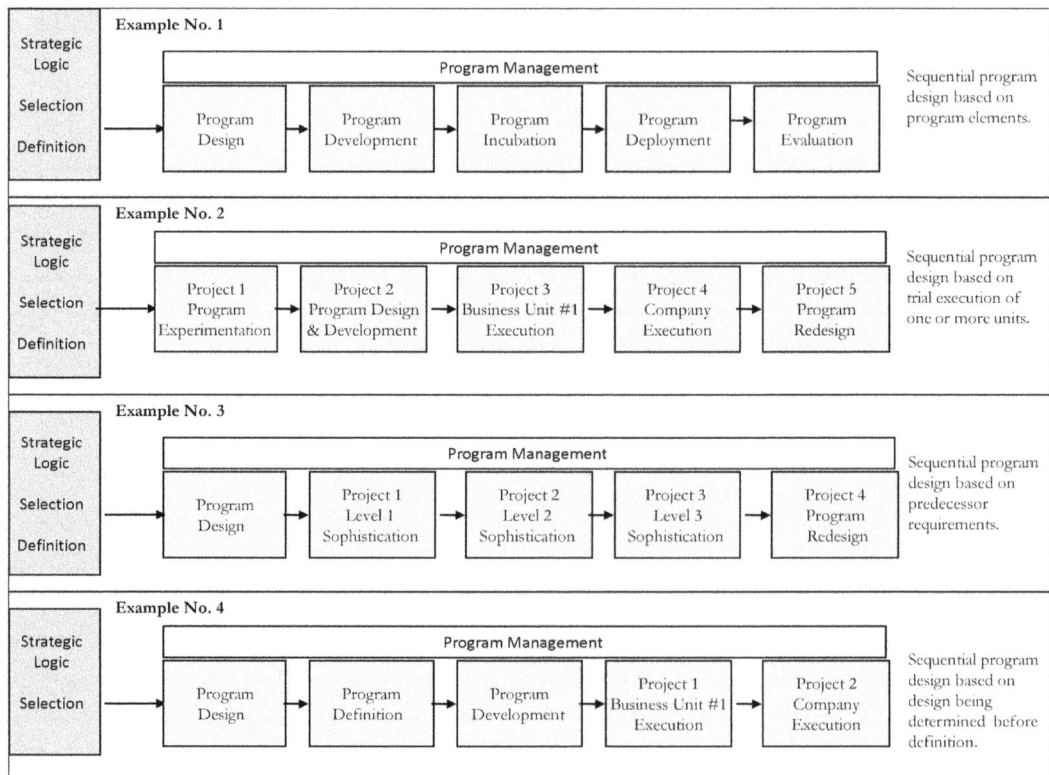

Figure 5.6 Selected examples of sequential forms.

downstream flows that are dependent upon the results of the upstream actions and activities. The advantage of sequential flows is that the knowledge and learning of the upstream actions and can be beneficially incorporated and used in the downstream actions. For instance, in example Number 2, the first project is basically "an experiment" to learn the know-how and nuances necessary to actually engage in the rest of the program. Another advantage is that it is easier for participants to understand what is required and for program managers to correct problems and difficulties when actions and activities flow in series. The main disadvantages include taking significant amounts of time to establish and execute the flow of the program and being too cautious during the early phases. Per example Number 4, program design precedes program definition in order to acquire the knowledge to define the program requirements and ascertain the means and mechanisms. While such approaches may be necessary, a lot of time is usually consumed just getting the program started. In such cases, the initial elements or projects may simply involve setting the stage for the program. However, such approaches are often required when the program involves new-to-the-world developments in which there are limited experience and know-how about how to initiate the program or how to determine what is necessary and how to proceed. There may be numerous other sequential forms that may be used based on the underpinnings of the program and the actual situations with which program managers have to deal.

For large global corporations, especially ones having many business units, strategic leaders have to use parallel processing to the extent possible so that HSPs can be completed as quickly as possible. This is based on the recognition that it may take a decade or more to complete the program across the entire domain of the corporation and all of its business units and their enterprises. While it would be desirable in certain situations to implement across all business units at the same time, such approaches may not be feasible given the capabilities and resources available. Like sequential programs, there may be experiments and learning necessary before proceeding quickly from development through execution.

The concurrent program may have a form similar to the U.S. Space Program. Figure 5.7 depicts a program with several subprograms running more or less in parallel. The current approach works well when the subprograms are not dependent on each other for the most part; thus, work on subsequent subprograms can begin relatively early in the overall program. While doing as much as possible on a concurrent basis is preferred, there are limitations in the real world. There may not be the money or resources to do everything in parallel. Moreover, some subprograms are related to the outcomes of earlier subprograms; therefore, there is a need to mitigate risks or

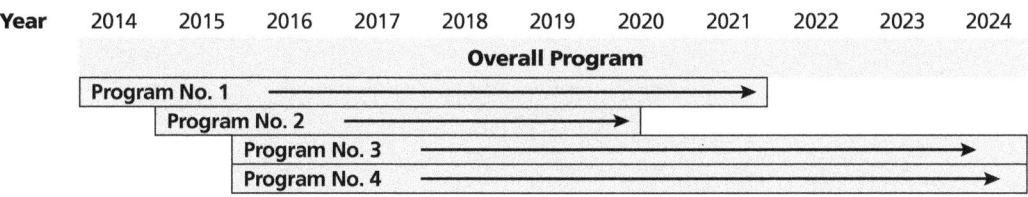

Figure 5.7 Example of a program with mostly concurrent subprograms.

160 ■ *Visionary Strategic Leadership*

customize the design. In general, this involves creating a hybrid of which there may thousands of forms or variations. Indeed, they are only limited by one's imagination.

Figure 5.8 provides an example of a hybrid form that may be useful for a corporation with several business units in which program execution requires the full support and engagement of the business units and their strategic leaders. The flow has linkages between the corporate level and the business units.

Program implementation and execution necessitate support mechanisms from program management and feedback from the participants at the business units. While it may be desirable to have one large project to execute the program, such an approach may be impossible for large corporations with many disparate business units that are extremely large entities themselves with far-flung operations. For example, United Technologies Corporations (UTC) has six business units that are multibillion-dollar entities with global reach and tens of thousands of employees.[16]

The main advantages of this hybrid form include the potential for strong support from the high levels of the organization, the concurrent development, demonstration, and deployment of actions at the business-unit level and the overall concurrent execution across the whole company. While it is always difficult to assure that a given framework and the related methodologies minimize the time required to complete the entire program, it is clear that the time duration will be shorter when many of the requisite

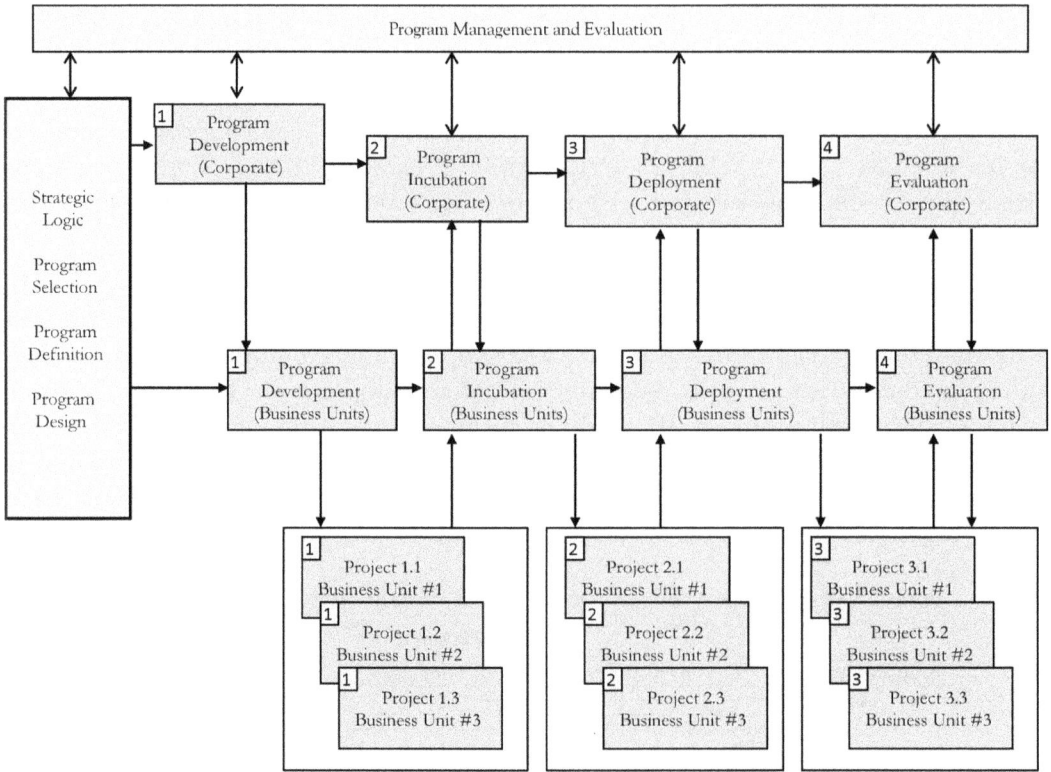

Figure 5.8 Example of a hybrid form tailored to large corporations with business units.

High-Level Strategic Programs ▪ 161

actions are completed in parallel. Moreover, program management and the corporate leadership play critical roles in providing guidance, support, and the resources to the business units as they participate in implementation and execution. This form can be expanded to include many more business units than suggested in Figure 5.8 without causing significant impacts on the overall duration and complexity of the program.

The main disadvantages include the difficulties in balancing the implementation and execution across the business units and the lack the necessary customization of the elements and subelements; the selected approaches may not fit the characteristics and requirements of one or more of the business units. Such approaches may work well for corporations that have similar business units like Nestlé, but they are not as appropriate for corporations like GE and UTC that have business units in different sectors and industries. The other disadvantage includes having to train numerous project managers who are only responsible for their own business unit. Unless there is appropriate sharing of information, knowledge, and lessons learned, the corporation may spend a considerable amount of money reinventing the wheel.

A hybrid form for a corporation with one or two business units is a variant of a sequential form in which the development, demonstration, and/or deployment elements are divided into functional areas and/or projects. Figure 5.9 provides the general flow of such a scheme.

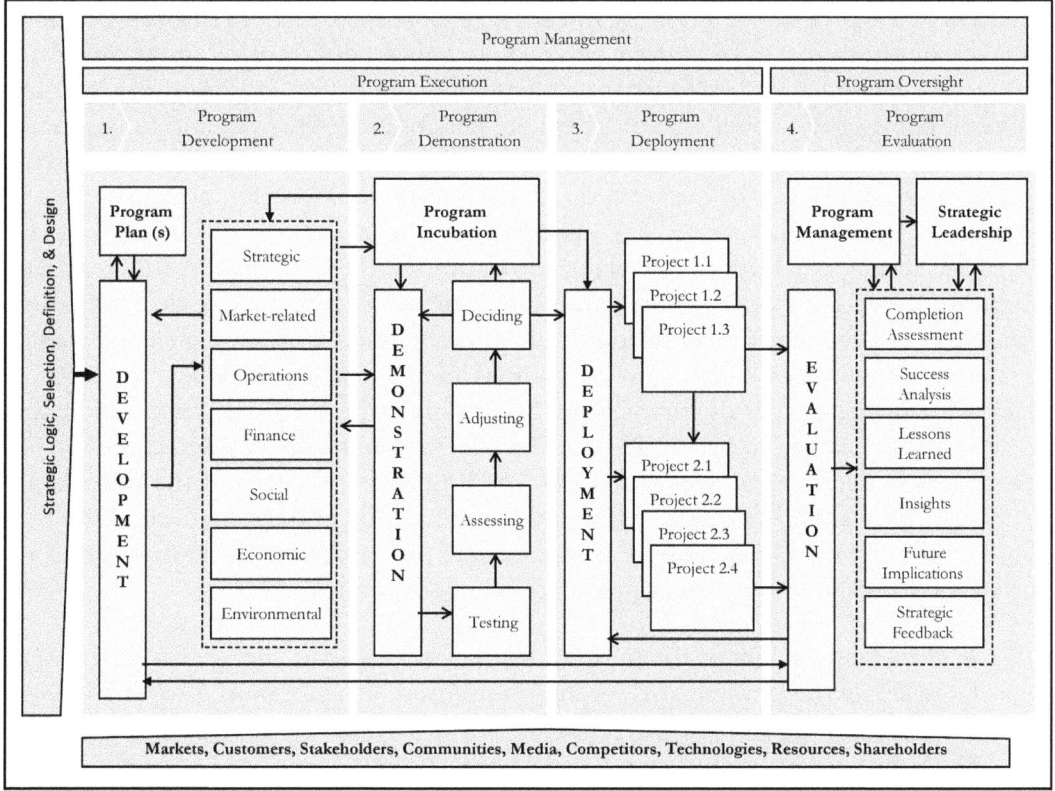

Figure 5.9 Example of a hybrid form tailored to small corporations.

The intent is to accomplish as much of program execution as possible using parallel processing. It is based on the recognition that some of the elements and subelements may have to be done in series, but there are many others that can be done concurrently. The main advantage includes reducing some of the time required to complete the program. Certain of the projects are done concurrently and some may be done sequentially. The main disadvantage is the possible lack of integration of program execution because functional areas and disciplines do their own actions rather than on an integrated team basis.

Ultimately, program design is actually what it means: design the program elements and subelements based on the strategic logic and the definition of the program. It implies that program management customizes the design to the needs of the external context and the corporation to the extent possible. This suggests that in reality there are few, if any, generic forms; the nature, requirements and specifications of a program are the main determinants in designing the program form. Since time is always important and it is often a key driver, speed usually dictates that as much as possible must be done concurrently, i.e., using parallel processing.

The layout of the program is the based on the expected or targeted external and internal outcomes. Program planning includes determining the flow of subprograms and/or projects using management constructs like project management and management reviews. The steering committee and program managers periodically review the progress of the program and the significant subelements thereof to provide guidance, to maintain oversight; to keep them on track, to correct deficiencies and problems, to reduce uncertainties and risks; to assure that adequate talent and resources are available and being used properly; to decrease the possibilities of failure; and to ensure the new opportunities and challenges are fully considered and managed. They basically review the performance of the program to determine its suitability, adequacy, and effectiveness. Reviews also address the need for changes to policies, objectives, and content. The strategic leaders or the steering committee often engage in the approval/disapproval decisions of the subprograms and/or projects and make determinations about how or even whether to proceed. In many situations, the strategic leaders and/or steering committee affirms the decision(s) of the program management, rather than actually making the decisions. The theory is that the program management and the participants have the best insights and understanding of reality and it is their perspectives and decision making that should be followed a majority of the time. Moreover, such philosophies empower the practitioners to be entrepreneurial and have a sense of being the architects of the program. The following are the main responsibilities of the strategic leaders/steering committee pertaining to reviews:

- Provide oversight of the programs, processes, actions and practices
- Evaluate the performance of the program(s), subprograms, projects, and activities
- Determine when the reviews are necessary and appropriate
- Ensure that the resources, capabilities, and communications are available and/or provided

- Make revisions and changes to assure ongoing success
- Communicate the results to senior management and board of directors

They ensure management commitment and ongoing support for the program. They drive design, development, and execution of the program. They play key, ongoing roles in program evaluation.

Program managers and the participants are the key players who engage in the program actions and obtain the desired results. However, when the road ahead becomes unclear, there may be a tendency for participants to slow down their efforts, to be fearful of making decisions, or even to stop making progress until they have a better sense of how to proceed. The fuzzier the pathway and actions required for obtaining successful outcomes, especially for a program involving new-to-the-world developments, the more important it is for the strategic leaders and steering committee to provide inspiration, guidance, information, and support.

Allocating the proper resources to ensure program continuity is a huge challenge that is based on order-of-magnitude estimates that are imprecise and usually obtained using comparison to previous efforts or those of peers and competitors. For instance, if it known that GE spent one billion dollars developing its SBD program, then it is reasonable to believe that it will require about the same amount of money to develop your program, if your size is similar to that of GE. While there are always nuances between the program of others and yours, the allocations may be simply based on a rough estimate of plus or minus 10 or 20 percent. An alternative is to allocate sufficient funds to design the program and to determine a more precise estimate during the early elements of execution. It is important to reiterate that estimates are usually redone periodically throughout the program. At program selection, the estimate is to provide a basis for determining the feasible of the candidate(s). While such determinations have to be as accurate as possible, they do not have the same impact on the company since the monies are normally not actually allocated until a later time. However, as time goes on and efforts are expanded, the estimates have to get much better.

From a strategic implementation perspective, building solid relationships among the leaders, managers, and participants is essential and should be initiated as soon as possible; however, it is imperative that everyone involved is a key player and proactively contributes in obtaining the desired outcomes. Moreover, it is incumbent upon the strategic leaders and program managers to develop with the participants a connectedness that engenders mutual respect and recognition. In more open-ended and fuzzy situations, command and control management constructs are difficult to orchestrate and they often lead to less success, not more. If strategic leaders and program managers are too dictatorial, then participants may go along with the dictates, but they may become less creative, adaptable, and more rigid. Therefore, cooperation and collaboration are essential and are often realized when people are personally and professionally connected. While strategic leaders typically pay a lot of attention to the investment(s) and the resources required, success or failure often depend more on the people involved. It is also important to keep in mind that programs are social endeavors requiring astute and dedicated leaders and contributors who can work well together in complex and often inadequately articulated situations. The goodwill and capabilities of the key contributors may overcome many of the inherent challenges when engaging in HSPs.

Program design is based on specifications that satisfy the social, economic, technical, and functional objectives and produce the desired outcomes. The design focus is predominately about architecture and the tools and techniques available for executing the program. The latter include the analytical methods for making good decisions. The specifications are derived from the external needs and expectations and the internal targets, requirements, resources, and capabilities. Most importantly, value creation as discussed earlier is central when determining the specifications.

From an external perspective, the value proposition is pivotal in mapping out how to obtain the external outcomes and what they mean to customers and stakeholders. Without such insights and perspectives, a program may achieve the established internal outcomes, but fail to successfully satisfy customers and stakeholders. People want value when they engage business entities. Moreover, they engage in transactions, exchanges, and activities that result in solutions and expected outcomes. The notion of a value proposition is straightforward; people expect to get positive outcomes from the solutions without any significant negatives. They want the best solution possible that exceeds their purposes and expectations. True value is derived through having positive outcomes (both tangible and intangible) with a sense of well-being and avoiding negative effects like having defects and burdens. For instance, people buy soap to clean themselves, not to enjoy owning the soap itself. They seek the outcomes, not the products. Value maximization is an essential consideration when designing a program. The intent of a program is to create successful situations so that everyone can maximize value to the greatest extent possible. While it is difficult to prescribe the actual flows and realizations of value for every entity and everyone, it is clear that customers want valuable solutions with maximum benefits. Stakeholders usually expect positive outcomes without significant problems; suppliers want fair and appropriate exchanges; and related industries want positive relationships and outcomes in supporting value creation and the value delivery systems. Overall, people want the best solutions possible given the realities of the world.

The means and mechanisms for improving the program architecture are numerous and every design decision may have a profound impact on the perceived value and program viability. Value analysis is a method used for enhancing design decisions. It evaluates the attributes as they pertain to customer wants and expectations. Attributes are features, functions, and benefits that customers find significant and advantageous. Customers want outcomes that bring them the most benefits. Attributes and value are provided through many means and mechanisms. Performance, quality, benefits, and flexibility are essential subelements of the program design decision-making. It uses customers' input to determine the most beneficial ways to obtain the targeted outcomes. The objective is to identify the essential characteristics and functions and ensure that they are provided using the most effective mechanisms. The following are a few of the suggested steps:[17]

1. ***Information Gathering***—The participants collaborate with external entities and individuals to determine what are the opportunities and challenges, why they are important, and what can be done to positively affect them; it also involves collecting information pertaining to the situations.
2. ***Brainstorming and Benchmarking***—Targeted or expected outcomes may be identified and examined in light of their possible contributions and positive impacts on program design and execution. They are compared to the prevailing mechanisms.
3. ***Technical Analysis***—Each option or potential outcome is assessed to determine its technical feasibility and economic viability. The list is narrowed to make subsequent work feasible.
4. ***Value Analysis***—The options are expanded to understand the implications of all of the attributes. Value analysis might take the form of a comparative assessment of the essential attributes.
5. ***Validation***—The selected targeted outcomes are tested to ensure that they are in line with real-world situation(s). The validation step may include management's review and approval.
6. ***Documentation***—The decisions are recorded and communicated to all of the program participants to assure that there is a universal understanding.

The external perspectives lead to the internal ones. Value innovation focuses on the dynamics of change, how to exploit opportunities through program outcomes, and how to create desirable ends. Value innovation involves ensuring that the strategic positions are enhanced, that the solutions are in line with reality, that actions are executed properly, and that sustainable success is realized. It involves the relentless drive to embrace positive change and gain significantly from it. In the context of a program, value innovation examines the ways in which new or additional value can be created through the next generation of solutions, radical breakthroughs, and/or new ways of achieving desired outcomes and success. Value innovation engages the innovative capabilities of the company to transition and transform its reality into a higher level of sophistication. Value innovation requires not only tangible aspects like resources and development projects, but intangibles like inspiration and encouragement. Participants have to be guided, supported, and rewarded on an ongoing basis to ensure that they continue to be creative, productive, and successful. It requires the personal involvement on the part of the strategic leaders and program managers who have to go beyond motivating people. They have to lead from the front, not just pushing from behind.

Configuration links the internal operating systems, the organization, its capabilities and the resources via a business model(s) or value delivery system(s). It involves the intellectual capital of the organization and enterprise and the strategic thinking and imagination of the leaders in translating program plans into external outcomes and sustainable advantages. Configuration includes the tangibles and intangible contributions made by all of the people and processes to fulfill the needs, requirements, and expectations and turn opportunities into valuable and sustainable outcomes.

The operating system(s)/value delivery system(s) include the functional and operational areas of the business unit(s). They are often the specifically designed systems with defined roles for the participants for executing business strategies and action plans. The operating system is the core operating level. Generally, the operating system is the lower-level management system designed and constructed to carry out the mission of the business unit. It includes all of the internal functional areas including supply chain management, production, assembly, marketing, service support, finance, and the complementary areas that support the actions plans. It concentrates on existing conditions and meeting the market, technical, and financial requirements of the organization. It is usually supported by the product and process innovation capabilities for updating and improving performance. The core operating level is usually supported by well-established management constructs that produce results through well-defined processes. The historical construct for managing the operating level focused on the resources deployed within the system and the organizational elements engaged in converting inputs into outputs.

The value delivery system incorporates the internal functions and links them with the extended enterprise. It focuses on the tactical approaches for achieving results. The value delivery system and the operating system focus on: (1) market opportunities, customer wants and needs, and stakeholder expectations; (2) product attributes, product and process specifications, product innovation, and marketing requirements; (3) the interrelated effects and impacts of customers, consumers, stakeholders, related industries, and competition; (4) day-to-day operations, functional strategies, and tactics; and, (5) the use of fundamental management methods for making sound business decisions. Tactical aspects involve translating inputs into outputs that are valuable and desirable solutions. Table 5.5 lists the specific areas that might be considered.[18]

Generally, outputs are designed, produced, marketed, and distributed for customers who require solutions to their social and economic needs and wants. While traditional operating systems include production, marketing, finance, human resource management, product development, supply network management, and essential support functions like information management, the other critical areas may include legal, stakeholder management, asset management, waste management, and government relationship management. The list is not intended to be comprehensive; it identifies some of the most important considerations. It is not the purpose of this text to provide a detailed discussion of the operating systems, nor of all of the techniques and methods used in the execution of business on a real-time basis. The managers and supervisors who engage in day-to-day actions have to be adaptive and creative in the fulfillment of their roles and responsibilities.

TABLE 5.5 Important Considerations Pertaining to the Operating System(s)

Areas	Specific aspects	Key considerations
Markets	Target markets and customers Value proposition Basis of competition Driving forces	Segmentation, locations, sophistication, and relations Value creation, customer success, and affordability Pressures, power, positions, know-how, and adaptability Social, economic, technological, political, and ecological
Value system	Supply network connections Stakeholders Related industries Infrastructure Competitors	Capabilities, resources, knowledge, and relationships Positions, power, requirements, mandates, and interests Support, linkages, relationships, positions, and value Support, logistics, and technological sophistication Number, power, size, strategies, and actions of rivals
Product line	Product line mix Uniqueness of positions Designs Cost structures	Mix of products, depth, breadth, scope, and life cycle Power, differentiation, quality, value, and sophistication Knowledge, insights, developments, and durability Inputs, conversion processes, volumes, and overheads
Marketing	Product strategies Pricing strategies Promotion and advertising Distribution channels Customer service and support	Brands, sophistication, quality, and reliability Premium, affordable, market-based, and discounts Theme, message, media, timing, honesty, and clarity Direct, retail, wholesale, and intermediaries Responsiveness, service support, quality, and timeliness
Operations	Production capabilities Capacity and planning Processes and equipment Supply management Quality management Workforce management Waste management	Volume, processes, utilization, and sophistication Facilities, locations, layouts, scope, and scheduling Lean production, machines, and technologies Procurement, outsourcing, and relationships Process control, quality outcomes, and six sigma Empowerment, labor practices, methods, and policies Pollution prevention, waste reduction, and compliance
Finance	Costs of capital Revenues and cash flow Budgeting Financial control/reporting	Funds, approvals, metrics, sources, and uses Sales, cash flow, margins, profits, and returns Costs, expenses, investments, cycles, and controls Accounting, accuracy, control, audits, and reports
Management	Leadership Entrepreneurship Management and commitment	Vision, inspiration, authority, duties, and talents Creativity, knowledge, experience, and insights Competencies, risk taking, flexibility, and people skills
Human Resources	Recruitment and retention Training and development Work processes Rewards and recognition	Nature of work, pleasure, compensation, and benefits Knowledge, learning, skills, and opportunities Structure, processes, flexibility, and adaptability Respect, awards, promotions, and new positions
Information	Information system Hardware and software Security and recovery	Structures, linkages, networks, and support services Technologies, data processing, automation, and design System, processes, backup, protection, and procedures
Development	New products and services Capabilities enhancements Research/knowledge creation	Product development and process improvements Alliances, partnerships, and cross-functional teams Learning, building, creating, and new ventures

BOX 5: ELECTRIC BOAT AND THE USS VIRGINIA-CLASS ENVIRONMENTAL COMPLIANCE PROGRAM: PIONEERING THE WAY TOWARD SUSTAINABLE DEVELOPMENT

In 1989, the U.S. Navy (Navy) selected Electric Boat Division (EB) of General Dynamics Corporation to design a new fast-attack submarine, the USS Virginia-class ship (Virginia-class). The goal was to design and develop a superior military system that is both cost effective and environmentally sound.[a] The Virginia-class development program became one of the first major Department of Defense (DoD) acquisition programs to apply life cycle thinking and management during design and build phases. Environmental management was elevated to a critical design factor in line with performance, safety, affordability, reliability, and risks. The main primary objective was to design a state-of-the-art weapon system that would exceed the Navy's mission requirements while at the same time minimizing environmental impacts during construction, service, and retirement. The design philosophy was to achieve superior mission performance, and balance all of the essential design parameters and objectives without compromising any of them.

The rise of international conflicts and terrorism had dramatically changed the defense needs of the United States since the end of the Cold War. The potential threats to national security were more difficult to identify, analyze, and defend. These conditions required DoD and its major defense contractors to pay close attention to the time, money, and resources needed to develop and implement new programs. In an environment of uncertainty and limited funding, major defense contractors were seeking innovative ways to satisfy the needs of the military and the associated stakeholders using state-of-the-art technologies and sophisticated design and development principles, processes, and practices. This phenomenon was especially important for weapon systems that are technically complex, expensive and produced in very small numbers.

The design and construction of a nuclear-powered submarine is one of the most complex and challenging technological innovation programs in the world. The design parameters are more demanding and complicated than those required for designing and building aircraft like the Airbus A380 or the Boeing 787. A submarine must be capable of meeting all of the operating requirements and regulatory mandates during peacetime and fulfill its military missions as well.

When DoD and the Navy contracted with EB to design the Virginia-class submarine, the specifications included complying with environmental, health, and safety (EHS) laws and regulations, but they did not specify having a special subprogram for ensuring that the best solutions were designed and deployed. However, shortly after the start of the Virginia-class development program, the Navy and EB realized that they needed to pay particular attention to EHS considerations and find new solutions for eliminating many of the burdens and impacts that affected previous classes. Managing toxic substances and hazardous wastes and reducing the costs of disposal of obsolete submarines were high priorities. The Navy authorized EB to establish the Virginia-class Environmental Acquisition Program as a subset of the overall acquisition program. It became known as the Environmental Compliance Program (ECP). The purpose was to minimize environmental impacts during the ship's full life cycle.

A BRIEF HISTORY OF ELECTRIC BOAT

EB was founded in 1899 through the merger of Electric Storage Battery Co., Electric Vehicle Co., Electro Dynamic, and Electric Launch Co. The primary reason for the merger was to complete the construction of the USS Holland, the world's first practical submarine. During World War I, EB's delivered 85 submarines to the Navy. EB did not own a shipyard. It designed the boats and subcontracted the construction to various other shipyards. However, in 1924 EB established a shipyard on the Thames River in Groton, Connecticut. During World War II (WWII), EB work force grew from 2,300 to approximately 12,400. By the end of the WWII, EB had produced 74 submarines; more than any other shipyard in the country.

After WWII, EB continued to design and develop innovative submarines. In 1954, it launched the world's first nuclear powered submarine, the USS Nautilus. During the 1970s, EB began construction of the Los Angeles-class (SSN-688) nuclear attack submarines and the Trident-class (SSBN) ballistic missile submarines. In October 1995, EB delivered the last of the 33 Los Angeles-class submarines that it built. The last Trident-class was completed in 1996. The Seawolf-class (SSN-21) was the successor attack submarine class; however, due to high costs and other issues, the Navy ordered only three of the original twenty-nine that were expected to be built. The lessons learned from the Seawolf-class set the stage for the development of the Virginia-class program. With the Virginia-class, EB and the Navy established objectives to improve the cost, performance, development and production cycles, and EHS considerations.

The USS Virginia (SSN-774) was commissioned in October 2004. The Virginia class is being built at both EB shipyards and those of Northrop Grumman Newport News in Virginia. Today, EB enjoys an outstanding reputation as the premier designer and builder of submarines.

THE STRATEGIC LOGIC AND PROGRAM IMPLEMENTATION
The Driving Forces Behind the Virginia-Class Program

One of the most critical challenges facing EB during the design of the Virginia-class program was to control costs of the final product. EB and the Navy had a mutual need to achieve a viable new design. EB needed to design a ship that would sustain its production capabilities and resources. The Navy required a cost-effective submarine built in sufficient numbers to provide an effective force that minimized construction costs, operating expenditures and end-of-life considerations. A prime requisite of the design was to ensure affordability across the entire life cycle. Life-cycle costs are extremely high for a class of ships having small numbers, such as the three Seawolf-class ships.

EB has been producing state-of-the-art nuclear-powered submarines since the launch of the USS Nautilus. However, the basic design process had changed very little prior to the design of the Virginia-class development program. While the technologies that were built into the submarines were very sophisticated, the design and development techniques were basically the conventional approaches used for several decades. The shortcomings of old design methods added to the high costs and the poor interactions between the design groups, contributing to construction problems, and adding additional economic wastes and environmental burdens.

The design of the new ship had to include high performance and low cost. The design philosophy was to achieve all objectives without making trade-offs and compromises. Through the application of the CATIA system, a state-of-the-art electronic computer-aided design and computer-aided manufacturing (CAD/CAM) technology, EB designed the Virginia-class with the ability to identify and resolve engineering problems and economic challenges early in the design sequences, avoiding problems, added costs, and unexpected waste streams. CAD/CAM was only part of the revolutionary changes made during the design process. Eighteen design-build teams comprised of all functional departments, important suppliers, and Navy personnel provided an integrated and collaborative perspective. The objective of these teams was to improve efficiency and effectiveness by eliminating the traditional walls between the design groups and the manufacturing units.

The Virginia-class incorporated modular construction concepts for maximum flexibility. Modular construction facilitates manufacturing efficiency by allowing entire deck assemblies to be built and tested before being mated with the hull. This means that a ship can be modified in the future to accommodate new technologies or meet new requirements. The Virginia-class has the capability of being updated without enormous expense, allowing the Navy to prevent the premature obsolesce of its ships.

The Virginia-class development program focused on preventing pollution and minimizing wastes in compliance with federal laws and regulations, Executive Orders (EO) of the President, and DoD directives. While the requirements included the International Convention for Prevention of Pollution from Ships, known as MARPOL,[b] and various federal laws, EO 12856[c] was one of the most significant driving forces. It mandates that federal agencies comply with right-to-know laws and pollution prevention requirements. It mandates that all federal agencies conduct their facility management and acquisition activities so that (to the maximum extent practicable) the quantity of toxic chemicals entering the waste stream, including any releases to the environment, are reduced as expeditiously as possible through source reduction; that generated waste is recycled to the maximum extent practicable; and that any wastes remaining are managed in a manner to protect public health and the environment. EO 12856 was implemented through DoD Directive 5000.2-R.

Establishing the Environmental Compliance Program

The Navy began the Virginia-class ECP by establishing an Environmental Management Team (EMT) with representatives from groups across the ship's full life cycle. The EMT included the Acquisition Program Manager and representatives from the Navy Policy and Legal Office, Facility Command, Navy Technical Design Codes, Maintenance Organizations, Shipbuilders, Design Agents, Operating Forces, Supply Command, Navy, Disposal Shipyards, and PARMS.[d] ECP was an essential part of the Virginia-class for supporting the pollution prevention directives of DoD and the Navy. The purpose of the pollution prevention strategy was to identify hazardous materials so that contractors and suppliers could find alternatives. The Navy's program manager stated the policy as:[e]

> The new attack submarine program is fully committed to ensure that the next class of attack submarines will be designed and constructed so that the operation, deployment, maintenance, overhaul and ultimate disposal of the submarine will meet all applicable environmental requirements.

EMT addressed environmental considerations in material procurement procedures and in transactions with the design/build teams as they worked on the development program, helping to integrate pollution prevention into system engineering.

The ECP became a reality because the Navy's program managers and EB management were committed to its success from inception and provided the resources to ensure its execution. Mr. J. Welch, President of EB, regarded environmental programs as essential for the long-term success of EB and its products. He sent a letter to all employees stating:[f]

> Electric Boat recognizes protection of the natural environment as among the highest of its priorities. We are conducting our operations in a manner that safeguards the environment and preserves natural resources.

EB formed an Environmental Compliance Team (ECT) with professionals from various disciplines to integrate environmental considerations into the design and development phase of the acquisition program. Unfortunately, ECT was organized several years after the beginning of the overall Virginia-class Acquisition Program. Given the late start, the ECT did not have the opportunity at the beginning to work with the design/build teams on a concurrent basis. Design/build (D/B) teams were cross-functional teams that linked downstream activities with upstream decision making. The design/build teams had to meet the technical/performance requirements of the product's mission. Design/build team members established the basis for performing the work, set the priorities, specified the design and development activities, assessed the alternatives, and evaluated the results. The knowledge of the downstream capabilities and limitations allowed the teams to select solutions that were appropriate for the needs and requirements of the program.

From an EHS perspective, D/B teams considered the entire life cycle of the submarine as they selected materials for use in the ship's systems. They identified the important issues, analyzed the situation, incorporated pollution prevention and life cycle management concepts wherever possible, and pursued innovative solutions to environmental concerns and impacts. Designing for recycling, reusability or disposal was an essential consideration. ECT coordinated the efforts and provided technical support and analysis, but the D/B teams were responsible for program implementation. ECT collaborated with D/B teams to perform the essential elements of life cycle assessment (LCA). The D/B teams had the skills and capabilities to execute the program requirements, but often obtained specialized knowledge from ECT when confronted by difficult EHS issues. ECT's primary responsibilities included providing

EHS awareness training to the D/B teams, mapping the hazardous materials, working on the environmental analysis, performing selected impact analysis, and conducting the vendor studies.

ECT assessed the laws and regulations affecting the procurement and construction phases by identifying the need for permits at the construction sites of the Virginia-class submarine. The assessments included determining anticipated permitting requirements and estimating the potential emissions, effluents, and waste streams governed by federal and state environmental laws and regulations. The ECT also evaluated the potential impacts of the various waste streams.

The Environmental Compliance Program Management

The management framework consisted of program management, environmental implementation plan, and performance improvement actions. According to the ECT program manager, EB structured the program so that all of the participants would understand the essential objectives and elements of the program. The environmental mission statement was:[8]

> The environmental compliance program mission is to facilitate and coordinate the Virginia-class life cycle environmental analysis and ensure the integration of design alternatives to minimize the environmental impact without compromising other program and customer objectives.

ECP management set the stage by articulating the philosophy of the program and integrating environmental considerations into the system design process. The philosophy during the design phase was to build in solutions for compliance with all laws and regulations; to improve the environmental profile of the Virginia-class; and to solve life cycle problems. In essence, this innovative program merged the fundamentals of compliance, pollution prevention, and design for the environment into a program focusing on sustainable development. The ECP framework offered guidelines rather than hard rules. It covered the design considerations and material selection from an environmental perspective. Figure 5.1A depicts the grand scheme.

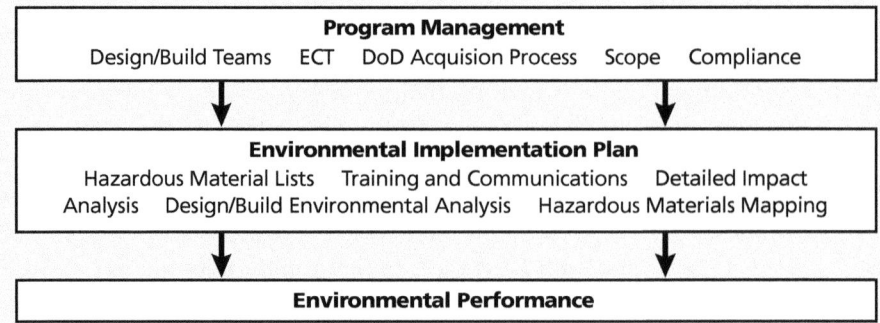

Figure 5.1A Simplified program management schematic.

The scheme included pollution prevention, liability containment, compliance issues, EHS aspects, and waste management. The program included environmental assessments based on the laws and regulations, waste minimization, identification of material requirements and specification, and the selection of materials that imbue pollution prevention. The purpose was to identify appropriate areas for improving the design considerations with respect to environmental risks and liabilities. The program baseline established the boundaries, methods, costs, and schedule of the activities, and set the stage for the comparative analysis for impacts and improvements.

The DoD Acquisition Process spelled out the requirements for completing the LCA. The purpose of LCA assessment is to identify, quantify, and evaluate the materials and energy employed used during the design/build phases and over entire life cycle. LCA was the fundamental tool used to analyze the inventory of materials and processes, their impacts, and the opportunities for improvement. The starting point was to define the purpose and scope of the assessment. The intent of the LCA was to analyze environmental issues and to discover pollution-prevention opportunities. Whereas LCA covers a cradle-to-grave view, ECT decided to limit the scope of their efforts. For example, 70 hazardous materials were selected for analysis and only 20 tier-one suppliers were included in the program. The scope of the program centered on areas that were within the immediate control of EB during the design/build phases and the Navy during the life of the ship through decommissioning. These boundaries clearly set forth the limits, making the process doable and cost effective. Figure 5.2A provides a representation of the scope of the LCA. It is a multi-stage input/output model that examines all of the inputs and their impacts, and all of the outputs including products, derivatives, by-products, and wastes and their impacts.

Material Acquisition		Boat Construction	Operation and Maintenance	Decommission	Disposal
Natural resources	Materials and part vendors	Groton and other locations	Open Sea and Navy facilities	Portsmouth and Puget Sound	Waste disposal
Not included in the analysis		Virginia-Class Life Cycle Considerations			Not included in the analysis
1	2	3	4	5	6
Resource Extraction	Manufacture of Materials	Top 20 Vendors	Construction of Submarine	Operations and Maintenance	Ultimate Disassembly and Disposal

Figure 5.2A LCA boundary options.

ECT used LCA to evaluate the design considerations and explore the possibilities for systematic improvements. ECT established material balances as a fundamental method for analyzing the processes and discovering opportunities to minimize waste streams. A material balance defines inputs (required materials) and outputs (product and waste streams generated) of an entire process. Material balances help determine the characteristics of amounts and components of a waste stream.

NOTES
a. Graduate students, Diba Khan-Bureau and Kurt Cramer, made significant contributions to the example. Originally known as the NSSN Program, the official ship class designation was changed to the Virginia-class on EB correspondence in November 1998.
b. MARPOL regulates the discharge of wastes from ships. It prohibits the discharge of plastics at sea and limits oily waste discharge of waste streams to those containing less than 15 ppm. It establishes special areas in which no discharge is permitted. Navy ship compliance with MARPOL is implemented by the Marine Plastic Pollution Research and Control Act. Submarines had to be in compliance by 2008, early in the operational phase of the Virginia-class life cycle. The significance of these laws for the Virginia-class is that the ship had to be designed to comply with all regulations during peacetime operations. The Virginia-class has to be able to discharge fluids that contain no more than 15 ppm oil, to retain waste oils and all plastic wastes, and to retain all wastes for the duration of anticipated operations.
c. Executive Orders are the formal means through which the President of the United States prescribes the conduct of business in the Executive Branch. Executive Orders12856 directs the Executive Branch to comply with existing environmental laws. The Executive Branch departments must establish means by which they are to comply with those laws.
d. PARMS are the DoD Participating Managers responsible for the overall system-level integration of the Command, Control, Communications, and Intelligence System subsystems.
e. "NSSN Design for the Environment Guidelines," EB, Environmental Compliance Team, D441, p3.
f. The Green Team News, Volume 3.4, December 1997, p3. Mr. Welch has since retired from Electric Boat.
g. Electric Boat Corporation, Environmental Compliance Team

Reflections

Strategic implementation though HSPs is a critical element of CSM and VSL. An exciting vision and great corporate strategies are of little consequence unless strategic leaders engage the organization and the extended enterprise to achieve positive results and sustainable success. HSPs involve converting strategies and goals into desired outcomes through program design and development, resource allocations, and various other means and mechanisms.

Strategy formulation and strategic direction set the stage for strategic implementation through program selection, definition and design, which set the stage for program execution and overall effective program management. Program implementation and execution for HSPs are difficult and complicated, because they include many elements and requirements that are open-ended and in many cases new to the company and even new to the world. While strategic leaders can orchestrate a general framework for implementing and executing HSPs, a significant amount of the actions and activities have to be determined during definition and design.

HSPs often involve numerous development projects within the programsand usually take ten or more years to reach maturity. Unlike most company projects that have starting points and ending dates, HSPs span across time and the business landscape with great uncertainty and unpredictability. While there are great challenges involved, there are also great opportunities and possibilities, especially for programs involving major transformations of strategic positions, corporate capabilities, and leadership and management sophistication. The general aspirations are to leapfrog peers and competitors and to become the architects of the future.

Strategic leaders, program managers, and participants who engage in program implementation and execution are usually pressed into dual roles and responsibilities of accomplishing their normal work and at the same time engaging in making the program real and achieving the targeted outcomes. They have to be careful not to just focus on pressing needs and requirements of the present, especially the short-term priorities, since such activities often overwhelm the situation and cause strategic implementation and execution to suffer. Moreover, there are more people engaged in program implementation and execution than in strategic formulation. Unlike strategic formulation, one of the main difficulties associated with program implementation and execution is that many of the people involved are ill-informed about the program plans and their roles and responsibilities. Most importantly, they often don't understand that many of the subelements cannot be fully articulated and have to be developed along the way. Unlike conventional management and business practices in which most of the systems, processes, tasks, and activities are clearly defined and developed and there is usually a tremendous depth of knowledge and experience in achieving the desired outcomes, program implementation and execution necessitate creativity, insights, imagination, and the courage to proceed along uncharted pathways.

This chapter focused on the front-end of the overall program framework. The next chapter continues the discussions with the elements of program execution and program evaluation.

Notes

1. http://spaceflight.nasa.gov/history/
2. Id. "After the last lunar landing, total funding for the Apollo program was about $19,408,134,000. The budget allocation was 34 percent of the NASA budget."
3. Id.
4. Steven Wheelwright and Kim Clark, *Revolutionizing Product Development* (Boston, MA: Harvard Business School Press, 1992, p34).
5. Project Management Institute, *A Guide to the Project Management Body of Knowledge, Fourth Edition* (Newtown Square, PA: Project Management Institute, 2008, p42).
6. Id, pp352–356.
7. Project Management Institute, *A Guide to the Project Management Body of Knowledge* (Newtown Square, PA: Project Management Institute, 1996, p29).
8. Gary Hamel, *Leading the Revolution* (Boston, MA: Harvard Business School Press, 2000, pp244–271).
9. David L. Rainey, *Enterprise-wide Strategic Management: Achieving Sustainable Success through Leadership, Strategies and Value Creation* (Cambridge, UK: Cambridge University Press, 2010, p440). The graphic is adapted and modified.

10. James Collins and Jerry Porras, *Built to Last: Successful Habits of Visionary Companies* (New York, NY: Harper Business Essentials, 1994, pp91–114).
11. Id, p94.
12. David L. Rainey, *Product Innovation: Leading Change through Integrated Product Development* (Cambridge, UK: Cambridge University Press, 2005, p232)
13. David L. Rainey, *Sustainable Business Development: Inventing the Future through Strategy, Innovation, and Leadership*, pp456–457.
14. Id, p461.
15. David L. Rainey, *Enterprise-wide Strategic Management: Achieving Sustainable Success through Leadership, Strategies and Value Creation*, p470. The graphic was adapted and modified.
16. http://www.utc.com/About+UTC; UTC is a diversified company that includes UTC Climate, Controls and Security, especially Carrier heating and air conditioning, Hamilton Sundstrand aerospace systems, Otis elevators and escalators, Pratt & Whitney aircraft engines, Sikorsky helicopters, and UTC Power fuel cells. In 2010, UTC had net sales of $54.3 billion and net income of $4.4 billion. It had 208,200 employees and international sales were 61% of total sales.
17. There are many similar constructs. The process is stated as generic because it contains the common elements of the standard methods. A refined approach might include benchmarking or similar methods.
18. David L. Rainey, *Enterprise-wide Strategic Management: Achieving Sustainable Success through Leadership, Strategies and Value Creation*, p485.

References

Collins, James and Jerry Porras (1994) *Built to Last: Successful Habits of Visionary Companies.* New York: Harper Business Essentials.

Hamel, Gary (2000) *Leading the Revolution.* Boston, MA: Harvard Business School Press

Project Management Institute (2008) *A Guide to the Project Management Body of Knowledge, Fourth Edition.* Newtown Square, PA: Project Management Institute.

Project Management Institute, (1996) *A Guide to the Project Management Body of Knowledge.* Newtown Square, PA: Project Management Institute.

Rainey, David L. (2010) *Enterprise-wide Strategic Management: Achieving Sustainable Success through Leadership, Strategies and Value Creation.* Cambridge, UK: Cambridge University Press.

Rainey, David L. (2006) *Sustainable Business Development: Inventing the Future through Strategy, innovation, and Leadership.* Cambridge, UK: Cambridge University Press.

Rainey, David L. (2005) *Product Innovation: Leading Change through Integrated Product Development.* Cambridge, UK: Cambridge University Press.

Wheelwright, Steven and Kim Clark (1992) *Revolutionizing Product Development.* Boston, MA: Harvard Business School.

6

High-Level Strategic Programs

Execution and Evaluation

Introduction

Program execution requires that program managers and participants provide concerted efforts and great contributions, and that strategic leaders provide outstanding leadership and oversight. Unlike the typical project management scheme as discussed in the previous chapter in which project managers map out the sequence of activities, develop a schedule, and try to maintain tight control over the execution of the project among numerous essential aspects, program execution is much more open-ended. It necessitates flexibility to manage the possible changes during the duration of the program. For instance, as the program unfolds, new requirements may evolve, the business environment may change dramatically, or the company's strategic or financial positions may worsen, as well as many other positive or negative possibilities, all of which could warrant significant modifications during program execution. Given such possibilities and the prevailing realities of the business world, program managers and participants have to be agile, adaptive, and innovative. Yet, they and the strategic leaders and the steering committee have to ensure that the program is managed and properly controlled so that the objectives are realized and the specifications and desired outcomes are met. The desired/targeted outcomes are the critical determinants, not the plans, actions, and activities. While program execution can be laid out as a framework with an articulated flow of elements, subelements, and projects, it is essential that the strategic logic, objectives, specifications, and criteria as discussed in the previous chapter are used to provide direction and guidance in moving toward the targeted outcomes, both in the near term and in the long term. The more complicated the program requirements, the more challenging the specific actions, and the longer its duration, the more likely there will be significant changes in the business environment and market spaces. Moreover, changes also increase the probabilities for mistakes, miscues, and catastrophic problems within program execution that may cause rethinking and redesign of the overall program or the subsets thereof. Since it is virtually impossible to contemplate all of the profound changes and unexpected events that might happen, program execution cannot be precisely configured and rigidly structured with all of the activities laid out. Program management has to be able to respond to the requisite changes as quickly as possible. Agility is a key to success.

Program managers are the principal leaders who provide the hands-on direction, guidance, and support. It is imperative that program managers act more like directors of the production of motion pictures than directors of Broadway plays. A movie is based on a screenplay and scripts, but the actual execution is circuitous with many changes and uncertain pathways to the outcomes. Moreover, the actual sequence and flow of actions have many variations depending on the outcomes of upstream actions. The schedule of activities usually has many adjustments and modifications. While there may be pressure to complete the filming of the movie at a certain date, the primary agenda is usually more on the quality of the acting and the scenes and the value of the end product than keeping to the schedule or within the budget. The filming is just one part of a number of subelements that all have to be done very well if the movie is to obtain the intended outcomes and the value proposition. The acting and filming are usually followed by editing the film, which is then followed by production, marketing, and distribution. Some of the activities associated with the latter two efforts might be done in parallel with filming and/or editing; thus, many more possible variations. The Lord of the Rings and the Hobbit movies are great examples of the focus on outcomes and not the subelements like costs and scheduling.

On the other hand, stage plays have precise scripts, schedules, sequences, budgets, and expected outcomes. There is little tolerance for changes during the play and the director's role is to ensure that the performance goes off without any variations and in accordance with the specifications. While the movie-play example involves actions and outcomes having relatively short durations, strategic leaders and program managers usually have significantly bigger challenges since the expected durations are much longer. They have to have the capabilities, willingness, and mindset to accommodate new requirements, dramatic changes in the actions and activities, and even wholesale swings in the strategic direction and expected outcomes.

Program development involves creating the solutions, developing the outcomes, and producing the related management constructs. It is very difficult to articulate all of the development considerations necessary to obtain the requisite solutions and outcomes, especially ones based on new-to-the-world technologies and approaches. Determining what the solutions are and what is necessary to produce them is not always readily apparent. It often takes many interactions among the participants and numerous iterations of certain activities before it becomes clear on how to develop the solutions and realize the expected outcomes. For most high-level strategic programs (HSPs), development is the most challenging and wide-ranging element. While the upstream elements discussed in the previous chapter may take many months or even a year or two years to complete before moving on to the downstream elements of execution, program development itself may take many years to engage in and to fully realize.

Program demonstration/incubation involves the validation and testing of the results produced during program development. If hardware is developed, then demonstration involves testing it to verify and certify the outcomes. One of the major goals of validation and the related testing protocols is to assure program management and the participants that they can achieve all of the objectives and targeted specifications. When human health and safety are concerns, extensive testing is necessary to ensure that every precaution has been taken to mitigate the possible risks.

Incubation is an optional approach when testing is not possible or demonstration techniques are not fully effective. It is also useful as a supplement to demonstration. The purpose is to ensure that all considerations and alternate views have been heard and that any contrary perspectives and positions have been identified, examined, and rectified before proceeding along the selected pathways. It involves taking the time and effort to assess the results and outcomes of the development(s) and to carefully think through and reflect on what has been achieved or failed to be accomplished. It may simply be a time of reflection and thought. While time is always important, program managers, in particular, may need to spend some time thinking through the activities and expected outcomes to assure that they will meet all of the expectations in the future. Even if testing was done and the results were favorable, incubation is usually a fruitful method and time well spent for assuring that success will be realized and big mistakes are avoided. Incubation invokes the precautionary principle that strategic leaders and program managers have a duty to ensure the well-being of participants and those who are expected to deploy and use the outcomes, especially potential customers and stakeholders. Incubation may also include scrutiny by selected and knowledgeable outsiders who have no invested interests in the program. They may provide peer review of the development(s) and potential outcomes and their implications; thus providing valuable insights about the suitability, usefulness, and safety of the outcomes in the market spaces and the business environment. Such feedback may help to achieve the best outcomes possible given the realities of the time and efforts and the prevailing state of the art.

Deployment involves introducing the solutions and/or outcomes to the business world. Like program development, program deployment varies considerably. For large HSPs with a national or international launches, deployment may also require many years to fully execute. Deployment often takes the form of sequential or parallel projects rolled out by region, country, market segment and/or business unit. In such cases, the program simply becomes real as the areas or business units engage in deployment and realize the targeted outcomes. Deployment involves the convergence of the program subelements, projects, people, and resources into a fully integrated system that proceeds down the pathways to success. Deployment requires an integrated perspective about the effects and implications of customers and markets, supply networks, stakeholders, related industries, infrastructure, and the potential responses from competition. It necessitates a high level of awareness on the part of program managers and participants pertaining to the actions and activities to achieve the objectives and desired outcomes.

Program evaluation is really an ongoing part of program implementation and execution. The methods, techniques, and metrics used to evaluate HSPs, the elements and subelements thereof, include continuously monitoring the progress being made and providing feedback to the strategic leaders, the steering committee, the program managers, and the participants. Program evaluation involves preempting problems, mistakes, and miscues before they happen, taking appropriate actions to eliminate the problems and difficulties, and taking corrective actions, if necessary.

The chapter includes the following main topics:

- Determining the means and mechanisms for program execution
- Discussing the main perspectives, methods, and insights about program evaluation

Program Execution

Framework for Executing High-Level Strategic Programs

The framework for program execution is even more difficult to map out than the framework for the upstream elements. Program development, demonstration, and deployment are highly dependent on the situations and circumstances of the business world and program implementation, thus making a general model difficult to articulate. Figure 6.1 highlights some of the key elements and subelements of program execution. It also includes program evaluation.

Program execution involves the actions and activities that result in achievements and the attainment of the objectives. Execution must be both rigorous and adaptive. Program managers are responsible for all aspects of program execution. They make appropriate decisions to adapt the program plans to fit the changes in the strategic aspects and in the external business world, when and if necessary. Without the ability to modify the program plans, the whole flow could become static, i.e., frozen in the time that the plans were conceived; the lack of flexibility might cause execution of the remaining elements and subelements of the program to drift out of synch with reality.[1] However, major changes, especially those affecting the strategic logic and desired outcomes, usually have to be approved by the strategic leaders and steering committee. Thus, it is absolutely necessary to allow for flexibility in the program since rigidity makes program management more difficult, not less. Moreover, since it is usually impossible to specify every detail associated with program execution during program design, program managers and participants often have to determine subsequent actions and activities as accomplishments are realized and the subsequent requirements become more apparent.

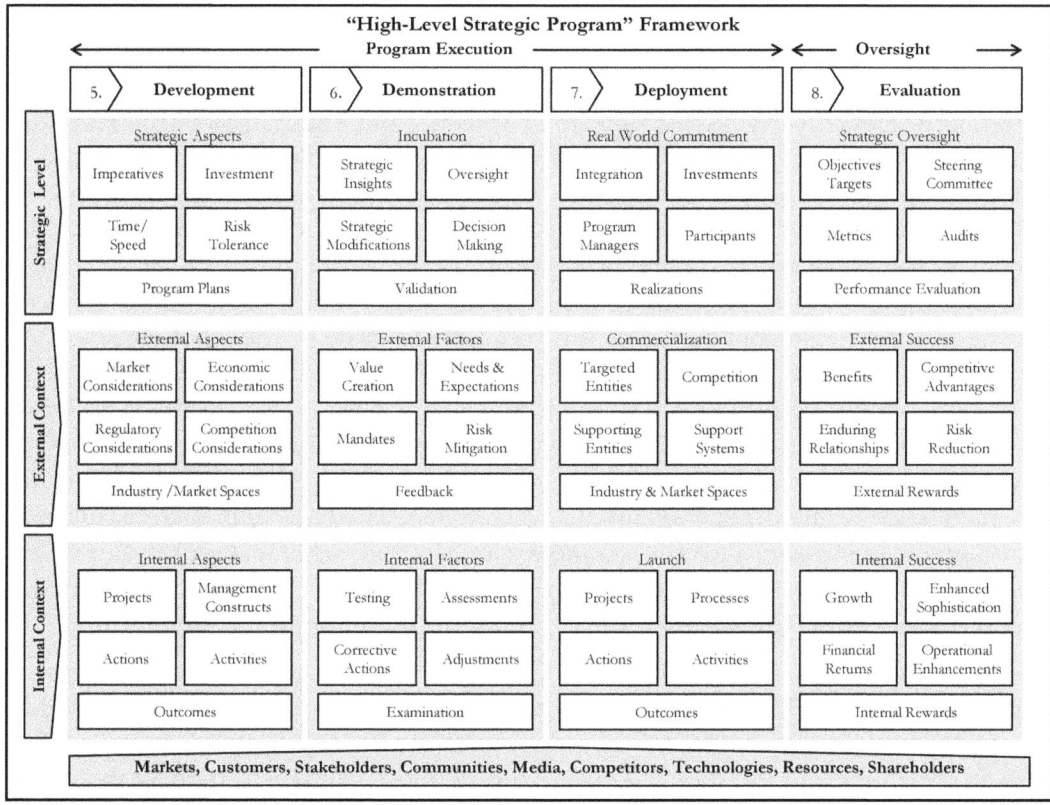

Figure 6.1 Key elements and subelements of program execution.

Program managers have to be willing to take responsibility for their decisions and accept criticism for results that are less than expected. They have to resolve conflicts within the organization and with partners as quickly as possible. They also encourage participants to be innovative and diligent in producing results and obtaining the targeted outcomes in the most expeditious ways possible without violating ethical principles and good practices. It is results and outcomes that are important, not intentions or even good efforts.

A capable program organization is one that understands what has to be done and how to do it, has the resources and knowledge to execute, has the willingness to engage in the actions, and knows how to succeed.[2] Such an organization typically has effective collaborative teams that have the skills, capabilities, talents, and behaviors, and use best practices, methods, and techniques to realize desired outcomes. Good organizations know that outcomes are important, not just activities.

Developing the Program and the First Actions of Program Execution
Strategic Aspects of Program Development

At the strategic level, strategic leaders and the steering committee continue to provide guidance and oversight during program execution. They are fully engaged in the program and have direct involvement. Most importantly, they constantly scrutinize the imperatives and the strategic logic of the program. Remember, the imperatives involve "the why" question and are the overarching reasons for the program. For instance, a program to create a sustainable enterprise requires the integration of the extended enterprise and the adoption of sustainability and sustainable business development (SBD) within the company as discussed in Chapter 1. The imperative is to create a totally integrated enterprise, i.e., a sustainable enterprise, based on the principles, perspectives, solutions, systems, structures, and strategic innovations of SBD. Becoming a sustainable enterprise requires a paradigm shift from doing what is possible based on the resources and capabilities of the company to those of the whole business enterprise, including all of the contributors and recipients. A sustainable enterprise includes the corporation with all of its internal strategic business units (SBUs) and their value-delivery systems linked with all of the value-added entities (contributors) of the supply networks, related industries, partners, and all of the relationships with customers, stakeholders, and other constituents (recipients). The basic approach for building a sustainable enterprise is to create value streams for the customers, stakeholders, and the organization that exceed social, economic, ethical, technological, and environmental expectations and requirements in the short term and in the long term.

Strategic aspects include examining how well the program plans are being managed and executed. The program managers reflect on how the estimated investment is tracking and how it is expected to fare over the course of program execution. They also examine whether the speed of program execution is sufficient to meet the expectations of the objectives and the targeted outcomes. These are keys to success that are monitored throughout the program.

External Context and Considerations During Program Development

From an external perspective, program development is primarily based on the market and economic considerations as identified and specified as targeted outcomes per the program design. Market considerations are critical even for programs that focus on internal aspects like improving the sophistication of the leadership and organizational capabilities. A main reason for many HSPs is to improve the connectedness, interactions, and relationships with the external business world. Markets considerations are among the most important inputs into the development actions and activities. Some of the intended outcomes are to serve customers in more innovative and fruitful ways and to enjoy mutual successes in the market spaces. While it is hard to generalize, program development from market space perspectives goes beyond traditional marketing methods and campaigns and reaches out to develop exciting new opportunities and the means and mechanisms to realize success. For example, Unilever has very ambitious HSPs to increase its strategic positions in developing countries. According to Chairman Michael Treschow, Unilever has programs to enhance its penetration of new markets. In Unilever's 2010 Annual Report and Accounts, he states that:[3]

> The focus of the Board in 2010 has been on strategy and governance. The strategy was reviewed in detail by the Board during a visit to Brazil with an emphasis on sharpening the

Group's vision and on the choices needed to enable Unilever to win in increasing competitive markets. A key element of the strategy is the enormous growth opportunities offered by emerging markets of Asia Africa and CEE [Central and Eastern Europe] and Latin America. These markets already account for more than 50% of Unilever's business. We start from a strong base therefore in reaching the growing number of people in these markets who share the same aspirations as consumers in the West.

Unilever's development program has global perspectives involving most of its business units and product lines and broad-based geographical reach and market-wise spread across many regions and countries. Furthermore, strategic leaders and program managers realize that doing business in emerging markets requires numerous high-level transitions and transformations so that the company and business units are in concert with the location conditions (culture, history, traditions, weather, climate, etc.) and the norms in the targeted markets. Development programs for reaching emerging markets involve the global connections and resources, and such programs may take a decade or so to reach their full potential.

Program development is highly dependent on the economic conditions and trends of the country and the global economy. Economic aspects cover a broad array of considerations from the state of the economy(s) and growth rates to the availability and costs of labor and capital among numerous others. Macroeconomics focuses on production and consumption (supply and demand) of goods and services, international trade, the resources required, and their availability, especially land, labor, and capital. Economic considerations involve the scarcity resources and how strategic leaders and program managers make economic decisions when confronted with insufficient time, labor, capital, energy, and natural resources to meet program requirements. Economic decisions are often made on the basis of cost-benefit or benefit-to-cost analysis. The latter is preferred since the most important factors pertain to the benefits. Benefit-to-cost (B/C) analysis, using a B/C equation, depicts the sum of the benefits of a course of action relative to the sum of the costs; the equation can be expressed as: $B/C = \Sigma$ benefits (B) $\div \Sigma$ costs (C) or $B/C = \Sigma B - \Sigma C$, i.e., ratio of expected beneficial outcomes to expected costs and the value of the benefits minuses the costs, respectively.[4] However, the economic considerations include many other factors like living standards, people's income and savings, trade, logistics, foreign exchange, concentration of wealth, land ownership, availability of capital and labor, and application of investments.[5] The state of a given national economy depends on many factors and it is a critical question relating to program development given that recessions and expansions are part of the normal cycles of macroeconomic conditions.[6] Since HSPs are expected to take considerable time to develop, demonstrate, and deploy, it is realistic to expect that there may both expansionary and recessionary times during the duration of the program. While business leaders generally favor business expansions and dislike recessions, neither may be exactly the best situation for program execution. For instance, recessions may be the best time to engage in program execution since it may be possible to employ capabilities and use resources that might otherwise be unproductive. While most companies tend to reduce their efforts to save money during such times, it may the very time to leapfrog peers and competitors and market expectations by being proactive in obtaining new solutions, higher levels of sophistication, and other competitive advantages.

Furthermore, program managers and participants have to understand that many of the conventional theories and practices of mainstream business management are not appropriate when managing and executing HSPs. For instance, using conventional management constructs such as discounted cash flow calculations to determine a rate of return of the investment may lead to inaction and even termination, if the outward cash outflows continue for years before the cash inflows begin a decade or so later, only after the program is fully deployed. The typical present-value calculations suggest that the future cash inflows are not very valuable and the expected program outcomes are not worth the investment(s). However, there are many inaccuracies when using such conventional thinking and methods. Firstly, the future cash inflows and positive effects may be significantly greater than anyone could ever contemplate. Think of the enormous wealth created by Intel and Microsoft; could anyone have foreseen such outcomes in 1968 or 1977? Secondly, the investment(s) may have tangential benefits across the company's enterprises that are impossible to calculate or even envision, such as the ability to survive and prosper in difficult times or to leapfrog the competition. For instance, the company may have gone bankrupt or may have become a target for acquisition, if it did not engage in HSPs to change its product portfolios in light of the Great Recession. Thirdly, certain uneconomically feasible programs may actually be precursors to future money-making programs that are absolute necessary in the sequence of strategic innovations and corporate developments. For example, Bill Gates and Paul Allen developed the operating system for IBM's early personal computers (PCs) for a very attractive price, knowing that Microsoft would make a lot of money in the future by selling its software to the clones. Gates and Allen clearly understood the business value for PCs was more in the software than in the hardware. It was relatively easy to copy the hardware, but much more difficult to make one's software the standard. The proof is in the outcomes; Microsoft has become a very wealthy corporation, whereas most of the PC producers have gone bankrupt or their business has been acquired by other corporations like Hewlett Packard's acquisition of Compaq or IBM's sale of its PC business to Lenovo.

Economic considerations also include a complex array of actions, transactions, interactions, and relationships among the contributors and recipients that are necessary to fully develop the program. Whether in developed or developing countries, positive economic conditions and overall stability are crucial for long-term growth and program success. However, conventional economic forecasting is usually insufficient for providing global perspectives about HSPs, since the extended time frame (ten years or more) often makes forecasting impossible or subject to too many assumptions that usually become irrelevant or inaccurate after a few years. Therefore, strategic leaders and program managers may have to use scenario planning (as detailed in Chapter 4) to explore the long-term economic aspects. Scenario planning helps to shape strategic thinking about the future and the potential changes that might be necessary. It also helps identify opportunities, challenges, and risks across the business enterprise over time and how strategic decision makers can make the best choices given the wide range of possibilities. It relates directly to the roles and responsibilities that visionary strategic leaders and program managers have in transforming or transitioning the company into a more viable and successful entity through HSPs; ones that are moving ahead of the rate of change and developing more sophisticated capabilities and new means and mechanisms based on the realities of the business environment. Scenario planning provides insights about what can be done or what has to be done in the present and in the future.

Regulatory considerations are critical mandates that have to be continuously revisited from the selection of a given program through execution. Regulatory mandates include the laws and regulations that specify directives, rules, protocols, control mechanisms, and reporting requirements, i.e., what must be done and how it is to be accomplished. They also provide certain incentives and disincentives. Laws and regulations are usually initiated by social-political forces to balance the needs and objectives of the political unit(s) and society with those of business enterprises. Regulations are usually codified, documented, and readily accessible to program managers and participants. They are usually written in the language of regulators and enforced by government officials of the responsible agencies. They are often complicated, making it difficult for untrained practitioners to understand the mandates and to follow them. The degree of uncertainty pertaining to regulations varies depending on the laws and the regulatory agencies. For many global corporations the implications of noncompliance are great and the precise (legal) interpretation of what is required for proper execution is paramount.

The outcomes of a given program have to be in concert with prevailing regulatory realities and the expected changes over a decade or even two. From a strategic perspective, the anticipated changes in laws and regulations are critical for success. Like the underpinning of scenario planning, the future implications have to be considered, not just the prevailing aspects. Compliance is a never-ending, difficult challenge that is always a key consideration, especially for HSPs that may take decades to fully execute. Nestlé provides its global perspectives:[7]

> Compliance with applicable laws and international conventions such as the Universal Declaration of Human Rights and strong support for the UN Global Compact, as well as our internal standards and regulations [policies and rules], is the foundation of our business. Beyond compliance, our business is based on sustainability, ensuring our activities protect the environment for future generations. Yet, we believe we need to go further, creating shared value for both the Company and society in areas where shareholders' and society's interests intersect-nutrition, water and rural development-are the focus for this strategy...

> Our objective is to be recognized as the world leader in nutrition, health and wellness, trusted by all stakeholders, and to be the reference for financial performance in our industry; this objective demands from our people long-term inspiration, to build the future, and short-term entrepreneurial actions, to deliver the necessary performance today.

Nestlé's perspectives have profound implications for program development. The underlying objective is to not only consider the possibilities of new laws and regulations, but to go beyond compliance and make the regulations irrelevant in terms of the program and the intended outcomes. While such efforts may not be easy, they make business realities a lot simpler. For instance, if the program managers and participants eliminate all toxic substances, then all of the regulations pertaining to toxic substances and hazardous wastes are nonfactors. Compliance is assured and future regulatory requirements do not affect the program outcomes because they do not apply.

Competitive considerations are always important. While most companies spend incredible time, effort, and money during program execution, strategic leaders, the steering committee, and program managers have to be concerned about what competitors and possibly peers are also doing in their related programs and initiatives. From a program development perspective, a key to success is obtaining valuable outcomes and sustainable competitive advantages. The pursuits for sustainable advantages and uniqueness are relentless. Over the last twenty years, most large corporations have become more sophisticated and have improved their product lines, brands, systems, processes, and performance. One's main competitors rarely stop developing new products, processes, systems and management constructs and improving business value and performance. Some of the main initiatives focus on lowering cost structures, improving the quality of products and services, enhancing product and process innovations, finding new market opportunities, establishing new businesses, and becoming global corporations.

Competition analysis is an important tool used during strategic formulation and implementation to determine the possible relevancy and effectiveness of the company's business strategies, operations, and outcomes. The focus is usually on specific competitors and the typical analysis is relatively narrow, targeting those competitors that might influence or negatively affect the company's outcomes. From a HSP perspective, competition analysis examines existing and emerging competitors to determine their expected strategies, responses, and innovations in light of the targeted outcomes. The competition analysis should result in an assessment and understanding of the expected competitive responses that allow program managers to deal with the challenges, make preemptive determinations, and take positive actions about how to achieve the desired competitive advantages. The basic approach is to have a good sense of the competitors and their capabilities so that decisions can be made about the prospects of the program, i.e., whether to proceed, to modify, to change, or even abandon the program. Some of the key questions include:[8]

- Who are the most significant competitors who might threaten the outcomes or usurp the potential competitive advantages of the program?
- What are their strategies and counter-efforts to negate the positives of our programs?
- What are their anticipated responses to our programs and their expected outcomes?
- What are the advantages and disadvantages of potential competitor efforts and responses?
- What constraints or limitations do they impose on our efforts?

The initial step is to identify and list the existing and potential competitors. Identifying the current competitors is usually easy; determining the potential or emerging competitors is obviously more difficult. From the list, the next step is to select the ones that are the most challenging. An assessment of the advantages and disadvantages of competition in the intended market space(s) provides a means to gain additional insights about what the program has to deliver to achieve success. The intent is to enhance the development of the program, not to become overly concerned about competitors. It is important to be realistic about the positions that competitors occupy. Their potential efforts provide a sense of the possibilities for achieving success in the market spaces. They also provide information about development options. Such information and data are usually readily available from the public disclosures by competitors, especially those on the Internet. Other rich sources include reports to or by government agencies, industry and media reports, and independent surveys and research. The goal is learn as much as possible about each of the competitors. Some of the most important considerations are the criticality of speed and time-to-the-market and the desired customer and stakeholder attributes as perceived by the competitors.

When engaging in program development and possibly even earlier during program selection, definition, or design; strategic leaders and program managers have to reflect on what the expected outcomes provide in terms of business value and sustainable advantages. The big concern is that good outcomes may not be good enough. If a competitor trumps the company's development(s) and gains the competitive advantage(s), achieving the program objectives, targeted specifications, and desired outcomes may not result in success, but in failure. For example, Kodak improved its chemical-based photography businesses with new products and enhanced capabilities, but those efforts were of little consequence due to the revolutionary changes of digital photography. Moreover, K-Mart and other discount retailers increased the size of their stores by a factor two times the prevailing norm, but they were still disadvantaged when Walmart employed its "big box" strategy and built superstores that were quadruple the size of the competitors or more (250,000 square feet); in 2011, Walmart had 2900 superstores with average size of 185,000 square feet.[9] Success is transient and competitive advantages are difficult to secure and maintain. Walmart is now trying to catch up with its global competitors like Carrefour and Tesco that have large numbers of neighborhood stores in the largest metropolitan areas like Rome and Shanghai. Their stores are customized to meet the specific needs of the local consumers and are very efficient in the utilization of space and resources. Size is not the only determinant. Effectiveness is critical as well. For instance, Fred Smith, the founder and Chief Executive Officer (CEO) of FedEx, created enormous business value and sustained competitive advantages by developing the "hub and spike" overnight delivery system that was very effective in controlling outcomes using the Memphis Airport as the central point.

Program development requires an ongoing reflection of the business environment and the market spaces. As previously stated, the business world is constantly changing and program managers have to ensure that the external changes are accommodated in their thinking and actions. If modifications are necessary, the sooner they are affected the better the expected outcomes. The potential tragedy is that the hard work and dedication of all of the participants fail to provide competitive advantages or to achieve substantial gains in the future because the targeted outcomes are no longer relevant due to radical changes in the external business environment.

Internal Context and Considerations During Program Development

The internal aspects of program development are varied and considerable. Program development normally has a high level of uncertainty and involves numerous strategies, actions, and activities to realize the targeted outcomes. It usually involves unique means and mechanisms and even new-to-the-world approaches. Given the diversity of the ways for executing program development, an effective management construct is to subdivide the development scheme based the requirements and necessary actions into sequential and parallel projects. These can be developed and managed using project management techniques for the more common requirements and company-specific approaches for the more profound aspects. This allows program managers to enlist the management support of project managers and delegate certain roles and responsibilities to more specialized professionals and subject matter experts to deal with specific development aspects. For instance, if certain new hardware is necessary for specific functions and the hardware has to be developed, then it is appropriate to have engineers and technical specialists handle the requirements as an engineering-related project. Indeed, the overall program managers can concentrate their efforts on the main development aspects and have subsets or specific projects developed concurrently without disrupting the overall flow of the program. Obviously, such projects have to be coordinated and integrated into the overall program so that program execution is effective, efficient, and successful.

Given that program development cannot be generalized, it is difficult to identify all of the essential elements of a management system for developing the specific actions and activities. Thus, there are many pathways for developing the subelements, and they are generally uncharted. For instance, the invention and development of new technologies or the next generations of existing technologies may take years to complete. They are often part of a company's strategic innovations as discussed in Chapter 4 under the domain of the research and development (R&D) organization. Such R&D projects are often part of HSPs as well. Think about what Kodak had to do to develop its digital camera business. It had to develop a new business unit with its own organizational structure. It needed many R&D projects to develop the technologies. The R&D efforts had to be transferred to product development programs for building prototypes and devices to be demonstrated and tested. It required training programs and marketing campaigns. Developing these kinds of programs is complicated and often requires building complex systems, structures, and relationships. Many subelements, projects, actions and activities overlap, and often subsequent actions or activities have to begin before the predecessors are completed. Program development occurs like cascading flows with many subelements being developed separately and then integrated into the overall program at the appropriate time and places. Program managers have to ensure that the subelements are linked together and that progress is made at the proper rate across all of the subprograms and projects. Such subprograms and projects often need people with unique skills and talents who love challenges and are not afraid of failure.

Program development focuses on translating objectives, targets, and specifications into practical solutions and the desired outcomes. The development of the solutions includes the integration of knowledge, insights, and imagination that has to be transformed into outcomes. The effects of social impacts, environmental degradation, resource depletion, and waste generation are important considerations in developing outcomes. Moreover, developments should not be based on making trade-offs; they must reflect the total solutions required by the external business world and the internal aspects. Total solutions and effective outcomes provide total satisfaction for customers, stakeholders, and others. Program development provides opportunities to rectify the problems of the past and to create new, more sustainable paradigms for the future.

Demonstrating the Solutions and Outcomes of the Program
Strategic Aspects of Program Demonstration and Validation

Demonstration and incubation are really ongoing efforts to ensure that the decisions and the development are in line with expectations and that the risks and vulnerabilities have been minimized to the extent possible. Both involve taking appropriate and necessary actions to fulfill the fiduciary responsibilities of strategic leaders and program managers as well as the company obligations. Assurance must be given that all reasonable precautions have been taken to ensure that the expected outcomes are of the kind and quality that the external business world expects and the board of directors and shareholders desire. The proper demonstration of the outcomes can and should be done periodically from inception through final deployment. Demonstration is also essential near or after the completion of program development because the expected outcomes are usually fully manifested at that time and it may be relatively easy to determine their overall suitability and viability. Moreover, it is important to assure that everything is in order before starting deployment, since deployment is normally the point at which most of the details of the program become public and open to outside scrutiny. It is better to be critical of one's own efforts and outcomes than to have outsiders do it for you. Taking corrective actions within the company is usually significantly less costly and embarrassing than having to do so after customers, stakeholders, and the public are involved and knowledgeable about the program or before they identify any problems and difficulties.

Incubation involves the non-specific events, actions, activities and thought processes in which strategic leaders, program managers, and participants take time to reflect on what they have done, how the outcomes were achieved, and whether the outcomes fit the objectives, targets, and expectations. Incubation can occur before, during, or after the actions and activities to demonstrate that the program is on track and the outcomes are appropriate. Furthermore, incubation is about thinking about all aspects of the program as it relates to the broader principles, policies, and practices of the company and the social, cultural, ethical, economic, technological, and environmental forces in the business environment. While the intent is to take time to reflect, assess, and double-check, the purpose is to gain confidence so that the program can move ahead knowing that appropriate steps and actions have been taken to achieve the proper outcomes.

Strategic leaders and program managers play key roles in assuring that the efforts are valuable contributions. They are expected to use their insights about the whole company and the business environment and market spaces to decide what has to be demonstrated, validated, and tested. They are ultimately responsible to everyone; therefore, it is incumbent upon them to provide strategic oversight about what has been accomplished and what needs to be examined before moving on to the next element. Strategic leaders, in particular, have to determine that the expected outcomes are going to make the company successful and achieve the strategic objectives. The worse possible case is when everything was accomplished in accordance with the strategic and program plans and executed flawlessly only to discover in the future that the wrong program was selected or that the program was based on the incorrect perspectives, strategies, and objectives. For example, the construction of the Maginot Line by the French government and military prior to World War II was well executed and it had many state-of-the-art features that made it a high-technology wonder of its day. However, the great success of implementing a defensive line of fortresses along the French-German border did nothing to stop the German panzer attack through the Ardennes Forest of Belgium in 1940.[10] While the construction of the Maginot Line was a very successful program, the French military and political leaders, i.e., the strategic leaders, failed to think about the broader implications of defending their country and all of the possible solutions that might have prevented a military defeat. In a business setting, there are many sad stories of strategic leaders trying to do the right things, but failing to reflect on the overall business context they were facing. For example, AT&T, Pan American, Sears Roebuck, and numerous other American companies built large corporate headquarters to show their power and prestige during their "high flying" days instead of investing the money into HSPs that would directly enhance their business prospects. As an aside to such comments, Ken Iverson, the CEO of Nucor Steel from 1965 to 1998, transformed a small specialty steel company into a significant player in the U.S. steel industry by assuring that HSPs were based on money-making investments that improved the strategic positions and capabilities of the company. He never wasted precious resources (money) on big corporate offices, company planes, and fancy automobiles. The story of Sam Walton, the founder of Walmart, has a similar tone. With all of his billions, Walton still drove his old pickup truck as he put his money into opening more stores, developing innovative technologies, and producing highly efficient and effective operations.

Validation involves testing the decisions and outcomes. Validation includes examining the most significant elements and subelements of the program to reduce uncertainties and risks. The aim is to duly consider and eliminate any barriers and limitations to full deployment and success. Validation provides evidence that the potential outcomes are worth the investment and that there are no undue concerns about completing the program. This is particularly appropriate when most of the investment is expected to be spent during deployment. If strategic blunders or miscues are determined or suspected, then strategic leaders can take action and make modifications at the strategic level to rectify the deficiencies. For instance, strategic leaders at McDonalds recognized that they had to invest into updating existing stores to improve their business prospects, not just building new stores and expanding the reach of the company. While the McDonalds story includes many facets including focusing more on nutrition, it indicates that strategic leaders have critical roles in HSPs that go beyond what program managers do. This is particularly true when strategic direction is involved and radical changes have to be made.

External Factors Involving Demonstration and Validation

Demonstration of the external context involves obtaining formal and informal feedback from the key external contributors and potential users of the outcomes. First and foremost, external validation is about obtaining inputs about the value of the potential outcomes and the value propositions. Various research methods may be employed to determine the suitability and viability of the targeted outcomes from market-related considerations and from customer and stakeholder perceptions. The purpose is to assure that the outcomes provide the appropriate benefits given the prevailing market conditions and trends and current and future expectations. The feedback from potential customers may be used to refine or modify the program before continuing. The research methods might include formal testing of the expected outcomes using customer surveys or obtaining feedback from direct contacts with selected individuals. Personal interviews are most appropriate when confidentiality is a necessity, which is often the case when there are still many years of required actions before the program may be fully disclosed to the public. The decisions to test and/or validate the development(s) and potential outcomes are often based on factors like the uncertainties, the unknown risks, extended time-to-deployment, the costs of testing and validation, the influences of competitors, and the potential benefits of the information and knowledge gained. Potential negative impacts can be minimized by expeditiously demonstrating or testing the subelements and expected outcomes. In some cases, spending more money to obtain the required feedback as quickly as possible may reduce the overall costs of the program, accelerate the full deployment of the program, and lower the uncertainties and risks.

Validating outcomes using external entities and individuals, especially potential customers, is not without risks. It is always difficult to get fair and representative feedback. The outsiders may not fully understand the underlying factors and their implications. Their views may be skewed to existing realities rather than future perspectives. They may not have the technical knowledge to offer the proper insights. While experts may have the knowledge to give good opinions, their inputs may be at one of the extremes. For instance, technocrats may like complexity and favor the more complicated outcomes, yet common people may eschew such outcomes. Another important concern is the potential that competitors may obtain crucial information about the program from interviewees who are also their customers or allies. Such information may allow competitors to develop a similar program or take countermeasures to limit the success of the company's future actions and outcomes. The feedback and information obtained from customers and others must be sufficiently valuable to warrant the exposure to any countervailing forces; such forces include stakeholders who may wish to stop the program before it is deployed. With that said, validation and testing should include stakeholders (who might be negative) to obtain their comments so that modifications may be made to rectify any critical issues, if appropriate. The avoidance of mistakes and miscues and the elimination of potential issues through testing and validation are difficult to quantify objectively, but such efforts can often result in significant enhancements and savings of time and money. Fortunately, most organizations have knowledge and information about the potential stakeholders. The program is usually related in some way to the underlying nature of the company's businesses. However, there are situations in which HSPs are new ventures or pertain to new market spaces with unfamiliar stakeholders. In such situations, a careful examination of stakeholders and their potential concerns, issues, and possible impacts is absolutely necessary.

Testing stakeholder responses is often the domain of specialists. Whereas it is highly desirable to formally assess stakeholder concerns and responses to the program, such testing is usually more of an ad hoc than a systematic process. The first step is to identify the critical stakeholders and their issues and how they could impact the program. The next step is to select the concerns and issues that could have a large potential impact on the success of the program and establish mechanisms for testing what roles they might play during deployment and thereafter. The third step is to craft a test plan that includes the important questions pertaining to stakeholders and the related issues and concerns. The aims are to assess the views of the key stakeholders and to ensure that the program incorporates appropriate solutions and outcomes that address the stakeholder perspectives. If it is impossible to address every critical question, the focus should be on the dominant issues and the main risks and vulnerabilities. The testing might address the following:[11]

- Identification of the most important stakeholders and the critical issues and concerns
- Determination of stakeholder requirements and the program's ability to satisfy and/or manage them
- Assessment of the constraints that might limit the targeted outcomes due to stakeholder issues
- Evaluation of the potential impacts of the program on stakeholders, the business world, and society
- Risk assessment of the potential stakeholder impacts and the program's vulnerabilities to those risks
- Mitigation approaches for reducing or eliminating the most significant real or perceived problems

The demonstration and deployment of the solutions and outcomes of the program often start with suppliers, and suppliers of suppliers, many years before potential customers or even stakeholders become involved. For instance, Mercedes-Benz at its

Sindelfingen Works near Stuggart, Germany built an integrated business system linking all of the suppliers seven deep in the supply chain to understand its total supply chain. The program consisted of implementing an information technology (IT) system that covered its entire global supply network. Mercedes-Benz initially employed a pilot introduction of the IT methodology to test the effectiveness of the IT system before it proceeded with implementation. Demonstrating one's capabilities to manage the supply networks and their implications is a difficult validation situation.

The logic for validation or the related testing is similar the discussions above. The main concerns include the following pertaining to supply networks:[12]

- Disruptions in the flow of necessary inputs or the lack of availability and affordability of key resources
- Dramatic increase in the cost of critical materials and parts or ones that have a major influence on the value propositions of the program
- Negative impacts on the quality, yield, and timeliness of the purchased and manufactured parts, components, and products
- Significant shifts in the prevailing realities about the supply and logistics such as a dramatic increase in the costs of transportation

Program managers might examine the most complicated or vulnerable parts of its supply chain and distribution channels. If the number of unanswered questions about specific needs or requirements is relatively high, it makes good sense to mitigate the uncertainties and risks by spending time and money on discovering the potential problems and taking corrective action to cure the problems before proceeding. For example, if successful deployment depends on integrating suppliers, and suppliers of suppliers, into a comprehensive IT system like the Mercedes-Benz example, testing might include finding unforeseen barriers that might prohibit the necessary linkages with all of the entities. Validating such concerns and potential problems also tends to be ongoing, rather than just at a distinct point during demonstration. However, there are many situations in which it is useful to have a double-check of the implications pertaining to the supply networks to ensure that any assumptions about the supply of materials and parts are valid.

Demonstrating the availability, affordability, and usefulness of the external infrastructure is not normally considered, but there are good reasons for determining the ability of the infrastructure to respond to the needs and requirements of the program. This is especially the case if deployment is expected to include emerging markets that have big challenges and uncertainties regarding their external infrastructure. If there are questions pertaining to key requirements, the critical aspects of the infrastructure should be tested. The testing instrument should address the following:[13]

- Identification of the infrastructure requirements and their potential availability, quality, potential negative impacts, and the resulting consequences on the solutions and expected outcomes

- Assessment of the constraints that might limit the effectiveness of the infrastructure
- Risk assessment of the potential impacts on program deployment
- Mitigating approaches for reducing or eliminating the most significant real or perceived problems

Demonstration might include examining competition is to ascertain the expected responses of the most critical competitors. To some extent, such testing would be part market-space testing, since it difficult to consider competition separate from market-related aspects. If market testing includes expected competitors' responses, then separate competitor-related testing may useful, but unnecessary. The objectives are to determine as soon as possible the potential impacts that key competitors might have. The questions relate to their expected strategies and actions. The following are a few sample questions:

- Which competitors are the most likely to respond negatively to the program outcomes?
- What are their expected responses and countersolutions and programs?
- How might competitors change their strategic positions, strategies, and related programs?
- How might they block our expected competitive advantages?
- What competitive advantages do they seek?

The bottom line of the demonstration and incubation is to determine whether the opportunities and outcomes of the program can be realized in an effective and efficient manner. The inherent focus of the demonstration is on mitigating uncertainties and risks. This is especially true for high-level strategic programs that stretch the state of the art, have new challenges, and include many unknowns. Uncertainties are usually relatively high at the beginning of a program and tend to diminish over time, especially if the implementation and execution are managed properly. The true power of program management is the systematic development of information and knowledge over the course of a program, thus reducing the unknowns and potential problems associated with the external and internal factors and reducing uncertainties and risks. The following are a few of the most important considerations when exploring the implications of uncertainties and risks and their influences on decision making:[14]

- Do program managers and participants truly understand the needs and wants of potential customers; both the tangible and intangible aspects?
- Do they have the requisite competencies and capabilities to manage external aspects?
- Are expected outcomes aligned with customer and stakeholder needs and expectations?
- Are the market and technical requirements for achieving success identified and managed properly?

- Are the expected/targeted outcomes properly positioned in the market spaces so that there are distinctive advantages and benefits with unique customer value? Is there a well-defined value proposition?
- Are there well-established means and mechanisms for deploying the solutions and outcomes that are efficient and effective?
- Have important stakeholders and their key concerns and issues pertaining to the program been addressed and handled appropriately?
- Have government laws and regulations been identified, assessed, and complied with?
- Have influential competitors and their expected responses been adequately addressed and have counteractions been prepared?
- Are the market, technical, and business risks mitigated?

The above list simply highlights some of the most crucial factors that have to be addressed, validated, and resolved. Uncertainties are reduced by systematically obtaining, analyzing, and understanding information, data, and insights, and making informed decisions about the external factors. Whereas perfect information and knowledge never exist, the investments of time, effort, and money should produce tangible results that mitigate uncertainties and risks. Thus, program managers and participants execute their responsibilities with courage and conviction.

Internal Vactors Involving Demonstration and Validation

The internal factors pertaining to demonstration and validation focus on examining the outcomes created during development. The first examination might include a simple determination of the advantages and disadvantages of the expected outcomes. This could be followed by a real-world examination of the suitability and durability of the solutions and outcomes and how they might relate to internal aspects as well as the external ones. Such an examination can take many forms from testing under simulated conditions to pilot testing of the solutions in a quasi-deployment situation using internal test mechanisms and/or potential customer applications. The degree of testing and the conditions used depend upon the uncertainties associated with the solutions and outcomes and the potential for serious defects, problems and/or mistakes. If the program involves new-to-the-world developments or it involves a significant departure from conventional methods, means, and mechanisms, then serious considerations have to be given to testing all aspects of the solutions and expected outcomes under very stringent conditions.

The internal testing has to validate that the program can achieve its objectives including the solutions and the targeted outcomes within the required time frame and the estimated investment. The expected outcomes should include having the right means and mechanisms, creating business value, having excellent value propositions, creating the ability to exceed customer and stakeholder needs and expectations, and being able to mitigate risks. It is not easy to achieve such difficult and often opposing outcomes or requirements. Testing may be enhanced by assessing specific subjects that might involve significant challenges. Such assessments mainly examine internal capabilities and resources to carry out the development and deployments. The assessments of the business portfolios, product lines, solutions, operations, marketing, and finances are among the other considerations that might require significant examinations. The analyses are prepared on the basis of the requirements of the program and the expectations for the assumed time horizon for the planning period, typically ten years or more. The assessments examine each of the businesses and/or product lines to ascertain the strategic positions and the prospects for successful development and deployment. They explore the geographic coverage(s) of the businesses and the requirements for the future. The assessment of businesses involves determining the areas where the organization enjoys powerful positions and what has to be done to enhance weaker positions, to exploit the positives, and to reduce the negatives. The focus may also include understanding what new businesses are required and/or what existing businesses might have to be enhanced, changed, or eliminated.

Like many development and demonstration considerations and questions, there are no simple answers. Each situation has to be analyzed and carefully thought through before arriving at an appropriate conclusion. In high-risk situations, prudence usually necessitates a high degree of testing and validation. Moreover, testing usually requires added time and effort—potentially delaying deployment. It is difficult to predict the total effects and impacts of internal testing, but the simple approach of reducing the amount of testing to save time and money is not always the right answer. The added time may be offset by enhancing the confidence in achieving the outcomes, improving the probability of being successful, and increasing the speed for completing the program.

Assessing the partnerships and alliances involves a similar view except that the analysis includes all of the partnerships, alliances, consortia, coalitions, and strategic linkages. It starts with an identification of all such relationships and prioritizes the importance of each in the present and in the future. The assessment links the relationships with the businesses and explores the advantages and disadvantages. It reflects on the purpose and power of each relationship, determines the logic for each, and how well the alignment is working. Such assessments lead to a better understanding of the improvements and changes necessary to deploy the program. This includes corrective actions and adjustments that are required to eliminate any potential limitations and constraints.

Deploying the Solutions and Outcomes of the Program
Strategic Aspects of Deployment

Deployment as previously discussed involves introducing the program outcomes to the external business world. This can take many different forms from a single worldwide launch to individualized deployments in selected market segments or business arenas. Deployment opens the door to the broader business communities and makes the program real from an external perspective. It also immensely expands the scope of actions and the implications of the program. While most of the elements include both internal and external factors and considerations, the externally-based efforts usually overshadow internal aspects during deployment and thereafter. Figure 6.2 depicts the basic scheme of the flow of a HSP and the implications pertaining to deployment.

High-Level Strategic Programs ■ 197

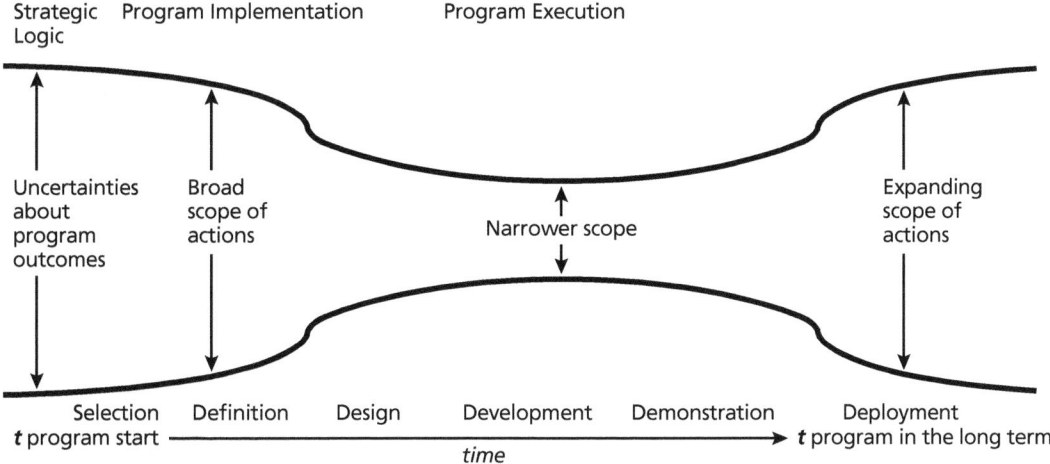

Figure 6.2 Relative scope of actions during program implementation and execution.

During selection and definition, the scope of actions and activities tends to be broad with many internal and external considerations. As a program focuses more on design, development, and demonstration, the scope of actions generally narrows as more of the actions relate to the internal aspects of the program. However, during deployment the scope of actions increases dramatically and the focus shifts more toward external considerations and activities as noted above. While it is impossible to generalize about deployment since there are incredible numbers of required actions and possibly many more ways to execute them, deployment involves bringing the expected outcomes and the benefits and value thereof into the mainstream of the business world and making them real. Even in the situations that are highly focused on specific agendas, deployment involves a multiplicity of entities and individual contributors and the potential users of the outcomes.

For instance, companies like General Electric (GE) and Motorola that created six-sigma capabilities and outcomes, engaged in many developments before they were able to fully deploy six-sigma for their customers in the form of enhanced products and services. The full realization of their six-sigma efforts from an external perspective included marketing campaigns promoting the exceptional quality and enhanced warrantees pertaining to reliability and longevity.

Deployment can take various forms including using projects to execute specific areas of the program. Such projects may be linked in terms of the related actions and activities with some done in parallel, while others that depend on predecessors are done in series, and, there are numerous hybrids. The main considerations are the integration of the internal and external contributors and how they interface and interact with each other to deploy the targeted outcomes. The integration includes the connections and relationships with the recipients, i.e., the intended audience-customer, stakeholders, the value networks, etc. The projects might be rolled out based on product portfolios or SBUs with lead product lines and/or business units initiating the deployment to obtain lessons learned, or alternatively all of them deploying their projects in parallel.

Other schemes include taking functional approaches with the lead projects focusing on operations followed by marketing and sales, etc.

Deployment is often the most costly part of the overall program given the expanding scope of the actions and activities and the increased fuzziness of how the expected outcomes play out in the real world. While there are always concerns about the total investment, most of the actual cash flow for the typical programs, if they are managed properly, occurs during program execution. It is imperative to keep track of the investment over the course of the program, especially during deployment, and there are numerous techniques for managing the financial implications. However, as a given program proceeds from the upstream elements of program implementation to those of program execution, especially deployment, the ability of program managers to control the expenditure of funds often becomes more and more challenging. The estimates made during selection of the program are subject to many forces that can substantially change over the course of time. Having a substantial portion of the investment(s) occurring during deployment is important from a financial management perspective, since the future value of such funds on a discounted cash flow basis is generally lower than the future value of the earlier expenditures. Great care has to be exercised when making projections that indicate steady or stable conditions; expected cash flows and business conditions can change radically in a short amount of time. Program managers have to continuously examine their financial plans and ensure that they reflect reality. Investment estimates and projections often miss the target.

Program managers and participants are the prime contributors during deployment and their efforts and contributions become even more open-ended than during earlier elements. Given the potential for changes in the business environment and the wide latitude of expected events and situations, they have to have flexibility in managing the program and have the authority to change, if necessary. It is also important that they are accountable for their decisions and actions and that there is management control over the program. Obviously, this is akin to "walking a tightrope." Customers and competitors may have significant influences on the conditions and trends in the market spaces and what the outcomes actually mean and what is possible. There are many examples of programs failing because program managers did not anticipate changes. For example, in the late 1980s and early 1990s, Motorola and its venture partners decided to create a global satellite-based wireless phone system that would allow users to receive and send calls anywhere in the world. The Iridium System consisted of 66 satellites orbiting the planet at 17,000 miles an hour. When the program was conceived, a satellite-based system seemed to have merit; however, over the subsequent ten-year period until the system was fully deployed in 1998, global telecommunications changed significantly, making the Iridium System obsolete even before program managers initiated their marketing efforts. It is always challenging for extremely large HSPs like the Iridium System in which there are many individual projects for program managers to maintain overall direction and control. While there are many conventional management theories, practices, and techniques, program managers, project managers, and participants have to determine what the best means and mechanisms are for their program(s) and requirements. It is not possible to articulate a standard approach like project management methodologies for those engaged in project work.

External Context Related to Deployment

External deployment is about producing successful outcomes, i.e., turning objectives and targets into real results and enduring success. It involves fully integrating the program with the external business environment and the specific market spaces being addressed. While deployment is not necessarily the end of the program, it is the essential element in which desires and expectations become realities and the expected benefits and rewards are realized over time. While the focus is generally on customers and stakeholders, there are many others who may benefit from the results, including society in general. Moreover, while execution often means getting results and being rewarded accordingly, HSPs may have extended periods of upfront deployment-related actions and activities before the company obtains its sought-after outcomes like unique competitive advantages, positive cash flows, and powerful market positions.

External deployment is more than just producing deliverables; it requires achieving positive outcomes and making real improvements for all external contributors and recipients. For very large programs, external deployment is multifaceted and may require many individual projects to initiate and execute all of the specific requirements. Using individual projects makes external deployment more doable and often allows participants to contribute within their comfort zones and capabilities. Furthermore, it provides program managers with the mechanisms to execute more of the requisite actions and activities on a parallel basis. For example, a company launching a SBD program across its business enterprise must engage in many actions and activities that have to be carried out. Every part of the organization and its extended enterprise has to be involved. There are so many requirements that it is impossible to do them all under the direct banner of a single program, never mind a single project. Multiple projects may be used by a company to make its transformation from conventional approaches related to the business environment and market spaces to ones that embrace SBD and sustainability. The transformation involves redefining and revamping the strategic positions and management constructs of the company through dramatic developments and strategic innovations that create extraordinary value and new value propositions for both the internal and external contexts. Transformation requires big departure(s) from the prevailing situations using innovative ways of providing solutions and achieving success. The outcomes have to be achieved using well-planned projects based on the overall strategies, action plans, and initiatives.

Project management techniques make big transformations possible during deployment, if the actions and activities can be divided into logical projects that can be managed and controlled. For instance, the market-related actions can be assigned to a group focusing on marketing and sales. The supply chain and logistical requirements can be affected by a project team from operations. All of the other critical deployment actions and activities can be managed using similarly organized projects. Many of the individual projects can be executed on a concurrent basis. However, specifying exactly how all of the requirements are going be executed through projects and configuring the projects to minimize overlap are arduous efforts. It is also a huge challenge to integrate all of the projects into a cohesive deployment, if there are more than just a few projects. Coordination and integration of the efforts and control over the outcomes are paramount for achieving success and keeping the overall investment in line with expectations, i.e., approved funding.

Keep in mind that this is just one perspective of the thousands of possibilities. Given the differences and diversity among all of the types of programs and the companies involved, generalizations are difficult. Trying to prescribe a general framework or arrangement for external deployment would require models that are so intricate and detailed that it would take many volumes to spell out all of the variations. However, established guidelines and standards can be used to provide a general sense of what has to be done and the criteria for doing them. While this is a complex task, it is much more doable than specifying all of the protocols and processes for engaging in the actions and activities. The guidelines are intended to provide help and assist in developing and implementing the requisite aspects of the programs and projects.

Program Evaluation

Evaluating High-Level Strategic Programs

Evaluation is a critical element and ongoing part of program management. It is a fundamental management responsibility that relates to good governance and oversight. The approaches and metrics used to evaluate programs and projects include performance evaluation, continuous monitoring, reviews, and periodic auditing, along with providing feedback and reports to the strategic leaders and the steering committee. Monitoring progress involves tracking actions and activities; taking proactive steps to avoid difficulties and problems before they happen; and taking actions to resolve or dissolve the underlying potential difficulties and challenges that may result in unacceptable outcomes and negative impacts or the failure to obtain the proper results. Reviews are usually formal assessments of the outcomes or progress achieved in terms of the program plans. Reviews may be done at the end of each element or at crucial points in the program when big decisions have to be made or significant investments have to be approved.

Program managers typically use metrics and/or measures to keep track of progress and for ascertaining performance. Traditional metrics like profitability, cash flow, return on investment, customer satisfaction, on-time outcomes, yield, quality, efficiency, productivity, cycle time, and market share provide measures for determining the potential for success; but some of them may not be leading indicators about how well the actions and activities are working. Many of the traditional metrics are good ones. However, they are often lagging indicators that describe what has happened over some period of time. They do not usually provide early warning about the lack of progress or the presence of difficulties. Strategic leaders generally desire leading indicators to determine whether overall progress is sufficient to keep the organization on track. Leading-edge metrics should be determined and used. Although more difficult to determine, they provide a greater sense of how well the organization is implementing and executing program elements and subelements in real time. Some of the leading indicators include an evaluation of the degree of program integration, the degree of organizational learning, the degree of innovativeness, and a sense of value creation.

The performance evaluation provides a general sense of how good the decisions are, and provides a degree of confidence that the program is on track, and that it can be expected to achieve the intended outcomes. It gives a snapshot of the realities and expectations. While there is usually a lack of precision and thoroughness, since only ten to twenty metrics might be used, performance evaluation offers insights about the actions and activities required for meeting targets and objectives and/or for taking timely corrective actions, if necessary. Performance evaluation also includes measuring actual performance against the expectations of customers, stakeholders, the community, the regulatory agencies, and other constituencies. While performance evaluation is often quick and not comprehensive, the power of performance evaluation is that it can be done frequently so that what might be missed on one day may be ascertained the next day or a week later. For instance, metrics can be examined every day through a formal reporting mechanism that allows program managers and steering committee members to find potential difficulties within less than an hour.

Program auditing is a technique used to ascertain performance on a periodic basis. It is usually used by program managers and strategic leaders to determine how well lower-level managers are performing their roles and responsibilities as well as how they are carrying out their actions and activities. Strategic leaders use audits to ensure that program and/or project managers and participants are doing what is necessary to achieve success, while at the same time giving the responsible managers the freedom and flexibility to get the job done in the most efficient and effective ways possible. In particular, program and project managers are empowered to execute the program(s), but strategic leaders and/or the steering committee can periodically audit to ensure that execution is being managed properly, prudently, and in accordance with the laws and regulations, company polices, principles, standards, rules, and the program plans. This obviously includes ensuring that the funds are managed properly and the procurements are made appropriately. Keep in mind that auditing is a lagging control mechanism that examines past performance and outcomes. It is based on trust relationships among the leaders, managers, and participants. It is also based on the perspectives that everyone is expected to do what is right and appropriate; people have good intentions; know that mistakes may be made by even the best individuals; and that strategic leaders have a fiduciary responsibility to the board of directors and the shareholders. The leaders ensure that everything is progressing as well as possible and that corrective actions and preventive measures are duly taken. While many people view audits as negatives, they should be perceived as supportive, at least in the context of good governance and program management.

Evaluating External Outcomes and Success

Evaluating external outcomes and determining the successes enjoyed by customers, stakeholders, and others are always critical management constructs that are nebulous at best. While there are numerous feedback mechanisms that may be effective for existing situations like querying customers whether they like existing products or not, it is extremely difficult to get good feedback from the external recipients, especially for programs with new-to-the-world outcomes. Customers and stakeholders may indicate they think that the outcomes are valuable and beneficial, but they may be unclear or have reservations about the long-term implications. For instance, customers and certain stakeholders may respond favorably to banks eliminating the verification of income when determining the person's qualification to obtain a mortgage, but such changes led to many unhappy situations and wholesale criticisms of the banking industry when some of the unintended outcomes turn negative. Many individuals prior to or during the Great Recession who obtained mortgages without the conventional income verification ended up losing their houses when they were unable to keep up with the payments.

An effective way to ascertain external feedback is to continuously monitor customer and stakeholder activities and patterns of behaviors as the program unfolds, especially as deployment moves into the mainstream. Generally, the best inputs come from what people do, not just what they say. For instance, if a company institutes a SBD program, certain shareholders like senior citizens who want safer returns may increase their investments in the shares of the company. Tracking their participation may provide evidence that the program is fulfilling the intentions, i.e., making the company more sustainable. Moreover, if certain customers like True-Blue-Greens increase their purchase of the company's product lines based on the SBD program, then it may be reasonable to ascertain that the program is meeting the objectives and targeted outcomes.[15] True-Blue-Greens are customers and environmental activists who are willing to pay more for "green" products; ones that are more sustainable. Such insights have to be used and validated over time.

Strategic leaders and program managers have to use out-of-the box thinking about how to evaluate success. One approach is to use a modification of Eric von Hippel's work pertaining to lead users. In *Sources of Innovation*, von Hippel, Professor of Technological Innovation at Massachusetts Institute of Technology, describes how lead users can provide insights and confirmation about new ways of creating and using products.[16] He was an early advocate of using external sources for innovation and for creating new solutions. Strategic leaders and program managers can use the lead-user concept to evaluate the potential and sustainability of the benefits of the external outcomes of the program(s), especially during the early stages. For instance, during early days of six-sigma initiatives, program managers could examine the needs and expectations of the most demanding customers to ascertain the benefits they wanted and the value that would be derived from higher levels of quality. The obvious candidates were manufacturers and users of airplanes, military vehicles, computers, and space-related devices like satellites that had to function flawlessly for years without human intervention; just to suggest a few. Obtaining feedback from such entities or individuals could be used to evaluate the decisions and progress and/or lead to improvements and changes. It is important to reiterate that it is positive external outcomes that lead to progress and create success. Often program managers think in terms of deliverables like project managers do. While deliverables are good, they are steps in the progression toward success. Ultimately, success is based on what the external entities and individuals obtain in terms of value and benefits.

Evaluating the relationships that strategic leaders, program managers, and participants have with customers, stakeholders, suppliers, distributors, related industries, and other supporters is vital for obtaining and ensuring success. Relationships are the glue that connects people and the elements of value systems and the extended enterprises to obtain positive outcomes and extraordinary benefits for the recipients and contributors alike. Strategic leaders have to be the lynch pins for building relationships and connecting the people who engage in developing, producing, delivering, supporting, and/or using the outcomes. Strategic leaders have the high-level responsibilities for building relationships with leaders in the business environment who are or might be affected by the outcomes of the program. Strategic leaders and program managers have to map out how they are going to create solid relationships with the people involved and how they can evaluate the positive and negative aspects. Most strategic leaders have a sense of what the critical relationships are or have to be by knowing the strategies, objectives, and desired outcomes of the program and what is required to achieve success. Moreover, they use the broad external-based agendas such as social and economic aspects, significant issues and challenges, the need for standards and connections, public policy concerns, and the overall common good, as areas that they must be engaged in, and build relationships with other key leaders. Relationships are built on connectedness and person-to-person dialogue. People respond more positively when there are common interests and a sense of being part of the greater good.

External evaluation includes examining the realities of the competitive advantages sought or obtained. It is imperative that strategic leaders seek external confirmation about the realities of the competitive advantages. The outcomes may result in certain competitive advantages, but they may not be as powerful or enduring as desired or perceived. They may have limited usefulness or may only apply to certain situations or market segments. For instance, Barnes & Noble (B&N) might believe that it has huge competitive advantages being the largest bookseller in the world with more than 700 stores in the US.[17] However, such present-day advantages might become disadvantages in the future as alternatives like e-books, e-readers and Internet-based publications increase in availability, affordability, and popularity.

Getting accurate external information about the competitive advantages is an arduous task given the lack of effective mechanisms. This goes beyond obtaining feedback from surveys and questionnaires. Unfortunately, the views that people have are often based on their opinions and perceptions. They may believe what they are saying, but their responses may be off base. For instance, people may indicate they like going to B&N stores to shop for books, magazines, and other products, but in reality they are just perusing what is available to determine what they want, then they try to get their selections from the least expensive sources using the Internet.

A simple method for evaluating the external perspectives of the competitive advantages of a program is to have unbiased subject matter experts provide assessments of the prevailing situation and the expected changes over the duration of the program and the life cycle of the outcomes. Another method is to examine the rewards obtained or expected to be obtained from the competitive advantages. Again, an unbiased approach is best. University researchers or professionals could do a comparative assessment of the advantages versus the competitive alternatives or substitutes. Regardless of the methods, the evaluation must be based on evidence and viewed from both the short term and the long term.

Risk reduction is always a critical factor in ensuring success and obtaining the desired rewards. Strategic leaders and program managers have to assure that actions are turned into positive outcomes and not into negatives that create liabilities. Indeed, one of main reasons for evaluating the external context is to mitigate risks and to ensure that the risks are within the company's tolerance for risks. No prudent strategic leader will bet the well-being of the company on a program unless the rewards are incredible or the situation is dire and there are no other acceptable options. Risk mitigation is discussed in more detail in the next chapter.

Outcomes and successes have to be viewed in terms of the rewards in the short term and the long term. If the investment has a very positive rate of return, the program is usually determined to be successful. If the program enhances customer satisfaction and loyalty, the program is deemed to be successful, especially if it is also financially rewarding. There are numerous ways to obtain rewards from personal satisfaction based on contributing to the greater good and to the rewards provided to shareholders based on market capitalization, earnings, and dividends. Examining the rewards is based on the corporate goals, the program objectives, and the desired outcomes. It includes both tangible and intangible results. For instance, survivability is a crucial requirement in today's business world. The outcomes may not present a positive cash flow over time, but they may allow the company to continue being successful in its other endeavors. In such situations, the program may be deemed successful and rewarding even though not from a conventional sense.

Evaluating Internal Outcomes and Success

Evaluating the internal context involves assessing the outcomes and the progress and comparing it to the expectations of internal objectives and metrics for business growth, enhanced leadership and management sophistication, improved operational capabilities, and greater financial performance and returns among numerous other objectives and measures. Various methods are used to ascertain the outcomes from the situation.

Firstly, simple checks can be used to determine if outcomes or metrics have been realized or will be realized as the program proceeds. For instance, an increasing number of small failures and mistakes may be indicators of broader program difficulties. While such problems may be viewed as inconsequential from an individual point of view, evaluating them in the aggregate may suggest that the overall program is tracking off course and that corrective actions are required. Program managers may not even be fully aware of small glitches because they are managed at the higher levels of the program. However, effective management and control at the program management level necessitates tracking the lower level as well as the significant difficulties. In many situations, especially when parallel projects are used, the project managers, team leaders, and participants face and experience identical problems and often make similar mistakes. If such difficulties are not tracked at a higher level, the lessons learned and the ability to reduce the number of problems and negative events are not realized and the overall program takes more time and money to complete.

Secondly, testing throughout the program, not just during demonstration, is another effective mechanism used to determine that the actions and activities have been completed properly and the outcomes have been validated to be correct and appropriate. Testing is generally costly and time consuming, but it provides a higher level of confidence and an assurance that the outcomes will meet the expectations of the real world. There are numerous examples of programs reaching the later stages or even the end points at which the leaders and managers realize that there are fundamental problems that cannot be corrected. Generally, the sooner problems and difficulties are addressed, the more likely the outcomes will be positive. The converse is also true. Testing outcomes of the major subelements based on real-world conditions is an effective way to discover hidden problems well before they become apparent during later elements. Such tests provide program managers and the participants with information and data that allow quantitative assessments of the results and a more precise determination of the prospects for success. For example, General Motors experienced problems with batteries catching fire after customers had accidents with their Chevy Volts. While the situation is under investigation to determine causality, it is much more effective and efficient to examine such possibilities early on in the program.

Thirdly, measures and metrics provide a sense of achievement on an ongoing basis. Participants in HSPs that take decades to implement and execute need positive encouragement and rewards along the way. Evaluating the outcomes at any point, and comparing them to objectives, measures, and metrics, and communicating the results to participants provides positive feedback that encourages and inspires them to go forward with enthusiasm and dedication. For example, if the outcomes of the program meet expectations and such outcomes are validated, such successes give participants a sense that their actions, activities and contributions are converging toward overall program success even though the program is expected to take many more years to reach the final stages. The evaluations provide the participants with small wins. Such evaluations may also provide information and data to prepare calculations about the cash-flow expectations. If projections suggest that the required investment has significantly increased, then the program may have to be re-evaluated, modified, or terminated. The objective of using metrics or making such evaluations is to discover potential problems as early as possible and take corrective actions.

Effective evaluation allows management to track and determine performance and to keep the program on schedule. The evaluation should be dynamic, yet flexible, in order to respond to changing business conditions. The quantitative measures might be determined from previous programs or by benchmarking the competitors, peers, and companies in related businesses. It is important to have a reasonable number of measures/metrics to provide balance so that evaluations and assessments are not skewed toward financial aspects or timing—achieving a given objective in one area while at the expense of performance in another. Again, the aim is to find potential problems and solve them. Much of the data and information to support the measurement process such as risk assessments, financial data, and inventory data may already exist as a result of the routine operations of the organization. Information and data of known and verifiable quality can be used to provide a basis for evaluating the performance of the program.

Ultimately, the purpose of evaluating internal outcomes and performance is to determine the likelihood of achieving success and obtaining the desired rewards of the program. The intent of most programs is to enhance the positives of the company: growth, sophistication, financial performance, and operational and tactical capabilities. The related objectives and the outcomes are generally ongoing and never-ending. Many high-level strategic programs like the vision of the company are never completed, but they are simply morphed into new programs that take up the opportunities and challenges at an even higher level and continue on into the distant future.

BOX 6: GEORGE DAVID'S HIGH-LEVEL STRATEGIC PROGRAMS AT UNITED TECHNOLOGIES CORPORATION[a]

George David was the CEO of United Technologies Corporation (UTC) from 1994 until 2007. UTC is a global corporation based in Hartford, Connecticut. It is comprised of UTC Aerospace, Pratt & Whitney (P&W), Otis Elevator, UTC Climate, Control and Security, Sikorsky Aircraft, and United Technologies Research Center (UTRC). In 2006, UTC had approximately 220,000 employees at 4,000 worldwide locations in 62 countries. It had revenues and net profits of $47.8 and $3.7 billion, respectively.[b] UTC's product lines include space exploration and propulsion systems, jet engines, elevators, escalators, heating, ventilating and air conditioning systems, helicopters, aircraft ancillary parts and systems, and alternative power systems such as fuel cells and gas turbine engines for marine and power applications. Operations include research, design, engineering, manufacturing, repair and maintenance in-house and at customer sites, and sales and administrative operations.

During his tenure as CEO, David held a practical view on how sustainable development (SD) played a key role in UTC's success. It was based on the perspective of consistently maximizing value for customers and stakeholders. David knew that customers want product reliability, safety, durability, quality, energy efficiency, long life spans, and superior service and support at a reasonable cost. He made sure that UTC delivered value and positive outcomes. He believed that UTC did not need to prove the usefulness of SD practices, because they are inherent in a well-managed company with a loyal customer base.[c] David suggested that SD came naturally to UTC, since it focuses on exceeding customer and stakeholder expectations.

UTC was recognized a SD leader. It was selected as one of the top 100 sustainable companies in 2004 and 2005 by Corporate Knights, Inc. and Innovest Strategic Value Advisors, Inc.[d] UTC was named to the Dow Jones Sustainability World Index every year from 1999 through 2007. KLD Research & Analytics, Inc. named UTC as one of the top 100 companies in its Global Climate Index.[e] KLD promotes investments in businesses that demonstrate leadership in developing solutions to climate change. David foresaw many SD opportunities when he tapped Bill Sisson, UTRC Research Director, to represent UTC as a co-chair with LaFarge Industries (cement products) in the World Business Council for Sustainable Development's (WBCSD) Energy Efficiency in Buildings (EEB) initiative. UTC joined WBCSD as a member in 2004.[f] Member companies realize that global energy demand is expected to double over the next 50 years and 80% of the world's energy is currently generated from fossil fuels. Unprecedented levels of carbon dioxide are predicted unless people make major changes. Participants in EEB include GE Energy, Habitat for Humanity, electric utilities, many residential and commercial building development firms, and manufacturing companies. EEB participants aim to conserve resources through energy efficiency, materials recycling, low impact materials manufacturing, and where possible, energy self-generation. EEB's long-term goal is to have energy self-sufficient buildings with zero emissions.

UTC instituted environment, health and safety (EHS), and quality policies as the basic framework for its SD initiatives. UTC has management systems, procedures, instructions, and practices in place to enable the achievement of these policies. The EHS policy calls for "unmatched" performance through injury-free workplaces, safe products and services, regulatory compliance, and pollution prevention. The common theme among the policies is the creation and delivery of world-class products and services. However, because UTC products and services differ substantially, each division has its own quality policy. The systems, programs, and practices described below are excellent examples of initiatives for achieving these lofty objectives.

UTC has developed top-level management systems that incorporate elements of ISO 9001, ISO 14001, and OHSAS 18001. The systems require strategic leaders to allocate adequate resources to quality and EHS initiatives and hold managers accountable for quality and EHS objectives; specify employee roles and responsibilities; validate that processes are documented and audited; ascertain that deficiency root causes are identified and appropriately corrected; and ensure that programs are evaluated annually.

UTC developed a continuous improvement system known as Achieving Competitive Excellence (ACE). ACE provides the basis for the operating systems to standardize and continuously improve processes across the company. The goals are to reach and maintain the following outcomes: delighting customers; fulfilling employees; growing financially; and, producing quality products and services. ACE techniques include "5S" inspections, benchmarking, customer market feedback analysis, quality control, process control, and root cause identification techniques, mistake proofing, process management and certification, and standard work.

In 1996, David challenged all UTC divisions to reduce employee injuries, waste generation, and energy and water use ten-fold (10X) by 2007. This was known as the 10X challenge. Some divisions managed to cut energy consumption by 15–20% despite doubling in size over the 10-year challenge period.[8] Employee teams at each division used many of the techniques and programs described in the list below as well as ACE initiatives to achieve the desired reductions. The following provides some examples of the programs and initiatives deployed under the 10X challenge that were realized during David's tenure:

"Green" Programs

The Green Engine and Green Factory programs began at P&W in the 1990s in response to developing regulatory requirements to reduce toxic materials in production processes and end products and to reduce waste generation. The two programs have since been merged and include other UTC divisions. The program objectives include:

- Minimizing energy and water consumption, waste and air emissions during manufacturing, operations, maintenance, and repair.
- Minimizing noise during operation.
- Involving green suppliers and partners.
- Manufacturing with green materials and processes: certain toxic chemicals are prohibited from use or are restricted from use in manufacturing and servicing products until suitable alternatives can be identified. These chemicals are known to have adverse effects to human health and the environment. Efforts are made to reduce raw material volume purchased and processed.
- Designing for extended lifespan, serviceability, reusability, and recyclability. This effort includes a practice known as human factors engineering. It involves the design of products and components that can be easily assembled, operated, serviced, and maintained. Factors include weight, visibility, accessibility, sharp edges and burrs, number of fasteners and force-fitted parts. Ergonomic injuries are the most common work-related challenges. Human factors engineering aims to design out the causes of such injuries by making products easier to produce.

EHS Gatekeeper Program

The divisions utilize a proactive system to evaluate proposals for modified and new equipment, machinery, processes, and chemicals, as well as changes to existing buildings and proposals for new buildings. The program objectives include identifying and addressing potential EHS hazards like toxic chemical use and emissions, waste generation, regulatory requirements, and safety considerations before the changes are implemented. As a continuous improvement tool, the program also focuses on opportunities to increase process efficiency, and reduce energy and water use.

Design for EHS (DFES)

DFES is a technique for integrating EHS considerations into product design, production, and use. The key steps in producing the product are mapped to identify potential EHS hazards. Hazards are evaluated for risk using quantitative rankings for severity and frequency. The risk assessment is then used to focus resources on addressing the concerns to deliver the maximum business value and to reduce overall risks. Identified risks are thought of as opportunities for innovation. The benefit of DFES is that it integrates business, market, and EHS concerns to provide value for customers while minimizing negative EHS impacts.

Hazard Risk Assessments (HRA)

UTC requires that all divisions evaluate existing processes from office work to manufacturing, distribution, and field services for EHS hazards and risks. The evaluations are documented and control measures are specified for each significant hazard and risk. Employees are trained and equipped to follow those control measures and supervisors are held accountable for ensuring that such measures are used effectively. HRAs are modified whenever a process is changed or a hazard and risk control measure is determined to be ineffective.

Supplier Alliances

UTC focuses on creative sustainable initiatives with suppliers. One successful initiative involved Dell Inc. Dell delivers computers packed in reusable plastic crates, eliminating approximately 66 tons of cardboard wastes from about 25,000 computers delivered in one year. Purchasing and CIO magazines recognized UTC for this initiative as did the U.S. Environmental Protection Agency.[h] P&W partnered with ISO New England to supply power to the local public electric grid during times of peak power demand. P&W has excess capacity from its own industrial gas turbine engine. The engine produces enough electricity to power the electricity needs of 30,000 people. ISO New England provided P&W with $1 million as an incentive.[i]

Competitor Alliances

P&W worked with competitors on several projects to best meet customer needs. In each case, the separate companies did not have sufficient core competencies to provide the value proposition that was needed to meet customer expectations. In one such project with GE, P&W provided maintenance and repair services on GE aircraft engines. On another project, a team including participants from Volvo and MTU developed a geared turbo fan for smaller regional jet services.[j]

Strategic Innovation

UTRC is the company's technology incubator. It supports each of the corporation's divisions with design and test product development. In existence for over

75 years, UTRC receives about $2.5 billion annually from company and customer funding for R&D.[k] The following examples summarize some of UTRC's most recent initiatives that support UTC's financial success by providing innovate solutions for customers:

- With Otis, UTRC developed the "Gen-2" elevator that is 75% more energy efficient than comparable models of only a decade ago.
- UTRC helped Carrier improve residential air conditioning energy efficiency 30% from the previous model. Carrier was first among its industry to adopt the new Federal Seasonal Energy Efficiency Rating standard of 13. The team worked on systems that capture waste heat to power air conditioning, refrigeration and dehumidification, as well as heat water.
- UTRC worked on developing fuel cell technology with UTC Power.

Community Outreach

UTC was heavily involved in community activities and services including education, arts, culture and sustainability. In the Hartford area, corporate involvement included sponsorship in local sporting events, donations to the arts, and community clean-up days. In addition, the company encourages employees to volunteer for Habitat for Humanity "Days of Caring" and tutoring in local schools. Similar initiatives took place globally, including working with Conservation International to restore forests in the mountains of southwest China and partnerships with many other public, nonprofit, and academic groups providing education and resources to combat climate change and advocate sustainable business practices.

Employee Fulfillment

The company conducts and takes action on annual employee fulfillment surveys. Senior management worked on these issues and employee fulfillment scores increased. People inside and outside the company looked favorably on the generous UTC Employee Scholar program that offers free education, paid time away from work, and company stock upon receiving a degree. Since program inception in 1996, UTC has spent roughly $500 million on employee education and nearly 18,500 academic degrees have been awarded.[l]

Governance

The UTC Corporate Responsibility website includes a section on governance. Securities and Exchange Commission report filings, the company code of ethics, governance guidelines and bylaws are included, as well as information about the board of directors. The company has an ethics office and employees are required to participate in business ethics training annually. During David's leadership, eleven of thirteen Board of Directors members were independent and periodically met alone. The Board's Nominations and Governance Audit and Compensation committees were made up independent directors. The UTC Vice President of Business

Practices regularly reported to the Audit Committee with respect to compliance and ethics issues. The Board's Public Issues Review Committee provided oversight on public policy issues such as health, safety, the environment, equal opportunity employment, government relations, and contributions to charitable organizations. Institutional Shareholder Services and Governance International, an organization that evaluates corporate governance programs, ranked UTC better than 95% of S&P 500 companies and 10 out of 10, respectively.[m]

Global Programs

Nearly 61% of UTC's 2005 revenue was from international operations and 67% of its employees resided outside the US.[n] UTC operations conducted business in over 180 countries. The majority of the company's major acquisitions have been outside the US. Strategic planning focused on rapidly developing markets like India and China. As a truly diverse, global company, UTC instills a corporate culture of continuous improvement and SD practices despite very different laws and regulations, business practices and customs, and often a lack of outside resources.

Outsourcing Programs

The UT500 program began as an effort to control non-product procurement costs in 2001. Efforts focused on material and service pricing and volume purchased mostly from North American Operations. The $500 million savings was quickly realized and the effort expanded to include overseas operations and use of ACE tools for continuous improvement opportunities that reduce operational costs.[o]

UTC has realized that alliances with suppliers must encompass many operational issues to achieve sustainable cost controls, quality, and EHS performance. UTC divisions address supplier product and service quality, delivery, continuous improvement, standard work, and environmental issues as partners. Through its Supplier Quality Assurance program, UTC has systems and protocols for assessing supplier quality and EHS practices, risk ranking suppliers, and auditing suppliers based on risk scores.[p]

Open, regular communications with all stakeholders are important elements of SD at UTC. Bad news is presented in light of a bigger picture of continuous improvement and learning from mistakes so that the risks of damaging the company's reputation are minimized. It is not an easy task, since bad news often comes quickly with little time to prepare communications. Some of the bad news included employee injuries and deaths, environmental permit violations, un-permitted toxic material releases, quality deficiencies and the suspected brain cancer cluster among P&W employees. In 2005, P&W paid $1.32 million in fines and penalties associated with an explosion that resulted in a subcontractor's death.[p] None of this news seriously affected UTC's reputation or stock value because the information was disclosed promptly with regular updates on the investigations and corrective and preventative actions. UTC also has demonstrated that over the long term the severity of such bad news is declining. Like most other old-line manufacturing companies, UTC has been responsible for chemical contamination in soil, water, and building structures from past practices. Although not illegal at the time, these practices are no longer permitted in most countries.

The best indicator that UTC's SD efforts are appropriate and effective is the corporation's long-term steady growth under David. UTC successfully balanced shareholder and stock analyst expectations for short-term profits with practices that sustain success and maximize value to customers and stakeholders. UTC's 2005 Annual Report probably best summarizes how UTC achieved a balance between short-term objectives and sustainable growth.[q]

> External forces challenge us to learn and grow. We define ourselves by how we respond. Globalization, productivity, technology and corporate responsibility will challenge us forever. They're how we get ahead and stay ahead of the competition. Our commitments define who we are and how we work. They focus our business and move us forward.
>
> These commitments are: outstanding performance, strategic innovation, personal and professional development, social responsibility and shareholder value—the core aspects of SD.

NOTES

a. This article was written by Gregg Gabinelle, EHS Manager, P&W Power Systems.
b. UTC 2006 Annual Report, p15.
c. Interview with Tom Swarr, UTC Environment Program Manager, July 20, 2006.
d. Innovest Strategic Value Advisors Press Release: *World's 100 Most Sustainable Companies Announced at Davos: Benchmarking Study Showcases Sustainability Premium.* Undated.
e. UTC Press Room: *UTC Names to 2006 Global Climate 100 Index.* February 20, 2006. KLD is an independent investment research and index provider.
f. UTC Press Room: *Top Global Companies Join With WBCSD to Make Energy Self-Sufficient Buildings a Reality.* March 29, 2006.
g. UTC 2005 Annual Report
h. UTC Press Room: Green Solution; Deliver the Computers, Skip the Boxes. December 21, 2005.
i. UTC Press Room: *Facilities and Services Helps Ensure Reliability of Regional Electric Grid.* July 28, 2006.
j. Presentation by Steve Finger, PW President, and Eilene Drake, PW VP Quality & EHS, to PW Quality and EHS employees, August, 10, 2006.
k. UTC 2005 Annual Report
l. UTC 2005 Corporate Responsibility Report.
m. Id.
n. UTC 2005 Annual Report
o. Corporate Update: *UT500 Two Years and Counting (the Savings That Is),* May 19, 2003,
p. UTC 2005 Corporate Responsibility Report.
q. UTC 2005 Annual Report

Reflections

Program execution is generally even more challenging and difficult to articulate than program implementation. HSPs require great fortitude and perseverance in order to achieve sustainable outcomes and success. Unlike many corporate or business unit programs having well-defined agendas that are targeted on specific areas and/or outcomes such as R&D programs for developing new-to-the-world technologies, HSPs necessitate global perspectives and involve diverse participation. Most importantly, they require sophisticated leadership, program management, enterprise integration, and strategic innovations. They are often about doing the undoable, achieving extraordinary results, and realizing impossible dreams.

Program management requires a dynamic perspective of the whole business world and the future possibilities. It involves making real the vision, strategic direction, and corporate objectives. It is based on the recognition that the world is ever-changing and that corporations have to transition and transform themselves into more capable and sophisticated entities. It requires visionary strategic leaders who are willing to lead change and are courageous in creating the future through new businesses, technologies, products, methods, and techniques.

Figure 6.3 depicts some of the most critical aspects of program management. The intent is to highlight the global perspectives and not to suggest that they are the only crucial aspects for achieving sustainable outcomes and success. In reality, everything is important and it is impossible to simply program implementation and execution to just the key elements.

Visionary strategic leadership (VSL) is the pivotal linkage for achieving sustainable success. Strategic leaders invigorate the organization and the participants to have the fortitude to invest the time, effort, and money over the decades to realize the desired outcomes. It takes exceptional vision and inspiration to integrate all of the participants into a unified team. The commitment to the program has to be solid so that the progress continues as transitions and transformations take place as well as the trials and tribulations that happen along the way. However, many corporations have difficulties maintaining the momentum of HSPs when new leadership takes over the helm. Extraordinary outcomes and outstanding accomplishments are usually realized only if the efforts are compounded over time and the subsequent elements and subelements leverage the experience, knowledge, and learning of the previous ones. Moreover, successful outcomes are based on the integration of the whole organization and its extended enterprise. Insights and profound thoughts are often the synthesis of inputs

Vision	Perspective	Linkages	Focus	Outcomes	Perspective
Visionary	New to the World	System/Structures	Relationships	Transformations	New Solutions
Strategic	Long-Term Success	Value Networks	Contributors	Transitions	Technologies
Inspirational	People	Markets/Applications	Recipients	Performance	Success
Visionary Strategic Leadership		**Enterprise Integration**		**Strategic Innovation**	

Figure 6.3 Essential aspects for managing high-level strategic programs.

from many participants. It is rare when a single person has all of the right insights and perspectives. Strategic leaders define and institute the systems and they integrate the whole enterprise.

Enterprise integration requires holistic thinking using cradle-to-grave perspectives about the linkages and relationships that are essential for establishing a framework that is inclusive and includes wise decision making and astute evaluations. While it is virtually impossible for strategic leaders and program managers to comprehend and manage the multiplicity of issues, concerns, problems, and impacts, it is possible to establish management systems to realize such ends with the contributions of all of the participants. The desired/targeted outcomes are achieved through VSL, enterprise integration, and strategic innovations. While VSL involves dynamic perspectives, strategic innovations provide the dynamism that focuses on making progress and being adaptive to the changes. Strategic innovation focuses on enhancing the positives and eliminating the negatives. Creating new businesses, new technologies, new products, new processes, and new means and mechanisms are the lynch pins for creating future realities that are superior and sustainable; ones that provide great solutions and competitive advantages.

Notes

1. David L. Rainey, *Enterprise-wide Strategic Management: Achieving Sustainable Success through Leadership, Strategies and Value Creation* (Cambridge, UK: Cambridge University Press, 2010, p486).
2. Id.
3. Unilever 2010 Annual Report and Accounts, p4.
4. David L. Rainey, *Enterprise-wide Strategic Management: Achieving Sustainable Success through Leadership, Strategies and Value Creation*, p176.
5. Id, p177.
6. Id.
7. Nestlé 2010 Annual Report, p8. The Principles of the Global Compact are:
   Human Rights
   - Principle 1: The support of and respect for the protection of international human rights;
   - Principle 2: The refusal to participate or condone human rights abuses.

   Labour
   - Principle 3: The support of freedom of association and the recognition of the right to collective bargaining;
   - Principle 4: The abolition of compulsory labor;
   - Principle 5: The abolition of child labor;
   - Principle 6: The elimination of discrimination in employment and occupation.

   Environment
   - Principle 7: The implementation of a precautionary and effective program to address environmental issues;
   - Principle 8: Initiatives that demonstrate environmental responsibility;
   - Principle 9: The promotion of the diffusion of environmentally friendly technologies.

   Anti-Corruption
   - Principle 10: The promotion and adoption of initiatives to counter all forms of corruption, including extortion and bribery.
8. David L. Rainey, *Product Innovation: Leading Change through Integrated Product Development* (Cambridge, UK: Cambridge University Press, 2005, p177). The questions are adapted from those pertaining to product innovations programs.

9. Walmart 2011 Sustainability Report, p8.
10. Stephen Weir, *History's Worst Decisions and the People Who Made Them* (New York, NY: Metro Books, 2008, pp126-130).
11. David L. Rainey, *Product Innovation: Leading Change through Integrated Product Development*, p177. The questions are adapted.
12. David L. Rainey, *Enterprise-wide Strategic Management: Achieving Sustainable Success through Leadership, Strategies and Value Creation*, pp266–304. The questions are adapted.
13. Id.
14. Id.
15. http://greenu.org/true-blue-greens/ Roper ASW is a leading market research and consulting firm headquartered in New York which has been providing global marketers options and opportunities for the last 80 years. Roper ASW publishes a report named the Green Gauge Report that serves as a guide for those involved in green concepts and sustainability. The population is divided into 5 segments based on their likelihood to buy green and some of the segment names include Basic Browns, True Blue Greens and Greenback Greens. True Blue Greens are a sector of the market that is keenly and truly interested in environmental issues. These consumers are typically well educated, belong to a higher income group, and are dedicated and able to influence other consumers.
16. Eric von Hippel, *Sources of Innovation* (New York, NY: Oxford University Press, 1988, pp106–107).
17. http://www.barnesandnobleinc.com. Barnes & Noble, Inc. (B&N) is the world's largest bookseller and the nation's highest-rated bookselling brand. As of April 30, 2011, the company operates 705 retail bookstores in regional shopping malls, major strip centers and freestanding locations in 50 states, and 636 college bookstores serving more than 4.6 million students and faculty members at colleges and universities across the US. B&N stores average 25,000 square feet and carry up to 200,000 titles.

References

Collins, James and Jerry Porras (1994) *Built to Last: Successful Habits of Visionary Companies.* New York: Harper Business Essentials.

Rainey, David L. (2010) *Enterprise-wide Strategic Management: Achieving Sustainable Success through Leadership, Strategies and Value Creation.* Cambridge, UK: Cambridge University Press.

Rainey, David L. (2005) *Product Innovation: Leading Change through Integrated Product Development.* Cambridge, UK: University Press.

von Hippel, Eric (1988) *Sources of Innovation.* New York, NY: Oxford University Press.

Weir, Stephen (2008) *History's Worst Decisions and the People Who Made Them.* New York, NY: Metro Books.

7

Enterprise-Wide Risk Management

Introduction

Managing risks has been a mainstream consideration from the early days of business management. During most of the nineteenth century and early twentieth century, risks were usually managed on a case-by-case basis. While high-risk situations were identified and mitigated to the extent possible, in many business situations the associated risks were assumed to be inherent aspects of doing business. For instance, during the nineteeth century train collisions were viewed as an unfortunate, but normal, part of providing the transportation services. In other more responsible business situations, risks were either avoided or transferred to other entities such as insurance companies. Insurance companies like the Travelers and Hartford Steam Boiler Insurance Company became highly successful and very profitable by writing insurance policies for high-risk situations like those involving high-pressure steam boilers that had significant occurrences of explosions, and then the insurance companies mitigated the risks through operational audits and employing innovative safety measures. While such approaches were effective and improved business performance by reducing the potential for adverse outcomes, many negative aspects continued to find their way into business operations, processes, products, and services. While physical risks were usually deemed to be important, many corporate leaders viewed underlying financial risks as the primary considerations. Early risk management approaches focused on reducing the financial risks and how strategic leaders could reduce, eliminate, or transfer the potential effects and impacts of the risks.

Given the fact that negative aspects and business risks, not just financial risks, had significant impacts on business success and led to bad, if not catastrophic results, corporate leaders in the latter part of the twentieth century adapted *"integrated risk management"* (IRM) methodologies to systematically uncover and mitigate risks and the related negative aspects. IRM became an essential element of strategic management and ineffective tool of operations management. There is not a direct correlation between the evolution of IRM and the shifting of strategic leadership from an economic-based view of supply and demand to a more holistic view pertaining to the broader perspectives associated with market-centric perspectives and sustainable business development (SBD). It is important to recognize that there are critical connections between being market-oriented and sustainable and mitigating or eliminating risks and the negative aspects.

Most strategic leaders and their business enterprises made dramatic improvements in strategic management and operations during the second half of the twentieth century. New perspectives and enhanced techniques like six sigma quality, lean business practices, and value systems, focused on satisfying customers and stakeholders, enhancing business performance, and achieving more beneficial outcomes. However, most of the improvements focused on making the positive side more efficient, effective, productive, and rewarding. Many business leaders followed the mainstream theories of the day such as exploiting their core competencies, improving customer satisfaction, improving quality on a continuous basis, expanding revenues, growing businesses, and maximizing profits and cash flow. While such perspectives are usually viewed as appropriate and often lead to reasonable improvements, there are several limitations in just using such management thinking. The approaches tend to be single sided, i.e., the positive side; they are narrow in scope and company-centric, rather than focusing on market spaces, the extended enterprise, and the business environment. The strength of focusing on the positives opened the door to the limitations.

Firstly, the general perspectives are on the company's positives, its strengths, and what it is good at doing. While it is appropriate to be optimistic and aggressive by concentrating on the positive side, such thinking may lead to being shortsighted. For instance, exploiting company strengths may achieve good success in the short term, but it may leave the company unprepared to meet the challenges of future situations. Unchecked problems, difficulties, and weaknesses often fester into uncontrollable risks and/or vulnerabilities that cause havoc, chaos, and worse. For example, General Motors (GM) exploited its wide-range product line of sport utility vehicles (SUVs) during the 1990s. While such products were in high demand and very profitable for about ten years, GM's failure to significantly improve fuel efficiency and to make more affordable cars resulted in disadvantages during the early 2000s as fuel prices increased and the demand for SUVs dropped.

Secondly, such strategic thinking has a narrow perspective focusing the direct economic aspects like customers and revenues. While the concept of customer satisfaction is appropriate and generally market-oriented, it is limited in scope and tends to overemphasize customer needs instead of the broader requirements and expectations of the whole extended enterprise and business environment. Such narrow thinking often leads to improper views of realities, opening the door to limited thinking about all of the requirements and expectations of customers, stakeholders, suppliers, and other contributors. For example, Nike provided good products to its customers during the 1980s and early 1990s and its internal operations were outstanding. However, it lacked a holistic view of its business domain that resulted in severe criticisms by various non-governmental organizations (NGOs) about the working conditions in its suppliers' factories. Fortunately, Nike responded to the demands to improve working conditions at its suppliers' facilities and instituted a code of conduct for suppliers and joined with international organizations like the Fair Labor Association to foster worker's rights and to improve working conditions.

Thirdly, the typical business goals are often self-centered or company-centric ones. They are generally based on what the company wants and desires. Growing the business and making more profits are usually viewed as appropriate objectives, but they may not be sufficient to sustain the business in the long term, if risks are not managed and mitigated properly. For instance, expanding output in order to generate more revenues may create new difficulties like excess inventories and overproduction. Trying to maximize profits may cause strategic leaders to avoid spending money on reducing risks until they are readily apparent and obviously causing severe consequences. To offset such potential problems, goals and metrics should be balanced, including ones pertaining to achieving successful customer and stakeholder outcomes, organizational learning, enterprise-wide achievements, risk management, sustainable success, among numerous others.

Fourthly, continuous improvements of one's strengths tend to involve incremental innovations that may not be significant enough to keep pace with or ahead of changes and risks in the business environment and the market spaces. The concept of continuous improvement has it roots in total quality management (TQM). Continuous improvements involving ongoing initiatives to improve quality and to reduce product and process defects are good, but they may not be sufficient, i.e., simple improvements may not be good enough. While such initiatives are sensible, gains tend to be easy during the early stages of deploying the associated initiatives as there are often many opportunities to make improvements; it typically becomes much more difficult to continue to make gains during the later periods after the easy improvements have been realized. In many business situations, continuous improvements must be coupled with dramatic developments to leapfrog over the problems, to resolve the underlying causes, and to eliminate the risks to the extent possible.

Overall, many of the prevailing theories are narrow, short-term oriented, company-centric, and/or customer-focused at best, rather than being broad based, long-term oriented, and externally-focused, based on the whole business environment. Moreover, careful deliberation must be given to the negative side of business activities, operations, and outcomes. The financial meltdown of recent times provides solid evidence that companies and strategic leaders have to pay more attention to negatives: the risks and vulnerabilities. In many business sectors, the negative side often grows with the positive side or in some cases it actually expands at rates greater than the rate of growth of the positive aspects. As business operations and product portfolios increase, a company may also become more susceptible to radical changes in the business environment, unexpected negative events, dramatic downturns in the economy, and other undesirable business realities.

In today's business world, uncovering risks and reducing their impacts and consequences requires substantial management constructs that go beyond simple risk management theories and practices of the past. They must include *enterprise-wide risk management* (ERM). ERM involves examining the all aspects of the company, its extended enterprise(s), and the business environment and assuring that risks are identified, understood, assessed, managed, and mitigated.

In this regard, mainstream management constructs have to morph into global perspectives like those associated with visionary strategic leadership (VSL), SBD, and sustainable enterprises; ones that are comprehensive, inclusive, and integrated from the beginnings of the supply networks to end-of life considerations. It is imperative that risks be explored in-depth and mitigated to the extent possible to create value, to enhance it, to assure that it is maintained, and to sustain it over the long term. ERM is essential for achieving and sustaining success. It involves making dramatic improvements and even radical developments to both the positive and negative sides to reduce and/or eliminate potential and real problems, difficulties, issues, concerns, and liabilities.

The chapter includes the following main topics:

- Discussing the concepts and realities of risks and the ERM framework
- Articulating the elements of ERM and how they are developed and deployed

The Concepts of Risk and the ERM Framework

Fundamentals of Risks

Risk involves the exposure(s) to the probability of experiencing an injury, a loss, an adverse situation(s), and/or a negative outcome(s). Risk is a multifaceted concept with many definitions, possibilities, and implications. From a business perspective, risks are mainly viewed from the external context, i.e., the risks of doing business or making an investment. Generally, risks are perceived to be related the possibility of experiencing unfavorable situation(s) and outcome(s) and the potential negative impacts and consequences. Risks include experiencing an undesirable result(s), the likelihood of not achieving goals and objectives, not experiencing a favorable event or outcome, failing to obtain certain advantages, and/or experiencing unwanted problems and disadvantages, among numerous others. Risks pertain to the amount of information and knowledge one has or does not have about the situations and potential outcomes, i.e., uncertainties about reality and outcomes. If uncertainty is high, then the perceived risk about the negative aspects is assumed to be likewise high.

The general perception in the business community is that risks are inherently bad and should be avoided, if possible. However, such a perspective is not always accurate. While many strategic leaders want low risks, low risks often mean low or little rewards.

Since risks are part of business and management, if there are no risks there are often very few good opportunities. Moreover, there are very few situations in which one can be guaranteed good outcomes without any risks, say a given financial return without some elements of risks. Even "risk-free" government securities typically have some negative aspects that may impact the perceived rewards. For instance, if inflation runs rampant, the value of certain investment instruments like government bonds may be significantly lower. The holders of such instruments have the risk that the true value of their holdings could be less in real terms as inflation erodes their expected returns.

Risk is a function of stability and change. Stability in the business environment and market spaces is an essential condition for achieving success in many business ventures. It relates to the degree of certainty that business leaders and professionals have in the information and data, facts, factors, and knowledge pertaining to the decisions they have to make, the strategies and actions they formulate and implement, and how they take advantage of opportunities and challenges. Formulating strategies and action plans and making decisions under certainty are expected to result in situations and potential outcomes that are more predictable. Thus, strategic leaders and professionals have a higher degree of confidence and comfort. However, the notion of certainty is always somewhat nebulous in a business setting. While there are many predictable situations and outcomes like the amount of pollution generated from a given process or technology, great care has to be exercised in assuming that there is a great deal of certainty when the business environment is subject to many forces that might change quickly or new forces that might develop rapidly. For instance, the dramatic downturn in most stock markets around the world during the Great Recession is an indication that assuming that there is a certain degree of certainty about market conditions and the information and data thereof has to be taken carefully. Moreover, while certainty and stability do not guarantee success, the lack of either one or both is usually a harbinger of increased risks and vulnerabilities.

Strategic leaders may perceive risks to be low in many situations, but such thinking is often based on the assumption that the driving forces and key other factors are within a limited range of variability. Such assumptions may be good most of the time, but it is important to realize that the underlying forces and the risks are dynamic. For instance, prior to the Great Recession most companies in the automobile industry would have contemplated a downturn in sales to be around ten percent or less; few strategic leaders or professionals would have considered a thirty to forty percent drop in sales and revenues. In today's business world with the numerous global changes, the actual risks may be much greater than the perceived risks, since there are many more forces and factors involved in the situations than what is apparent to most strategic leaders. Again, taking global perspectives help to identify the true nature and number of risks involved. For instance, banks typically analyze the risks in providing loans to individuals and corporations based on credit scores and the credit worthiness of the companies, respectively. However, the risks go beyond the individuals or corporations; they involve numerous other factors including the state of the (global and/or national) economy, the long-term value of the underlying assets, and the stability of the markets, among many other factors.

The quantitative view of risk involves the probability of occurrence, the severity of the outcome(s) or impact(s), and the capability to mitigate the potential negative outcomes. Risk is a function of how bad the results may be and what mechanisms are available to reduce or eliminate the impacts. The latter are called safeguards, means of mitigation, and/or detection mechanisms. Risk also depends on the entities or individuals involved and their knowledge and capabilities. Sophisticated companies and knowledgeable strategic leaders may have a lower level of risks given an identical situation than ones that are unsophisticated or lack detailed information, capabilities, knowledge, and experience. For example, companies with a well-connected and properly functioning extended enterprise may be in better positions to deal with negative events or economic downturns since they are more fully integrated and better understand the complexities and realities of the business environment. They are better linked with customers, stakeholders, suppliers, and distributors and can often respond to the new needs or changes in demand more quickly than their less sophisticated competitors. One relatively simple mechanism for reducing risk is to assure that there is no overproduction and that products are provided on an as-needed basis. For example, Dell Inc. was better able to manage market risk, when it sold directly to customers based on orders and precise customer requirements. Selling though distributors and retailers as it does now involves more uncertainties given that Dell may have less knowledge about who is buying its products, when the purchases take place, and what the customers' true needs are. This usually results in more risks given the market situations and customer expectations.

Uncertainty involves the lack of or limits on information and data and the potential wide variability in outcomes. These include inadequate information, data, knowledge, and/or the possibilities of extremely wide variations in situations and outcomes that are difficult to understand and predict. It also includes the possibilities of having unknowns and hidden aspects. Uncertainty is a normal situation. Outcomes are rarely predictable with a high degree of certainty; most situations involve probabilities of occurrences with a relative large number of possible outcomes. For instance, there is always a probability that severe weather conditions will cause damage to property and life in a given place within a certain time frame. For instance, the likelihood of experiencing a hurricane is greater in Florida than in New York, and, outcomes tend to be worse in Florida than in New York. Yet, Hurricane Sandy that hit New York and New Jersey on October 29, 2012 is an example of how relatively rare occurrences affect seemingly safe locations and populations. Uncertainty is a complex subject with many potential implications. It is based on unknowns. It also involves knowing or not knowing what is unknown. Uncertainty leads to risks. One can reduce the effects from uncertainty by improving one's understanding of the known and unknowns, obtaining more knowledge, information, and data, and taking precautionary measures to avoid the potential for severe outcomes.

Basic Types of Risks

Risks can be subdivided into the types of risks: voluntary and involuntary; objective and subjective; static and dynamic; and absolute and relative. Voluntary risks are those that are assumed by the people who have the freedom to choose whether or not to engage in the activities or to be subject to the risks. When strategic leaders engage in developing new technologies and new products, they assume voluntary risks. They know that such endeavors have risks and the potential outcomes have a degree of uncertainty and that many such initiatives in the past have ended in failure. On the external side, consumers have historically bought and used many products that are known to have negative effects and have one or more risk elements. Gasoline is a great example. It is flammable, toxic, and subject to potential dangerous outcomes. Yet, people willingly assume the risks and use the product. Obviously, they do so because they own products like cars that have gasoline engines.

Involuntary risks are just the opposite. They are generally imposed upon the people involved without their consent or even in certain situations without their knowledge. For instance, consumers may be exposed to certain health risks when consuming processed food, if the food processor did not have proper sanitation or the conditions in the processing plant were not sterile. Because of the faulty practices, the people involved may be at risk of becoming ill or worse. In such cases, they are not aware of the threats nor would they take on such risks if they know about them. Strategic leaders may involve customers and others with involuntary risks when they make decisions based on incomplete and/or deceptive information and data from their suppliers or other contributors. For example, toy companies in the United States suffered significant losses because they incorporated parts manufactured in China that were painted with lead-based paint, making the products hazardous; especially dangerous for young children. The U.S. companies were unaware of the problems and so were the parents who bought the toys and games until information became available through various sources. Some strategic leaders may force their customers to assume certain risks when their companies fail to disclose the full details about the negative effects and impacts of the products or how to use the products safely. Involuntary risks are usually significant concerns, since the people involved have no knowledge or voice in such situations. Clearly, one way to reduce involuntary risks is to eliminate the underlying causes or to provide full disclosures.

Objective risks are those that can be quantified or determined scientifically, based on prior knowledge, scientific experiments, and the like. They are rationally based using generally accepted technical methods and statistical techniques. For instance, the safe exposure rates or harmful concentrations of many manmade chemicals are usually documented; there is a body of knowledge about the risks involved. While perfect knowledge is rare, there are usually details available to make adequate determinations about the associated risks. Objective risks can also be specified in terms of a range of possibilities. For instance, the risks of driving along interstate highways under normal conditions in the United States is fairly well determined, if the drivers follow prescribed safety measures issued by the government; assuming the driver is going around the speed limit (65 mph). Otherwise the risks may increase dramatically as one either goes too fast or too slow.

Subjective risks are based on the perceptions of the people involved and how they interrupt the risks. They are typically based on the individual's or expert's judgment and views about how risky a situation or event is or may be. In the case of strategic leaders, some decision makers may perceive a new product development (NPD) program to have high risk, if they have limited experience in the required technical disciplines, especially if they have to also develop new-to-the-world technologies. As an aside, many strategic leaders have a tendency to underestimate the risks in developing new products that are related to their core competencies, i.e., with what they are familiar. On the other hand, they may overestimate the risks when developing new products, processes, and technologies that are beyond their core competencies and capabilities. There are many more risks beyond the technical risks. Focusing on areas in which the company has experience, knowledge, and capabilities may appear to be low risks. However, if the specific areas are becoming less important to the external business world, especially if the related technologies, products, and processes are obsolete, then the actual risks of following conventional approaches may be extremely high because the outcomes are most likely to be irrelevant to customers and stakeholders. There may seem to be great challenges and risks in developing new products, technologies, and core competencies. However, the company may face even higher risks associated with possibilities of not developing the requisite new solutions, competencies, and capabilities, especially if the external business world requires such innovations and changes. For instance, many strategic leaders tend to overestimate the risks of engaging in strategic innovations and underestimate the risks of doing nothing. They view risks from their own perspectives, rather than the broader external context.

Risks may be viewed as static and dynamic. Static risks are those that do not change much over time or from situation to situation. For instance, the effects and impacts of heavy metals are well known and remain fairly constant. They are poisonous and have detrimental effects on people and other living species. Dynamic risks, on the other hand, change over time and depend on situations and circumstances. They may become greater or lower as time marches forward. For instance, the risks associated with pollution and wastes tend to increase as more of these negatives are generated and put into the environment. The opposite can be true as well. For example, the negative effects of using certain products like gasoline often decrease over time. Such risks tend to moderate as more information, knowledge, and experience become available and people take appropriate actions and safeguards. As real-world experience is gained and more knowledge becomes part of the public domain, the application risks are reduced. This is especially the situation with new technologies and new products as the associated potential negative effects and impacts become better known as people learn how to use them. However, there are many exceptions.

Risk can be classified as absolute or relative. Absolute risks are fixed and do not vary from situation to situation. The risks of fire in buildings made of combustible materials are preordained. Likewise, the dangers involved in using explosives are well established and fixed to a certain extent. Relative risks are the opposite. They are dual-sided with possibilities for positive outcomes and negative ones. The risks in developing new products fit this very well. While there are risks of being unsuccessful with NPD programs, there are many upside possibilities that can lead to great success. Many strategic leaders often think that radical innovations (quantum leaps) are more risky product innovations (incremental improvements), but they neglect to recognize that the more significant risks in certain situations involve simply failing to make the requisite changes to meet the business situation, i.e., what customers and stakeholders want and expect.

Risks are part of everything people do. Business conditions and trends can change quickly and have unexpected impacts and consequences. Even in stable situations, the business environment has many unknowns and open-ended factors. Knowledge is usually based on limited views of the whole and subject to many gaps. Many of the factors are based on what people believe to be true and can be swayed by opinion, faulty information and data, and the lack of precision in understanding reality and the risks therein. Risk and uncertainties exist because not everything is known or considered. While there is a plethora of information and data, especially in the developed countries, not all of it is accurate or complete. If facts mislead decision makers into thinking that they understand reality, then decisions may be skewed or improper since they were based on false perspectives and conclusions. Dealing with future requirements is even more challenging since our understanding of the future is imprecise at best.

Enterprise-Wide Risk Management Framework

The definitions and realities of risk management vary considerable from organization to organization and from institution to institution. Risk management involves assessing, determining, understanding, mapping out, and mitigating key concerns, difficulties, issues, potential problems, and the related aspects pertaining to risks. It also involves establishing a framework and/or management system to assure that the proper strategies, actions, methods, techniques, and approaches are crafted and executed to significantly reduce, if not eliminate, risks and their impacts and consequences. Risk management includes designing the system(s), assessing existing and potential risks, formulating risk responses, implementing risk mitigation, measuring and monitoring progress, and communicating results to contributors, customers, and stakeholders.

The main perspective herein is on ERM. The intent is to examine, explore, understand, mitigate, and manage risks across the strategic landscape of the company, its business units and operations, and the whole extended enterprise. ERM involves protecting the health, safety, and well-being of people as they relate to the company, its business enterprises, and new ventures, and to the well-being of the company itself. It also includes preserving the resources, capabilities, and assets of the company and enterprise(s), and developing and safeguarding its connections and relationships with all of the other entities and individuals with whom the organization deals. It involves protecting and enhancing the social world and natural environment to the extent possible. ERM is based on the external context of the business world and the internal management systems, capabilities, resources, and leadership of the organization.

The logic and aspirations of ERM involve achieving sustainable success and creating exceptional value that exceeds the implicit and explicit needs and requirements of all of the contributors and recipients of the company. ERM focuses on providing the best ways to achieve positive outcomes without jeopardizing anyone's well-being or harming the natural environment and the social world. These are the most important considerations. ERM also focuses on assuring that the property, resources, and physical goods of the company and the other tangible and intangible aspects like its reputation and image are sustained and enhanced over time. ERM is an evolving methodology that involves assuring that the unique solutions provided by the company and the people involved are not threatened, harmed, reduced or rendered useless by the negative side.

The ERM framework provides guidance for establishing a risk management system through the identification, articulation, and development of the main elements of the ERM and making it clear what is necessary and appropriate. It presents how the elements are linked, but it does not prescribe the precise flow of activities. Given the wide diversity of business entities, especially global corporations, and the complexities of most organizations, the ERM framework is intended to provide a map of what should be included in providing direction and guidance to strategic leaders, the business professionals, and key practitioners without prescribing an exact way of doing risk management that might not fit everyone's specific situations or constrain their systems and solutions. The ERM framework is intended to be flexible. Strategic leaders have to craft their own system(s) and process(es) that reflect the realities they face, especially those related to risks.

ERM should be integrated into the mainstream strategic management system and operating systems so that it is a system within the system(s), i.e., part of an embedded management system with various levels and elements. This is especially important when most of the risk exposures of a company and its extended enterprise have important strategic implications. Risks are said to be strategic when they have the potential to negatively impact the success and/or survival of the company and its ability to formulate and implement strategies and solutions and to its realize objectives and sustain success. The ERM framework includes three main sections: risk management system; risk assessment; and risk strategies and actions plans. These sections and the elements are highlighted in Figure 7.1. The main sections have subsystems.

The upfront risk management system involves defining the strategic logic and overarching perspectives, mapping out the areas where risks might occur, and crafting the system design. Risk assessment includes identifying the critical risks, assessing their importance and potential impacts, and evaluating what has to be done. Risk strategies and actions include the examining the risk responses, forming risk mitigation action plans, and monitoring and communicating results. While there is a logical progression of the elements, the ERM framework provides a sense of what is required and not necessarily the way in which the elements have to be or must be carried out. For instance, some companies might start with designing, developing, and establishing the risk management system before mapping out the perceived risks, while other companies may want to articulate the main areas of risks before contemplating what the system should

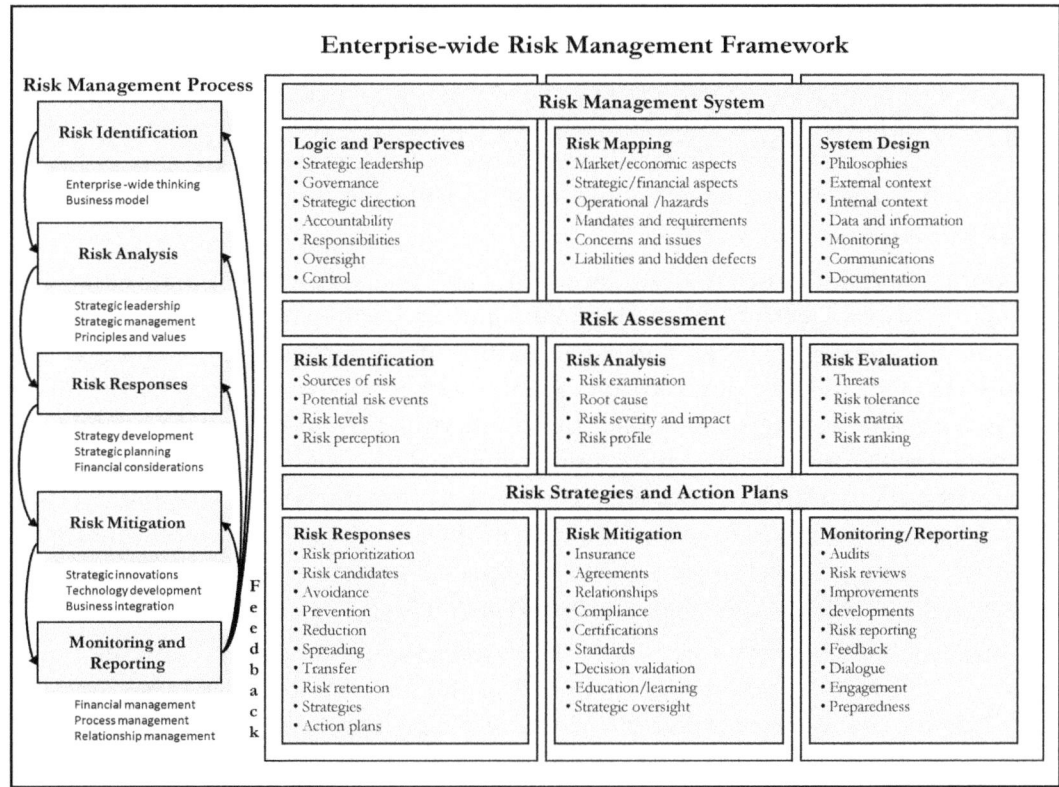

Figure 7.1 Main elements of the ERM framework.

be. However, in most cases the first three elements listed in the ERM framework are managed currently; that is, what makes it a framework rather than a process.

Once the risk management system is established, it may not be necessary to reexamine the first three elements every time. ERM becomes a continuum in which of the subsystems and elements are managed on an ongoing basis. Over time some of the main elements may become incorporated into a process that is managed systematically. The ERM framework is used to assure an understanding of the key elements and to create the system. The process is used to facilitate execution.

Main Elements of ERM

Risk Management System

Strategic Logic and Overarching Perspectives

ERM has several overarching aspects that are embedded within the risk management system. They are strategic leadership, corporate governance, strategic direction, accountability, responsibilities, oversight, and control. Most of the details of these elements were discussed in previous chapters. Strategic leaders across the organization and extended enterprise have the primary duties for assuring that risks are identified, assessed, mitigated, and managed. Each is an absolute obligation for ensuring the well-being of the organization, the enterprise, and people. Strategic leaders have to assure that risks are reduced or eliminated to the extent possible. They are duty-bound to protect the assets of the company and to preserve its survival and success. They must aggressively pursue the aspirations of the company, yet be prudent in the exercise of their power and authority. They must never risk the fortunes of the company or the health, safety, and well-being of people for short-term and long-term gains or for personal recognition and rewards.

Corporate governance is an underpinning and management imperative that cuts across the whole spectrum of the company and its business units. Strategic leaders have an obligation to exercise due care and diligence when making decisions and to ensure that they use best practices and prudent judgments when engaging the affairs of the company. They are compelled to do everything in good faith and to use the test of reasonableness and appropriateness when making decisions and taking actions, especially ones that involve risks. Strategic leaders are agents of the shareholders and the company and have to exercise risk mitigation in every endeavor, yet they must act decisively and aggressively to stay ahead of expectations and realities. These are some of the major tensions involving the decisions and actions of strategic leaders.

Strategic leaders have a strict duty to make assessments of the prevailing and future situations and considerations and to use all of the means and mechanisms available to realize the best outcomes possible. Astute strategic leaders are never willing to risk sustainable success or the long-term well-being of the company to maximize short-term financial performance. While profitability and positive cash flow are important regardless of the time frame, they are the results of doing well, not just the results of attaining the financial objectives. Strategic leaders are expected to achieve a balanced array of objectives, including sustaining success, enhancing learning, and transforming the company into a more vibrant entity.

The strategic direction of the company is a crucial consideration when engaged in risk management. Strategic leaders must ensure that the proper strategic direction is set forth and used to guide the organization toward a sustainable future. If the strategic direction of the strategic leaders is very aggressive, then ERM becomes even more important as fast-paced transitions and transformations open the door to more uncertainties and additional risks, especially in new areas in which the strategic leaders are not familiar. Thus, strategic leaders must establish the means and mechanisms to assure that all risks are well understood and managed. They must assure that due precautions are taken. Strategic leaders have to be accountable and must accept responsibility for their decisions and actions. Accountability includes, but it is not limited to, the following:

- Ensuring proper governance and well-being of the organization
- Protecting the health, safety and well-being of the organization, enterprise, and humankind, and preserving the natural environment
- Satisfying customers and stakeholders and promoting their success
- Creating value and protecting the assets and capital of the shareholders

- Rewarding capital investments through wealth creations and above-average returns
- Developing new capabilities and leaders and acquiring and using resources
- Reporting on financial, social, economic, and environmental performance and success
- Auditing results and mitigating risks and impacts

Accountability means standing tall when facing challenges, taking the high road in decision making, using good judgment, and being personally involved in ensuring that outcomes are appropriate.

Responsibility is an imperative of leadership and risk management, in particular. Strategic leaders have responsibilities to the whole enterprise to ensure that risks are identified, categorized, assessed, evaluated and mitigated using the capabilities and resources of the organization and enterprise to the fullest extent possible to ensure sustainable outcomes. Such responsibilities are usually dependent on the industry settings and the nature of the operations. For instance, strategic leaders operating a nuclear power plant must ensure that the people in the surrounding communities are knowledgeable about the safety systems and how to deal with emergencies. Moreover, strategic leaders of such facilities have responsibilities that exceed requirements and expectations to assure that such plants do not impose risks on the people and even whole countries.

Oversight and control are two of the more difficult elements to fully articulate. While it is easy to understand what they mean, it is difficult to prescribe exactly how they should be properly managed. Too much oversight and control may stifle creativity and empowerment within the organization. If they are carried to the tightest extreme, employees and lower-level managers simply wait until they are told what to do. On the other hand, too little oversight and control may result in catastrophic outcomes as people become accustomed to dealing with risky situations and fail to take actions to eliminate the root causes of the potential difficulties and problems. For example, Lord John Browne, the former chief executive of BP plc, was a great visionary strategic leader who was transforming BP from a petroleum company into an energy company with good intentions and some successes. Yet, he was criticized for failures to provide safeguards against accidents like the fire and loss of life at BP's Texas City, Texas refinery in 2005. Great strategic success can be nullified due to the lack of operating controls or the failure of strategic leaders to provide adequate oversight and control.

Risk Mapping

Risk mapping is an essential part of the risk management system and it is also generally one of the first steps in the risk management process. It involves determining the key risk areas and categorizing the potential risks therein. It also involves selecting the main targets that must be and/or should be addressed. Risk mapping involves the fundamental building blocks of risk management that allow strategic leaders to understand what needs to be managed. It is the precursor to designing the risk management system.

As stated earlier in the chapter, risks are a natural part of doing business. There are always risks and uncertainties in any situation because perfect information and knowledge are rare, if they actually exist. Strategic leaders have to make judgments and determinations based on what information, data, and knowledge that is available. Risks are the price strategic leaders pay when they make decisions to obtain rewards for the company knowing that they cannot wait forever. They realize that risks have to be managed and that it is unlikely the all risks can be eliminated. Generally, high-potential rewards (positive outcomes like profits) involve higher risks (negative outcomes).

Table 7.1 provides examples of some of the more important risk mapping categories. It is subdivided into two main categories of risks: those pertaining to external context and those pertaining to internal context. The order of the key elements is generally based on a flow from the broadest to the more specific ones. The risk categories cut across all spectrums of the business world and beyond. Risks arise in every part of the business environment and within the company and its extended enterprises. It is usually appropriate to start with the external context first, since the external business environment is dynamic and beyond the control of the company and its leaders. Some of the external categories are very broad like those pertaining to complex topics such as globalization and climate change. While the internal context is within the domain of the company, it is critical to realize that internal risks are just as dangerous as those related to markets, stakeholders, political forces, and all of the other constituents. Moreover, while the internal risk categories and areas are often viewed as controllable, internal context is not always easy to manage and there are often many areas that require stringent controls to manage the risks. For instance, modern accounting and finance methods have to deal with complex business transactions and outcomes that are not easily characterized.

The categories and the risk areas listed represent only a microcosm of the multitude of ones that strategic leaders have to contemplate and manage. It is imperative to seek out risks wherever they may be and to identify them so they can be analyzed and managed accordingly. While some strategic leaders are fearful of finding too many risks that cannot be handled, it is critical to map out all of the risk areas so that the design of the system is comprehensive and it is able to account for all of the specific risks. ERM is about making appropriate determinations about all of the risks and carefully executing the action plans, initiatives, operations, and processes to mitigate and manage them. As discussed later, not all risks can be mitigated, but knowing about the risks does provide a degree of risk management in itself. Indeed, one of the risk responses is called risk retention. It simply involves understanding and accepting certain levels of risks and managing them accordingly.

Risk management covers the gamut of business endeavors. However, there are several fundamentals that must be adhered to regardless of the situations. One of the most obvious and important involves compliance with laws and regulations. There are often severe penalties for failing to comply with the laws and regulations; therefore, the risks are significant. While laws and regulations spell out what has to be done, it is not always easy to fulfill such mandates and ensure that all of the requirements are met.

TABLE 7.1 Examples of Some of the More Important Risk Categories (Areas)

	External Context		Internal Context
Category	Key Elements	Category	Key Elements
Natural world	Weather, natural disasters, climate change, loss of biodiversity, depletion…	Governance	Failure of compliance, lack of oversight and control, lack of due diligence, vulnerabilities…
Social world	Pandemics, poor conditions for workers, economic chaos, political instability…	Corporate	Reputation, image, capital, litigation, failure to make sound decisions, bad decisions, harm to people…
Business environment	Globalization, conflicts, terrorism, chaos, uncontrolled expansion…	Strategic business units	Implementation of strategies and actions plans, lack of new opportunities, risks….
• Social	Disease, poverty, illegal drugs, lack of education, hunger, limited housing…	Enterprise	Severe competition, eroding markets, problems in the supply networks, lack of available materials…
• Political/legal	Corruption, bribery, loss of freedom, human rights violations, instability…	Financial	Profitability, cash flow, credit, liquidity, tax liabilities, poor accountability…
• Regulatory	New regulations, conflicting rules and requirements, barriers to foreign entities…	Innovation/R&D	Lack of creativity, too little innovation, maintaining the status quo, fear of change…
• Ethical	Lack of universal standards, lack of general accepted principles, unfair practices…	Human resources	Trained employees, turnover, competencies, knowledgeable workers, safety concerns…
• Technological	Disruptive new technologies, hidden issues, obsolescence, rapid technical change…	Physical assets	Fire, destruction, obsolescence, capacity utilization, capital recovery…
• Environmental	Lack of water, poor air quality, degradation, spills, accidents, wastes…	Marketing/sales	Building relationships, customer satisfaction and success, new challenges…
• Economic	Financial instability, trade barriers, lack of economic freedom, insecurity…	Operations	Quality defects, hidden defects and burdens, health and safety problems, soundness…
Market	Downturns, lack of credit, limited demand, falling prices, limited purchasing power…	Wastes	Hazardous wastes, proper disposal, safe handling of wastes, recycling…
Stakeholders	Adverse agendas, restrictive actions, boycotts, lobbying, conflicts, intervention…	Pollution	Pollution prevention, regulatory compliance, controlling the negatives…
Competition	Emerging competitors, new strategic actions, substitutes, severe rivalry, predators…	Hazards	Accidents, spills, toxic substances, negative health effects, long-term problems…

Generally, the business environment has many opportunities that are usually deemed to be positive. But, there are uncertainties and risks in identifying and determining which ones to pursue. Strategic leaders can make a "type one" mistake by taking on the wrong opportunities or a "type two" mistake by failing to pursue the correct ones. Likewise, companies usually have a sense of what their main problems, challenges, and vulnerabilities are, but they may not have the wherewithal to fix them. The risks may be high since strategic leaders are generally expected to correct known defects, problems, and burdens, especially if the risks and severity of the impacts and consequences are high. Inaction is not an option. Strategic leaders have an absolute duty to correct such situations.

Hidden defects and problems are particular concerns and challenges. They cause risks and uncertainties, because it is difficult to know what you do not know. Such risks may be high since hidden defects can cause significant damage, destruction, and the like. At least with hidden defects and problems, it is not always possible to blame the strategic leaders for their failures in this arena, if they take proactive efforts to seek out and rectify hidden problems to the extent possible. However, there is always the argument that strategic leaders should have known.

There are many other fundamentals risk areas that require attention, especially ones that have lingered for years. Externalities are external costs that are related to the effects and impacts of pollution and residuals from operations, products, and processes of businesses borne by stakeholders, communities, and society. Externalities are latent problems that impact others in the short term, but may be charged back to businesses in the long term. They are high-risk areas since the potential implications are usually unknown. The costs of handling the effects and impacts could be extremely high and negatively affect the company in the future when it may be unable to handle the costs. For example, for many years before there were stringent regulations pertaining to hazardous wastes, companies often used simple landfills to dispose of their toxic wastes. Such practices saved money during the earlier times, but created huge liabilities that cost incredible amounts of money in the future after governments forced such companies to remediate the landfills. Saving money and profit maximization in the short term resulted in very expensive liabilities that reduced profitability in the long term.

Lagging difficulties are similar to externalities except that they pertain more to internal effects and impacts. Product defects and unchecked problems may not be manifested immediately, but may be apparent later. It is often a matter of time before the information, data and/or statistical analysis provide overwhelming evidence that there are difficulties and the associated risks. Often it is only after the number of problems experienced by customers, employees, and others become very large that strategic leaders recognize the problems; and then it is often expensive to fix the problems and eliminate the causes. Such defects may give rise to forced product recall and government-imposed corrective actions that require huge expenditures. For example, Ford Motor Company (FMC) spent about three billion dollars to replace all of the Firestone tires that were originally installed on its early Explorer models. It became apparent that there were significant problems with the tires after there were many accidents that could not be explained by driver errors.

System Design

System design identifies and articulates the subsystems and processes and how they flow from inception though full execution. It must be inclusive and properly connected with the other systems of the company, especially the strategic management system and the operations. System design includes all external and internal aspects necessary for ensuring that risks are managed and mitigated to the extent possible.

Risk management philosophies provide the organization and other participants with the company's underlying principles and the basic tenets of the system. They are the high-level guidelines for developing the subsystems and the processes and implementing the overall system. The design philosophies are the rules, codes for behaviors, and the criteria for decision making that define what is acceptable and not. They involve ways to limit the risks that company's face since they set parameters on what can be done. The details of the underlying principles, codes, etc. were discussed in Chapter 2.

System design begins with examinations of the external and internal contexts. Table 7.2 is an overview of the essential preliminary steps. System design is dependent

TABLE 7.2 Preliminary Steps in System Design

Items	Steps
Scoping Understanding reality and determining the driving forces in the business environment [External context]	• Identifying the driving forces in the business environment • Identifying the regulatory mandates that pertain • Determining key stakeholders throughout the flow of goods and information • Identifying key issues and concerns • Benchmarking important peers and competitors • Identifying trade associations and industry groups and their standards • Obtaining related research from academic communities • Understanding the needs and expectations of customers and stakeholders • Determining the uncertainties and risks
Goal Setting Defining and establishing the short-term and long-term goals [Internal context]	• Reviewing internal reports to determine the critical needs and concerns • Determining the social, economic, environmental, technological, and ethical goals • Reiterating the corporate goals and business objectives • Identifying the information requirements • Determining organizational capabilities • Identifying the specific elements for the risk management process • Defining objectives for reducing uncertainties and risks
Designing Developing and instituting the design elements and the requisite subsystems and processes	• Establishing protocols and the design criteria • Determining the key subsystems and processes and the linkages • Creating successful short-term outcomes to build momentum • Changing attitudes about the expectations • Building a spirit of cooperation, collaboration, and commitment • Determining the process, actions plans and long-term initiatives

on the main elements as discussed in subsequent sections and the particulars of the company and its business environment.

Design criteria establishes the specifics of what is acceptable and places conditions on how far decision makers can go in assuming levels of risks and what they must do to mitigate risks. The system is articulated through system design that identifies and defines the subsystems and processes and how they flow from inception though full execution. The system design must be inclusive and properly connected with the other systems of the company, especially the strategic management system and the operations. System design is based on external and internal contexts and the leadership of the company.

ERM involves a systematic design that is holistic and dynamic, rather than the typical piecemeal approaches, in which risks are managed by the separate parts of the organization. For instance, traditionally the marketing functions would be responsible for customer or market risks and manufacturing functions would be responsible for supply chain risks and health and safety ones. However, in the past, because risks were managed by the functions or individual disciplines, there was little integration, and often ill-defined or hidden risks were not managed at all. Under ERM, risks are managed on an integrated basis using cross-functional teams, intra-company cooperation, and enterprise-wide integration. System design links ERM with all aspects of the company. Thomas Barton and his colleagues in *Making Enterprise Risk Management Pay Off* provide the following guidelines about risk management:[1]

1. A cookbook recipe for implementing enterprise-wide risk management is not feasible because so much depends on the culture of the company and the change agents who lead the effort.
2. To manage effectively in today's business environment, companies should make a formal, dedicated effort to identify all of their significant risks.
3. Various techniques are available to identify risks, and once identified, the process of identification should be dynamic and continuous.
4. Risks should be ranked on some scale that captures their importance, severity or dollar amount [financial implications].
5. Risk should be ranked on some scale of frequency or probability.
6. Measure financial risk with the most sophisticated and relevant tools available.
7. Develop sophisticated tools and measures that meet the organization's needs and that management can easily understand.
8. Know your company's and shareholders' appetite for risk.
9. Apply more rigor to measuring nonfinancial risk whenever possible.
10. Companies are choosing various combinations of acceptance, transfer, and mitigation to manage risk.
11. Decisions regarding control (an application of mitigation), acceptance, and transfer are dynamic-they must be continuously reevaluated.
12. Seek creative solutions and transfer risk where economic opportunities exist.
13. Organizations should adopt an enterprise-wide view of risk management.
14. Consultants, if they are used, should supplement, not replace, senior management involvement in the risk management effort.
15. Successful companies are good at managing silos' [separate risk items] risk. ERM offers them more effective risk management at potentially lower costs.
16. Making risk consideration a part of the decision-making process is an essential element to ERM.

17. Risk management infrastructures vary in from but are essential to driving throughout the organization the idea that decision makers should consider risks.
18. A prerequisite for implementation of ERM is the commitment of one or more champions at the senior management level.

Their insights are very useful when designing the system. ERM takes a global perspective, since it includes all participants from the origin of the raw materials to end-of-life considerations.

Again, the external context should be the initial starting point. It is necessary to understand the risks in the business world and their ramifications before the internal risks can be clearly spelled out. The key is to examine the social, political, regulatory, economic, environmental, technological, and ethical dimensions in the market spaces for inherent and potential risks that require responses and mitigation. Each area may presents risks that must be understood and managed. Moreover, some may have risks that could lead to significant impacts on the company. These are the risk imperatives. For instance, customer preferences may dramatically change in light of economic conditions resulting in insufficient demand of the company's products. The loss of social stability may result in less capable or dependable work force(s), making production quality and outcomes less predictable. Social discord may also result in threats to the safety of employees or destruction of company properties. Political upheavals may make investments in plants and equipment in certain locations or countries at risk to government takeovers, and higher taxes and fees that reduce the business value. Regulatory changes may impose new restrictions or prohibitions on the manufacture and sale of certain products or the use of sensitive processes that cause environmental problems.

Economics are always important. The major concerns are the possibilities of a large decline in the economic value of one's contributions and assets, i.e., products and services and capitalization of one's enterprise. For example, the subprime mortgage disaster caused a large drop off in business activities in the banking industry as well as having huge impacts on the market positions of many of the large financial institutions in the Unirted States.

Technological change is a critical factor that can have very positive and very negative implications. The impacts are often dependent on where one is situated. Technological advancements might introduce whole new enterprises at the same time wipe out the viability of many of the existing business using old-line technologies. For example, Kodak had to reinvent its businesses because digital technologies made most of its chemical-based technologies irrelevant. Ethical aspects often intercede as new norms and standards cause changes in stakeholders' perspectives and acceptable behaviors.

Internal context involves the multiplicity of internal capabilities, resources, and ways of doing things within the company's systems and processes that could be at risk or produce risks. They typically involve the numerous means and mechanisms on which a company depends to achieve successful outcomes; ones that might have hidden flaws that only manifest over time or ones that seemingly work well until a tipping point is reached and the negative aspects become apparent. For instance, many companies profitably used asbestos in their products for decades until it became widely known that asbestos caused cancer and thousands of workers suffered the ill effects. The possibilities for risks include the interrelationships and connections between internal and external entities and people and their abilities to engage properly and achieve desirable outcomes. Every event, situation, and action within the internal context and within the external context represents both positive possibilities to realize success or negative aspects that might increase the risks of the company. Robert R. Moeller, author of *COSO Enterprise Risk Management: Understanding the New Integrated ERM*, identified the following internally-based risks:[2]

- *Organizational and management-related risks.* [Ability to obtain, develop, and retain leaders, managers, and personnel]
- *Information security risk.* [Exposures to loss data and information, confidentiality, availability, integrity, and security]
- *Production, process and productivity risks.* [Interruptions and disruptions in the flow of key processes, activities, and outcomes]
- *Profitability, market, and operational risks.* [Variability and unpredictability in revenues, margins, market conditions, pricing, operations, and results]
- *Business disruption risks.* [Loss of business operations and outcomes due to natural, political, or business-related problems or lack of resources and capabilities]
- *Project activity risk.* [Failures to manage and execute new product programs and other large projects; poor project management]
- *Contract and product liability.* [Litigation due to poor performance or failures to meet specification, especially safety-related aspects]
- *Crisis situations.* [Catastrophes or severe unexpected events due to natural or manmade like severe accidents, blunders, or mistakes]
- *Illegal acts.* [Criminal behaviors lead to huge fines and other consequences]

His list could go on to include many other items, but the point is clear: there are numerous areas where there are existing or latent risks. In designing the system, it is important to include all aspects so that a comprehensive view is possible.

External and internal contexts represent the starting point and the points of ongoing reflection. They include positions, situations, circumstances, and events. Potential or actual risks are often hidden until they are thrust on the realities of the world. Astute strategic leaders design a system so that all risk can be identified and mapped out properly per risk mapping, vetted through risk analysis, and resolved through risk strategies and action plans. Most importantly, knowing about the external and internal risks is meaningless unless proactive approaches are taken to mitigate or eliminate them via risk responses and risk mitigation. Monitoring and communications make up the last elements of design. They ensure that the system is dynamic and has ongoing improvements and developments. They are listed as the last elements, but they are two of the most important elements because ERM is a continuum. While ERM includes an IRM system and may have a risk-management process, it can never be viewed just as a strategic requirement that is done once a year or considered periodically with start and end dates like preparing budgets. It is a continuum with periodic assessment and reviews.

Risk Assessment

Risk Identification

Risk identification is the first part of risk assessment. Risk identification involves developing an understanding of the potential risks facing the company through a qualitative understanding of the risks and a quantitative characterization of each of the risks. This includes uncovering the sources of risks; determining potential risks and possible events that could give rise to additional risks; characterizing their effects and impacts; and evaluating the possible consequences (determining who or what is at risk and ascertaining when the risks may possibly manifest themselves in unwanted outcomes). The business environment drives change and VSL ensures that the organization and the entire enterprise understand the risks involved and that they have the capacity to manage the implications. Risk identification entails an important subsystem within ERM. Table 7.3 provides a suggested flow of the main steps.

The first step of risk identification includes scanning and monitoring the external context to find sources of potential problems, difficulties, and defects, etc. that could cause serious losses, harm, or worse. Scanning involves the broad exploration and examination of the driving forces and internal aspects to understand the conditions and trends and potential issues and concerns that could result in risks for the organization. Monitoring involves delving into specific areas for further examination to discover negative patterns and potential worrisome areas that could lead to risks and negative impacts. It also involves tracking selected factors that might result in adverse situations or could harbor hidden defects and difficulties.

For internal context, risk identification involves scrutinizing the capabilities, weaknesses, limitations, challenges, and questions associated with the business strategies, operations, functional areas of the organization, and those of the key extended enterprise entities. It explores the inner workings of the company, its organization, enterprises, programs, projects, etc. to identify possible situations, events, and/or negative aspects that involve risks or could lead to risks and negative consequences. While there are several variations to the risk identification (a subprocess of the risk management process), it is imperative to develop a broad a sweep of potential risks as soon as possible. It is also critical to explore all of the risk categories/areas per Table 7.1 to ensure balance and thoroughness.

Often strategic leaders skew their perspectives by concentrating on selected business risks like financial or market-related ones. While those risks are crucial for success, there are many other areas that are equally important, if not even more crucial, for success. Moreover, risk areas that are neglected are occasionally the ones with the potential to do the most harm or ones that fester over the years into intractable problems. For instance, for years many companies that generated hazardous wastes paid little attention to the impacts and consequences associated with disposing the residuals from their manufacturing processes. In the long term, some of the companies, especially those involves with toxic chemicals, had to spend millions of dollars to remediate the landfills and other sites contaminated with hazardous wastes. Small investments in prevention would have saved huge amounts time and money in the long term.

TABLE 7.3 The Risk Identification Process

Steps	Broad perspective	Specific areas
1. Determine risk areas (scanning and monitoring)	Determine the most significant areas that represent significant risks and/or potential risks	Examine market segments, customer wants and needs, stakeholders, competition, supply networks, infrastructure, and related markets, internal operations, health and safety aspects, strategic initiatives, programs, projects, and numerous others.
2. Make a preliminary list of risks	Identify risks from readily available information and data using existing sources	Conduct an initial study to obtain existing information and data from internal records, the Internet, government sources, research organizations, etc. of risks and candidates for potential risks.
3. Benchmark related other companies	Obtain information from other companies to determine a sense of their risk areas	Companies in a given industry often face similar risks. Identify what other companies perceive to be risks and select the ones that may be important in the company's setting.
4. Brainstorm possibilities and options using internal and external participants	Obtain ideas about risks from employees and external contributors who are most familiar with the areas of concern. Learn from their perspectives	Brainstorming is a popular way for exploiting the organization's knowledge of its business environment. Employees from selected areas of the organization or, in certain cases, all employees and external contributors are solicited to provide suggestions about risks. Brainstorming requires an open exchange of ideas without negative feedback or adverse consequences.
5. Do a gap analysis	Identify additional requirements not available through existing means	Conduct a gap analysis to identify the missing information or details about risk areas. Prioritize the needs and requirements and determine how to obtain the data and information.
6. Determine the relevant options	Determine the research methods and options that are likely to provide immediate results and meet the goals	Develop a research design. Generally, standard statistical methods are used to ensure the results are valid. Develop a questionnaire or other data collection mechanisms.
7. Identify means	Determine the resources and time constraints	Examine the requirements and the time frame to complete the research; identify the constraints and develop a schedule.
8. Evaluate methods	Evaluate options in terms of time, costs, and benefits	Assess the requirements and determine the most advantageous means to achieve the results in terms of time, money, and impact.
9. Select methods	Select the appropriate research design	Select the best research mechanisms for the situation and develop the research methods.
10. Execute study and analyze the results	Execute the research and obtain the information and data. Analyze the data and evaluate the implications	Conduct the research as formally as possible to eliminate bias and improve validity and reliability. Select the information and data that meets the design goals and study the implications. Determine the implications.
11. Interpret the results and characterize the risks	Prepare a list of all of the potential risks. Determine what they imply. Present the results	Characterize the risks and quantify the details to the extent possible. Interpret the results and think about implications. Obtain management approval of the selected risk candidates. Articulate and record results.

Once the risk areas have been established, the second step is to identify all of the prevailing risks and to list them in terms of the categories. This step entails conducting a study(s) or doing research about the external and internal aspects that could involve risks and determining the sources of risks and the specifics about them. This step involves characterizing the known risks; ones that become obvious after conducting passive research and examining the external information and data.

The third and fourth steps are not always necessary, but are good methods for expanding the discovery of potential risks. Benchmarking other companies may result in finding or contemplating risks that may not be prevalent within the company or its enterprise, but could be hidden or in the early stages of manifestation. For example, the Bhopal catastrophe at Union Carbide's plant in India provided insights for other chemical companies that many of the industrial processes were not as safe as originally believed by managers and engineers. Benchmarking involves studying similar risk areas from an external perspective. It includes engaging other business leaders and professionals and listening and learning about their views and challenges. It involves using industry knowledge about risks and applying it to the company's situations and processes. Benchmarking should be conducted in accordance the American Productivity and Quality Center's Benchmarking Code of Conduct.[3] There are other standards that may apply as well.

Brainstorming is similar in certain respects in that it is open-ended and involves listening and learning from key contributors. However, rather than obtaining input and considerations from strategic leaders and practitioners at external entities, brainstorming involves internal employees and enterprise participants. They have specific knowledge and insights about potential risks, especially ones pertaining to their fields of expertise and responsibilities. Brainstorming works well when participants can speak their mind openly and freely. The best contributions may come from employees who express perspectives, beliefs, and opinions that are not shared by their superiors or ones that are not part of mainstream thinking. Whether the approach is brainstorming or something similar, it is crucial that as many practitioners as possible are given opportunities to discuss their views about potential risks. Moreover, such activities must be carried out in risk-free atmospheres, in which the individuals are not subject to sanctions because they shed light on risk areas that are never discussed or even kept secret.

The next steps include determining the gaps that might exist in finding sources of risks or identifying potential or hidden risks in the various risk categories and defining and executing specific research program(s). The suggested protocol is highlighted in Table 7.3 per steps 5 through 11. Again, it is difficult to generalize the approaches that are necessary to find hidden or unknown risks. However, it is critical that strategic leaders take all of the means and mechanisms possible to explore all aspects pertaining to potential risks and uncover risks that might cause significant difficulties.

Ultimately, risk identification provides the strategic leaders with a comprehensive list of the risks facing the company and business units. The list should provide a description of each of the risks, the sources of the risks, the known characteristics pertaining to the risks, the likelihood of occurrence, and the person(s) in the organization who are responsible for taking action(s). Such a list is often called a risk register.[4] It typically includes a prioritization of the risks and the preliminary game plan for dealing with the risks. While prioritizing the risks in terms of seriousness or required actions is a reasonable management approach, great care must be exhibited to assure that all steps are taken to mitigate and manage the risks. The main concern pertaining to risk prioritization is that risks given a low priority may not get the proper attention or no attention at all. Prioritization is often done on the basis of current thinking about what the risks are and not how they may change over time. The big concern is that today's low priority risks may cause tomorrow's huge crisis.

Risks can be prioritized in levels rather than in a sequential listing. The highest level involves those risks that require urgent attention, i.e., immediate actions have to be taken without delay. For instance, if there is an immediate threat to human life and safety, it is unacceptable to tolerate such situations even for the shortest time. If there is an eminent danger, then all actions and precautions must be taken including stopping the operation or terminating the product or process. The subsequent level involves those risks that have the potential for severe outcomes, but the probability of occurrence in the near term is relatively low. The next level involves those risks that are serious, but they do not require an urgent response. They might involve risks to the business and its financial and strategic success. A systematic approach can be taken to deal with them. These required responses and requisite actions are elaborated in more detail under risk strategies and action plans.

Risk identification may take the form of being part of a process as suggested, but it should also be ongoing. Strategic leaders have a duty to continuously evaluate what is happening and to seek ever opportunity to find risks if they exist. The risk management process is dynamic rather than static or periodic and if it is used it should have many iterations. Risk identification should be executed carefully with sufficient time and effort being provided to reflect on the possibilities and results. It takes insightfulness to uncover hidden or potential risks, especially ones that are not in the normal perspectives and day-to-day operations of the company. Moreover, unless risks are identified properly, it is highly unlikely that the subsequent actions will be executed.

Risk Analysis

Risk analysis is the second and most detailed part of risk assessment. It involves examining the causes and effects of the identified risks, determining the severity and probability of occurrence of the risks, and discerning the potential impacts and their consequences. Actual risks are often difficult to determine and calculate precisely. Risk analysis includes qualitative and quantitative methods to determine the underlying aspects about the risks, their seriousness, and possible implications. Generally, risks are mapped out in terms of severity of the risks and probability of occurrence. The analytical analysis may start with a broad perspective using qualitative approaches to provide insights and an understanding of the actual or potential threats. Qualitative analysis provides a general sense of the critical aspects of the risks involved and allows a quick determination about what is appropriate for dealing with the risks. Those with a relatively low severity and low probability of occurrence may be deemed to be relatively easy to manage; they may be handled by the professionals directly associated with them. Those with severe impacts and a high probability of occurrence are strategically important; they are candidates for comprehensive quantitative analysis. Those with potentially severe impacts and a low probability of occurrence may be serious concerns as well; they require more careful analysis.

Qualitative analysis includes determining the characteristics or qualities of the risks elements to provide insights about what has to be done. A qualitative view provides a relative perspective on the risks and maps out the risks in terms of their importance and potential impacts and consequences. If the specific risks or the risk elements are well known and are an ongoing part of the operations and activities of the company or enterprise, then a qualitative analysis may be sufficient to shed light on the risks and to properly map out the implications. For instance, a company engaged in developing new products faces numerous risks associated with executing the NPD process. There are market-related risks, technical risks, program-related risks, stakeholder risks, financial risks, and strategic risks, among others. If the company has a long history of developing similar new products and the NPD programs have many common elements including the risk elements, then the company may have a well-established database and understanding of the associated risks. For the well-documented risk categories, the strategic leaders may simply perform qualitative analysis to obtain an understanding of the nuances for the particular NPD program and save the time and money for the lesser known and more challenging risks. The following are a few of the risk areas that might be well known, requiring only a qualitative approach.[5]

- **Market-related risk**—the potential of a significant unexpected event occurring or a failure to understand one or more of the essential market requirements. The biggest market-related risk is usually the product failing in the marketplace due to a defect, causing claims under product liability and a loss of reputation.
- **Technical risks**—a function of the internal design and development processes. It includes the failure to develop an essential component of the product or product and/or the inability to secure the appropriate resources to build the product. There are many forms of technical risks.
- **Business or program risks**—the failures of the business units or program elements to meet their objectives. One of the most crucial is the failure to meet the schedule and the target launch date. Program risks are often difficult to manage, but the implications are actually the simplest to understand.
- **Stakeholder risk**—a relatively new area for risk analysis associated with products, services, and operations. Stakeholder problems may arise during the product life cycle, making risk assessment difficult to determine unless there is a concerted effort to understand the potential impacts. Stakeholders may have adverse reactions to the company based on what they believe to be problems.

242 ▪ *Visionary Strategic Leadership*

- **Environment, health, and safety risks**—the failures to protect environmental requirements and ensure the well-being of people. Such failures include the lack of compliance with the laws and regulations.
- **Financial risks**—the inability to meet the expected economic and financial results, especially the desired objectives, outcomes, and rewards.
- **Strategic risks**—the potential negative impacts on the organization and entire enterprise. They include the possibly of a serious or even catastrophic failures that would significantly damage the strategic positions and reputation of the organization and its ability to carry out strategic innovations and high-level strategic programs.

Many of the risk elements in developing new products, technologies, and/or businesses or in executing growth and expansion programs can be viewed as normal (inherent within the context of the business environment) for sophisticated business enterprises. Such risks should be explored and reaffirmed in terms of scope, content, and specifics, but strategic leaders must have sufficient understanding of such risks so that only qualitative analysis is necessary.

Qualitative analysis is often used to determine whether more rigorous approaches are necessary to understand the seriousness of the risks and what needs to be done to mitigate and manage the risks. For the more serious risks, quantitative approaches are used to delve into the depths of the implications and potential impacts.

Figure 7.2 provides a relative sense of when qualitative and quantitative techniques are used. The perspectives offer a general sense and they are not intended to be definitive. Great caution should be exercised; it is never an either–or situation.

Quantitative analysis employs a more thorough analysis of the risks. It explores the causes, effects, and potential impacts of the risks. Most importantly, it examines the severity of each risk and the probability of occurrence. Failure mode and effects analysis (FMEA) is one of the frequently used quantitative techniques for assessing risks. It involves identifying all potential failure modes and prioritizing them in terms of severity, probability of occurrence, and risk ranking. A failure mode is a mechanism that may cause the product, process, or operational aspect to fail to meet specifications

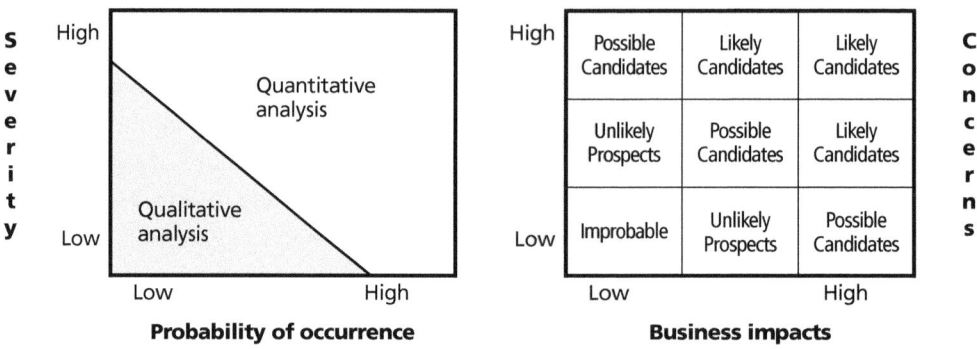

Figure 7.2 Simplified perspectives associated with risk-analysis methods.

or requirements. The potential for a fire or explosion is example of a failure mode. An *effect* is something that is produced by an action or cause. It results in an impact on the downstream processes, activities, products, and services and even on a customer, if the failure mode is not prevented or corrected. For instance, the effect of birds flying into a jet engine could produce a failure that might result in a crash. Effects and potential impacts represent problem areas that could lead to higher cost, excessive defects, poor reliability, inferior performance, increased liability, and/or catastrophic loss. They also represent opportunities for improvements and risk responses. The *cause* of the failure is the deficiency resulting from the failure mode. Negative impacts usually have adverse consequences.

FMEA methodology determines overall risk by examining each failure mode and determining its potential effects in terms of severity, probability of occurrence, and the potential to detect and prevent the occurrence. The method focuses on analysis and the elimination of the cause of potential failures. The analysis is expressed using the following terms to determine the seriousness of the failure:

1. **Severity (S)**—What are the potential effects and how significant are the problems if they occurs? (property losses, injury to customers or workers, death)
2. **Occurrence (O)**—What is the probability of an occurrence? (likelihood of occurring)
3. **Detection (D)**—What is the possibility of discovering the problem? (ability to detect the causes or failure modes if they occur?)

The construct of the analysis is relatively simple. It is a mathematical formula using each of the components (severity, occurrence, and detection) scored on a scale between 1 and 10 (one is the lowest, ten is the worst). For each failure mode, a risk priority number (RPN) provides an indicator of the risk potential. ***RPN = Severity × Occurrence × Detection.*** Higher numbers indicate a greater concern. Ideally, the construct usually provides a significant difference between the problem areas with minimal concerns and those with the greatest potential for difficulties.

The RPN is a way to identify and prioritize items or areas that need immediate planning and action that result in significant improvements. Any RPN higher than a certain number (between 70 and 125) requires action; any severity 7 and higher requires immediate action as well. FMEA is an effective tool for understanding potential failures but it is meaningless unless leaders and managers take the requisite actions. Further details about FMEA are presented in Chapter 7 of my book, *Product Innovation: Leading Change through Integrated Product Development* (2005, Cambridge University Press, ISBN 0-521-06601-3).

Risk Evaluation

Risk evaluation is the third part of risk assessment. It involves determining the requirements for risk responses and risk mitigation. While it is desirable to eliminate all threats and risks or at least mitigate them to the extent possible, it is also unrealistic to assume that all risks can be mitigated, especially immediately or in the short term.

Even with very aggressive approaches and proactive strategies, there may be risks that cannot be addressed quickly. Risk evaluation requires wisdom and good judgment on the part of the strategic leaders to determine the ranking of the risks and the potential order in which they are expected to be handled. Based on external and internal contexts, risk evaluation leads to a definitive understanding about the risks and what has to be done in the subsequent steps under risk strategies and action plans, especially those pertaining to risk mitigation.

Significant threats are examined in light of the organization's tolerance for dealing with and managing the risks. Risk tolerance is the company's abilities and resources to deal with the various risks. Risks that involve business and/or financial success are critical, but most are normal risks associated with transactions, investments, developments, operations, and activities. Well-endowed companies with vast resources may have the ability to tolerate higher levels of risks in these areas. However, risks that involve the health, safety, and well-being of people cannot be tolerated and must be immediately eliminated. Moreover, risks that threaten the survival of the company have to be responded to and mitigated to the extent possible.

Businesses engage in risk taking because it is rare when there is a risk-free situation. If an opportunity is risk free, surely everyone would want to get in on the situation; thus, changing it from risk free to possibly high risks anyway. In the real world, risks are often measured on the basis of risk to reward. Even the most affluent companies examine risks in terms of level of risk to level of reward rather than just costs or threat criteria. High risk requires high reward. Low risk often means low reward. The overall approach is to manage the level of risk and to keep it in an acceptable range. The acceptable level of risk varies from company to company and program to program. There is usually a relationship between the level of risk and the expected reward. It is difficult to generalize on the exact values that are appropriate, but the concept is easy to portray.

Figure 7.3 presents the construct in its simplest form. It examines the relative level of risk to the relative level of reward. The relative level is measured based on factors pertaining to a base condition or expected outcome. For instance, the factor of one for the relative level of reward might be equivalent to the required rate of return from a financial perspective. If the required rate of return is 10%, than the factor of two and three equals 20% and 30%, respectively. In a simple view of the risk profile, the relative level of risk would be multiples of the total investment. While such a view does not fully characterize the level of risk, the concept provides a reasonable perspective.

Zones A through C are areas of unacceptable reward. Zones A and B simply do not meet expectations in terms of reward regardless of risk. Zone C may have acceptable rewards, but the risks are too high for the relatively low level of reward. Zones X, Y and Z are acceptable based on the level of risk. In particular, Zone Z represents an area where the reward is substantial relative to the level of risk. Zone X and Zone Y represent risk-to-reward areas that are reasonable, but just adequate. The former has low risk and lower rewards; the latter has higher risks and higher rewards. This methodology is simply a means to delineate and understand the level of risk versus reward.

Enterprise-Wide Risk Management ▪ **245**

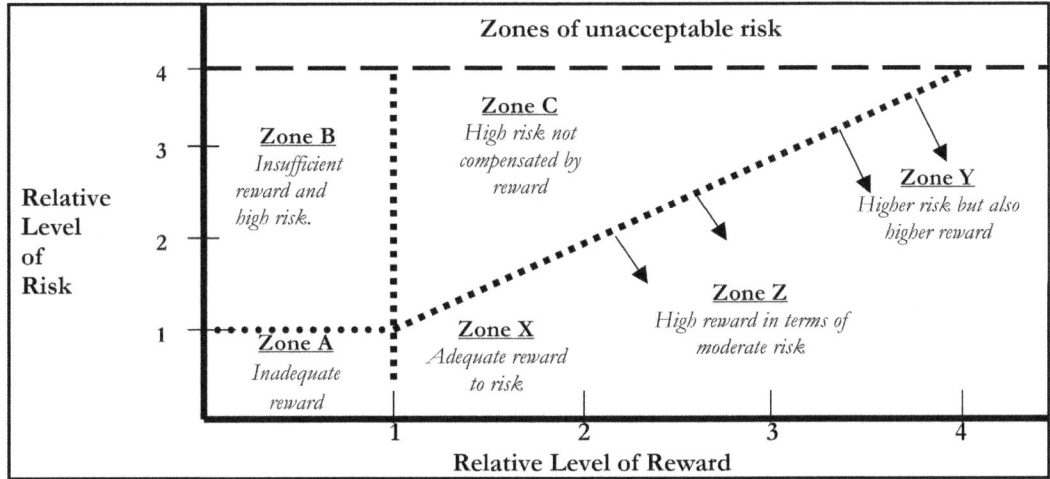

Figure 7.3 Relative level of risk-to-reward matrix.[6]

It is intended to provide guidance in making determinations about risk to reward. It is not to be construed as providing an absolute sense of what is acceptable or not.

Similar constructs can be used to assess risks in general. The perspective simply changes from a financial one to more general view. Again, the construct suggests that it may not be worth investing a lot of money into efforts to make small improvements to areas with low risks, but low rewards. However, it does suggest that certain risks in Zone B, Zone C, and Zone Y might be examined regardless of the rewards, if the severities are high. Like most constructs it provides some insights, but leaders have to use judgment based on their situations and realities. It is impossible to have a single construct that fits every situation. Furthermore, it is not intended to be prescriptive.

Risk ranking involves strategic thinking about the risks that have been identified and analyzed and determining what courses of actions are appropriate and necessary. Risk ranking includes fine-tuning the list of candidates for risk responses and risk mitigation. Risk ranking is always an arduous task. There is rarely a best way to accomplish the end result. The preferred approach is to have the capacity to manage all risk instantaneously or to have all risks given immediate and equal attention and action. However, such approaches are rarely possible given the realities of the business situations. With that said, risk ranking can be affected using the tiered approach starting with the most significant and serious to the least. This is similar to the levels discussed earlier. Based on ranking the candidates, there may be many options to obtain improved situations and positive outcomes. A four-tier approach can be used.

Tier 1 represents the must take action risks that have high severity with the potential for significant negative impacts and consequences. Tier 1 risks require proactive strategies and action plans and the risks have to be mitigated as quickly as possible, especially ones that affect the surrounding communities and people or those that are mandated under laws and regulations. Great care must be taken to ensure that all such risks are managed and mitigated. For example, chemical companies have to ensure that none of their toxic substances have the potential to be released to the atmosphere, the waterways, or ground since such outcomes will negatively affect the communities or worse. They have to take every precaution to assure the safe handling, use, management, and disposal of such agents. No one has the right to risk the well-being of other people.

Tier 2 represents the have to take action risks that have medium levels of severity and high to medium probabilities of occurrence with the potential for negative impacts and consequences. Tier 2 risks also require immediate action, but the risks are less severe and the chances of an adverse outcome are a little less likely. They usually have high priorities. Such risks may result in serious damage and loss to outsiders and the company and its people, assets, and reputation. For instance, NPD programs are always challenging with the potential for adverse outcomes. There may be hidden defects that could lead to products' liabilities. As part of NPD, efforts have to discover potential difficulties and eliminate them. Companies use extensive in-house and external testing to examine new products and reduce the potential for hidden problems.

Tier 3 represents the should take action risks that have the potential for undesirable outcomes that could negatively affect the success of the business. Tier 3 risks are likewise critical, but the potential outcomes are more likely to affect the fortunes of the company rather than the well-being of people. The risks may still be significant but they involve mostly financial burdens. For example, customer preferences could change quickly, resulting in obsolete products and significant cash flow and profitability losses.

Tier 4 represents the would like to take action risks that might have adverse outcomes, but ones that are in the normal range of potential effects and impacts. They involve the potential for less desirable outcomes, but ones that would not have a significant impact on the company or the business environment. For instance, old machinery always has the potential to break down and affect production. However, if the equipment has been well maintained and there are no indications that failures might occur, then the risks are low. Moreover, while there are risks associated with using old machines, clearly the decision makers have to use judgment about such situations. They would like to replace old equipment in many cases, but such actions are not pressing.

Risk ranking may also have to be taken within a tier, especially for the more critical tiers. Moreover, the actual tier selection is often dependent on the situation or circumstances. For instance, there is always the potential for businesses that are connected to the power grid to lose electricity due to storms and the like. On one hand, if the company has a lot of frozen food that could spoil during an unexpected long outage, such risks may be assigned a higher tier than for a company involved in bookkeeping that could be done at any location or any time. In one case, electricity is a critical factor; in the other case, it is necessary supporting mechanism, but it is not something that would have catastrophic outcomes or losses. In the former, the potential reward for investing in a backup generating system may be well worth the money. In the latter, if the probability of occurrence is low, it may not be worth the expense of having a risk reduction mechanism.

Beyond the logic of the tiers, public perception plays an important role in how strategic leaders rank and manage risks. Certain risks receive much greater public attention and scrutiny requiring strategic leaders to elevate them to a higher tier than a rationale analysis would necessitate. This includes pressure from government officials and politicians. In such situations strategic leaders have to consider the pulse of public sentiment and take actions to reduce the concerns that people may have. People's perceptions about many of risks are not based on science or logic and in some cases their views do not accurately reflect the true nature of the risks and how serious they may be. Nevertheless, public perception is vitally important and must be properly considered and managed. Such situations vary considerably from local and regional to national and global. For instance, building an aluminum recycling facility in a neighborhood may have few real risks, yet the local population may perceive many negatives due to their knowledge of problems associated with an automobile dismantling operation in the adjacent community that has many environmental problems. On a broader scale, people may believe that the climate change phenomenon is causing the severe weather in their region and they blame certain businesses like electric utilities for the effects and impacts of the severe weather. Even though strategic leaders believe that they are blameless or that they are not significant contributors to the problem, it is incumbent on them to take such issues seriously, give them high rankings, and take proactive actions. On a global basis, the meltdown of the Fukushima nuclear power plants in Japan after the earthquake has caused other nuclear energy providers and the national governments to engage in serious examinations of their reactors. For instance, a Bloomberg Business Week report dated March 23, 2011 stated that Germany is "set to abandon nuclear power for good" because of the inherent risks.[7] One serious event can change the dynamics of an entire industry on a global basis. It may also change people's perceptions about the severities and the probabilities of events and outcomes.

Beyond public perceptions, strategic leaders must also understand what shareholders, employees, customers, and stakeholders believe to be important risks; ones that are deemed to be beyond the normal risks of a business. For instance, shareholders understand that there are always financial and market risks in doing business and they accept them as part of the business environment. However, they may not be willing to accept extraordinary risks such as building manufacturing plants in certain developing countries with unstable or dictatorial governments. Similarly, stakeholders may perceive the risks associated with new-to-the-world technologies to be much greater than an objective assessment might suggest. For instance, various U.S.-based stakeholder groups have argued that conventional nuclear power is "too unsafe" to deploy in the United States, yet France obtains more than seventy-five percent of its electricity from nuclear power and the French industry's safety record is outstanding.[8] Americans tend to accept generic engineering, while Europeans tend to boycott the related products. It is important to understand the risks tolerance of shareholders, customers, and stakeholders as well as those of the strategic leaders. Such understanding helps strategic leaders determine the most appropriate risk responses.

Risk Strategies and Action Plans

Risk Responses

Strategic leaders and strategy professionals ultimately have to select the best strategies and action plans for effectively managing risks within their business enterprises. The initial step is to determine the best risk response(s) for each risk. Some of the possible responses include risk avoidance, risk prevention, risk reduction, risk spreading, risk transfer, and risk retention (acceptance). From the potential responses, risk strategies and action plans are developed. It is the intellectual part of ERM in which strategic leaders, professionals, and practitioners examine the best ways to abate and/or mitigate the risks. They use insights and their imagination to determine the best solutions.

Risk avoidance is easy to understand, but it is often difficult to implement. It is logical and inherently sensible in situations that cannot be changed, satisfactorily modified, rectified into acceptable outcomes, or eliminated through new designs or strategic actions. For instance, most electric utilities have not built new nuclear power plants in the US, because they cannot reduce the public's perceived risks and the real risks associated with making large capital investments in a turbulent and uncertainty business environment. Risk avoidance often involves not taking on the risk-producing strategies, actions, operations, or activities. A more poignant example is not engaging in business in countries where bribery and corruption are rampant and where strategic leaders might become embroiled in illegal activities that are viewed by local participants as normal practices. Simply avoiding such situations is an effective risk response, since there are myriad ways in which unlawful or unethical behaviors can lead to bad outcomes like damaged reputations or even criminal charges against the company and its strategic leaders. Risk avoidance is most appropriate for risks that have a high severity and a high probability of occurrence, especially when the means and mechanisms to mitigate the risks are lacking or may themselves introduce additional risks.

Risk prevention involves examining the causes of risks and taking actions to prevent the causes from occurring. The main theme is to prevent or eliminate the exposure to the risk; therefore, the downside of the risks is decreased or eliminated. For instance, toxic substances used in various products have the potential to cause difficulties during the production processes and customer applications and after being discarded. There are always the possibilities of contamination and improper use. Risk prevention in such cases involves finding non-toxic substitutes that eliminate the risks altogether. Risk prevention may also involve restricting the sale and use of certain products to only those who have the knowledge and capabilities to apply the products properly. For instance, it is incumbent upon companies engaged in alcoholic beverages to insure that underage people do not buy and use their products; they must take measures to ensure that their customers use the products safely and understand the limitations in consuming such products. Risk prevention is appropriate for all severities and probabilities of occurrences, especially for high and medium severities with medium to high probabilities.

Risk reduction involves lowering the potential severity and/or probability of occurrence, especially in those situations in which risks are inherently part of the doing business and, even with extraordinary efforts, some risks still remain. For instance, product safety is a major consideration in the United States and other countries as well. The risks in using cars, airplanes, and other devices have been dramatically improved over the last century. However, with all of the actions taken and the added safety devices, there are still significant risks associated with such products. It is seemingly impossible to make the perfect product; therefore, the grand scheme is to reduce the risks on an ongoing basis, especially as new products are developed and commercialized. Risk reduction involves the efforts to make outcomes better, safer, and more ideal with recognition that perfection is a distant dream. Such responses are commonplace. Risk reduction is often relatively easy and cost effective. For instance, establishing safeguards, monitors, and other mechanisms to warn people of potential adverse situations may significantly reduce the severity of an adverse event like a fire in a building without substantially changing the economics or the functionalities involved. Given that society values people over things, if the threats to human well-being are significantly reduced or eliminated, then the potential severity of the risks can be lowered. Risk reduction is appropriate for all severities and probabilities of occurrences.

Risk spreading is similar to risk reduction except it involves sharing the risks with other entities or through diversification of businesses and activities. Companies can form associations, cooperatives, joint ventures, and the like to obtain large numbers of responsible entities and/or individuals; thus, improving their abilities to withstand an adverse situation. For instance, electric utilities in the United States and elsewhere understand that they are all exposed to the possibilities of severe weather, such as winter storms in the Northeast, hurricanes in the Southeast, and tornadoes in the Midwest. They form arrangements among the partner companies to provide mutual assistance in such situations that lowers the potential severity of the impacts or consequences and allows each company to have good responses without having excess equipment and manpower just to handle the potential for such events. There are numerous ways to spread risks, especially from a financial perspective. Such instruments are covered in the next section under risk mitigation. Risk spreading is appropriate for all severities and probabilities of occurrences, but it is most useful for high severity with relatively low probabilities. Given low probabilities of occurrences, others may be willing to share in the risks in many situations, especially if it can be done at reasonable costs.

Diversification of the business portfolio is another way to spread risks. From a strategic perspective, it involves having large numbers of products and operations that reduce the potential effects of a problems or negative impacts in one product line or business sector causing the whole corporation to decline or collapse. However, more products, operations, actions, and activities may also mean more risks and increased probabilities of something going wrong. This is especially a concern if the risks are linear, i.e., they increase with increasing numbers.

Risk transfer is a more formal way to share risks with other entities. It normally involves financial instruments that allow the company or entity at risk to pay someone to assume the potential impacts, especially the financial ones, associated with the adverse outcomes. Risk transfer simply means that some other entity is willing, for a fee, to underwrite the exposure(s). It may also involve stipulating who is responsible for certain risks in executing a contract or in the purchase and use of a product. For instance, a manufacturer may state that the customer is responsible for certain aspects of the product or that certain potential problems are the responsibility of the buyer. It is commonplace that producers do not guarantee wear parts or certain applications like using the products in severe conditions. Risk transfer is appropriate when the companies, entities, or individuals do not have the capacity to manage all aspects of the risks. For example, there are always the possibilities of accidents in most endeavors and in some cases the severity of the outcomes are beyond the capacity of the entity(s) to manage them. The U.S. nuclear industry during its early days (the 1950s) got the Federal Government through the Atomic Energy Commission to assume the financial risks of a potential catastrophe (meltdown) beyond a certain point ($540 million).

Risk retention is one of the primary responses taken when other options have been examined and the most effective way to respond is simply to accept the risks and their implications. It is most effective when the cost-to-benefit ratios of other approaches are not very favorable or that there are relatively few options overall. It is also used when the risks themselves cannot be adequately identified and articulated. For instance, businesses and other types of entities across the world face the threat of terrorism, but it is extremely difficult, if not impossible, to clearly define what are the risks, severities, and probabilities. Given the high degree of uncertainty, trying to determine the proper risk response is difficult and possibly too costly. Risk retention may also be appropriate for situations in which the severities and probabilities of occurrence are relatively small. There are many risks in the Tier 4 category that are deemed to be almost insignificant in the grand scheme; therefore, they are recognized as such and they are simply accepted.

Another form of risk response that is similar to risk avoidance is to make strategic changes in the company's businesses and operations. Strategic changes involve high-level decision making that significantly transitions or transforms the business portfolio(s) and the associated risks thereof. Such changes may include new initiatives that have the potential to dramatically improve the well-being of the whole company. For instance, General Electric (GE) established a "six sigma" philosophy to improve quality and reduce defects and the associated costs; United Technologies Corporation (UTC) developed its Achieving Competitive Excellence (ACE) program that includes quality and lean business practices to enhance efficiency and effectiveness; and, many companies have instituted SBD. In each case the strategic leaders focused on reducing, if not eliminating, defects, burdens, and problems; thus, providing improved responses to the inherent risks.

Strategic risk response involves strategic management and corporate leadership formulating and implementing proactive business strategies and action plans to affect positive outcomes. At the highest level strategic leaders can resolve or eliminate risks and problem areas by creating new solutions. For instance, developing clean technologies that eliminate hazardous wastes and pollution is an effective way to eliminate certain risks. Investing into strategic innovations and new capabilities are often cost-effective ways to reduce risks. If leaders, managers, and employees have more knowledge and know-how, they are more likely to make good decisions and have few difficulties. Mistakes are often the results of inadequate preparation, training, and education.

Strategic change may also involve divesting or withdrawing from certain businesses or operations that are deemed to be too risky. GE sold off its insurance businesses because it believed that exposures to adverse weather conditions and events were increasing, especially damage to property. Severe weather and the potential effects of climate change negatively affect the business opportunities and GE's strategic leaders selected strategic change as ways to handle the risks. Thus, when potential exposures are deemed to be too high, divesture is an option when the negative side of the businesses outweighs the positive side, i.e., the risks become higher than the potential rewards.

Outsourcing is often viewed as a mechanism for reducing risks. While the company's legal responsibilities for the risks may be reduced through outsourcing, its enterprise risks may actually increase since it is more dependent on its suppliers and partners and their abilities to perform and act in appropriate manner. For instance, Lego outsourced its North America production to a company in Mexico that ultimately was unable to successfully produce the products. While Lego successfully mitigated the related problems, it had to take extraordinary means and mechanisms to rectify the situation. Outsourcing may ultimately result in more risks, not fewer ones.

From an operational point of view, strategic leaders can use emergency preparedness and contingency planning as special ways to respond to risk. Rather than taking specific actions or implementing actual responses, emergency planning simply involves preparing for the likelihood of adverse situations or events and putting the means and mechanisms in place to affect positive outcomes, if necessary. It involves many complicated methodologies and techniques to prepare for the possible undesirable event like an accident, toxic substance spill, or other types of adverse situations. Emergency planning involves more than planning; it includes obtaining the capabilities to respond, creating awareness and know-how, and communicating the plans to the broad communities of employees, neighbors, and government officials.

Risk Mitigation

Risk mitigation involves the implementation of the ERM programs to positively affect (lower or eliminate) the risks. It includes all actions that may be or must be taken to diminish or alleviate the risks via externally based approaches and internally based ones. The number of such approaches may be endless, based on the full participation of the organization and the extended enterprise. Risk mitigation may be viewed from a strategic level down to the operational aspects. Most importantly, risk mitigation has to be integrated, not fragmented or done on a piecemeal basis. W. Edwards Deming, one of the greatest TQM gurus of the twentieth century, suggested that fragmentation of efforts was one of the big difficulties associated with achieving improved quality and productivity:[9]

Efforts and methods for improvements of quality and productivity are in most companies and in most government agencies fragmented, with no overall competent guidance, no integrated systems for continual improvement. Everyone, regardless of his job, needs a chance to learn and develop. In a climate of fragmentation, people go off in different directions, unaware of what other people are doing. They have no chance to work to the best advantage of the company nor with themselves, and little chance to develop.

Risk mitigation is a function of VSL, which must be exhibited at every level of the organization and enterprise. Leaders are ultimately the ones who set the stage for risk mitigation and ensure that the efforts are integrated and not fragmented. Efforts must be integrated up and down the organization and across the enterprise. ERM requires dedicated attention to finding the underlying causes, understanding the implications of the risks, and instituting integrated approaches for affecting positive changes and improvements. The potential number of risk mitigation actions is extensive. They include obtaining insurance, buying hedges against risks, making agreements with other entities to reduce exposures, building relationships, ensuring compliance with laws and regulations, obtaining certifications, and achieving standards. It also includes validating decisions, educating people, and providing strategic oversight. Risk mitigation has to be based on knowledge, learning, and concerted team-based efforts across the entire enterprise.

Buying various types of insurance from third parties is one of the simplest external approaches. Insurance is most effective for protecting the company against financial exposures. Such actions usually transfer or spread the risks rather than truly reducing or alleviating them. They are absolutely necessary if the potential losses or impacts are beyond the financial means of the company to sustain. Insurance is used for many normal business exposures such as property losses, liabilities associated with accidents and unexpected events, and many other situations involving the company's responsibilities related to potential negative outcomes. However, insurance does not lead to risk-free operations and results. It implies a "trust." The insured party depends upon the insurance provider to fulfill its contractual responsibilities, if an adverse situation occurs. This assumes that the insurance providers remain solvent and can provide the required financial protection. However, as the experiences of the financial crisis of 2008 indicate, some insurance companies like AIG may not always have the wherewithal to fulfill their obligations, if there are overwhelming negative situations and events. Like most risk-mitigation approaches, there are usually residual risks that require ongoing management and possible mitigation.

Hedging is a popular way to reduce financial risks like price escalation and/or inflation by buying financial instruments that stabilize future costs or prices at a certain level. While there are many forms of hedging, one of the most often used is to buy options or fixed-price contracts that provide protection against negative changes in costs and prices. Hedging is also used to fix currency fluctuations during the execution of a project or commercial contract when doing business across borders. It allows the purchaser to fix the exchange rate at a certain point so that the funds flow from the project or contract can be ascertained precisely.

Risks can be mitigated to some extent by simply defining business or contractual responsibilities better. Detailed contractual agreements are excellent ways to mitigate risks by stipulating who is responsible for what actions and what the remedies might be for failure to execute or if there are unexpected outcomes. They are also the instruments used to enforce insurance policies and other risk-mitigation techniques. They map out exactly the scope of the responsibilities and relationships between the parties and the implications thereof. While nothing is perfect and there are always the possibilities of loopholes, formal contracts take the fuzziness out.

Compliance with government mandates provides controllable ways to mitigate risks by ensuring that the company meets external expectations. Compliance involves understanding the laws and regulations and having the capacity to meet the expectations. Certifications of acceptance by government agencies or independent third party auditors provide evidence that the products, operations, etc. are of the kind and quality suitable for customers and stakeholders. While such certifications do not alleviate risks, they do indicate that the company was proactive in ensuring the risks are mitigated. Codes and industry/government standards provide a basis for risk mitigation by expressing what the requirements are and establishing a definitive set of criteria for determining what is generally acceptable practices and/or outcomes. While following codes and standards does not guarantee positives outcomes, it does reduce the risks involved by avoiding deviant behaviors. It may limit liabilities in some cases, since there is the defense that one used best practices.

In addition to externally based approaches, there is a myriad of internally orchestrated mechanisms. Validating decisions is one of the most effective ways to lower the risks of doing business. Leaders and managers might use analytical techniques to authenticate the inputs and outputs of their decision making processes. They may use TQM and six-sigma principles and methods as suggested by Deming and other quality gurus to assure that they fully understand the underpinnings and the implications of their decisions. If difficulties and concerns are discovered and identified, strategic leaders can mitigate negative aspects by ensuring that corrective actions are taken immediately to rectify the situations and eliminate the causes. Affecting positive actions and taking corrective actions are usually operational actions to eliminate product and process defects, problems, and nonconformance. However, they may also apply to strategic issues and concerns that make the business situation more tenuous. For instance, the lack of attention to resource depletion may lead to increased business risks; such situations may be corrected by instituting initiatives like SBD.

Strategic oversight is an excellent mechanism to affect risk mitigation through ongoing "supervision" in the broad sense or periodic reviews of strategies, businesses, systems, programs, operations, processes, etc. to assure that they are in control and are performing in accordance with mandates, standards, specifications, management criteria, and related metrics. The "art and science" of strategic oversight provide operational latitude while at the same time maintaining control. Strategic oversight is especially effective when lower-level managers and practitioners have the freedom and flexibility to make decisions and act expeditiously based on well-established rules and guidelines and within the parameters that are well defined and observable. Managers and practitioners know that there is strategic oversight and act accordingly. "Trust but verify."

Some special risk mitigation techniques include peer review, life-cycle thinking, the precautionary principle, and VSL as discussed in Chapter 2. Peer review involves having outside professionals, subject matter experts, and/or groups of impartial customers and stakeholders provide input or feedback on proposed actions and activities before they are initiated. Peer review includes soliciting constructive criticisms, obtaining alternative perspectives on the topics, and/or gaining mainstream acceptance.

Life-cycle thinking and assessment are relatively new and evolving management methodologies for examining, assessing, and improving products, processes, and operations. They involve exploring all of the effects, impacts, and consequences of the organization and extended enterprise from a "cradle to grave" perspective. The underlying constructs are to validate the positive benefits (value added), to discover hidden problems and potential risks and to eliminate them before they become significant. Life-cycle management and assessment are comprehensive methods that are explained in detail in *Sustainable Business Development: Inventing the Future through Strategy, Innovation and Leadership*.[10]

The precautionary principle is one of the underpinnings of the scientific method. From a decision-making perspective, it simply involves not taking actions that are extremely risky unless there is compelling evidence that the potential dangers, harms, negative effects, and potential impacts are well understood and can be or are mitigated through reasonable and sustainable actions. It implies that strategic leaders have an absolute duty to people in general, and to employees and customers in particular, to assure that the potential impacts and implications of the decisions are clearly understood and managed. Moreover, it obliges strategic leaders to err on the side of safety and well-being and not to take risks that are beyond their control. For instance, developing new-to-the-world technologies and products often involves novel situations in which there is a lack of knowledge and experience in dealing with all of the potential risks. In developing genetically engineered food products, the long-term health effects are not always clear. The innovators must do a significant amount of real-world testing before they commercialize such products. It is unreasonable to risk the well-being of potential customers or employees if there are concerns and unknowns. If there are significant concerns, strategic leaders must exercise caution and take every effort to obtain additional information and proper answers. If the right answers are not forthcoming, then the program should be terminated or stopped until such time as the information and data becomes available and proper judgments can be made.

VSL is the quintessential risk mitigation approach. It takes good and dedicated strategic leaders who fulfill their fiduciary responsibilities to the company and the well-being of people to ensure that risks are mitigated and there are no unreasonable risks being taken. Strategic leaders must assure that the organization and enterprise have the capabilities, knowledge, and resources to manage and mitigate risks in a prudent and generally accepted manner. They must put the safety and well-being of people and the natural world first and foremost. Great strategic leaders have the courage and conviction to mitigate risks and reject unacceptable actions and behaviors.

Risk Monitoring and Reporting

Risk monitoring is the ongoing efforts by strategic leaders, managers, and practitioners to obtain acceptable outcomes, to deliver outstanding performance, to get the best outcomes possible, and to assure success. It includes strategic control, audits, reviews, reporting, dialogues, and engagements among countless other mechanisms. It involves the never-ending challenges to keep business risks within the acceptable zones as shown in Figure 7.3.

Strategic control is a broad management construct that involves protecting the assets of the company; assuring its strategic positions and successes; enhancing intellectual capabilities and physical and financial resources; maintaining sound and effective operations; and avoiding the potential to do or to be harmed. It also involves realizing solid performance; achieving high levels of quality; assuring good management rigor; and promoting leadership development through the proper delegation of authority, effective learning, and good judgment, and wisdom. Strategic control requires effective strategic leadership to assure that the solutions, systems, structures, methods, and practices are performing properly and within acceptable parameters. The parameters are generally articulated by strategic leaders who have the overall fiduciary responsibilities to assure the well-being of the company and all of the people that it touches. They include defining what are the performance targets, how much variation is acceptable, and who is responsible for assuring success.

As discussed earlier, strategic control is complicated because it is difficult to precisely define how to accomplish it. Too little control often leads to risk exposures due to the lack of attention and action. On the other hand, too much control may stifle agility and/or a sense of individual responsibility, i.e., the person (or team) involved does what he or she is told to do and nothing more, because the individual is fearful of being out of the norms of acceptable behaviors and actions. Strategic control can be affected through performance evaluation and auditing.

Performance evaluation is the process of measuring, reporting, and taking actions to obtain, improve, and/or assure that performance exceeds expectations. Performance evaluation of ERM is similar to the constructs discussed in the previous chapter. It involves a real-time examination of the risks and the risk-management techniques. Performance evaluation provides immediate insights about the risks and whether they are acceptable or not. It gives strategic leaders indications about what actions have to be taken. The main advantages of performance evaluation are the results and implications are available in real time and actions can be taken immediately. The main disadvantage is that the breadth and depth of the evaluations are often limited. It is difficult to get a comprehensive understanding (the full picture) of a complex situation by just examining the key metrics. For instance, profitability is often used to measure risk mitigation and if profitability suffers, what are the causes? Is it due to the company's ERM programs or other factors? In some cases, the metrics confound the evaluation.

For example, Lucent Technologies (Lucent) had a surge in business during the late 1990s just before the collapse of its served markets in March 2000. The seemingly good news of enhanced revenues and profitability did not foretell the business risks in the markets nor did it provide the underlying causes of the good performance. While the story is complex due to the "Y2K" phenomenon, Lucent's extraordinary performance was not sustainable and was due in large part to its customers buying new equipment before they normally would do so because of their fears about "Y2K." Customers were simply accelerating their equipment replacement cycles, which resulted in a subsequent period of serious decreases in sales and profits.

Auditing is a complementary methodology for examining the systems, processes, activities, and outcomes. It includes tests and confirmations of the procedures and practices to ascertain compliance with laws and regulations, the functioning of the management systems, adherence to standards and codes, and assurance that the organization is capable and responding in accordance with the values, policies, guidelines, and requirements of the organizations. It also is used to assure that strategic leaders are fulfilling their fiduciary responsibilities to provide proper control and oversight so that risks and liabilities are mitigated to the extent possible; that the management system(s) are effectively improved, transitioned, and/or transformed; and that significant improvements are made to every facet of the businesses.

Auditing has the advantage of being more comprehensive and thorough. Its main disadvantage is that it requires considerable time and effort to execute; thus, audits are performed infrequently. In many cases there is a relatively long cycle between audits, say three years. Moreover, auditing requires well trained and unbiased professionals who have the depth and breadth of knowledge, know-how, and subject matter expertise. Auditors must be independent of the areas and subjects being audited and have the ability to convey the results in a constructive manner that facilitates corrective action and adjustments in performance and organizational learning. Auditing has to be positive in helping people.

Risk reviews are among the most effective ways to ensure effective outcomes. They involve either periodic or ongoing reviews of the ERM and the specific risks confronting the company. They are a function of management at all levels. Senior management often focuses on the most serious risks with other levels of management involved with the more general risks. For instance, certain operational risks may be delegated to functional managers and professionals. Regardless, strategic leaders still assume the responsibilities for the whole ERM, the systems, and all of the risks. In large companies, a Chief Risk Officer (CRO) or an equivalent may be assigned to manage the systems and to provide specific attention on assuring the all risks are managed and mitigated. The actual approaches are dependent on the types of risks and their potential severity, impacts, and implications. Risk reviews must be forceful in most situations and done frequently. It is difficult to specify the time frame for such reviews, if they are conducted on a periodic basis. It is not unreasonable to have monthly or weekly reviews. In some cases they should be done daily. For instance, petroleum or chemical companies have to have very sophisticated systems and review processes given the nature of the businesses and extreme hazards involved.

Risk monitoring is part of the ongoing efforts to assure that the most effective and efficient outcomes are realized. It is not the end of the risk management process, but an essential ongoing element to keep risk management at the forefront of everyone's attention. It is easy for people who live with certain risks everyday to become accustomed to the risks and fail to keep up the necessary diligence. Even with an outstanding ERM, there are always residual risks that remain.

Risk reporting is an essential element that is also an ongoing rather than an end point. Risk reporting can take many forms such as formal quarterly and annual reports to shareholders, stakeholders, and especially to government agencies and internal participants and enterprise partners. It involves certain disclosures pertaining to ERM, the effectiveness of systems, the risks, and the results obtained. It highlights the pluses and the minuses and the ongoing efforts to make improvements. It provides feedback to all of the contributors so that they can enhance performance in the future.

ERM is also about building solid relationships with the external entities and people and engaging them in constructive ways to reduce the severities and probabilities of the inherent and potential risks of doing business. It requires open and honest dialogues with people and ensuring the all sides of situations are open to scrutiny; the positive aspects and the negatives. In particular, it is imperative that the negative aspects are highlighted and dealt with as quickly as possible.

Reflections

ERM is a sophisticated management construct that is philosophically and practically aligned with the underpinnings of VSL, SBD, and higher levels of management sophistication. Risk management is a critical responsibility of all leaders, managers, and practitioners. It is the ongoing, never-ending approaches taken to identify, analyze, evaluate, strategize, mitigate, and monitor risks. It is one of the most critical functions of leadership and management focusing on the negative sides and possibilities of harm and undesirable outcomes. Great achievements and extraordinary financial successes can be undone by a few mistakes or blunders pertaining to hidden or unabated risks.

ERM involves many approaches beyond those discussed in the chapter. Leaders, managers, and practitioners have to be diligent and continuously mindful of the risks in their businesses and enterprises. Risk management includes the process as indicated in Figure 7.1, but it is more than a process. It is the ongoing awareness of the strategic and operational risks and continuous attention to mitigating those risks. ERM is a continuum. It is the full-time, real-time efforts for assuring sustainable success. While much of the discussions about risks focus on the negative side, ERM is really about positives. It involves creating and sustaining value; it involves realizing gains and improvement and keeping them over the long term. It is clear from the debacles of the financial meltdown of 2007 thru 2009 that decades-long financial success can be wiped out in a matter of months. ERM also involves business resiliency; being able to weather storms and misfortune and rebound. Strategic leaders implicitly know that there are business cycles and that economies and markets have ups and downs. Strategic leaders have to prepare to take advantage of opportunities and to minimize the effects of the challenges and threats to both short-term and long-term success.

ERM, VSL, and operational leadership entail creating and sustaining success. The prime motivation is the obtainment of financial, market, strategic, enterprise, and sustainable success. Businesses have to make money and have positive cash flows to sustain their well-being. They have to satisfy and sustain their customers and stakeholders. Unless external contributors and recipients are successful there are threats to the existence of the businesses themselves. Businesses have to grow, develop, and become more sophisticated and capable to meet the ongoing expectations and challenges. Strategic success necessitates more advantages and fewer disadvantages; more sustainable positions with a brighter and more enduring future. The same must be the case for the whole extended enterprise. Ultimately, ERM is about creating, growing, and managing an organization and enterprise.

Notes

1. Thomas L. Barton, William G. Shenkir and Paul L. Walker, *Making Enterprise Risk Management Pay Off* (Upper Saddle River, NJ: Prentice Hall, 2002, pp12–32).
2. Robert R. Moeller, *COSO Enterprise Risk Management: Understanding the New Integrated ERM Framework* (Hoboken, NJ: John Wiley & Sons, 2007, pp98–100).
3. http://www.apqc.org/sites/default/files/files/CLGResearch/Bmkg_Code_of_Conduct.pdf
4. Tony Merna and Faisal F. Al-Thani, *Corporate Risk Management* (Hoboken, NJ; John Wiley & Sons Ltd., 2008, p72).
5. David L. Rainey, *Product Innovation: leading Change through Integrated Product Development* (Cambridge, UK: Cambridge University Press, 2005, pp536–538).
6. Id, p540
7. http://www.businessweek.com/ap/financailnews/D9M4U7300.htm
8. http://www.world-nuclear.org/info/inf40.html, dated March 7, 2011.
9. W. Edwards Deming, *Out of The Crisis* (Cambridge, MA: MIT Press, 1982, 1986, pp465–466).
10. David L. Rainey, *Sustainable Business Development: Inventing the Future through Strategy, Innovation and Leadership* (Cambridge, UK: Cambridge University Press, 2006).

References

Barton Thomas L., William G. Shenkir and Paul L. Walker (2002) *Making Enterprise Risk Management Pay Off.* Upper Saddle River, NJ: Prentice Hall.
Deming, W. Edwards (1982) *Out of The Crisis.* Cambridge, MA: MIT Press.
Merna, Tony and Faisal F. Al-Thani (2208) *Corporate Risk Management.* Hoboken, NJ; John Wiley & Sons Ltd.
Moeller, Robert R. (2007) *COSO Enterprise Risk Management: Understanding the New Integrated ERM Framework.* Hoboken, NJ: John Wiley & Sons.
Rainey, David L. (2006) *Sustainable Business Development: Inventing the Future through Strategy, Innovation and Leadership.* Cambridge, UK: Cambridge University Press.
Rainey, David L. (2005) *Product Innovation: Leading Change through Integrated Product Development.* Cambridge, UK: Cambridge University Press.

8

Reflections and Concluding Comments

Introduction

Visionary strategic leadership (VSL) and corporate strategic management (CSM) involve creating and sustaining the vision; leading and managing the organization and its business enterprises; and inspiring the organization and external contributors to transform existing positions and capabilities into more exciting realities. Such strategic leaders engage people throughout their business enterprises; imbue their organizations with an awareness of and commitment to the goal of sustainable success; and shape the knowledge, understandings, capabilities, and actions necessary to lead change and support higher levels of sophistication.

Leading change requires visionary strategic leaders who have the insights and imagination to think globally across the full scope of the enterprise. They inspire people through innovativeness to create new landscapes for exceeding the needs and dreams of all contributors, customers, stakeholders, and constituents. Innovativeness ties the internal organization and external entities through exceptional solutions and integrated value system(s) that reach beyond the prevailing business situations to create a more sustainable business world. Staying ahead of needs, expectations, and changes in a turbulent business world is a huge challenge.

Today, visionary strategic leaders must possess broad knowledge and appreciation about every facet of the business environment and the market spaces. They must engage in VSL and CSM and be generalists and multi-specialists who have the know-how, skills, talents, and capabilities in many technical subjects, management disciplines, and leadership competencies. They also must be able to formulate, implement, and execute strategies, actions plans, and operations. They must make wise and decisive decisions that improve the prospects of their business enterprises at a rate greater than their peers and competitors. VSL involves the profound ways of strategic thinking and leading people based on global perspectives of the exciting opportunities and real-world challenges. VSL is about what true corporate leaders have to be. It includes competencies and capabilities for leading change, setting the strategic direction, crafting strategies, and leading people. In doing so, corporate leaders advance the well-being of their organizations and business enterprises by ensuring that the future is brighter and more sustainable than the present. Such leaders seek exceptional outcomes and extraordinary performance that exceed requirements and expectations and ensure that everyone is successful from the newest employee to the most influential customers or shareholders. They make informed, balanced, wise, and meaningful strategic decisions that place the greater good of the enterprise(s) above their own self-interests. They are the fiduciaries of the company and their enterprises who have the overarching duties to assure sustainable success from every perspective. CSM involves the compelling means and mechanisms for managing the strategic aspects of a corporation and ensuring that it achieves its aspirations and desired outcomes.

Visionary strategic leaders are selfless individuals who are exceptionally competent and exhibit outstanding qualities of strategic leadership and personal integrity. They are committed to their organization's endeavors, confident in their capabilities, courageous in their decisions and actions, and concerned about all of the people involved. They have big dreams for their organizations and enterprises, but they are not arrogant or engage in self-promotion and self-aggrandizement. They realize that everyone is important and that it takes the entire enterprise to create value and achieve success.

Visionary strategic leaders spend the majority of their time and efforts formulating plans and directions for the future and assuring that they are carried out in the most effective and efficient ways. They employ intellectual capital across their organizations to contemplate the future and develop innovative strategies and actions for realizing their aspirations. While visionary strategic leaders engage in establishing the vision and strategic direction, they also have obligations to assure that the actual programs, actions, and activities are executed properly and successfully from every perspective. Ultimately, high-level strategic leaders of any organization are responsible for everything that happens or fails to happen. They are generally viewed to be at the apex of the strategic leadership of an organization, but in reality they are the foundation of the leadership structure. It is their obligation to support others and to contribute to their success. Given the broadness of such a scope of global perspectives and strategic actions, it is impossible to articulate all of the roles and responsibilities of visionary strategic leaders.

Visionary strategic leaders have the awesome duties to chart the course for the future, to steer the organization in the right direction, to maintain the well-being of the organization, to achieve the expected performance, and to avoid corruption, blunders, and other forms of destructive behaviors. While mistakes are made and there is no such thing as perfection in business, visionary strategic leaders know how to uncover potential difficulties, take corrective actions, and quickly mitigate challenges, risks, difficulties, and problems. Most importantly, great visionary strategic leaders ensure that leaders and managers at every level of the organization are well prepared and are competent to perform their roles and responsibilities and that the future generation of leaders and managers are being developed, mentored, and given opportunities to learn and lead.

This chapter highlights some of the most crucial aspects of VSL. The main topics include:

- The overarching qualities of visionary strategic leaders.
- Reflections on visionary strategic leadership.
- The linkage between visionary strategic leadership and sustainable success.
- Concluding comments.

Being a Visionary Strategic Leader

Visionary strategic leaders are ordinary men and women who aspire to achieve extraordinary outcomes for the benefit of people and the organizations that they serve. They are not aristocrats with preordained positions acquired at birth. They are not elites who set themselves apart from the rest of the organization. They do not place themselves in superior positions of privilege and respect. They are often just regular men and women who develop certain qualities that focus on making contributors and recipients successful. They have the mindset that it takes the whole organization and enterprise to be successful and that it is the duty of the strategic leaders to inspire and support others. Most visionary strategic leaders have many qualities; some are inherent and many are developed. Outstanding visionary strategic leaders work exceptionally hard at self-improvement and in becoming the kind of person that is competent, trusted, and respected.

Visionary strategic leaders are **open-minded**, have **wisdom**, and exhibit good **judgment**. They challenge the prevailing views and are willing to invest into change mechanisms. They avoid making too many assumptions or just following the mainstream thinking. For example, over the last decade many corporate leaders outsourced much of their supply chains to companies in China under the assumptions that they would achieve low-cost production. They also assumed that the cost of logistics would continue to remain very low. However, as energy costs escalate some of their assumptions are proving to be inaccurate. Moreover, some of their key suppliers are shifting from being key contributors to major competitors. Great visionary strategic leaders think about all of the implications and the future consequences of their decisions. They implicitly understand that change is ever present and that few strategic positions and competitive advantages endure without active participation and strategic actions on the part of the strategic leaders. They take every opportunity to understand the inputs and listen to the voices of all of the contributors and recipients. They thoroughly analyze their situations, make strategic determinations about the facets, and then take decisive actions based on the totality of the business environment and their business enterprise(s). This does not necessarily mean that everyone can be accommodated or that every detail has to be obtained and scrutinized, but it does imply that astute visionary strategic leaders take broad perspectives and seek win-win outcomes. They avoid making trade-offs in which one person, contributor, group, or market segment wins and others lose. For instance, some strategic leaders focus so much on satisfying customers that they harm their suppliers or forget about stakeholders and employees. Moreover, visionary strategic leaders subordinate their rewards to those of employees and shareholders.

Visionary strategic leaders have **courage** and **conviction**. They set the stage and show the way even when the pathway to the future is unclear and fraught with many uncertainties and risks. Visionary strategic leaders lead by example and are willing to be out front in taking initiatives and implementing change. Too often some strategic leaders are happy to formulate new strategies and initiate new solutions, but fail to put their own personal reputations on the line during implementation and execution. It takes courage to personally engage in the strategic actions that may be radical or out of the ordinary. Moreover, visionary strategic leaders have to have conviction that their vision and strategic direction are right and that they will result in the positive gains envisioned. They have to be committed to the long term even when difficulties arise and the organization experiences some of the typical challenges during the early stages in which efforts require significant investments of time and money without corresponding rewards. For instance, many strategic leaders often encounter what could be called the "V-shaped phenomenon." There is great enthusiasm when the new strategic innovations and high-level strategic programs (HSPs) are announced. Most people are onboard. They are excited. However, as time marches on, the challenges mount and the positive outcomes tend to lag. On the left side of the "V," major efforts tend to result in seemingly small gains and advancements. People work hard and make improvements, but the rewards are often significantly less than the efforts. On the downward side of the "V," outcomes are typically less than what was invested; it is akin to investing a dollar and getting fifty cents back at the end of the year. People become discouraged and start challenging the wisdom of the leaders and the programs, initiatives, and changes. The processes seem to be inefficient and the investments are perceived to be ineffective. However, often it is simply the typical phenomenon involving radical innovations and transformations; the process cannot be expected to be linear. It takes time to obtain the big positives. Moreover, it takes great VSL to keep the organization on track and moving toward the right side of the "V," in which the gains outweigh the efforts and the rewards increase dramatically. For example, in 1968 Reynolds Metals started its aluminum recycling business. During the first few years, the company lost money on the new venture and it seemed that the aluminum recycling business was financial nonsense. But, the venture broke even in 1972 and ultimately Reynolds Metals made hundreds of millions of dollars in aluminum recycling. It took David Reynolds, a wise and courageous corporate executive, to provide the stewardship to keep employees inspired and moving toward the strategic goals during the early years of hard work and few rewards.

Success is never guaranteed, but it is often just around the corner. The more dramatic the change and the more involved the HSPs, the more likely it will take considerable time and efforts to realize the desired outcomes. Visionary strategic leaders have to stay the course knowing that the organization can succeed. As an aside, in Virgil's epic poem, *Aeneid*, Aeneus sets out from the destruction of his home city of Troy to establish a new city-state. When he was convinced that the vision of finding a new Troy (Rome) will be fulfilled upon arriving on the Italian peninsular, he had his warriors burn all of the ships. From then on they could only go forward into the future; there was no going back. While it may be unwise or imprudent for visionary strategic leaders to sell off or spin off all of the old businesses or completely embrace the strategic direction without a well-planned transformation, it is imperative that they are committed to the future and ensure that the associated action plans and initiatives are fully implemented. Without strong strategic leadership, many organizations tend to support the prevailing situations even when it is apparent that change is necessary. It takes great VSL to get people to stay the course toward the future. It is common for people to lose confidence and commitment during the long duration of the strategic innovations and HSPs, if success is not readily apparent. As in the case of many disastrous military campaigns of the past in which the army lost heart, broke ranks, and scattered, business organizations have to reaffirm their commitments and dedication to the goals on an ongoing basis.

In American history, Patrick Henry was one of the most powerful advocates for leading change. He was a vocal radical during the American Revolutionary War period; his famous speech that he gave in the Virginia House of Burgesses on March 23, 1775 saying "give me liberty or give me death" inspired people across the colonies. He continued to be a great advocate of change during his entire life. Possibly his most important contribution to liberty and freedom came during the ratification of the U.S. Constitution. He was a leading challenger to the adoption of the Constitution, because he thought that it gave too much power to the federal government. He believed that citizens were sovereign and endowed with fundamental rights. His beliefs and convictions resulted in his being the most influential supporter of the Bill of Rights. He had the courage to disagree with powerful men like James Madison who believed that the Bill of Rights was unnecessary. Henry had the fortitude to overcome the obstacles and the perseverance to stay the course, because he knew that his perspectives were proper and necessary. He prevailed and the Bill of Rights became amendments to the Constitution. Interestingly, the Bill of Rights has become more important over time as the federal government expanded its reach and power. Henry may have known that he was protecting future generations, not just his contemporary one.

Visionary strategic leaders have exemplary ***personal values***. They are honest and truthful. They have personal integrity and never risk losing it for the sake of personal or professional gains. Great visionary strategic leaders always put the well-being of people first. They are open and transparent in their communications and actions. They are ethical and embrace proper behaviors. They go beyond what is mandated by laws and regulations and ensure that they are following exacting standards. They firmly believe in universal principles of protecting human rights and preserving the natural environment.

They maintain the highest codes of conduct and ensure that their integrity is never compromised. They encourage and support these qualities in other people.

Visionary strategic leaders have outstanding *personal characteristics*. While not every leader may be handsome in the physical sense, outstanding visionary strategic leaders can always exhibit attractive personal characteristics. They present a professional appearance and have a pleasant personality. They respect other people and treat everyone with dignity and due care. They lead by example and never expect others to do something they are unwilling to do themselves; they do not exploit their subordinates or others in lesser positions. They are supportive of other people's objectives and aims. They listen to others and provide the proper considerations. They encourage change, but are not foolish enough to believe that all changes are positives. They are generally optimistic with positive perspectives, but they are also skeptical about possibilities until sufficient knowledge, understanding, and validation are available about the proper courses of action. They focus on opportunities to make significant gains and they also focus on eliminating challenges and the negative aspects. They are quick learners and devote time and energy to understand reality and the implications of their proposed plans and actions before they make decisions. They give credit to those who are deserving of such credit and ensure that rewards are fairly distributed. They never blame others for their mistakes or failures.

Visionary strategic leaders are *innovative* as discussed numerous times throughout the book. They seek new ways to solve problems, to demystify the complexities of the business world, to overcome what perplexes organizations, and to create solutions. They are the risk takers and the individuals who have the capacity and commitment in providing the requisite solutions. While visionary strategic leaders do not have to be inventors or design engineers, they have to be the architects, facilitators, and the overseers of actions, advancements, and achievements. Visionary strategic leaders are never satisfied with the prevailing level of achievements and seek ongoing successes and higher levels of sophistication. They invest heavily into learning, creating innovative solutions, and developing the most robust systems for enduring success. They use their insights and imagination to create a better world for people.

Visionary strategic leaders realize that everyone has personal strengths and limitations. They know that personal growth and professional development are never-ending challenges. They understand that great strategic leaders like great businesses take advantage of their strengths and mitigate their weaknesses. They know that the business world is ever changing. They realize that most *competencies and capabilities* become less powerful over time unless there are concerted efforts to stay ahead of change through learning and new experiences; ones that exceed expectations. They know that strategic leaders have a duty to be competent in their roles and responsibilities and exhibit the wisdom necessary for making good decisions. While in many professional fields like medicine and the law, there are examinations to verify professional competencies and there are certifications of qualifications by government agencies, there are no such measures for strategic leaders. Strategic leaders are often assumed to be competent based on their experience, knowledge, and positions as leaders of organizations. However, such assumptions are not always appropriate. The incumbent's experience may be relevant in one setting, but not another. He or she may be a good leader in maintaining stability and the status quo, but not really competent in leading change. For instance, an incumbent may be good at managing preset operations that have repetitive activities, but he or she may not be competent at managing HSPs involving new-to-the-world technologies. While it is difficult to prove that many business failures are attributable to the lack of experience and knowledge on the part of the strategic leaders or to poor and inadequate decision making, it is obvious that one has to be competent when undertaking any endeavor. Moreover, new strategic leaders have little time to become fully capable of fulfilling their responsibilities. Unlike the prevailing view of the past in which strategic leaders were often given a year or so to become competent, in today's fast-paced world the time frame may be measured in weeks or months, not years. Strategic leaders have to be competent and capable. If they cannot become so for whatever reasons, they should (must) forego their positions. As an aside, who would want to be a patient of a medical doctor who has no experience as a brain surgeon, but who thought that he could perform brain surgery because he studied medicine and worked at a hospital or that he or she would learn through trial and error? Unfortunately, there are business leaders who engage in areas, practices, and decision making in which they do not have the requisite competencies and knowledge.

Visionary strategic leaders have to *care for people*. It is one of the most basic aspects of VSL, but often one of the most significant challenges. Today's business world is driven by intellectual capital and the contributions of people. Success is predicated on having creative and capable people. If the strategic leaders do not take due care of the contributors and recipients, in the long term such people will find other opportunities to realize their outcomes and achieve success.

The final two qualities discussed herein are *passion and confidence*. They go together. Visionary strategic leaders have to have passion for making changes, engaging in the challenges, realizing opportunities, and improving everything within their domain. They must be dedicated toward obtaining outstanding results and balanced outcomes. They must ensure that sustainable success is achieved and that it is enjoyed by everyone to the extent possible. They have to be confident that they can set the proper strategic direction and formulate and implement strategies and action plans to realize their aspirations. Success is rarely guaranteed and it is often fleeting. While businesses focus on succeeding, failure is always a possibility, especially if strategic leaders are not passionate about their visions for the future and the desires to obtain extraordinary results. It takes great visionary strategic leaders to keep on track and avoid the pitfalls that lead to failure.

Reflections on Visionary Strategic Leadership

Philosophical Perspectives

VSL requires philosophical perspectives that include both the tangible aspects of the business world and the intangible aspects of one's mindset and beliefs. Great visionary strategic leaders work hard to understand reality and to determine the driving forces of change and the implications for the future. They have the uncommon abilities to avoid engaging in trade-offs when making strategic decisions and to ensure that short-term and long-term objectives and outcomes are balanced to the extent possible. They realize that decision making involves global perspectives and that simply maximizing one aspect, like generating profits, without regard to the other critical requirements, like making recipients (customers, stakeholders, etc.) and contributors (suppliers, employees, etc.) successful, may suboptimize the whole business enterprise and lead to less success in the future.

Great visionary strategic leaders depend on principles and personal values that underpin everything they do. VSL involves building solid relationships with people. Relationships depend on trust and integrity. Trust is the glue that connects people together. For instance, customers buy products from a given producer because they trust the brands and reputation of the company. Without trust, few people would get on airplanes or consume food products. No one wants to risk their well-being when trying to satisfy their needs and wants. They want the best possible outcomes with the least costs and risks. They rely on the trustworthiness of the producers and providers of the solutions when deciding upon the choices they have and using them beneficially.

Great leaders are truthful, accountable, and transparent. They provide the best solutions possible and are open and candid in providing all of the information necessary for people to make good decisions about the products and services that they buy and use or the ones that affect them. Great visionary strategic leaders provide information about both sides of the value proposition. They promote the positive aspects and disclose the negative ones. They actively encourage truthfulness and take every opportunity to discover the hidden defects and concerns that people may have. Moreover, they immediately rectify the negative aspects and eliminate the associated impacts. In those situations in which appropriate solutions cannot be found, feasibly be produced, and/or properly delivered, astute strategic leaders use the precautionary principle and develop alternate approaches or outcomes. They never risk anyone's well-being or success to make money or obtain personal or professional gains. Visionary strategic leaders support the development of their organizations and the employees therein.

Rhetoric and Reality

Great visionary strategic leaders are fairly rare. They have to have most of the qualities necessary for leading and inspiring people. They are visionaries who can determine what the future expectations are and how to create the required solutions, systems, and structures well before the needs and expectations are apparent. In the fast-paced business world of today, it is often too late if one waits until the needs, mandates, requirements, etc. become evident. Once they are obvious, the opportunities to gain competitive advantages or to obtain leading positions are usually lost.

Visionary strategic leaders must be comfortable in establishing the vision and strategic direction and formulating and implementing strategies and action plans. They must also know how to select the right constructs for leading change and managing the flow of actions and activities. They have to determine what the appropriate perspectives are and how to create the proper methods and techniques for obtaining the best outcomes and for achieving extraordinary performance. Visionary strategic leaders have to engage and empower people to recognize, accept, and carry out the explicit and implicit aspects of the vision and strategic direction. They have to establish and provide the means and mechanisms for realizing success. They have to allocate the right resources and ensure that people have the capabilities and skills necessary to perform well and achieve the desired outcomes. Moreover, they have to provide oversight and to continuously monitor and measure results. In addition, they must recognize and reward the key contributors.

Some strategic leaders craft exquisite vision statements that articulate almost everything the external world of customers and stakeholders wants to hear. However, such strategic leaders and their staffs often spend most of their time creating flowery words, developing outstanding plans, and promoting the strategic plans. Their basic schemes are self-promotion and personal gain, in which the strategic leaders take great credit for being visionaries, but they do not get engaged in carrying out the initiatives and actions. This is where reality often does not meet the rhetoric. Their plans and words are more of a marketing campaign, instead of a vision and actions for the future. Such strategic leaders know that it takes years to actually get results and that outsiders usually do not expect immediate outcomes. By the time outsiders expect to recognize the results of the plans and HSPs, such strategic leaders have moved on to bigger and better things or retired. They obtain the benefits of the audacious vision using rhetoric, but they lack the commitment, efforts and hard work to actually implement and execute the actions and initiatives.

A variation to the scheme is to create a grandiose plan with a few big strategic initiatives and many smaller programs. The former are fully funded and are fully implemented. The strategic leader takes full credit and publicizes the achievements. The other programs are left to the lower-level leaders who struggle to obtain the necessary resources to carry out their programs. In some cases, lower levels of the organizations are starved of resources, especially money, to pay for the high-level strategic initiatives. Moreover, in many such cases, recognition for the successes goes to the high-level strategic leaders and blame for failures goes to the lower-level managers.

Two common difficulties that even well-meaning strategic leaders have are spending too much time on the vision and not enough on managing the realities of the business world and alternatively not spending enough time and effort to implement the vision and strategic direction. Both may lead to major problems, even disasters. Right-minded and honest strategic leaders who believe in the vision, strategic innovations, and HSPs also have to be proactive in strategic implementation and execution. Moreover, some strategic leaders become so dedicated to the future prospects that they fail to pay sufficient attention to the realities of the current businesses. They fail to balance the near-term and long-term aspects. For example, Lord John Browne, former chief executive of BP, plc, was a great visionary during his tenure as the chief executive at BP. All of the evidence suggests that he really believed in the vision to turn BP into a diversified energy company instead of just being a petroleum company. The vision was audacious, his commitment was excellent, yet his success was tarnished by accidents and poor operations. Again, strategic leaders have to ensure that realities of the present are in good stead as well as being prepared for the future. It is never an "either-or" situation. Remember, oversight of strategic actions and actual operations is always necessary and absolutely critical.

Failure to implement and execute properly is the bane of many strategic leaders. Good intentions count for little if the organization is unable to carry out the strategic initiatives and action plans. The general problem is often the immediacy of the present. The current operational requirements and day-to-day operations often take precedent over the strategic plans and development programs. The problem is obvious: people do what is absolutely necessary first and then try to fit in the long-term aspects. If there is insufficient time and resources, implementing strategic initiatives often has to wait until tomorrow. The story is repeated day after day as tomorrow becomes tomorrow. The consequences of such failures are not felt immediately and by the time reality catches up with the lack of implementation, it is too late.

Visionary strategic leaders have to be credible. They have to create and espouse visions that lead to significant changes and enhancements. The business world is ever-changing and standing still actually means falling behind. Visionary strategic leaders have to use rhetoric to promote the vision and strategic direction and they have to ensure that everything articulated is being implemented and executed. They have to measure results, take corrective actions, and provide oversight on all of the strategic and operational requirements.

Great visionary strategic leaders *"walk the talk"* and set the examples. They have a responsibility to exhibit best practices and to follow the principles of acceptable behavior. For instance, visionary strategic leaders are duty bound to tell the truth, because people have to rely on their statements. If such leaders are not honest and trustworthy, then people are unable to make good decisions about their own situations and those affecting the organization. While deviations from the acceptable standards and norms are never acceptable, failures on the part of strategic leaders are the worst case because they destroy the confidence that people have in the organization and its strategic leadership.

Great visionary strategic leaders promote the highest standards across all the dimensions of their domain and time. They assure that ethical behaviors are followed regardless of the location or whether there are prescribed standards or government regulations. They are jealous about their reputations and do everything possible to assure that they are unblemished. They monitor the whole organization to assure that practices are in keeping with the principles. They set the stage by being role models for what is expected rather than assuming that they are exempt of the policies, basic rules, and standards of behavior because of their positions. It is difficult to get people across the organization and enterprise to accept the highest levels of standards of behavior when they see their strategic leaders flagrantly disregarding the generally accepted principles and practices.

Linkages between VSL and Sustainable Success

VSL is the alpha-omega of leadership with a virtual spiral of ever-increasing aspirations, objectives, expectations, and realizations. Visionary strategic leaders are the architects who create the means and mechanisms for achieving success and building enduring relationships with people. They shape the future aims and outcomes and empower the lower-level leaders, employees, and external contributors to maximize their intellectual capital, efforts, inputs, and decisions. Visionary strategic leaders concentrate on the planning and architectural aspects of the vision, strategic direction, and grand strategies. However, they delegate as much as possible to the other strategic leaders and key contributors, especially in the determination of the solutions, systems, and structures, and in the implementation and execution of strategies and action plans.

Visionary strategic leaders orchestrate the design and development of the solutions, value chain, value systems, extended enterprises, and business models, but they allow the actual efforts to be carried out at lower levels. They are an integral part of setting up the value networks and ensuring proper value deployment. They constantly monitor performance and take corrective actions. They are ultimately responsibility for everything that happens or does not happen. They integrate the whole enterprise and assure its success. They establish the high-level methods and techniques that are used to determine what has to be done and how to measure success. They provide the resources and ensure that contributors have the requisite capabilities to be successful.

VSL involves the relentless pursuit of perfection: the highest levels of sophistication and broadest perspectives of strategic development and achievements. While perfection is a distant dream, sustainable success and ongoing achievements can be realized over time as visionary strategic leaders continue to build solid relationships with the whole enterprise based on trust and integrity. People engage in exchanges with businesses because they have needs and expectations and they intrinsically believe that the solutions they select fulfill their objectives. There is never perfect knowledge about the solutions; therefore, people usually make their decisions based on certain underpinnings. The underpinnings involve their knowledge of the broader business environment including the economic and social conditions and trends. They involve their understanding and beliefs about the companies and their strategic leaders. In the short term, people have to connect with businesses to buy products and services and to have dialogues to promote their well-being and/or to resolve issues or difficulties. People base a lot of their views on the trust they have in the companies and the integrity that the strategic leaders have exhibited over time. Trust is developed by having the right mindset and ethical approaches based on an outstanding track record of solid performance over time.

Amartya Sen, winner of the Noble Prize in economics in 1998 and author of *Development as Freedom,* believes that successful capitalism depends on values and trust. He takes the global perspective that economic exchanges are multifaceted, in which businesses produce products and provide services that fulfill customer needs and wants and they make money by providing the best solutions possible. Rather than capitalism being based on businesses maximizing objectives and performance, i.e., maximizing profits, true market capitalism is multifaceted and depends on ethics, trust, and mutual gain. Capitalism involves win–win situations. Sen's views are expressed accordingly:[1]

> [C]apitalism works effectively through a system of ethics that provides the vision and trust needed for the successful use of market mechanism and related institutions.
>
> Successful operation of an exchange economy depends on mutual trust and the use of norms—explicit and implicit. When these behavioral modes are plentiful, it is easy to overlook their role [importance]. But when they have to be cultivated, that lacuna can be a major barrier to economic success...
>
> The need for institutional developments has some clear connections with the role of codes of behavior, since institutions based on interpersonal arrangements and shared understandings operate on the basis of common behavior patterns, mutual trust, and confidence in the other party's ethics.

Sen articulates the foundation upon which the business world lies. Trust links the internal with the external. Businesses are successful because they create and sustain trust with the markets, customers, and stakeholders. Trust is the most important underpinning that makes the businesses successful. Trust is difficult to obtain and often takes years of building awareness and acceptance of the company, its solutions (brands), and people who are part of them. One of the most important reasons for building trust is that it provides sustainable positions and enduring success. However, such positions require due diligence on the part of strategic leaders to sustain the trust within the enterprise and over time. One of the main concerns of any visionary strategic leader is that trust is difficult to obtain, but easy to lose. In such cases, it is incumbent upon strategic leaders to embrace openness, transparency, and honesty and ensure that all relevant information is made available to customers, stakeholders, employees and all of the other recipients and contributors. The ultimate bottom line is the well-being of everyone from customers to shareholders. It is their belief in the wholeness and integrity of the company that really is the crucial difference.

Sustainable success is based on doing everything well, not just focusing on certain core competencies or satisfying customers. Visionary strategic leaders may obtain competitive advantages in the short term using their strengths, but unless they and their enterprises have a balanced portfolio of competencies and capabilities, they may have difficulties maintaining their positions in the longer term. The underpinnings of sustainable success run the gamut from having a great vision for the future, establishing well-articulated strategies and action plans, managing strategic innovations and HSPs, ensuring fully-integrated strategic implementation and execution across the enterprise, and achieving the desired outcomes.

Sustainable success is the ultimate goal that visionary strategic leaders seek for their organizations and enterprises. It requires ongoing investments, efforts, and dedication. The driving forces in the business environment and market spaces are dynamic and require diligent attention to the details and specifics of what is expected and demanded. Sustainable success implies being ahead of the requirements, peers and competitors alike. It means taking advantage of all opportunities and mitigating or eliminating all challenges and risks.

Concluding Comments

Visionary strategic leaders play vital roles in their organizations and enterprises. They have the awesome obligations and responsibilities to make wise strategic decisions for their business enterprises. Moreover, they have implicit and explicit responsibilities to protect and preserve the well-being of the organization and its use of the natural environment. Visionary strategic leaders must have global perspectives that go beyond the traditional management construct of supply and demand or production and consumption. They must include the whole business environment, social systems and structures, external ecosystems in their strategic thinking, analysis, planning, and actions. They must think holistically and consider future aspects and implications as well as the prevailing ones. They must avoid "either-or" thinking and maximize the positives and minimize the negatives. They must consider every factor to sustain success over time.

Visionary strategic leaders have the duty to govern their organizations and enterprises. They are the agents of the shareholders with the profound duty to protect the assets and well-being of their companies and to ensure continued success. Their responsibilities are open-ended and all encompassing. It is impossible to specify in precise detail all of the opportunities, challenges, requirements, mandates, expectations, difficulties, and risks that they have to take advantage of, deal with, manage, resolve, and/or mitigate. Visionary strategic leaders establish the fundamental beliefs and determine the values and perspectives that guide strategic direction and decision making. They guide learning within the organization and enterprise and assure that they and all of the contributors learn faster than the rate of change in the business environment and the social and technical worlds. They assure that corporate performance exceeds expectations and that future performance continues to increase a rate greater than that of peers and competitors.

In today's turbulent business world, global corporations and small- and medium-size enterprises require well educated and knowledgeable visionary strategic leaders who can lead change and deal with the complexities of a global economy. This implies that there is no status quo and that resting on one's laurels or past successes is a prescription for disaster. It also implies that great strategic leaders have an implicit duty to develop the next generation of leaders to assure enduring success. Moreover, the future strategic leaders must be better prepared and more competent and capable than the incumbents of today given that the business world and opportunities and challenges therein are becoming more complicated and demanding. There may be millions of potential strategic leaders who can manage simple businesses, but there are the rare few who have the talents, skills, competencies, knowledge, and mindset to lead in difficult and turbulent times. Yet, such opportunities and challenges are the most exciting aspects of leading businesses today. Moreover, exceptional visionary strategic leaders think out-of-the-box and consider what should be done instead of just focusing on what is being done.

Visionary strategic leaders use their intuition, wisdom, and judgment about the business environment and social and natural worlds. True strategic leaders use their imagination to set the proper direction toward the future. They do not simply follow their peers or competitors. They chart their own course. While it is seemingly easier and less risky to follow in the footsteps of other business leaders, simply mimicking conventional approaches may be fraught with many dangers, since most of the mainstream constructs and ways of doing things are based on the past and not the future. Optimizing performance based on the past perspectives may result in suboptimized results in the future. Visionary strategic leaders have to be courageous and articulate a vision for the future that provides both strategic direction and sustainable success. The vision must be augmented by an overarching strategic perspective that links the future possibilities with the present realities. It is critical that the vision is viewed from the present going forward based on external and internal contexts as well as from the desired future state of success back to the prevailing capabilities and resources of the enterprise. If the vision is established based just on the current realities, it may lead to less than adequate achievements and the failure to keep pace with the driving forces in the business environment. On the other hand, if the vision is simply based on aspirations without reflecting on the realities, it may result in stretching the organization beyond its breaking point. Visionary strategic leaders have to be optimistic and realistic at the same time. Such challenges are not easy to accomplish and necessitate strategic leaders who reach out beyond the norm.

Visionary strategic leaders focus on the big picture through CSM. They formulate the grand strategies and overarching goals for their companies. They monitor achievements and ensure that their organizations maintain the hard work and diligence necessary to realize the desired outcomes. They establish the strategic management systems for the company and aid in determining the frameworks for the business units and their extended enterprises. They also guide lower-level strategic leaders in the selection of the management constructs that are used to facilitate tactical decision making and execution. Visionary strategic leaders should spend a considerable amount of their time thinking about the future and the implications of change. They should map out the various possible scenarios and reflect on the how they can influence the prospects for sustainable success. They should examine and consider the available strategic options and be proactive in selecting and implementing the most effective strategies based on the prevailing and expected realities. Visionary strategic leaders should spend time building solid personal and professional relationships with influential leaders and decision makers in the market spaces, the industry, business organizations, supply networks, stakeholders, communities, governments, media, and investment communities. They should also foster solid relationships with shareholders and employees.

Visionary strategic leaders must become proficient in understanding the broader aspects of their business environment. Too often business leaders just pay attention to the direct economic entities, markets, customers, and competitors. While this seemingly makes strategic sense, especially in the short term, an overreliance on the short-term opportunities may result in missing more profound future opportunities and trends that lead to new solutions and outcomes with superior value creation and extraordinary financial rewards. Visionary strategic leaders have to explore the social world to the extent possible to find additional opportunities and to reduce the risks associated with radical change. On the positive side, the social world is dynamic with new opportunities developing every day. For instance, there are billions of people in the emerging markets who need and want solutions that meet their situations. The business world of the twenty-first century is rich with possibilities and new participants. Visionary strategic leaders have to create the requisite solutions for such people. On the negative side, the social world has many challenges that could disrupt sustainable success, if they are not dealt with and resolved. Resource constraints, pollution, diseases, terrorism, and political instability are just a few of the concerns that have negative effects on global businesses that effective strategic leaders have to consider and deal with.

Visionary strategic leaders have to be knowledgeable about the natural environment and take appropriate actions to prevent degradation, depletion, and deterioration. They have to assure that the requisite resources are available and they have to mitigate resource depletion. They must protect the natural environment for future generations so that sustainable success is possible. They must work with other leaders in governments and communities to manage the ecosystems and eliminate the negative effects and impacts that businesses and people have on the natural environment. Such requirements are the duty of every leader regardless of position and agenda. While such implicit duties generally pertain to the common good and the well-being of humankind, it can be argued that they are also critical for the self-interest of businesses. Without resources or stable economic systems, businesses will have difficulties flourishing. Indeed in turbulent and disruptive times, there are often many business failures and it becomes difficult for strategic leaders to achieve their objectives. It is in everyone's interest to assure sustainable success.

The opportunities in today's business world are great; so are the challenges and risks. However, there are good reasons to be optimistic. The business world has made many great contributions to the social world over the last several decades. The technologies of today are superior to those a generation ago. For instance, personal computers have provided dramatic improvements in productivity and connectivity. The Internet has expanded communications and global reach. It facilitates international trade and the interconnections between companies and people. New technologies and products like cell phones and digital cameras have superior attributes and reduce wastes and pollution. There is a lot of good news, but there is also a long way to go to have truly sustainable solutions in every arena. Visionary strategic leaders have to continue to invest into strategic innovations and HSPs. They have to proactively lead change through new-to-the-world technologies and products that eliminate the problems and negative impacts associated with existing and past ones. Great new solutions do not just occur. They take competent and courageous strategic leaders to manage development programs and create value through innovativeness.

Success does not just happen. While good luck and fortuitous events may play a part, success is achieved due to the intellectual capital of the leaders and organization and their capabilities and willingness to orchestrate positive change. It takes dedicated and hard-working strategic leaders and people to realize the vision and the overarching objectives. It also takes fully-articulated strategies, great solutions, integrated systems, and well-constructed business model(s) to ensure everyone in the organization and across the enterprise knows what is expected and how to perform and execute.

Visionary strategic leaders use insights and foresights in managing their enterprises and leading change. They go beyond what may seem obvious about events, situations, and positions. They think through the superficial aspects and determine the essence of what is happening. They focus on the underpinnings of reality and the driving forces of change. Moreover, they think about the both the present aspects and the future implications. They are aggressive and prudent at the same time. They realize that success is obtained by leading change, yet they know that strategic leaders never risk catastrophic failures for the sake of short-term rewards. They know that they have a duty to the whole and that they must subordinate their own rewards as they secure gains for the organization and its shareholders.

Great visionary strategic leaders are competent, confident, courageous, forceful, influential, and dynamic; yet they are personable, reasonable, and uphold the highest values. They are respectful of superiors and subordinates alike. They have empathy for others and take due consideration in protecting and preserving the social world and the natural environment. Visionary strategic leaders are fanatics about learning and recognize that they must be knowledgeable about the underpinnings and implications related to the decisions they make. They understand the power of building solid relationships with contributors and recipients. Great visionary strategic leaders realize that there are no magic formulas for achieving success; that today's strengths may become tomorrow's weaknesses. They know that success depends upon leadership, intellectual capital, dedication, and commitment, and that true power rests not with capital assets, machines, production, marketing, or finance, but with people.

Visionary strategic leaders are ordinary men and women who understand the essence of business and endeavor to achieve successful and sustainable outcomes. They appreciate that the essential ingredients of success are intangibles like trustworthiness, honesty, integrity, and hard work. They are selfless and aspire to make the world a better place. Their true rewards are being recognized as great visionary strategic leaders with impeccable integrity and outstanding reputations.

In summary, VSL is about people and CSM is about things. Visionary strategic leaders take global perspectives and they are the architects of their organizations and enterprises. They design and develop the solutions, systems, and structures. They create the vision, determine the strategic direction, inspire people, generate enthusiasm, build relationships, provide governance and oversight, monitor outcomes and sustain success. They engage in the never-ending challenges of achieving success and moving beyond present realities to higher levels of positions, capabilities, and performance. They set high standards and map out the pathways toward creating value and realizing the aspirations, knowing the journey is long, arduous, and fraught with potential challenges, difficulties, and risks. Yet, visionary strategic leaders are very optimistic and excited about the future. They know that sustainable success is both the aspiration and the means to a more exciting reality.

Note

1. Amartya Sen, *Development of Freedom* (New York, NY: Anchor Books, 1999, pp263, 265).

Reference

Sen, Amartya (1999) *Development of Freedom.* New York, NY: Anchor Books.